D1207458

REGENERATION THROUGH EMPIRE

France Overseas: Studies in Empire and Decolonization
Series editors: A. J. B. Johnston, James D. Le Sueur, and Tyler Stovall

REGENERATION THROUGH EMPIRE

*French Pronatalists and
Colonial Settlement in
the Third Republic*

Margaret Cook Andersen

University of Nebraska Press
Lincoln & London

A version of chapter 3 was originally published as "Creating French Settlements Overseas: Colonial Medicine and Familial Reform in Madagascar," by Margaret Cook Andersen, in *French Historical Studies* 33, no. 3 (Summer 2010): 417–44. A version of chapter 4 was originally published as "French Settlers, Familial Suffrage, and Citizenship in 1920s Tunisia," by Margaret Cook Andersen, in *Journal of Family History* 37, no. 2 (April 2012): 213–31.

Library of Congress Control Number: 2014952326

Set in Minion Pro by Renni Johnson.

To Brett, Katie, and Lexie

CONTENTS

ILLUSTRATIONS

Figures

Tables

ACKNOWLEDGMENTS

Since I began researching this book a decade ago, many people and institutions have helped me along the way with their generous intellectual, financial, and emotional support. In these pages I can only begin to acknowledge my appreciation for everything they have done to help make this book possible.

Funding from a variety of sources was indispensable. A Florence Gould pre-dissertation grant from the Council for European Studies and numerous grants and fellowships from the University of Iowa funded the first years of research. At the University of Tennessee, a Professional Development Award and a semester of junior faculty leave helped me move forward with my research and writing. Finally, a summer stipend from the National Endowment for the Humanities enabled me to undertake the final research and prepare the manuscript for publication.

My initial curiosity in French history was sparked at Occidental College, where I was privileged to have dedicated professors who believed in me and inspired me during my undergraduate years. In particular, I would like to thank Nina Gelbart and Annabelle Rea for supporting my decision to pursue graduate school and encouraging me to study abroad. In addition to being one of the most meaningful experiences of my life, my junior year in Rennes and Toulouse sparked my interest in the politics and culture of the Third Republic.

The University of Iowa provided a collegial environment that facilitated my early work on this project. In the first years of my graduate career, Sarah Hanley advised me and provided warm encouragement. Classes with Jeff Cox, Jim Giblin, Sarah Hanley, Lisa Heineman, Glenn Penny, and Rosemarie Scullion provided insight and shaped my thinking. I am particularly indebted to my adviser, Jennifer Sessions. Always happy to answer questions about the odds and ends of doing research in France and to comment on my work, Jen gave me invaluable advice and pushed me to do my best work. She continues to be a supportive presence in my life, always available to talk about my project and read additional drafts. My friends at the University of Iowa are too numerous to list, but I would nevertheless like to thank Becky Pulju, who gave me sound advice about doing research in France, and Cari Campbell, who commented on drafts of each and every chapter. Other friends, including Annie Liss, Karen Ursic, Scott Perrin, Kristen Anderson, Mandy Trevors, Kathy Wilson, Anna Flaming, Melissa Moreton, and Dauna Kaiser, provided moral support through long months of writing and revising the dissertation.

When I arrived at the University of Tennessee as a new professor I was fortunate to find a vibrant intellectual community and supportive environment for my research. Along the way my work has improved thanks to advice from and conversations with my colleagues, including Vejas Liulevicius, Catherine Higgs, Lynn Sacco, Laura Nenzi, Shellen Wu, Marina Maccari, and Douja Mamelouk. In addition, the faculty and graduate students in the After Wars Seminar were particularly helpful by commenting on portions of the manuscript that I presented.

I would also like to thank the staffs at the Bibliothèque nationale, the Archives du ministère des affaires étrangères, the Archives diplomatiques, and the Centre des archives d'outre-mer (CAOM) for assisting me in carrying out my research. Daniel Gillies at CAOM was especially helpful in directing me to the collections I needed. My time in France was also enriched by conversations with friends I met along the way, including Renée Goethe, Farid Ameur, Amanda Shoaf, and Terry Young Hwa.

Feedback I received from colleagues I met at academic conferences, including the Council for European Studies, the Western Society for French History, and the Society for French Historical Studies, was especially instrumental in pointing me in new directions and identifying ways I could improve my work. Particularly helpful were comments I received from Elisa Camiscioli, Michael Vann, Sue Peabody, Natalia Starostina, Naomi Andrews, and Stephen Toth. Judith Surkis, especially, helped me refine my analysis of the myth of the prolific settler. I particularly want to thank Christina Firpo for reading and commenting on the entire manuscript.

My revisions of this manuscript were aided by the detailed comments I received from Carolyn Eichner and the anonymous reviewer at the University of Nebraska Press. I also want to thank Bridget Barry and the editorial staff at the press for all of their hard work.

Finally, I certainly would not be where I am today were it not for my family. First, I would like to thank my parents, who were my first teachers. From an early age they encouraged me to read and learn. They sent me to college and supported my decision to pursue a PhD in history. My parents, along with my brother, Mike, have spent countless hours listening to me talk about my studies and for that I am very grateful. I would also like to thank my husband, Brett, who relocated with me from California to Iowa and finally to Tennessee. I know he made many sacrifices so that I could pursue this career. Throughout the process, Brett has read multiple drafts of this work. He has also patiently tolerated living apart so that I could carry out my research in France, something that was especially difficult after we started having children. Most of all, he has spent countless hours listening to me talk about my work and giving me love and support when I needed it most. Last, but certainly not least, I would like to thank my daughters. Katherine was born while I was writing my dissertation, and Alexandra arrived while my manuscript was under review. Experiencing pregnancy and motherhood while working on this project gave me important insights into the history of pronatalism during the Third Republic. More significantly, my daughters serve as a constant reminder of what really matters in life.

REGENERATION THROUGH EMPIRE

Introduction

The race is hardly responsible for French depopulation
because, far away from the metropole and the artificial
influence of civilization and customs, French people
once again become prolific.

—CHARLES RAISIN, *La dépopulation
de la France*, 1900

F rench defeat in the Franco-Prussian War was swift; in less than two months of war, enemy troops had encircled Paris, captured the emperor Napoleon III, and left the government of the Second Empire discredited. This humiliating defeat in 1870 resulted in the unification of Germany, the loss of Alsace and Lorraine, the establishment of France's Third Republic, and fears that France was on the brink of becoming a second-rate power in Europe. The crisis that gave birth to the Third Republic would influence its political history throughout its existence; in the immediate aftermath of the war, patriotic French men and women turned their attention to their empire, the declining birthrate in France, and the comparative demographic strengths of rival powers in Europe.

It was therefore in the early Third Republic that Malthusian arguments in favor of fertility restraint were eclipsed by the growing belief that victory over Germany in the next war would require a higher birthrate. This conviction was shaped by statistical studies revealing the relatively slow growth of the French population over the course of the nineteenth century. For example, France's population grew by a mere 43 percent between 1800 and 1900; the population of the United Kingdom had increased by 164 percent during that same period.[1] One of the principal causes of this inferior population growth was France's modest birthrate, which, in 1888, stood at 23.1, in contrast to the birthrates of 36.7 and 36.6 reported in Germany and Italy that same year.[2] Growing numbers of pronatalists studied the causes and consequences of depopulation, pursued a vocal propaganda campaign, and convinced the government to pass legislation promoting population growth through a variety of means, including financial incentives, restrictions on women's work, and protection of motherhood. In the twentieth century, pronatalists would work closely with the government in extra-parliamentary depopulation commissions in 1902 and 1912; the Conseil supérieur de la natalité, formed in 1919 to advise the government on demographic matters; and the Haut comité de la population, created in 1939 to design new laws on the family and the birthrate.

As the trauma of the *année terrible* fueled the pronatalist movement in the first decades of the Third Republic, it simultaneously created a desire to overcome the humiliation of defeat by establishing a vast empire outside Europe. While commentators frequently described France's earlier colonial expansion as "accidental," there was nothing accidental about the colonial campaigns of the 1880s and 1890s when France acquired new territory in Africa and Southeast Asia, greatly expanding an empire that by World War I would be roughly twenty-five times the size of the metropole. In the late nineteenth century, colonial expansion and settlement enjoyed considerable support in France that extended beyond the usual colonial circles and impinged on political discussions that ostensibly had nothing to do with imperialism. Though representing distinct political movements with few prominent members in common, the colonial lobby and pronatalist organizations of the early Third Republic were nevertheless born out of the same crisis and reflected similar anxieties concerning France's trajectory and position in the world. As a result, the discourses of these two groups intersected and presented similar conclusions.

This book explores that intersection by showing, first of all, that pronatalist ideas were an integral part of how colonial propagandists and administrators pursued their goals of establishing a strong French presence overseas and making colonies profitable. Pronatalism influenced how the Union coloniale française recruited people for settlement; pronatalist thinking led governors in places like Madagascar to try to make their colonies more profitable through state-controlled population growth and managing colonial subjects' reproduction; in large settler colonies such as those in North Africa, colonial governments considered pronatalist policies designed to encourage reproduction and support settler families to be essential to establishing a strong and permanent French presence. Second, this book details how demographic thinking about empire shaped pronatalists' strategies and their proposed solutions to depopulation. In the early Third Republic, many social scientists saw colonial settlement schemes as a medical question based on a sophisticated understanding of demography, race, and acclimatization, a body of knowledge that would determine whether or not the French could reproduce adequately in the colonies. While many late-nineteenth-century experts outside pronatalist circles produced pessimistic assessments of French prospects for establishing large settler colonies, those prominent statisticians and demographers directly engaged in questions relating to depopulation were among the vocal advocates of French colonial settlement in the 1870s. As the pronatalist movement became more organized in the late nineteenth and early twentieth centuries, pronatalists increasingly understood their demographic crisis in terms that transcended the boundaries of the metropole and positioned their empire as a key component in their nation's regeneration. In short, not only were French pronatalists aware of France's empire, but they emphasized the potential demographic benefits of colonial settlement, studied the pronatalist initiatives of colonial governments seeking to make settler colonialism viable, and collaborated with analogous organizations in the settler communities. By incorporating sources from both the metropole and empire, including familialist journals from French settlers in North Africa as well as archival material specific to colonial pronatalist policies, this book explores precisely why pronatalists came to believe that the maintenance of a large empire with settler colonies would be central to establishing demographic growth and strength.

Until recently, many historians underestimated the significance of empire in metropolitan France and instead posited that prior to decolonization the French public's interest in empire was fickle at best.[3] Along similar lines, other scholars have argued that over the course of the Third Republic, the French public became increasingly aware of their empire but rallied around it only in times of crisis, such as in 1914 and 1939.[4] More recently, as part of the "imperial turn," scholars such as Gary Wilder have discredited the image of Third Republic France as "simply a self-contained parliamentary republic that also happened to possess overseas colonies."[5] In particular, historians have been interested in examining the significance of empire to daily life in France, concluding that it was neither remote nor irrelevant but, rather, figured prominently in the French imagination. For instance, recent studies have analyzed the images of empire and the colonial "other" that flooded the metropole in films, the penny press, advertisements, and postcards.[6] Colonial exhibitions such as those of 1889 and 1931 speak of the popular fascination with the empire and its people.[7] In the twentieth century, the colonial encounter was no longer even limited to those travelers who ventured into the empire or visited colonial exhibits in the cities; it also occurred in factories, brothels, cafés, and the streets of cities as large numbers of colonial migrants arrived to fill the labor shortage, serve in the army, or attend university.[8] Collectively, these examples of colonial encounters and colonial consciousness ranged from the spectacular to the quotidian, revealing the interconnectedness of metropole and empire. They further suggest that, political and economic considerations aside, French people were not only aware of empire, but many encountered it on a regular basis.

Although historians have convincingly portrayed public interest in empire during the Third Republic in terms of its impact on mass culture, few studies explore how this phenomenon in turn affected political movements that lacked any direct connection to empire.[9] In his study of French imperialism between the world wars, Martin Thomas explores public perceptions of empire among a group of people he dubs the "imperial community."[10] Moving beyond official colonial circles, such as the colonial lobby, Thomas applies the label "imperial community" to a group of people consisting of "politicians, bureaucrats, colonial administrators, manufacturers, traders, media commentators, educators, missionaries, lobbyists and settlers that dominated the political discourse of empire after the First World War."[11] This book demonstrates that while French pronatalists were concerned with political issues of a primarily metropolitan nature, namely, the national birthrate, their engagement with this question nevertheless brought them to discussions of empire that placed them clearly in the "imperial community." Visions of empire were so pervasive in France during this period that pronatalists looked well beyond the borders of the metropole as they imagined solutions to what would, at first glance, be construed as a strictly metropolitan problem.

The first English-language historical study to address France's crisis of depopulation was that of Joseph Spengler, written in 1938.[12] An economics professor at Duke University, Spengler began his study by situating this historical topic in the politics of his day. He argued that "within the next quarter century true depopulation—a persistent long-run excess of deaths over births—will manifest itself in nearly all the countries of Europe and in those non-European countries to which Western civilization has spread."[13] Spengler detailed the demographic trends over the last few centuries, providing a number of explanations for the low birthrate and echoing the arguments made by French pronatalists. Like pronatalists, Spengler attributed the low fertility rate to many factors, including urbanization, military service, women's work, and the desire for social mobility. More recent scholars have returned to Spengler's work when considering pronatalism as part of their studies of sexuality, the woman question, feminism, the crisis of masculinity, nationalism, immigration, and the rise of the welfare state. These studies collectively reveal the persuasiveness and importance of pronatalist doctrine during this period and the fears that depopulation engendered.[14] Departing from Spengler, they rightly emphasize, moreover, that the anxiety surrounding the birthrate reflected more than simply pronatalists' stated fears of military defeat and economic ruin; pronatalism was also a response to concerns about gender identities and the changing roles of women and men in society.

Though demonstrating the far-reaching implications of demographic thinking in Third Republic France, scholars have thus far analyzed pronatalism within a specifically European context, focusing on France's rivalry with Germany and making few references to the empire. The European focus most likely stems from the fact that fears of depopulation initially gained momentum following a specifically European conflict, the Franco-Prussian War. In many other European states, by contrast, pronatalism developed in the context of colonial expansion, and imperialism has consequently figured more prominently in historians' assessments of the topic in other national contexts.[15] Anna Davin's article on British pronatalism, for example, positions the Boer War as a key event that gave rise to concerns about depopulation in Britain.[16] In France, by contrast, the birthrate began declining at a much earlier date than in Britain and became a national crisis prior to the scramble for Africa and following a European conflict that had nothing to do with empire. As this book will show, French fears of depopulation, though born out of a European crisis, eventually evolved beyond such European rivalries to include empire.

When discussing French population growth, whether in France or in the colonies, race was central to how pronatalists made sense of the demographic crisis. In this respect, Alys Weinbaum's concept of the "race/reproduction bind" serves as a useful reminder that reproduction and race are intricately connected.[17] Applying this concept to France and French colonies, we can see that pronatalists were primarily concerned with the relative strength of their nation, something that they measured with data on French reproduction and population growth. A low birthrate among those they considered capable of transmitting French racial identity to the next generation would threaten the existing "social systems hierarchically organized according to notions of inherent racial superiority, inferiority, and degeneration."[18] Conversely, pronatalists would be inclined to interpret a high birthrate among outsiders, particularly those residing on French soil, as the propagation of a rival social system with the potential to eclipse that of the French. It follows, therefore, that race and reproduction were intimately connected in these larger concerns about national strength and maintaining a particular social order.

Still, having established that French pronatalists saw reproduction in racial terms, it is necessary to consider what they meant when refer- encing "the French race." Though seemingly self-evident in meaning, the concept of "the French race" that regularly appeared in pronatalist literature was an inherently unstable category, changing over time and subject to conflicting interpretations. As historians have shown, the notion of a coherent French racial identity was partly complicated by the legacy of the French Revolution, which established shared culture, language, and territory as the central elements of national identity. Nineteenth-century theorist Ernest Renan was famous for empha- sizing that constructs like race and ethnicity had nothing to do with defining the French nation; this was a voluntary and subjective form of nationalism that could be contrasted with the more biologically or racially based nationalism of Germany.[19] Though willing to acknowl- edge the impact of universalism on French ideas of national iden- tity and citizenship, historians no longer accept this idea uncritically and have instead assessed the importance of race as a social marker in modern French history, despite official proclamations to the con- trary.[20] For the purposes of this study, it is essential to recognize that throughout the Third Republic race was an integral part of how pro- natalists conceived of the French population as a unified entity and interpreted France's demographic strength in relation to other popu- lations. When discussing the need to increase the French population in France, pronatalists had very specific ideas about who was French, ideas that were guided by concepts of racial purity. For instance, after World War I, André Michelin, a pronatalist and major donor to the Alliance nationale, restricted family allowances to "French" employ- ees at his company, denying such benefits to workers from elsewhere in Europe or the colonies.[21] This policy exemplifies how pronatalist- minded Frenchmen such as Michelin saw reproduction in racial terms.

Michelin had no interest in encouraging foreigners residing and working in France to have more children, despite the fact that French naturalization laws made it possible for some of these children to become French citizens, thereby adding to France's overall population growth.[22]

While this would seem to suggest a hostile attitude to immigrants and foreign workers, this was not universally the case, as pronatalists' ideas about who could be French or contribute to French demographic strength were malleable, changing over time and differing from one context to another. The research of Elisa Camiscioli, in particular, has enlarged our understanding of how ideas of race intersected with gendered anxieties to shape pronatalist views on immigration following World War I.[23] Camiscioli shows that despite the largely nationalist character of their movement, interwar pronatalists welcomed the assimilation of select European immigrants, most notably Italians, into the nation as a means of strengthening the race as a whole. Empire and, more specifically, colonized populations were not a central part of the immigration debate, as pronatalists vehemently opposed the immigration of people from Africa and Asia, whom they considered incapable of being assimilated and consequently adding to "French" demographic growth.[24] Tyler Stovall notes, moreover, that it was the very presence on French soil of workers from the colonies that shaped evolving French views of "white" European immigrants after 1914. Contrasting the "white" racial identity of the latter workers with workers from the colonies, French immigration reformers were more receptive to the arrival of Italians and other Europeans whom they believed to have the requisite racial characteristics needed for assimilation and absorption into the French population.[25]

This book will show that even as pronatalists saw a potential danger in interactions between France and its colonies (namely, in the form of migration of colonial workers to the metropole), they by and large supported imperialism. This is because pronatalists believed that it was not enough to encourage French population growth solely within France's borders; true demographic prowess entailed extensive French settlement of the colonies and support for French families both in France and in the empire. Ultimately, by imagining France's regeneration within the larger context of empire, pronatalists moved toward more complex ideas about race and population growth more generally. For instance, pronatalist awareness of the superior birth-rates exhibited by French populations in the empire prompted them to think differently about the concept of French racial decline and the impact of gender on the larger phenomenon of "race suicide." Also illustrating pronatalists' evolving racial thinking were their responses to pronatalist measures introduced in certain colonies. In some cases, as in Algeria, Morocco, and Tunisia, pronatalist policies were focused almost exclusively on the French settler population. In Madagascar, on the other hand, where the settler population was relatively small, the colonial government introduced a different set of pronatalist measures aimed at decreasing mortality rates and increasing fertility among Malagasy subjects. Although the policies developed in Madagascar were strikingly different from those in North Africa, both in terms of their nature and origin as well as the racial composition of the populations at which they were directed, metropolitan pronatalists demonstrated strong interest in and support for both forms of colonial pronatalism. Making sense of this response requires recognizing that colonial forms of pronatalism were premised on the idea that the future of the French empire depended on developing demographic resources, be it French settlers or select populations of colonial subjects. As establishing and maintaining a strong empire was an objective that had everything to do with the depopulation crisis, it is clear that French pronatalism extended beyond a simple desire to increase the "French" population of France through a uniform set of measures.

Consequently, one major contribution of this book is the evidence it offers showing that pronatalists understood their demographic crisis in global terms and positioned their empire as an essential part of the national regeneration they envisioned. That they thought about depopulation in global terms is also evident in their mixed response to fears of "race suicide" among their European rivals. While France's population began declining at an earlier date than did the populations of neighboring European states, depopulation was not a uniquely French anxiety in the modern period. By the twentieth century most states in Europe had likewise witnessed an appreciable decline in their population growths and developed policies aimed at improving the "quality and quantity" of their populations.[26] In some states, such as Germany and Great Britain, governments introduced a more selective form of pronatalism by encouraging higher birthrates in certain segments of the population and, in Nazi Germany's case, actively preventing the population growth of those they considered social undesirables.[27] On the other hand, in Italy and Spain, fascist leaders Mussolini and Franco pursued pronatalist policies that more closely resembled those of France.[28] Such distinctions aside, most European states in the twentieth century developed fears of degeneration and population decline that led to a variety of attempts to bring population growth under state control.[29]

Pronatalists were well aware of such demographic concerns elsewhere in Europe, and yet, for two reasons, this knowledge did little to assuage their fears of depopulation. First, pronatalists asserted that France remained at a numerical disadvantage because its depopulation crisis had emerged earlier than was the case elsewhere in Europe. Second and more significantly, pronatalists were well aware that birthrates outside of Europe remained strong and feared that Europe's position in the world was weakened by its relatively small population. Initially, pronatalists' extra-European demographic concerns were more focused on Asian populations than on African and American populations. Throughout the Third Republic, discussions of *le péril jaune* ("yellow peril") were evident in pronatalist literature and typically took one of two forms. On the one hand were fears that Asia's population was so large that it would inevitably "overflow" into Europe and inundate Europe's population.[30] On the other were concerns that this demographic disparity left French and other European colonies in Asia particularly vulnerable.[31] In this respect, Japan, widely believed to have designs on French Indochina as well as other European colonies in Asia, was seen as the most formidable threat.[32] As both of these two responses to the "yellow peril" make clear, pronatalists presented this particular demographic threat both in terms of its implications for France and its threat to European or Western powers generally. Outside France, nationalists in other European and Western countries were equally concerned about the rise of Japan and the mass migration of Asian workers in the nineteenth century. For instance, policy makers in the United States, Australia, and South Africa evoked the "yellow peril" when crafting restrictive laws designed to limit or prevent Asian immigration.[33]

Despite the fact that this was a period of intense rivalry between major European countries and empires, and this competition represented much of the driving force behind French pronatalism, there was simultaneously a sense of a shared demographic crisis among rivals. Competitive impulses aside, French pronatalists identified with other Europeans as members of the same race and believed that inadequate "white" population growth in places like Britain or Germany had consequences for the race as a whole. One example of this sense of a shared "European" or even "white" demographic crisis is visible in a pronatalist brochure titled "The White Race in Danger of Death."[34] Through graphs, illustrations, and statistical charts, the authors of this brochure sought to persuade the public that declining birthrates in other European countries gave French people little reason to celebrate; far from diminishing the nature of the crisis, this development only made it more severe.[35] Another revealing picture in the journal of the Alliance nationale depicted Japan as a large Asian man with an excess of 943,000 births over deaths in the year 1926; Britain, France, and Germany, however, had a combined excess of 823,000 births over deaths that same year and were depicted collectively as a smaller European man (fig. 1). Underneath the picture, the caption explains: "The true 'Yellow Peril' will be born of Western European countries' insufficient birthrate."[36] When considering the global ramifications of French depopulation, the editors of the journal considered it more relevant to present the birthrates of these three European rivals as a group. In this way, as they promoted awareness of French depopulation, pronatalists simultaneously educated the public about similar developments elsewhere in Europe and linked France's fate to that of other European states. By studying French pronatalists' interest in empire and support for colonial settlement, this book further elucidates how pronatalists' anxieties about a shared European depopulation crisis could exist alongside the persistent demographic rivalry they felt with Germany and other European states. Once pronatalists expanded their vision beyond Europe's borders and conceived of the issue in global terms, they began to think differently about how they would strengthen the French birthrate. For one thing, this "imperial turn" in pronatalist thinking generated impassioned arguments in favor of developing colonies as a destination for French migration. Also, in various colonies this global perspective on French depopulation meant envisioning the growth of certain rival European populations and select groups of colonial subjects as part of larger efforts to safeguard France's interests.

Ultimately, by exploring French pronatalists' complex reasons for supporting empire, this study sheds new light on one of the many myths that was integral to French imperialism: the idea that the establishment of an empire made France's population one hundred million strong. As many scholars have pointed out, the empire represented more than vast expanses of land of geopolitical and economic importance; the empire brought some sixty million colonial subjects under the French flag, thereby representing a valuable population reservoir.[37] One early proponent of the "population reservoir" theory was Charles Mangin, who in his 1910 book *La force noire* argued that West Africa's abundant population, which he grossly overestimated, could provide much-needed soldiers for depopulated France's army.[38] Soon after, the benefit to the metropole of this population became readily apparent when large numbers of colonial soldiers fought in the French army during the Great War, filling the void left by those Frenchmen who had never been born.[39] During this same war, other men from France's African and Asian colonies arrived in the metropole to fill the labor shortages created by the departure of many working-class men to the front.[40]

While many contemporaries may have had their reservations about the demographic value that the colonies represented for the metropole in this respect, it is important to remember that few pronatalists regarded France's colonial subjects as anything more than a temporary solution to France's demographic troubles. In fact, the idea of

LE PÉRIL JAUNE
Excédents des naissances sur les décès
En 1926

Japon	Allemagne	491.000
943.000	Grande-Bretagne	279.000
	France	53.000
	Total	823.000

Le véritable « Péril Jaune » naîtra de l'insuffisance de la natalité dans les pays de l'Europe occidentale.

Le nombre, c'est la force

Fig. 1. "Le péril jaune," *Revue de l'alliance nationale contre la dépopulation*, July 1928, 208. Reproduced courtesy of the Bibliothèque nationale de France.

being permanently reliant on colonial subjects to fill France's population void elicited numerous comparisons with ancient Rome. This comparison was not surprising given that, as Patricia Lorcin and Jonathan Gosnell have shown, French imperialists often presented the French empire as the next great Latin empire, continuing where ancient Rome had left off in not only Gaul, but also North Africa.[41] French pronatalists made additional historical connections; the French empire was not only "descended" from that of Rome but was threatened by a depopulation crisis similar to that which had weakened Rome.[42] Like France, Rome had been obliged to import foreign workers because of a labor shortage, the Roman countryside became subject to "peaceful colonization" by foreigners, and Rome increasingly relied on colonial soldiers to maintain the large empire that could not be defended with Roman soldiers alone. Drawing on the example of ancient Rome, French pronatalists were convinced that the loyalty of colonial soldiers could never be truly ensured and that being outnumbered by, and excessively reliant upon, France's colonial subjects was a sign of weakness, not a solution to depopulation.[43] Even if pronatalists saw some advantages to drawing on the demographic resources of the colonies during times of crisis, occasionally filling the ranks of the army and supplying workers to factories, their racial views led them to reject any notion of depending on non-European populations to compensate for France's low fertility. Instead, to pronatalists the demographic potential of empire resided in another myth, the myth of the prolific settler, or a belief that French settlers on average had a higher birthrate than their metropolitan compatriots. Ultimately, pronatalists saw the demographic potential of empire less in terms of offsetting France's numerical inferiority by bringing millions of colonial subjects under the French flag, and more as an important step on the road to encouraging a more robust French population growth, both in the settler communities and the metropole.

Methodology and Chapter Outline

Given the prevalence of demographic anxieties in Third Republic France and the sheer number of people who in one way or another engaged this question, it can be challenging to determine who was a pronatalist and what this label meant. Three considerations must therefore be kept in mind. First, it is important to recognize that the term *pronatalist* can be broadly applied to encompass individuals who, though not members of pronatalist organizations, were nevertheless involved in causes intersecting with demographic questions, something that led them to collaborate with such organizations or employ pronatalist rhetoric in their own arguments. For instance, activists seeking the abolition of regulated prostitution saw their cause as a moral crusade against a practice that corrupted men and degraded women; moreover, they presented regulated prostitution as a cause of depopulation due to its association with adultery, the spread of venereal disease, and women engaging in non-procreational sex.[44] In addition to social-reform movements can be added the Roman Catholic Church, whose leaders, cognizant of the declining influence of religion in French society, presented depopulation as the consequence of a secular government and a less observant population. They joined many pronatalists in asserting that religious faith was critical to replacing decadence and individualism with notions of morality and duty. Although the pronatalist movement was by and large male-dominated, in that its leaders were men and its committees predominantly composed of men, feminists were very assertive in demanding that pronatalists consider women's opinions. They were quick to emphasize the absurdity of a group of men assembling to develop recommendations on breastfeeding, maternal health, and child care without including mothers in these discussions.[45] Many feminists became active members of the pronatalist movement, attending meetings and giving presentations at pronatalist congresses and, through their activism, emphasizing the social importance of women's political participation.[46] To this end they presented their own goals, such as state support for motherhood and reforming married women's legal incapacity, as conducive to improving population growth.[47]

Despite the multiplicity of voices engaging the demographic debate in the metropole, my research revealed that individuals who published books about depopulation, were active members of pronatalist organizations, or were directly involved in promoting colonial settlement were the most inclined to present imperialism as a solution to French demographic decline. The Catholic Church in France was an active participant in discussions about the birthrate, but it largely addressed this issue separately from that of empire. Catholic missionaries in the empire, though very important in establishing French influence in the colonies, seemed similarly disinclined to treat the two questions simultaneously.[48] In addition to their active engagement of demographic questions, feminists were interested in empire, whether that meant investigating the condition of colonized women or attempting to carve out a greater role for women in the public sphere. Yet, with the exception of Mme Léon Pégard, whose work will be discussed extensively in chapter 2, feminists generally treated depopulation and imperialism separately. The most likely reason why feminists and Catholic clergy did not articulate the demographic question in this particular way is that the birthrate was only one of many issues with which they concerned themselves, and they generally only engaged this question insofar as it related to their primary objectives. Pronatalist organizations, on the other hand, established with the goal of devoting all of their energy to finding ways to improve population growth, were subsequently at the forefront of identifying a wide array of potential solutions to depopulation, solutions that included colonial emigration and drawing inspiration from colonial initiatives. It is for this reason that this book focuses mostly on those individuals and organizations primarily involved in either promoting colonial settlement or developing reforms to address French demographic decline.

Second, within the organized pronatalist movement there were many different organizations and approaches to achieving the mutual goal of stronger demographic growth. For instance, the Ligue pour la vie had Catholic roots, whereas the Alliance nationale pour l'accroissement de la population française had a strong secular and republican tone under the leadership of Jacques Bertillon, though it did move in more conservative directions during the 1920s.[49] Within these and related organizations there was a diversity of opinion as some activists focused their energy almost exclusively on finding ways to increase the birthrate and others, suspecting that such measures were not particularly efficacious, prioritized reforms that would reduce infant mortality. Most pronatalists developed agendas combining both approaches, and, as will be seen in this study, empire impinged on discussions about both decreasing infant mortality and increasing the birthrate.

Also crucial to this study are organizations that were familialist as opposed to pronatalist. According to Paul Smith, one of the key differences between the two ideologies is that pronatalism was "quantitative," in that its adherents sought measures that would boost population growth.[50] Familialists, on the other hand, were more concerned with the moral quality of the French family and with representing the interests of the *famille nombreuse* (large family). Familialist organizations typically restricted their membership to people with a designated number of children, something that distinguished them from the Alliance nationale, and were focused primarily on securing reforms intended to alleviate the financial challenges of raising a large family and to elevate the social importance of fathers of many children. These differences aside, familialists and pronatalists shared many of the same objectives and collaborated with one another during and after the Great War. Pronatalists considered policies extending financial assistance to large families an integral part of raising the birthrate, and they promoted the idea that people who had large families deserved to be respected and commended for their sacrifices. Familialists shared pronatalists' concerns about the declining French birthrate and lamented how few French people were willing to follow their example and have numerous children. It is for this reason that in chapters 4 and 5, which focus on the decades after World War I, this study utilizes both familialist and pronatalist sources.

The third and final consideration is that pronatalism, as a concept and a program for political reform, evolved considerably during the seventy years examined in this study. In the first decades of the Third Republic, pronatalist reformers built on the existing impetus to reduce high rates of infant mortality and saw their greatest success in introducing legislation designed to protect young children, most notably two laws in 1874 that strengthened government oversight of the wet-nursing trade and placed restrictions on child labor. In the 1880s and 1890s, pronatalists increasingly advocated measures that would encourage a higher birthrate as opposed to simply reducing child mortality. Many of the proposals during this period reflected the growing focus on motherhood and aimed to limit how many hours per day women could work outside the home, restrict pregnant women's work before and after the delivery, and assist indigent and unmarried mothers. The focus on "protecting" mothers, regardless of the circumstances under which they became pregnant, is most evident in the 1912 law allowing *recherche de la paternité* (paternity suits), a measure that enabled unmarried mothers to seek financial support from their child's father. The extreme loss of life during World War I, as well the war's impact on gender roles and family life, marked a new phase in the pronatalist movement as it made the depopulation crisis more urgent and compelling to the French public and the nation's leaders. In addition to seeing a growth in their memberships in the aftermath of the war, pronatalists and familialists in the 1920s increasingly asserted that the family, as a unit, had rights distinct from the individual, and with such arguments they successfully secured greater benefits and financial advantages for fathers and large families. The new concept of family rights was most evident in the campaigns for the family vote in the 1920s and 1930s. During this period there was also a renewed emphasis on discouraging family planning, most notably with the 1920 legislation banning the sale and advertisement of contraceptives and strengthening penalties for abortion.[51] Generally, the pronatalist movement moved in more-conservative directions during these years, particularly after 1934, when organizations such as the Alliance nationale increasingly worked with right-wing groups.[52]

Using these larger developments as a backdrop against which to assess the impact of imperialism on French pronatalism, the chapters that follow, organized chronologically, collectively demonstrate that pronatalists supported colonial emigration and settlement as solutions to French depopulation, studied the pronatalist initiatives of colonial administrators, and collaborated with analogous settler organizations. The first two chapters focus specifically on migration. Chapter 1 explains how and why settler colonialism became an essential part of the pronatalist agenda. It was the desire to establish healthy patterns of migration in order to trigger population growth that turned pronatalists into proponents of colonial expansion and settlement. This development had its origins in academic debates in the 1860s and 1870s about the impact of migration on individuals' family-planning decisions. Prominent demographers, led by Louis-Adolphe Bertillon, theorized that colonial emigration improved the demographic health of the nation but worried that France lacked a suitable destination for its emigrants because few French colonies were located in temperate zones where colonists acclimatized easily. This view changed in 1880 with the publication of Dr. René Ricoux's statistical study revealing that French settlers in Algeria had a birthrate exceeding that of the metropole. These findings not only produced more optimistic assessments of France's prospects for establishing a large settler colony in Algeria but also gave birth to the myth of the prolific settler. This image of colonial demographic strength was based on gendered ideas about individuals' family-planning decisions that ultimately shaped pronatalist arguments in favor of colonial expansion and settlement throughout the Third Republic.

Ideas about the causes of depopulation and the demographic benefits of colonial emigration resonated beyond pronatalist circles and influenced French efforts to recruit men and women for colonial settlement. As chapter 2 explains, relatively few French people migrated to the colonies in the late nineteenth century, a problem that the Union coloniale française (UCF) attributed in large part to the low birthrate. Focusing on the 1890s and the first decade of the twentieth century when the UCF was active in encouraging migration to the colonies, this chapter explores how the UCF expanded the myth of the prolific settler by developing ideas about why it was in the colonies that the French were likely to achieve what seemed difficult in France: a more stable gender order and a higher birthrate. They constructed the male colonial settler as a symbolically powerful countertype to the urban, metropolitan man who displayed all the wrong qualities thereby contributing to both the low birthrate and France's failure to settle its colonies. Through this image of colonial masculinity, both imperialists and pronatalists expressed their class-based and gendered anxieties about modernity. Concerns about depopulation also impinged on the UCF's efforts to recruit more women for colonial settlement, leading them to focus on women who struggled to find husbands and employment. In contrast to how the UCF appealed to prospective male settlers, the Société française d'émigration des femmes (SFEF) presented itself as a charitable organization that would provide women, who in this modern society struggled to fulfill their traditional roles as wives and mothers, with jobs in the empire. Although their first priority was matching these women with careers, it was expected that women would marry soon after arriving in the colonies and that their migration would contribute to the growth of French settler populations.

As these two chapters indicate, late-nineteenth-century pronatalists, like many French people, often thought about the empire in abstract terms, bringing together diverse peoples and administrative units into a single geographic space as they promoted the benefits of migration to "the empire." This vision of the empire was not entirely fictional, as the government did take some steps toward centralizing the colonial administration in the late nineteenth century by establishing a ministry of colonies as well as the École coloniale to train civil servants for colonial posts.[53] In the twentieth century this unified, abstract idea of empire would be expressed in the term "greater France," the notion of an expanded French nation of which both the metropole and colonies were integral parts.

That said, when it came to population policies in the colonies, pronatalists were well aware that methods of rule and administration varied substantially from one colony to the next. My research revealed that certain colonies were of greater interest and symbolic value to pronatalists than were others. This study draws on the example of recent studies that focus on the role of select colonies in shaping larger policy, rather than looking at the empire as a whole or studying a single colony in isolation.[54] To that end, chapters 3, 4, and 5 are structured as case studies focusing on population policies introduced in those colonies of particular interest to pronatalists and analyzing how, as they developed strategies to encourage French population growth, pronatalists understood colonial developments. Although there were French settlers all over the empire, and colonial authorities introduced pronatalist policies in a number of different places, the developments in colonies such as French West Africa seemed to generate relatively little interest among French pronatalists.[55] In fact, pronatalist discussions of empire mostly focused on four places: Algeria, Tunisia,

Morocco, and Madagascar. That Algeria would play a role in shaping French pronatalism is not surprising given that this colony was always exceptional in the French colonial imagination. Its conquest, initiated in 1830, marked the beginning of France's pursuit of a new empire. By the Third Republic the colony was seen as part of France due to its administrative assimilation, its large French settler population, and its proximity to the metropole. For the purposes of this study, Algeria was an important destination for French colonial emigrants, although pronatalists did envision French settlement of other colonies as well, and, even after French colonial migration declined in the early twentieth century, settlers in Algeria continued to shape larger debates about family rights in the 1920s and 1930s. Also significant to French pronatalists were Tunisia and Morocco. Joining France's empire in 1881 and 1912, respectively, these two protectorates were frequently associated with Algeria, as all three formed part of France's North African empire. Morocco and Tunisia were nevertheless seen in a different light, since they had fewer settlers and were administered indirectly, with residents-general reporting to the Ministry of Foreign Affairs. As that relationship suggests, these protectorates were never imagined as an extension of France or even as colonies properly speaking. Still, they, like Algeria, were considered suitable for more extensive French settlement and played an important role in interwar debates about family rights and suffrage reform. Madagascar, seemingly the outlier in this study, being much further away from the metropole and a less popular destination for French migrants, was nevertheless significant because of the pronatalist decrees introduced there in the late nineteenth and early twentieth centuries. This colony joined the empire in 1896 and was ruled directly, unlike Tunisia and Morocco, with an appointed governor-general reporting to the Ministry of Colonies.

Chapter 3 begins in the 1890s, a time when French pronatalists became more organized and sought to develop a comprehensive approach to encouraging population growth, one that initially focused on motherhood and protecting young children. For this reason, they took great interest in the work of colonial governments seeking to increase their respective populations and pave the way for future French settlement. The first such colony to shape pronatalism in this way was Madagascar. Declaring the island "underpopulated" and lacking a sufficient labor force, Governor-General Joseph Gallieni introduced a series of decrees between 1896 and 1905 designed to increase the population of the Merina people who lived in the central highlands of the island. Like pronatalists in France, Gallieni thought about depopulation in gendered terms, targeting Merina men and women in different ways and positioning motherhood as a centerpiece of his pronatalist decrees. Yet his initiatives were also informed by the colonial context in which they developed as well as his racialized thinking. Pronatalists eyed developments in Madagascar with interest and saw in Gallieni a "man of action" who was willing to address depopulation in a way that their own government seemed disinclined to do. Moreover, they considered Gallieni's reforms equally applicable to their efforts to confront the gendered causes of French racial decline. They therefore embraced Gallieni's population policies, despite the fact that these efforts were designed to increase a population that was not French. This shows that French pronatalism extended beyond simple efforts to increase numbers of French people. Addressing depopulation required solidifying France's position outside Europe, an objective that, it was believed, could only be accomplished by establishing demographically strong colonies.

By World War I, metropolitan pronatalists had become more successful at pushing proposed laws through France's parliament and witnessed a significant increase in their memberships. Yet, despite these achievements, birthrates continued to decline, and the loss of over a million young French men during the Great War rendered the pronatalist movement increasingly desperate to address the crisis by whatever means possible. As chapter 4 explains, it was thus in the interwar years that redefining citizenship by introducing familial suffrage, a system of voting in which parents receive supplemental votes to represent their children, gained credibility and dominated the pronatalist discourse of the period. Although familial suffrage was never enacted in France, it was introduced in Tunisia in 1922 and Morocco in 1926.

In their decision to implement familial suffrage, French officials in Tunisia and Morocco made clear connections between the strength of the French settler family and the maintenance of colonial rule. In each context, French settlers were outnumbered by both colonial subjects and other Europeans. Chapter 4 illustrates how pronatalist objectives could be more powerful and politically expedient in a colonial context. To colonial officials, the maintenance of colonial rule required encouraging French population growth. Because of the importance of the French settler family to these objectives, officials were inclined to think about political participation in familial, as opposed to individual or egalitarian, terms. This shift in political thought was particularly significant for metropolitan pronatalists, who urged their government to distinguish between male citizens on the basis of their contributions to overall population growth.

In the interwar years, the concept of family rights dominated the pronatalist movement. As the French state increasingly extended benefits to French families, benefits that many pronatalists considered to be fundamental rights, the disparity between raising a family in France and raising one in North Africa became all the more evident and acute. Chapter 5 explores the emergence of familialist organizations in the North African settler communities after World War I and shows how these organizations were focused largely on acquiring the same family rights as their compatriots in France. While in the nineteenth century pronatalists viewed the settler colonies in North Africa to be models of demographic stability, this perception changed in the 1920s due to the activism of the familialist movement and studies revealing a relative reduction in settler population growth. Fears of French depopulation in North Africa represented a departure from the optimism that Dr. Ricoux's study had inspired decades earlier; yet, pronatalists in France continued to see settler colonialism as an important component of their efforts to improve French population growth. In fact, during this period, metropolitan pronatalists were more interested in empire than ever before. This transformation can in part be understood as a reflection of the general growth of interest in empire seen in French society during the interwar years. Yet, as this chapter argues, metropolitan pronatalists' growing commitment to empire can be attributed equally to the emergence of settler familialist organizations. Despite many similarities between the groups, demographic concerns in North Africa differed fundamentally from those of the metropole. Nevertheless, because of the collaboration between these groups, the specific needs and concerns of the settler populations became part of the metropolitan pronatalist agenda. Studying this collaboration reveals, therefore, that French pronatalism should not be viewed as an exclusively metropolitan political movement that developed solely within France.

The conclusion explores the legacy of the myths, detailed earlier in the book, of the prolific settler and the influence of imperialism on individuals' family-planning decisions. It begins by looking at the introduction of the Code de la famille, a systematic approach to addressing depopulation that was introduced shortly before France's entrance into World War II and foreshadowed the efforts that Vichy officials would soon undertake to improve the birthrate and strengthen the French family. Following France's defeat in 1940, the French empire represented hope during these uncertain times, just as it had in 1871. While Vichy officials attributed French defeat to the inadequacies of the Third Republic and the decadence of French society, they saw settlers and colonial life in a very different way. Representing health and virility, colonial settlers were supposedly untainted by the decadence that characterized metropolitan life and were subsequently central to the national regeneration Vichy officials envisioned. Furthermore, despite France's defeat, many of the colonies were under Vichy's control and remained a symbol of French power. The history of colonial pronatalism and its interaction with that of the metropole thus sheds considerable light on why pronatalists in both France and the settler colonies later embraced Vichy's National Revolution. Ultimately, as this book demonstrates, pronatalists during and after the Third Republic believed that establishing and maintaining large settler colonies was essential to restoring demographic growth and safeguarding France's position in the world.

ONE

France's "Supreme Chance"

Migration and Pronatalist Visions of Empire

The growth of the French population and the extension
of our colonial empire are but two sides of the same
question . . . if the population does not increase, the
colonial empire is fragile, divisive, and useless; on the
other hand, our population cannot grow unless we have
colonies into which excess population can spread out.

—CHARLES RICHET, "La richesse et la population,"
Revue des deux mondes, 1883

When Charles Richet, physician and co-founder of the Alliance nationale, wrote these words, he expressed the commonly held pronatalist belief that depopulation and colonial settlement represented two facets of a single dilemma. In order to resolve the depopulation crisis in the metropole, France needed a secure empire with viable settler colonies; in order to solidify and strengthen the French empire, France needed to produce adequate numbers of emigrants to settle the colonies. At first glance Richet's equation of emigration with demographic strength would seem paradoxical. If emigration, by its very definition, suggests population loss, it would hardly seem logical for pronatalists to position it as a vital part of the population growth they sought. Yet, as this chapter will show, the desire to trigger demographic growth by establishing purportedly "healthy" patterns of migration was ultimately the decisive factor in transforming pronatalists into proponents of colonial expansion and settlement.

The pronatalist view that colonial emigration could produce a healthier rate of population growth in France has its origins in the 1860s
with the statistical studies of Louis-Adolphe Bertillon. Drawing on
eighteenth-century theories of population, Bertillon used statistical
evidence to argue that individuals restricted their fertility when they
believed that economic opportunities for their children were limited;
by opening up new and seemingly vast possibilities, settler colonies
encouraged a higher birthrate. Emigration to the colonies contributed
to this demographic strength, he maintained, as departures reduced
competition for resources and opportunities in the metropole and by
extension encouraged a higher birthrate at home. As a result of Bertillon's studies, belief in the theoretical benefits of colonial emigration
held sway in demographical, anthropological, and statistical circles
in the 1860s and 1870s. Though embracing these ideas, many of these
same social scientists expressed concerns that France lacked a suitable destination for its settlers. In 1880, Dr. René Ricoux intervened
in this debate with statistics showing that the birthrate for the French
population in Algeria had exceeded that of the metropole. This convinced metropolitan social scientists that emigration to Algeria was
not only feasible but also desirable from a demographic standpoint.
Following a flurry of discussion and interest, metropolitan pronatalists applied Ricoux's conclusions to their own theories about how to
influence individuals' family-planning decisions.

It was from Bertillon's theories and Ricoux's study, therefore, that
the myth of the prolific settler was born. One of many myths that
shaped French imperialism, the idea of the prolific settler was conceived in racial and gendered terms. First of all, in terms of the myth's
racial connotations, it is important to recognize that social scientists
understood acclimatization to be a racial characteristic that could be
identified through careful study of mortality and natality statistics for
French settlers, other Europeans in the colony, and colonial subjects.
Their analysis of this data led them to draw larger conclusions about
the relative aptitude of the French, as a race, to adapt to the Algerian climate. Once Ricoux established that the French had the requisite racial characteristics needed to thrive in this climate, and indeed

reproduce at a faster rate than in France, these conclusions impinged on debates about racial degeneration in France.

Still, despite the centrality of race to discussions of settlement and acclimatization, when Ricoux and the other social scientists examined in this chapter referenced "the French race," they were using a category of analysis that was neither as straightforward nor as neutral as they likely understood it to be. Scholars have noted the shifts that took place in French racial thinking in the second half of the late nineteenth century; influenced by the practice of empire, French identity was increasingly equated with "white" and European.[1] In colonial Algeria the idea that "the French race" was also white and European was particularly evident in discussions of acclimatization and demographic growth. For instance, when celebrating French fertility in Algeria, Ricoux and other social scientists were not referring exclusively to those settlers who were either from France or descended from French migrants. By contrast, Ricoux envisioned the French settler population absorbing some of the other European settlers through a combination of assimilation (for instance, learning to speak French) and scientifically guided intermarriage; ultimately, this would produce a "new white race" that was French.[2] This idea of French demographic growth excluded any possibility of intermarriage with the colonized Algerians, a practice that was in any case relatively uncommon in the colony.

Second, given the centrality of race to ideas about settler population growth, it is clear that Ricoux and pronatalists expected that French and other European women would migrate to Algeria, where their role would be, as in France, to reproduce the race. Though appearing as natality statistics in Ricoux's study, women were significantly absent from larger discussions about how migration and colonial life could affect individuals' reproductive choices, choices that accounted for the successful growth of the settler colony. This was not an aberration, however, as explanations about why men migrated and had more children in Algeria and other colonies were consistent with pronatalist thinking about family planning more generally. This was a set of beliefs about individuals' reproductive choices that shaped the myth of the prolific settler, a myth that ultimately inspired pronatalists to argue that the solutions to demographic decline could be found in colonial settlement.

Depopulation and Degeneration in Modern France

In order to understand the centrality of migration to pronatalist thought, it is necessary to begin with concerns about depopulation that developed in the eighteenth century when France was at the beginning of its "demographic transition," a steady decrease in fertility and mortality rates that would continue through the nineteenth century.[3] When Louis XIV ascended the French throne he ruled over the most heavily populated state in Europe. By the end of the seventeenth century, however, this picture of strength had given way to an image of demographic decline; many in the educated elite believed that costly warfare and the expulsion of Protestants after the revocation of the Edict of Nantes had reduced the population.[4] The perception that France was depopulated continued in the eighteenth century, shaping Enlightenment criticisms of both the monarchy and the Catholic Church. For example, as part of his criticism of despotism, Montesquieu argued erroneously that the world's population was substantially smaller in the eighteenth century than it had been in the ancient world.[5] Perceptions of depopulation such as these were not based on statistics, as royal efforts to quantify the population were fraught with error.[6] In fact, later statistical studies revealed that eighteenth-century France was not depopulated; its population increased substantially during this period, rising from roughly 22 million in 1700 to 28.1 million by 1801.[7] Yet this growth was due more to a reduction in mortality rates than an increase in fertility, something that made France unique in Europe. Consequently, it was in the eighteenth century that other European nations, whose rapid population growth resulted from both a strong birthrate and a reduced mortality rate, began to surpass France. While French people in the eighteenth century did not have access to statistics detailing these population trends, they nevertheless observed that families, particularly those in the upper classes, were smaller than in earlier generations and felt nostalgic for a time when people took pride in having many children.[8]

Eighteenth-century demographic anxieties stemmed from the widely held belief that the size of the population was directly connected to a kingdom's capacity to generate wealth; people consequently feared the economic effects of population decline.[9] Among the explanations given for the perceived depopulation of the eighteenth century was the depressed state of agriculture and industry, which reduced the majority of the king's subjects to poverty and thereby discouraged them from having more children.[10] Many Enlightenment thinkers blamed these problems on royal mismanagement and the lack of economic liberties.[11] However, consistent with the mercantilist thinking of the period, these writers also argued that France could only generate a limited amount of wealth until it expanded its territory. Consequently, many thinkers considered colonies an essential part of generating the prosperity that would in turn trigger population growth at home.[12] While this does represent a demographic argument in favor of colonial expansion, its proponents generally did not argue, as would Bertillon a century later, that the simple act of French migration to these colonies would also have a beneficial impact on the birthrate in France.

At the start of the nineteenth century, the earlier enthusiasm for population growth was displaced by Malthusian fears of urban overpopulation. For example, between 1800 and 1850, the city of Paris doubled in size, growing from half a million to a million people.[13] No longer inclined to see population as wealth, French elites saw the "dangerous classes" as a threat to their property and economic interests.[14] The rapid growth of French cities in the early nineteenth century generated middle-class anxieties about poverty, instability, disease, radicalism, and revolution. Fearing the effects of urban overpopulation, elites supported the Malthusian argument that unchecked population growth would condemn ever greater numbers of people to starvation and misery.[15] The famine in Ireland further bolstered such beliefs and convinced many experts, including Alfred Legoyt, who served as the director of the Statistique générale de France from 1852 to 1870, of the advantages of a low birthrate.[16] As in the eighteenth century, the French empire continued to shape proposed solutions to France's demographic ills in the mid-nineteenth century. Similar to

British plans to "shovel out paupers," many French social reformers saw in settler colonies, especially Algeria, an opportunity to relieve cities of redundant and socially undesirable populations. Emigration to Algeria would not simply reduce the social pressures in French cities; it would also establish a more permanent French presence in the colony. Ultimately, however, the urban workers recruited for colonial settlement proved to be ill-suited for colonial life, and such schemes were short-lived.[17]

The beginnings of France's transition to pronatalism can be seen in the final years of the Second Empire when writers continued to support Malthusian prudence but nevertheless worried that the population was growing too slowly relative to other nations. In the late nineteenth century, pronatalists would credit Léonce de Lavergne, who would later serve in the Senate, as being the first to identify and bring to the public's attention the danger that lay ahead. Writing in 1857, de Lavergne argued that France's population was no longer growing and that Malthusian caution, which he supported, had given way to an excessive "egoism" and "abuse of pleasures."[18] By the 1860s, arguments in favor of fertility restraint became increasingly rare in light of Prussia's growing power and influence in Europe. During this period, as in earlier decades of the nineteenth century, some thinkers considered Algeria a potential solution to the demographic crisis. For instance, in terms that pronatalists would later call "prophetic," journalist Lucien-Anatole Prévost-Paradol argued in 1868 that France had a "supreme chance" to increase its population and reclaim a respectable position in the world: the French colony in Algeria.[19] Ultimately, the gradual move away from Malthusian arguments was accelerated by France's catastrophic defeat in 1870. This debacle made clear the need to maintain a strong birthrate that would ensure adequate numbers of soldiers for the French army; it also discredited individuals, such as Legoyt, who had previously argued against population growth.[20]

In addition to being driven by nationalism, the desire for a stronger birthrate intersected with gendered and racial concerns about the supposed decline and "degeneration" of the French population. Beginning in the mid-nineteenth century, a number of scientists and writers became preoccupied with the idea that populations and races can become degenerate or progressively weaker, ultimately either dying out or being overpowered by another population. Sometimes such arguments focused on non-European populations whose degeneracy was supposedly evidenced by their dwindling numbers, the decay of their civilizations, or the ease with which Europeans conquered them. Simultaneously, the concept of degeneration became an expression of deep-seated fears about the quality of European populations and the impending fall of Western civilization. Paradoxically, these nineteenth-century fears of European degeneration coincided with a period of rapid colonial expansion in the late nineteenth century—expansion that was justified, in the minds of many Europeans, by the idea that they were racially superior to the populations under their subjugation. According to William Schneider, one way to understand this paradox is to see fears of degeneration as a consequence of Europeans' "overexpectations" in the advance of their civilization.[21] In other words, the optimism and faith in progress that characterized the era actually produced this pessimism because people observed what they considered to be a savage, backward existence persisting in certain segments of their own societies in spite of the advances of the age. In France, among the frequently cited symptoms of racial decline were an array of mental disorders, such as hysteria, insanity, and cretinism, and various social scourges, such as alcoholism, prostitution, vagrancy, syphilis, and tuberculosis. These symptoms of degeneration had a larger destabilizing effect as they contributed to crime, revolution, and pauperism. More importantly, many scientists emphasized that degeneration was self-reproducing and held dire consequences for subsequent generations. For instance, syphilitic mothers passed the disease on to their babies. Influenced heavily by the thinking of Lamarck, many French scientists also believed that criminal tendencies were likewise passed from one generation to the next as were other signs of degeneration like alcoholism and vagrancy.[22] Moreover, many of the afflicted were simply unable to produce viable offspring, their sterility being one more cause of the nation's low birthrate. As evidence that these ills were contributing to the larger decline of the

French population, writers and scientists pointed to statistics showing the number of army recruits unfit for military service because of
their stunted growth, their alcoholism, their hysteria, or other factors.
In some regions the rejection rate for army recruits was an alarm-
ing 60 percent, suggesting the rapid progression of French degeneration.[23] The fact that these symptoms of degeneration were supposedly
more prevalent among the lower classes was also a source of concern,
given that the poorest people often had the highest birthrates. While
in some European countries, such as England, class-based concerns
about racial degeneracy would make selective neo-Malthusianism and
eugenics more popular by the early twentieth century, in France pronatalism continued to predominate, the desire for a stronger birthrate
in all segments of the French population coexisting with deep-seated
fears about the quality of the population.

In addition to theorizing that there were medical causes behind
French racial decline, pronatalists emphasized the "voluntary sterility"
of the French population, thereby bringing attention to individuals'
reproductive choices. They presented the low birthrate as a symptom
of a larger moral crisis, drawing on an older set of concerns about gender identities and the welfare of the family. In explaining this crisis,
pronatalists sometimes attributed the problem to men who failed in
their social obligation to reproduce, something that indicated both a
lack of virility and honor.[24] Likening fatherhood to military service, for
example, pronatalist Jacques Bertillon wrote that a man's duty of producing three children was as important as his responsibility to defend
his country.[25] Pronatalists denounced men who ignored this "duty"
as they postponed marriage and fatherhood, ultimately producing
fewer than three children. They positioned the French *père de famille*
(father of the family) as the masculine ideal and emphasized his role
in national regeneration. Conversely, they described the *célibataire*,
or single man, as an irresponsible male type who lived a life of moral
depravity and decadence unburdened by familial expenses. Although
some married men also visited brothels, spread venereal diseases, and
abandoned their pregnant mistresses, pronatalists placed much of the
blame for these social problems on the shoulders of the *célibataire*.

FRANCE'S "SUPREME CHANCE"

Although many pronatalists condemned childless men, they recognized that financial considerations might compel some married men to limit their families to fewer than three children. Consequently, when discussing male "voluntary sterility," pronatalists often presented it as a rational, though problematic, decision. For instance, when members of the Société d'anthropologie discussed the low birthrate in 1874, they presented the problem as the "natural preoccupation of a father to assure the future of his children." Clémence Royer, the lone woman present at this meeting, critiqued this view for its presumption that men were the only ones involved in family planning, an idea that overlooked the influence of mothers.[26] Although Royer's opinions were largely rejected or ignored at the time, she was correct in identifying the widespread assumption that important family decisions were made by men, a view that shaped pronatalists' understanding of depopulation. This example also illustrates how pronatalists, even as they denounced family planning, were very concerned with why individuals made this choice and were careful to differentiate between what they considered legitimate reasons and purely selfish impulses. Because pronatalists believed that many married men made such decisions out of a desire to provide adequately for their children, some of the pronatalist legislation introduced later in the Third Republic would appeal to men as breadwinners by offering financial incentives.

Pronatalists understood women's reproductive choices in an entirely different light, and for this reason much of their outrage at French demographic trends was directed at women and what they saw as an unnatural gender order. As many historians have shown, nineteenth-century conservative thinkers drew on older notions of "nature" to describe women's fundamental differences from men and justify their relegation to the private sphere.[27] By aligning women's "natural" functions within the family, such as child-rearing and reproduction, with the welfare of the nation as a whole, conservatives both asserted the national importance of stable gender identities and increasingly legitimated state intervention into family life. In this vein, some pronatalist propaganda, particularly in the nineteenth century, scrutinized the behavior of mothers and connected high rates of infant mortality to women working outside the home, relying on wet nurses, ignoring the fundamentals of hygiene, or "morally abandoning" their children. The shortcomings of these mothers were not, however, the main focus of pronatalist propaganda.[28] Far more disconcerting and unnatural to pronatalists in the late nineteenth century were modern, independent women who chose to have few or no children. After the mid-1890s, this type of woman was increasingly in the public eye and became known as the *femme nouvelle* or new woman, a term borrowed from the American writer Sarah Grand.[29] Pronatalists viewed the rise in divorce after 1884 and the growing numbers of women entering the professions and institutions of higher education as contributing factors behind this phenomenon and the concomitant decline in childbearing.[30] Also of great concern was the feminist movement, whose members advocated a greater public role for women that included more equality within marriage and, especially after the Great War, political rights.[31] Expecting women to devote themselves selflessly to their families, pronatalists looked aghast at what they saw as rampant "individualism" in French society. By deciding, on the basis of their own happiness, needs, or ambitions, when or if to have a baby, some women acted more like autonomous individuals than as dutiful members of a family unit. Moreover, because such women showed that pregnancy was not an inevitable part of a woman's life but rather a choice that some rejected, they also challenged prevailing views about women's "natural" roles as mothers and wives.[32] Pronatalists challenged this attitude, equating some women's aversion to repeated pregnancies with mental illness.[33] Moreover, pronatalists cited leading doctors of the era whose studies concluded that a woman who avoided pregnancy did so at her own peril, as her body, made for producing babies, would sicken and weaken if prevented from fulfilling its natural role.[34]

Although they reserved their most severe criticism for the "new woman," pronatalists also had a great deal to say about married middle-class women who had few or no children. Whereas pronatalists could empathize with bourgeois men who limited their fertility due to the high cost of providing for a child, they took for granted that bourgeois wives were far removed from serious decisions about managing finances and funding their children's educations. Consequently, they alleged that married bourgeois women who avoided pregnancy acted out of selfish and vain interests that could include the refusal to take on additional responsibilities in the home, the desire to continue spending lavishly on entertainment and a stylish wardrobe, concerns about losing their beauty, and the fear of childbirth. The belief that it was primarily women's choices that were problematic was particularly evident in how the scale and progression of depopulation was assessed. Generally, pronatalists discussed the birthrate in terms of the number of births per thousand women within a particular age group rather than the number of births per thousand people in the population, an approach which implied that it was mostly women's choices and actions that yielded the low birthrate.[35] In an attempt to influence women's decisions, pronatalists unleashed propaganda elevating motherhood to the status of a patriotic duty and positioning single womanhood as an abnormality that threatened the future of the nation. This approach nevertheless reveals an interesting paradox in French pronatalism: although pronatalists militated against the idea of pregnancy as a choice, they recognized that many couples were treating it as such and proceeded to try and shape that choice. They opposed the practice of family planning yet sought to influence family-planning decisions with propaganda intended to persuade women to have more children for the good of the family and nation. This impulse to persuade nevertheless coexisted alongside more coercive proposals reflecting a desire to constrain women's choices and reestablish the patriarchal family. Over the course of the Third Republic, pronatalists consistently advocated reforms aimed at restricting women's employment and defining a woman's place in society primarily in terms of her role as a mother.

Theories of Depopulation and Migration

As they sought to comprehend and document individuals' reproductive choices, pronatalists were aided by a new statistical language for describing the population: demography. Efforts to not only measure the size of the population but also use a quantitative analysis to study its internal and external influences had their roots in the Old Regime. However, it was not until the combined effects of industrialization and revolution in the early nineteenth century generated significant interest in the "social question" that France entered what was known as the "era of statistical enthusiasm," a growing public fascination with numbers detailing the incidence of disease, criminal activity, and mortality.[36] The study of population took a distinctive form in France, where researchers viewed their country as a group of "virtual strangers" and devised new social aggregates in order to understand variations within the larger population. Rather than relying on averages, as did their English counterparts, French population researchers distinguished between the married and the single, the male and the female, as well as class and age groups.[37] The study of population had implications beyond the realm of social science, as it coincided with, and contributed to, the growth of the French state. By compiling data illustrating the interactions between different aggregate groups and their susceptibility to such external forces as disease, and then presenting these data in statistical tables, population researchers could make claims about collective interests as well as individual obligations to the larger group. As the Third Republic progressed, the need to defend the newly defined collective interests from destabilizing forces was increasingly used to justify state intervention into some of the most private aspects of women's lives: reproduction and child care.[38]

One of the key figures in the development of demography was the physician Louis-Adolphe Bertillon (1821–83). According to his children, who published a memorial about him in the *Annales de démographie internationale*, the inspiration for the new discipline of demography came in response to the failure of the June Revolution of 1848.[39] At this time, Bertillon was a young medical student who openly supported the Republican cause in the hopes that the revolution would emancipate the virtuous worker. Between the Revolution of 1848 and Napoleon III's 1851 coup d'état, Bertillon was arrested three times and met his future father-in-law, the botanist Achille Guillard, in prison.[40] In response to the upheavals that led to their incarceration, Bertillon and Guillard contemplated the social utility of developing a new discipline that would use statistics to determine the probability of misery occurring in human society. According to Guillard, *la statistique humaine*, which he would rename *démographie* in 1854, was the only science that definitively established "the state of the nation."[41] Throughout his career, Bertillon published widely on a variety of topics including infant mortality, birthrates, and marriage. He was one of the founding members of the Société d'anthropologie, served as the president of the Société de statistique de Paris, and held the chair in demography at the École d'anthropologie. In addition to his contributions to the establishment of these new disciplines, Bertillon was active in government, serving as mayor of the fifth arrondissement in Paris. Toward the end of his life he would lead the Paris statistical office and lobby for the creation of an analogous institution in Algeria. After Bertillon's death in 1883, his son Jacques continued his father's work in the Paris statistical office and expanded his father's campaign to reduce mortality rates and achieve a "healthy" birth index.[42]

In his writing about French population trends, Louis-Adolphe Bertillon argued that six social phenomena were central to understanding demographic change: marriage, death, birth, immigration, emigration, and internal migration.[43] One of the questions that preoccupied him was that of infant mortality, still relatively high during this period. Bertillon believed that simple figures detailing the incidence of infant mortality failed to indicate its causes. However, by using statistics to show a correlation between numbers of infant deaths in the city of Paris and use of the wet-nursing industry upon which so many Parisian parents relied, he showed that statistical aggregates could be used to illuminate otherwise invisible facts. In 1858 Bertillon presented his findings in a paper, "Étude statistique sur les nouveau-nés," which he delivered to the Académie de médecine and that was later published after his death in 1883.[44] At the time of the paper's presentation, relatively few people objected to the well-established practice of sending babies out to nurse. Many working-class women hired wet nurses out of necessity, as they could not breast-feed while at work. Wealthier families likewise engaged wet nurses because they wanted to give the mother time to recuperate and believed that it was healthier for a baby to spend his or her first months in the country. Yet as authorities and reformers became increasingly determined to reduce infant mortality, they alleged that the practice caused thousands of infant deaths each year as wet nurses sought to earn a living by accepting multiple babies simultaneously, knowing full well that they could not possibly feed them all. Critics alleged that wet nurses substituted cow's milk (which led to gastrointestinal illnesses), underfed their charges, or outright neglected them. Although Bertillon's 1858 paper did not have an immediate impact on legislation, it eventually inspired the Roussel Law, which introduced restrictions on the wet-nursing trade in 1874. When Théophile Roussel proposed this law in the National Assembly he drew heavily on Bertillon's publications, including the *Atlas de démographie figurée de la France*.[45]

In addition to his research on infant mortality, Bertillon published widely on the theme of migration, ultimately laying the theoretical foundation for pronatalist arguments in favor of colonial emigration and settlement. He compared statistics concerning birthrates and emigration for Britain, France, and Germany and concluded that there was a correlation between demographic strength and outward migration. While the idea of emigration as a solution to depopulation could appear paradoxical, Bertillon argued that a nation's ability to expand outward and fill sparsely populated regions of the world with its people was essential to its demographic growth.[46] This theory rested on a number of highly debatable assumptions, including the notion that economic factors, especially parents' assessments of their children's future employment prospects, determined individuals' reproductive choices. First, Bertillon argued that the departure of emigrants stimulated the birthrate in the home country by creating more room and opportunities for the next generation, something that in turn encouraged people to have more children.[47] Second, once a healthy pattern of migration was established, with sufficient numbers of people departing, that pattern became self-reproducing, since the initial increase in the birthrate following the first wave of departures would in turn produce more people who wanted to emigrate. According to this theory, it was therefore critical to have a preliminary group of people willing to leave the home country as well as a destination for these emigrants. Conversely, without a permanent current of emigration abroad, the population would remain stagnant and confined to reproducing itself within narrow, suffocating borders.

Finally, Bertillon theorized that French emigration would be most beneficial if it were directed to French colonies, so that migrants would remain part of the nation rather than being absorbed into foreign populations. Bertillon's analysis of statistical data therefore led him to advance the idea that France needed settler colonies in order to achieve stronger population growth, a demographic argument in favor of colonial settlement that would later complement the preexisting political and economic arguments for empire. Countering claims that colonial emigration contributed to depopulation by spreading the French population thin, Bertillon asserted that his conclusions were based on scientific evidence and statistics. Arguments to the contrary, such as those advanced by Enlightenment philosophers Montesquieu and Voltaire, were based on philosophy or "speculation" and were therefore, consistent with the thinking of the day, less credible than the conclusions of objective statistical studies.[48] That Bertillon used statistics to paint a very different picture of the role the French empire could play in efforts to achieve a healthy birth index in France shows that data detailing French population movements influenced not only metropolitan reform organizations but also questions relating to colonial expansion and settlement.[49]

Although Bertillon developed a solution for depopulation that many social scientists accepted in theory, it did not apply in practice to nineteenth-century France. In the seventeenth and eighteenth centuries, France sent many settlers to its colonies in North America, exhibited a high birthrate, and boasted the largest population in Europe.[50] By the nineteenth century, however, this was no longer the case, and proponents of colonial emigration stressed the relative lack of migration out of France.[51] As an example of how France's emigration abroad lagged behind that of its rivals, between 1820 and 1855 only 200,000 French people arrived in the United States, compared with 1.25 million German immigrants and 1.3 million British and Irish immigrants during the same period.[52] In addition to generally producing fewer migrants than rival European states, France also lost many of its departing emigrants to foreign countries such as Argentina, Chile, Canada, and the United States.[53] Scattered in this way, emigrants ceased to contribute to the growth of French populations abroad, as they were absorbed into foreign nations. Furthermore, the low birthrate in France encouraged the arrival of foreign immigrants who filled any vacancies created by emigration, thus eliminating emigration's potential for inducing demographic growth.

According to Bertillon, because of preexisting conditions, France failed to gain from either of the demographic benefits of colonial emigration: emigration did not trigger a stronger birthrate in the metropole, and it did not lead to growing concentrations of French populations abroad. This statistical dilemma led Bertillon to argue that France needed an empire with viable settler colonies in order to reverse these demographic trends. He concluded that in the interest of "soliciting our birthrate which languishes, to not lose annually our 15,000 to 20,000 emigrants who disappear, either in the United States or in the Plata basin, we also need a Victoria."[54] To Bertillon, the source of Britain's demographic strength was its strong settler colonies, most notably Australia, which gave Britain additional territory into which it could grow. Without viable settler colonies, France would continue to lose population to the Americas and would remain in its demographic slump.

Despite extolling the demographic benefits of colonial emigration and convincing most of his fellow social scientists of this theory, Bertillon stopped short of advocating colonial emigration in the early 1870s. Like the majority of anthropologists, statisticians, and demographers of his era, he saw an enormous obstacle to France's colonial settlement schemes: the problem of acclimatization, or the ability of people to adapt to climates other than their own. Statistical studies of birth and death rates among European populations in the colonies tended to support one of two views concerning the ability of French colonial settlers to acclimatize to a different climate. Those who adhered to the polygenist view believed that the human race had multiple origins and tended to emphasize the "non-cosmopolitism" of humanity; in other words, when individuals moved to a region of the world with a climate markedly different from their own, they lived shorter lives and produced fewer children. Proponents of monogenism, on the other hand, believed that the human race had a common origin and tended to emphasize the "cosmopolitism" of humanity; as a result, they believed that people would be able to live and reproduce equally in different climates.[55] Still, even if they accepted that eventual French acclimatization in the tropics was possible, monogenists generally saw it as a challenging process that depended on many variables, including the dissemination of medical expertise on colonial hygiene.

The question of acclimatization led French social scientists to the view that Britain's great advantage in the race for superior population growth was its large empire, which included vast territory in temperate zones.[56] Yet experts worried that few of France's colonies were located in regions of the world that were suitable for French settlement; acclimatization would be difficult in colonies such as Indochina and Senegal, for example.[57] That French officials failed to take acclimatization into consideration when establishing new colonies, thinking more in terms of the economic benefits of acquiring colonies of exploitation in the tropics, was, to Bertillon's way of thinking, a misguided approach that overlooked the real benefits that colonies could provide. Bertillon explained: "It is not spices that we need to defend ourselves against the rising Germanic tide: it is men and our race will never produce any in the tropics!"[58] France's history of colonial expansion consequently lacked a scientific basis and was determined more by economic priorities than a solid understanding of demographics and acclimatization.

Although demographic data suggested that the majority of French colonies were unsuitable for extensive French settlement, one colony seemed to offer some hope: Algeria. Whether or not the French would be able to tap into the demographic potential of this colony was a medical question concerning the acclimatization of French settlers in the North African climate. Data from the 1860s indicated that the Algerian climate had ceased to decimate Europeans as it did in the earliest years of colonization, though the mortality rate continued to exceed the birthrate.[59] By the 1870s population figures were more positive, and statisticians such as Frederick Passy and Louis-Adolphe Bertillon became convinced that acclimatization was under way, though by no means complete. Bertillon argued in 1873 that acclimatization had reached the third of four stages, which was marked by "an equilibrium between births and deaths, but at which the slightest circumstances stop or destroy the population's progress. It is only when a surplus of births becomes regular and the population follows a normal growth that acclimatization is complete."[60] As this definition makes clear, scholars such as Bertillon believed that acclimatization was advancing but hesitated to declare it a fait accompli, concluding instead that only time and observation would yield more concrete answers. Social scientists were also reluctant to draw definitive conclusions because they were constrained to work with incomplete and often outdated data. For instance, in an 1873 article comparing the French population of Algeria with the British population of Victoria, Bertillon explained that the census taken in Algeria in 1872 gave only an overall indication of the size of the population; the most recent year for which a more "analytical" study of the population had been undertaken was 1852. Consequently, for this article in 1873, Bertillon had to work with a twenty-year-old demographic study and statistical data that, though more recent, provided little information about the composition of the population.[61]

Because they lacked accurate, long-term data detailing population trends in Algeria, social scientists such as Bertillon looked to classical history for clues about whether or not French settlers were likely to thrive in the Algerian climate. Despite the vast number of centuries that separated the Roman Empire from nineteenth-century France, the fact that Bertillon and his colleagues would consider Roman colonization a relevant point of comparison was to be expected, given how the French understood their empire's place in history. French imperialists often presented their empire as a successor to that of ancient Rome, using this "foundation myth" and the idea of historical continuity to justify their presence in Algeria and ultimately in Tunisia.[62] From this perspective, France's territorial claims predated those of the

Arabs, whom the French considered to be the true invaders, a conclusion that shaped not only their sense of legitimacy but also their definition of a civilizing mission. While the combined effects of the Arab invasion and Rome's "temporary" withdrawal from North Africa had plunged the region into darkness, France's "revival" of the centuries-old Latin empire reintroduced civilization.[63]

Also viewing the ancient Romans as a racially similar population, many social scientists considered their survival and adaptation to the Algerian climate a litmus test of French settlers' ability to acclimatize. How successfully the Romans had settled Algeria and adapted to the climate was nevertheless a highly debated question and a source of disagreement within scholarly circles. Louis-Adolphe Bertillon, for one, argued that the Romans did not acclimate in North Africa and that this made long-term Roman colonization impossible.[64] This view was disputed by other social scientists citing evidence of long-term settlement of Roman civilians in Algeria. For example, one contributor to the *Annales de démographie* argued that archaeological excavations of a Roman graveyard attested to the acclimatization of the Roman population in North Africa. He explained that a third of the Romans buried in the tombs studied in El-Meraba died between 70 and 110 years of age. As unlikely as this longevity seems, the author nevertheless presented it as a "guarantee" that the French would successfully settle in this region.[65] Other contributors went so far as to claim that not only did Roman settlers survive in the Algerian climate, but their descendants continued to live in Algeria in the present day, a factor that could be taken as further proof that a Latin population could thrive in this region. For instance, René Ricoux engaged the ongoing ethnological debate over the origins of the Kabyle population by arguing that Romans and Kabyles had formed alliances against Arab invaders, intermarried, and produced a new race of which the present-day Kabyles were the descendants.[66] Jacques Bertillon nevertheless disputed this conclusion, stating that the fact that some Kabyles had fair hair did not establish that Latin populations could acclimatize, because "it is perfectly proven that these men are not of our race."[67] Though divisive, the interrelated questions of Roman acclimatization and the ethnological origins of the Kabyles underscores the importance that social scientists concerned about France's birthrate attached to the question of French acclimatization in Algeria.

Uncertainties about French acclimatization led many metropolitan thinkers to conclude in the 1870s that the process of acclimatization could be facilitated through intermarriage with other "Latin" populations. This argument in favor of engineering a new French racial stock that was better suited for colonial settlement was shaped in large part by Ricoux's research. Ricoux was a French doctor in Philippeville, Algeria, who would ultimately intervene in France's depopulation debate with his 1880 study of Algerian demographics. However, it was in 1874 that Ricoux first became known in the metropole with a study concerning the acclimatization of French settlers in Philippeville.[68] In this preliminary study, Ricoux set out to determine whether or not French settlers had the racial characteristics needed to thrive in Algeria.[69] Foremost among his conclusions was the belief that "artificial acclimatization," achieved through scientifically guided intermarriage between French and other European settlers, was essential to completing the process of acclimatization in Algeria and establishing a more permanent French presence in the colony. Ricoux analyzed the birth and death rates of European settlers, taking into consideration differences in nationality and, in the case of the French population, distinguishing between the regions of France from which settlers originated; he also made special note of instances of intermarriage between settlers from different regions or countries. He concluded that settler society in Algeria had produced a "new white race" composed of settlers from all over Europe, each to varying degrees suited, or ill-suited, to the climate.[70] The future of French rule depended, he concluded, on creating a resilient settler population by studying the unique proclivity of each nationality to acclimatize and in turn using these data to determine which nationalities should intermarry to produce offspring well suited to this climate. Ricoux went on to argue that marriage should be influenced by scientific facts rather than "sentimental inclinations derived from a stubborn and dangerous patriotism."[71] As an example of this "dangerous patriotism," Ricoux noted the "stubbornness" displayed by settlers from northern France, most notably Alsatians, who struggled to acclimate to the Algerian climate. His research indicated that Alsatians would be best off marrying and reproducing with Italian and Spanish settlers, but instead they preferred the equally ill-adapted German settlers.[72] As early as 1874, therefore, Ricoux advanced the idea that the feasibility of French colonial ambitions depended on a sophisticated understanding of demography, race, and acclimatization, a view seconded by many metropolitan social scientists, including Jacques Bertillon.[73]

In the 1870s, therefore, the demographic benefits of emigration to Algeria received reserved encouragement from the Bertillons, Passy, and their colleagues. That this group of social scientists remained cautiously optimistic about the possibilities of French settlement in Algeria is striking when compared to more negative assessments of French acclimatization seen in other academic circles. As Eric Jennings has shown in his analysis of studies written by military doctors and anthropologists (among them Alphonse Bertillon, Jacques's brother), French commentators in the second half of the nineteenth century were generally pessimistic about the possibilities of French acclimatization in either North Africa or the tropics.[74] Yet the research undertaken by Louis-Adolphe Bertillon and his fellow statisticians and demographers indicates that many social scientists, particularly those most engaged in questions relating to French depopulation, were inclined to present the possibilities of French colonial settlement in a more positive light. By the 1870s, the only factor that prevented Bertillon et al. from fully supporting colonial emigration was the lack of solid scientific data from which they could draw more accurate conclusions. No comprehensive study of Algerian demographics had ever been carried out, and the demographic benefits of French colonial emigration had yet to be definitively established.[75]

Ricoux and the Myth of the Prolific Settler

Dr. Ricoux's most important contribution to debates about French settlement in Algeria came in 1880 with the publication of *La démographie figurée de l'Algérie*.[76] In this study, Ricoux set out to determine precisely how valuable Algeria was for France by assessing the French population's adaptation and growth in the colony on a larger scale. He explained that this was a challenging task because official documentation was incomplete, imprecise, and published irregularly. Furthermore, prior studies of Algerian demographics were carried out by visitors from the metropole studying small segments of the population over short periods of time. As a member of the settler community, Ricoux believed himself well positioned to break new ground with a study of Algerian demographics on a large scale, over a number of years, and using consistent scientific methodology. In particular, he drew on Louis-Adolphe Bertillon's work on French acclimatization in Algeria.[77] Unlike many of his predecessors who produced statistics for the European population as a whole, Ricoux differentiated between segments of the population by nationality, age, marital status, and sex.[78]

Ricoux's study challenged the contemporary adage that the cemeteries represented the only growing French settlements in Algeria. In fact, Ricoux argued, Algeria's French settlers had not only survived but had become a thriving population with a birthrate surpassing that of the metropole. While in France the birthrate was only twenty-six per thousand, in Algeria the French had a birthrate of thirty-seven per thousand. Ricoux used this data to argue that French settlers had acclimated and to corroborate Bertillon's theories about the correlation between emigration and demographic strength. One critical difference, however, is that while Bertillon presented colonial emigration as conducive to population growth in colony and metropole alike, Ricoux only assessed this question in terms of Algeria. Still, Ricoux used his findings to argue that Algeria represented a valuable demographic resource for France. He concluded by urging the government to promote colonial settlement and to use Algeria as an outlet for French emigration.

Algeria as a Fountain of Youth

It was because of Ricoux's findings on Algeria that the French empire became an important part of how pronatalists envisioned restoring a healthy rate of population growth. Pronatalists and others inter-

FRANCE'S "SUPREME CHANCE"

ested in the depopulation question responded directly to Ricoux's work in their published books and editorials, repeating his and Bertillon's arguments about the connections between colonial emigration and demographic strength. The editors of the *Annales de démographie* argued that colonization represented the most certain way of increasing France's birthrate and presented Algeria as precisely the colony that would provide this demographic benefit to the metropole.[79] Also suggesting that there was something specific about Algeria that influenced individuals' reproductive choices, the political economist Paul Leroy-Beaulieu observed that "the Frenchman, who has lost his fecundity in France, seems to find it again in Algeria."[80] Charles Buloz, the director of the *Revue des deux mondes* and brother-in-law of pronatalist Charles Richet, affirmed Ricoux's assessment of Algeria as a "fountain of youth where the languishing birthrate of France must immerse itself."[81] Whereas these commentators focused their statements on Algeria, others applied the lessons learned from the Algerian example to French colonial endeavors more generally. They presented Ricoux's findings as proof that the French could acclimate and reproduce in other colonies and envisioned the eventual settlement of other regions of the empire.

One reason why Ricoux's study inspired so much hope is that it seemed to show that France's population was by no means degenerate or genetically predisposed to depopulation. In other words, the discouraging population trends were reversible. Presenting the issue in racial terms, Ricoux stated that the growth of the Franco-Algerian population proved that the French race was not doomed to continued decline: "Evidence to the contrary is bursting on the African soil where, after barely a half century, with its worrisome beginnings, we have achieved, not only the birthrate of twenty-six like in Europe, but that of thirty-seven!"[82] Echoing these sentiments, Jacques Bertillon stated that Ricoux's study showed that "sterility is not a characteristic of the French race."[83] Rather, as Victor Turquan and others concluded, French settlers in Algeria had shown that depopulation was simply a consequence of life in France and that French people became prolific once they left France to establish themselves overseas, whether in Algeria or in other colonies.[84] Echoing Louis-Adolphe Bertillon's theories, pronatalist Paul Ponsolle wrote in 1893 that the French race still had its vitality and that all that reformers needed to do was "to give it air and space, so that it can develop itself and grow vigorous branches."[85] To pronatalists, Ricoux had demonstrated that it was in the empire that the French could achieve the very things they appeared to find difficult in the metropole: the establishment of a French population whose birthrate equaled, and would eventually surpass, that of European rivals.

The theme of youth evoked in many of these editorials is an important part of how settler colonialism shaped ideas about French population growth. Pronatalists asserted that having this settler colony in Algeria allowed France to tap into the kind of youthful energy that was characteristic of new, emerging nations and also an important part of their demographic strength. This view was consistent with contemporary historical ideas about the rise and decline of nations. For example, in an 1886 book on French depopulation, the German Dr. Rommel explained that nations were like people in that they were not made to live eternally or remain permanently vigorous.[86] A declining birthrate, slow rate of expansion abroad, and minimal current of emigration, Dr. Rommel concluded, meant that France was like an elderly person who was no longer growing, no longer reproducing, and becoming increasingly decrepit and inclined to stay home. Although pronatalists were annoyed by the arrogant tone of the German's book, they were inclined to agree with many of his conclusions.[87] When, in January 1900, the bulletin of the Alliance nationale revealed that in the years 1890, 1891, 1892, and 1895 deaths in France had actually outnumbered births, many pronatalists saw this as evidence that France had moved beyond the stage of stagnant middle age; its shrinking size and dwindling energy meant that France had become elderly.[88]

In this context, the Algerian "fountain of youth" represented a means of reversing the trend of aging and transforming France into a growing, vigorous, and youthful nation. Like Louis-Adolphe Bertillon, pronatalists considered youthful nations' ability to expand outward and fill sparsely populated regions a critical element of their superior demographic growth. For this reason, they made numerous comparisons with the United States. Fully accepting the idea of Manifest Destiny, pronatalists believed that the great availability of land and opportunity in the American West encouraged families to have large numbers of children. Many Americans shared this view, most notably Teddy Roosevelt, who, in the early twentieth century, worried about falling birthrates among "native-born Americans." Roosevelt expressed nostalgia for the "true" American family whose vigorous character was shaped by the exigencies of surviving along the frontier.[89] Like many American proponents of Manifest Destiny, pronatalists often phrased their arguments for expansion in biblical terms, evoking the book of Genesis when telling French people to "be fruitful and multiply."

This image of the American West prompted pronatalists such as Roger Debury to argue that in order to grow demographically, France needed a steady current of emigration to the French empire.[90] They thus built on the earlier arguments of Louis-Adolphe Bertillon by adding statistical and demographical arguments for colonial expansion to the preexisting political and economic arguments. In this vein, Charles Richet concluded that the conquest of North Africa was the most important enterprise undertaken by any French government in the nineteenth century, because it had given the French "an immense territory where, like in Canada, a new French race can develop and grow."[91] Like many other pronatalists, Richet believed that France was too small for the population's needs; approaching its maximum potential in Europe, France's population would only grow if it were to expand outward into the empire. The development of Algeria into a successful colony and a French version of the American West represented the best means by which to minimize the effects of aging and transform France from an elderly nation into a youthful power.

Colonial emigration was also important to pronatalists because it would ensure French influence abroad by establishing prolific French populations in the colonies. In this respect, it is clear that their interest in colonial settlement schemes extended beyond the simple goal of increasing the French birthrate; they also equated demographic strength with French influence in the world. Jacques Bertillon, for example, wrote that when French people migrated to a region of the world where they could keep their language, they represented an asset to the *mère-patrie* (mother country).[92] In French colonies, migrants had large numbers of children, contributed to the development of the French language and race, and strengthened France's commercial interests abroad. Like Bertillon, colonial propagandist Eugène Poiré stressed the importance of France's former colony in Canada, where the French population had grown, solely by virtue of its birthrate, from ten thousand original settlers to sixty thousand when France lost the colony in 1763.[93] By the 1880s their numbers had surpassed a million, despite the "invasion" of the English language and continuous migrations to the United States.[94] While the average family size in France continued to decline, pronatalist commentators emphasized that among the Franco-Canadians, families with twelve or thirteen children remained common. French pronatalists therefore considered the French settlement in Canada proof that the French could be prolific when far away from the "corrupting" influences of the metropole. Yet, despite its symbolic value, Canada was no longer a French colony. It is also worth pointing out that when making claims about French fertility in Canada, pronatalists were unclear about which people in Canada counted as representatives of "the French race." Still, flawed as these assertions may have been, pronatalists hoped that Algeria and eventually all of North Africa would produce a large French population like that of Canada while remaining connected to the *mère-patrie*.

Other pronatalists viewed the establishment of large French populations abroad as critical population reserves that would ultimately ensure France's survival. Debury, for example, wrote in 1896 that the formation of strong settler colonies would lead to the birth of French children abroad who would reinvigorate and care for the elderly mother country.[95] In this respect, establishing French settler colonies was likened to starting a family; on both the individual and the national level, the future of the French population would be ensured. In Debury's worst-case scenario, these French colonies could survive the mother country should the declining birthrate of the metropole ever lead to

FRANCE'S "SUPREME CHANCE"

foreign invasion or conquest.[96] While most pronatalists did not make such pessimistic arguments in favor of colonial settlement, they did envision a continuous current of migration between colony and metropole that would ensure France's demographic health. Not only would France export emigrants to the colonies, but the colonies would in turn export migrants to France, and Algeria's "French children" would in this way maintain the strength of the *mère-patrie* through the demographic benefits of emigration.[97]

The Rural Exodus and Algeria

Another reason why Algeria was so important to pronatalists is that they saw in it the possibility of correcting existing patterns of migration within France. Instead of expanding outward and growing, which Bertillon and other demographers considered a vital part of healthy population growth, the French population seemed to be contracting inward and shrinking because of a phenomenon known as the rural exodus. As pronatalists saw it, over the course of the nineteenth century, the rural regions were drained of their life forces as their youth migrated to the cities in pursuit of employment opportunities outside agriculture. For instance, between 1851 and 1891 the total population of France grew by only 7 percent; however, the rural population dropped by 8 percent and the population in towns of at least ten thousand nearly doubled.[98] Although some scholars have challenged the idea that nineteenth-century migration patterns constituted an actual exodus, it seemed real to many people at the time and contributed to fears about national decline.[99]

Firmly convinced that the inward contraction of a population resulted in low birthrates overall, pronatalists considered rural migration patterns symptomatic of more serious problems. This was because birthrates differed from region to region. In fact, demographers such as Jacques Bertillon divided the French departments into "departments of death" and "departments of life."[100] All the departments in Normandy and in the Garonne valley topped the list of the departments of death because mortality rates exceeded the birthrate. On the other hand, Lozère, Ardèche, Aveyron, and all the departments of Brittany were among the few where births surpassed deaths, despite the fact that large numbers of young people also left these regions. Generally, urban populations exhibited lower birthrates than did rural populations, something that made these rural communities particularly critical. Many pronatalists borrowed the title of René Bazin's novel *La terre qui meurt* (The dying land) to describe the fate of the countryside where farmers, like the character in Bazin's novel, saw their children abandon the family and land to migrate to the Americas or to the cities.[101]

Some commentators feared that young peasants migrated under the misguided assumption that success and wealth awaited them but found misery instead. Once in the cities, these peasants postponed marriage and parenthood, had fewer children, and sometimes turned to prostitution, alcoholism, and the other social diseases commentators believed to be rampant in the cities. Numerous studies appeared claiming to show higher rates of urban criminality among the newly arrived.[102] Furthermore, this problem was self-perpetuating; young people were too ashamed to write to their families about their degrading situation. Other young people in the villages believed that their departed siblings and friends were striking it rich in the city and wanted to join them.[103] This migration therefore had disastrous effects on both urban and rural birthrates. Villages in prolific regions such as Brittany lost youth of childbearing age, and in the cities life was so hard that even those young people who did not become beggars and prostitutes were driven by fear of unemployment and hunger to the point that they chose not to have children. Pronatalists consequently considered the migration of peasants from prolific rural "departments of life" to big cities such as Paris to be particularly detrimental to the overall national birthrate.

Many pronatalists asserted that this current of internal migration should be redirected to the empire.[104] In fact, the acquisition of Algeria, as well as Ricoux's new findings on the success of acclimatization in the colony, meant that France had acquired another region with "departments of life" to which existing patterns of migration could be redirected. Encouraging peasant migration to Algeria and eventually elsewhere in the empire would establish the kind of healthy

FRANCE'S "SUPREME CHANCE"

emigration necessary for stimulating the birthrate and would also correct the existing "unhealthy" patterns of migration, thus solving two demographic problems simultaneously. Along these lines, Jean-Baptiste Piolet, the author of a number of colonial emigration guides, wrote that the rural exodus only "drives miserable people to an even greater misery. Thus, we must change the direction of it and orient it toward countries where, on the contrary, there are unoccupied spaces, where there is an absence of arms, and more importantly, an absence of intelligence, money, activity, industry."[105] Likewise, pronatalist René Gonnard, who published a number of studies on depopulation and emigration, wrote that because the country villages were losing population anyway and the arrival of peasants in Paris did little to increase the birthrate there, the migration of peasants to the colonies, where they would continue to work the land and give birth to large numbers of children, would benefit the colonies without harming rural or urban France.[106] Consequently, the French colonies represented a valuable space to which France could export individuals whose lives were unfruitful in the metropole but could be redeemed in the empire. Piolet was persuaded that "we will find in that outward expansion the most practical remedy to the terrifying decline of the birthrate."[107] Notably, many of these authors presented the colony as not only an extension of France to which the French population could easily be redistributed but also as an empty space awaiting their arrival. The colonized Algerians already residing in the colony did not factor into these theorists' arguments about the demographic value of these new "departments of life."

Gender and the Myth of the Prolific Settler

Taken as a whole, demographic arguments in favor of colonial emigration illustrate the emergence of an important myth in the French "colonial mind": the myth of the prolific settler, or a belief that on average settlers had a higher birthrate than did their compatriots in the metropole.[108] This myth encompasses the idea that French settlers overseas were a youthful population with a racial vitality contrasting significantly with that of the old, metropolitan French. Moreover, gender was central to how the prolific settler was imagined. This is because pronatalists believed that depopulation resulted primarily from "voluntary sterility," and consequently focused their agenda on influencing individuals' reproductive choices. Similarly, as the myth of the prolific settler illustrates, studies showing the correlation between colonial emigration and demographic growth reveal gendered assumptions about why individuals chose to migrate, a choice that ultimately had an impact on the birthrate. While men's migration centered on finding a lucrative position or means of earning a living, a woman's migration was assumed to be "matrimonial" in that a woman either followed her husband overseas or migrated alone in search of a husband.[109]

One of the best-known novels promoting the pronatalist agenda, Émile Zola's *Fécondité*, is clearly influenced by the myth of the prolific settler and positions men's choices as the critical factor in settler population trends. Zola paints a picture of an ideal French couple, intended to represent the French nation, fulfilling their patriotic duty by having a large family and correcting France's migratory trends. Instead of remaining in Paris, Mathieu and Marianne migrate to the countryside and farm the land, enabling them to have the kind of large family that would have been incompatible with city life. With twelve children, Mathieu and Marianne are able not only to replace themselves and sustain the population but also to repopulate the French countryside and, finally, the empire. While two children live in Paris and contribute to France's industrial wealth, the majority of the family remains in the countryside, where they have many children and work the land. In addition to emphasizing that rural life was conducive to strong demographic growth, Zola's novel suggests that it was overseas, in the colonies, that France would find a remedy to its low birthrate. Consistent with pronatalist thinking at the time, one of Zola's characters states that "in the colonies no race is more fruitful than the French, though it seems to become barren on its own ancient soil."[110] As evidence of this, Zola introduces Mathieu and Marianne's two youngest sons, Nicolas and Benjamin, who migrate to French colonies in Africa.

Nicolas, the older of the two, feels stifled among so many older brothers and sisters and decides to seek his fortune elsewhere. This reflects pronatalists' arguments about the familial conditions that inspired men to migrate. In such families, the younger sons found remaining in the crowded family home unappealing and were eager to strike out on their own. In this case, Nicolas departs to Senegal with his young French wife, Lisbeth, and later settles in French Sudan. Just as France's children in Algeria were more prolific than those of the mother country, Nicolas surpasses his parents by fathering eighteen children, instead of a "mere" twelve. Zola's choice of French Sudan instead of Algeria suggested that the prolific French population in Algeria was only the beginning of the French "race's" growth in the empire; pronatalists envisioned this population growth eventually spreading to other parts of the empire. The fact that few French people migrated to French Sudan or had large numbers of children did not discourage Nicolas. He explains that his large family has founded a whole new village that will soon become a city, thus emphasizing the power of individual men to single-handedly reverse the demographic trends. When the younger brother, Benjamin, decides to join Nicolas in French Sudan, another branch of the family tree becomes firmly rooted in the African soil from which, it could only be hoped, other branches will soon grow. Presenting colonial emigration as an investment in future demographic growth, Zola's narrator concludes: "From this day a new France is born yonder [Africa], a huge empire; and it needs our blood—and some must be given it, in order that it may be peopled and be able to draw its incalculable wealth from the soil, and become the greatest, the strongest, and the mightiest in the world!"[111]

Although Zola depicts this family's migration to Africa in terms of what it represents to both the family and France generally, he does this mainly through the eyes of his male characters. Nicolas comes across as a man of action securing his own destiny and establishing a colonial village. His wife Lisbeth, on the other hand, remains behind the scenes. Her primary role is reproductive as she supports her husband's goals by accompanying him to Africa and bearing his children; her thoughts and reasons for migrating remain largely invisible to the novel's readers. This depiction is consistent with Bertillon's studies, which emphasize that it is men's ambitions for lucrative employment and financial gain that will drive migration to the colonies and by extension the elevated birthrate among settlers. Because many of these men produced large numbers of "French" children after emigrating, it can be assumed that they either brought their wives with them or met French women upon arrival. Yet, despite the implication that there were French women in the colony, there is little indication in these studies about why women chose to emigrate or how their choices contributed to the strong birthrate.

In Ricoux's study, women also seem peripheral to his explanations of the Algerian colony's growth, the conception, birth, and survival of their babies being determined less by their own choices than by the culture in which they live and the attitudes of the men in their lives. For instance, Ricoux argued that in Algeria the high birthrate worked in tandem with a slightly lower infant mortality rate, particularly among illegitimate babies, to produce stronger population growth overall. This is significant, because in France the mortality rate for illegitimate babies was twice as high, a fact that pronatalists generally attributed to the social condition of unwed mothers and not to any initial physiological disadvantage. Unmarried pregnant women faced discrimination in the job market, were frequently disowned by their families, and were often abandoned by the fathers of their babies. Born into such a precarious situation, illegitimate babies were more vulnerable to starvation, life-threatening illnesses, and abandonment.[112] Whereas in France an illegitimate baby was twice as likely to die, Ricoux's study showed that in Algeria there was less of a distinction between those babies born to married couples and those born to single mothers.[113] Government data from the period suggest that this may have been partly due to the family situation of these babies, as roughly half of illegitimate children in Algeria were legally recognized by their fathers, a number that was greatly superior to that of the metropole.[114] Ricoux went a step further by arguing that, first of all, the settler community was more tolerant of unwed mothers and illegitimate babies than in the metropole. Consequently, unmar-

FRANCE'S "SUPREME CHANCE"

ried pregnant women were not forced to attempt an abortion or later abandon their newborns. Moreover, Ricoux explained, men wanted children and valued having a wife so much that it was common for a man to marry a single mother and raise her children as his own.[115] Following this logic, the key difference between the French populations in France and Algeria was determined not by the actions of single mothers but rather by men's choices about becoming a father and supporting a baby born out of wedlock. That women's choices were unrecognized in this discussion is hardly surprising, since these were women who, by having babies outside of marriage, had visibly broken with gender ideals of virtuous womanhood. Although in pronatalist reasoning such women could atone for their transgressions by becoming devoted mothers, pronatalists did not want to highlight their role in population growth. It is most likely for this reason that Ricoux and, later, Louis-Adolphe Bertillon were inclined to attribute the survival of these babies to male protection. Male commentators were far more comfortable arguing that these statistics could be explained by settler men having the right sense of duty and paternal instincts to marry these women and provide for the children; they were less comfortable ascribing virtue or independence to women who had had children out of wedlock.

Although Ricoux's claims about settler men's attitudes on marriage, fatherhood, and illegitimacy are difficult to prove, his conclusions were convincing to experts who read his work, including Louis-Adolphe Bertillon. Bertillon wrote an introduction to Ricoux's study in which he presented this research as a valuable lesson for metropolitan demographers and statisticians studying French depopulation. Representing a means by which to assess the growth and development of the French population in a different context, Ricoux's evidence confirmed many of the things that Bertillon had been arguing for years. For instance, the findings on infant mortality showed that it was not for physiological reasons that the babies of unwed mothers accounted for a larger proportion of infant deaths than those born to married women. Echoing Ricoux's sentiments about settler men's attitudes about marriage and fatherhood, Bertillon explained that the settlers of Algeria were more enlightened than their metropolitan compatriots, whose prejudice against unwed mothers deprived France of thousands of babies a year.[116] This is a statement that, again, emphasizes the importance of men's choices and male protection in the survival of these babies.

As these late-nineteenth-century works make clear, the myth of the prolific settler initially hinged on men's choices about migrating and starting a family. Still, as the next chapter will show, organizations involved in encouraging colonial emigration and settlement recognized that many men migrated to the colonies without wives and that the growth of settler colonies depended on the emigration of young, unmarried women. This led them to appeal to women directly as they sought to re-create the domestic ideal in the colonies.

Conclusion

In 1898 the new minister of colonies, Georges Trouillot, connected colonial settlement and metropolitan depopulation in a speech he gave in favor of colonial expansion: "Let us give our population, which has ceased to grow, an arena. Let us give ourselves a birth incentive so that we can once again become the world's foremost colonizing people."[117] As this chapter has shown, by the end of the nineteenth century the pronatalist movement had taken a decidedly imperial turn, presenting colonial settlement and depopulation as interconnected issues and envisioning colonial emigration as a birth incentive. This happened in part because, as Joshua Cole has shown, social scientists in this era had access to all kinds of statistical data detailing population trends. For our purposes, it was their confidence in statistical data concerning migration that inspired them to try to "correct" migration patterns that they considered detrimental to the birthrate. By redirecting population to regions and colonies that had stronger birthrates, pronatalists hoped to shape individuals'—in particular, men's—family-planning decisions. A critical part of this development was Ricoux's 1880 study demonstrating that the French population was not condemned to extinction and positioning Algeria as a promised land in the fight against declining birthrates. Not only had Algeria become a viable settler colony to which the existing current of emigration to the Americas should be redirected, but it was an extension of France with a growing birthrate and an emerging Latin race.

Ricoux's study demonstrated to pronatalists and others that there was nothing inherently wrong with the French race; its decline and decadence were the result of social transformations specific to the metropole. Colonial emigration thus represented a means by which French people could leave the corrupting influences behind, regain their birthrate of previous centuries, and contribute to France's repopulation, all while remaining part of the nation. Pronatalists viewed colonial emigration as an investment in the future; by giving up a small amount of population to the colonies, metropolitan France would gain down the road as arriving settlers gave birth to prolific populations and simultaneously stimulated the birthrate in France by creating vacancies to be filled by the next generation. As Gonnard wrote in 1898, it was in Algeria that France should work to multiply the French race, because "by touching the African land, our race has acquired a new vitality. Let us encourage emigration: for some thousands of French people that Europe would lose, there will be millions of Neo-French people that Africa will return to us one day."[118]

Eventually, pronatalists would move away from Bertillon's original assertion that the simple act of emigrating exerted a positive influence on the birthrate in the metropole; this view was less frequently evoked in pronatalist propaganda in the twentieth century. Nevertheless, one legacy of Bertillon's theories is that throughout the Third Republic pronatalists continued to regard emigration as a sign of vitality and strength and linked it to family-planning decisions. The fact that France sent few migrants to its colonies was both a sign of demographic weakness and a source of worry for imperialists concerned about maintaining colonial rule. The myth of the prolific settler that gained popularity with Ricoux's study did have a lasting influence. As the next chapter will show, this myth played an important role in colonial settlement schemes as members of the Union coloniale française sought to encourage the migration of French people to the colonies despite the low birthrate in France. This myth was so strong, in fact, that it persisted well after World War I, even after demographic studies indicated a reduction in the settler birthrate. For example, in 1923, Professor Louis Vignon of the École coloniale wrote to the director of Affaires indigènes (Native affairs) in Algeria describing the ongoing problem of depopulation in France, expressing his belief that birthrates were higher among Franco-Algerians than they were among their metropolitan compatriots and asking for specific information about birthrates and numbers of children per household among the French settlers of Algeria.[119] Though by this time birthrates among Franco-Algerian settlers had declined significantly from those Ricoux first presented in 1880, Vignon's letter demonstrates that people continued to think of Algeria as a place where the French could achieve what was difficult in the metropole: a high birthrate. Ricoux's 1880 demographic study made such an impact on pronatalist discussions of depopulation and the rejuvenating potential of colonial emigration that pronatalists continued to argue, long after twentieth-century statistical studies had proved otherwise, that emigration would give birth to prolific French populations abroad.

TWO

Recruiting Colonial Settlers

The Union Coloniale Française and the Non-Classées

In France, people only emigrate to the office.

—EDME PIOT, *La dépopulation en France*, 1900

In the late nineteenth century, pronatalist propagandists frequently presented colonial settlement as a sign of demographic strength and repeated the claim that French settlers were more prolific than their metropolitan compatriots. Still, this support for colonial emigration aside, the reality was that relatively few French people actually migrated to the French empire. According to members of the Union coloniale française (UCF, French Colonial Union), two primary factors accounted for France's meager supply of colonial settlers. The first, they maintained, was that the French government did not do enough to facilitate or promote migration to the colonies, a problem that could be rectified through administrative changes and additional funding. The second factor, on the other hand, was more insidious, as it stemmed from problems within French society. Demonstrating a keen awareness of France's demographic trends, the UCF argued that a depopulated and decadent country such as France was unlikely to produce large numbers of colonial settlers. With its restrained birthrate, France lacked the kind of population pressures that elsewhere pushed large numbers of people to leave home and hearth to find their fortune overseas. Yet this was not simply a question of numbers. Other forces were at work within French society that deterred

Frenchmen from choosing the life of a colonial settler. Sharing many of the same preoccupations as French pronatalists, members of the UCF expressed grave concerns about French masculinity and modern society, emphasizing factors such as the educational system, the decline of rural life, the expectation of social mobility, and family size in their explanations of why so few Frenchmen were interested in migrating to the colonies.

By looking at colonial emigration recruitment efforts in the final decade of the nineteenth century and the first decade of the twentieth, this chapter investigates the influence of pronatalism on the UCF's efforts to establish strong settler colonies. Similar to French pronatalists, the leadership of the UCF understood depopulation and its connection to colonial emigration in gendered terms. They consequently focused their efforts on individuals who failed to contribute to France's demographic growth as they postponed marriage and parenthood while seeking to enter the saturated liberal professions. In the case of Frenchmen, the UCF presented the problem as one of misguided ambitions as many men aspired to having the security of a white-collar job, ultimately languishing in a vocation that deprived them of the virility and vigor they would have developed by enduring hardships and working the land. As for the middle-class women the UCF hoped to recruit, their problems had less to do with their physical strength or any sort of life choices that they had made; rather, the UCF presented them in a more passive light, portraying them as victims who struggled to find husbands and subsequently sought employment out of desperation. Clearly influenced by the myth of the prolific settler, the UCF's leaders emphasized that because French people displayed a higher birthrate after migrating to the colonies, recruiting these individuals for colonial settlement would redeem lives that were otherwise fruitless and wasted in the metropole. In this way, they situated their own efforts to establish strong settler colonies within the larger debate about restoring demographic growth.

In addition to evoking the myth of the prolific settler as they sought to recruit people for colonial emigration, the UCF expanded this idea in their discussions of why the French were likely to achieve in the colonies what seemed so difficult in France: a more stable gender order and by extension a higher birthrate. Gender was consequently central to the advantages that colonial settlement was supposed to offer decadent and depopulated France. These concerns about gender intersected with underlying anxieties about modernity, with many pronatalists and imperialists simultaneously fearing and embracing its effects. Many French people worried that rapid progress, which they counted among the benefits of modern society, simultaneously fueled race suicide by upsetting stable gender relations, reducing the birthrate, and weakening the traditional family. While these trans-formations had supposedly given birth to a decadent society in the metropole, imperialists believed that rural settler societies had been spared many of these nefarious influences. That the UCF appropriated pronatalist arguments as they sought to encourage colonial settlement elucidates how empire factored into the gendered anxieties about modernity that were central to pronatalist fears of depopulation. This chapter shows, therefore, that arguments concerning the demographic benefits of colonial emigration resonated beyond pronatalist circles; this connection was also being made in political circles, such as the UCF, with which pronatalist organizations had very few members in common. Ultimately, the goals of organizations such as the UCF con-verged with those of pronatalists, as both groups saw colonial settle-ment and demographic growth as "two sides of the same question."[1]

Encouraging Colonial Settlement

France's relationship with its empire was full of contradictions in the last decades of the nineteenth century. Governments committed sub-stantial human and economic resources to securing the vast empire that many patriotic French people believed would play a central role in improving demographic growth and advancing France's position in the international arena. Yet imperialism was never a major gov-ernmental priority in France during the late nineteenth century, a fact best exemplified by the government's reluctance to promote or encourage colonial settlement. Critics emphasized the absurdity of conquering vast amounts of territory and then doing little to exploit the resources they contained, thereby opening the door to foreign corporations and settlers. They even asserted that in strong settler colonies, such as Algeria, the French population flourished in spite of the French government. Such criticism aside, certain opportunities did nevertheless exist for French people who wished to establish themselves in the empire. Prospective emigrants could obtain information about land concessions and employment from the government's Office de la colonisation and could also request free passage from the Ministry of Colonies.[2] However, imperialists worried that few French people were aware of such resources and that, without incentives, they would not even find colonial migration to be an appealing option. In response to apparent governmental disinterest in empire, an influential colonial lobby formed in France in the 1890s and became the most important force behind efforts to organize colonial emigration.

Stuart Persell defines the French colonial lobby as comprising both the *parti colonial*, an unofficial grouping of imperialist members of parliament, and representatives of colonial organizations and congresses in the metropole. United by their support for empire, these individuals represented a variety of social strata, political outlooks, and professions, including military officers, clergy, journalists, academics, and businessmen.[3] By the end of the nineteenth century the most important colonial organization in France was the UCF, founded in 1893 and presided over by Joseph Chailley-Bert between 1897 and 1914.[4] The goals of the UCF included finding means by which "to assure the development, prosperity, and the defense of the diverse branches of agriculture, commerce, and industry in our colonies; to unite all organizations and societies with these interests in common; and to examine and present all economic or legislative measures deemed necessary to the public powers and to disseminate them by publicity in newspapers, etc."[5] Although the journal of the UCF, *La quinzaine coloniale*, had only a modest readership, many of its articles were in major newspapers and reached a much larger audience.[6] The UCF also exerted significant influence on the government; Chailley-Bert himself was in the Chamber of Deputies, as were many other UCF members. Together with other colonial organizations and the *parti colonial*,

RECRUITING COLONIAL SETTLERS

the UCF's leaders lobbied successfully for the creation of a ministry of colonies, administrative decentralization for the colonies, and the 1889 establishment of the École coloniale to prepare bureaucrats for colonial administration.[7]

In their efforts to promote French colonial settlement, the UCF's leaders were careful to differentiate between "colonies of exploitation" and "colonies of settlement." According to these prominent imperialists, colonies such as French West Africa and French Equatorial Africa were predominantly colonies of exploitation. French efforts in these colonies centered largely on the extraction of natural resources, such as rubber, and because of the tropical climate, imperialists frequently discouraged large-scale European settlement. Although there were French settlers in these colonies, including women and children, the French population remained small compared to that of the "colonies of settlement." The UCF positioned New Caledonia, Algeria, Tunisia, and parts of Madagascar as potential "colonies of settlement" because the climates of these regions were particularly conducive to the establishment of familial agricultural enterprises. Whereas French pronatalists often discussed emigration to "the empire" in general terms, the UCF focused on specific colonies.

One of the biggest obstacles UCF members faced was the paucity of French colonial migration. In the May 1895 issue of *La quinzaine coloniale*, the editors explained that a mere 200 of the 5,586 people who left France in 1893 had migrated to French colonies.[8] One popular destination was Argentina, which attracted 230,000 French settlers over the course of the nineteenth century. In fact, there were more French people in Argentina than in any colony (except Algeria) in France's formal empire.[9] This migration to other parts of the world showed, the UCF maintained, that French people wanted to emigrate but that a lack of information, education, and governmental incentives prevented them from choosing the colonies as their destination.[10] Emigration organizations in North and South America were doing a better job of recruiting French emigrants for their territories than was the French government or even private French emigration organizations. In response, many promotional guides argued explicitly that life in a

French-speaking colony was more desirable. One 1899 brochure concerning Tunisia, for example, emphasized the harsh weather in the American prairies that were otherwise beautifully presented in brochures, concluding that America was not a promised land where the emigrant could get rich quickly from the abundant and fertile land.[11] Similarly, when receiving letters from French people interested in migrating to the Americas, the UCF sought to redirect them toward French colonies and stressed how miserable their lives would be in foreign countries.[12] This opinion was validated by letters the organization occasionally received from French settlers in North and South America complaining about their current situation and asking for assistance in relocating to Algeria.[13]

The UCF also lent its support to charitable and special-interest groups that were responsible for the emigration of small groups of people. In the early twentieth century, for example, a priest named Cros, at the abbey of Saint-Michel de Frigolet in Tarascon, received significant publicity in journals such as *L'expansion coloniale* and the pronatalist *Bulletin de l'alliance nationale pour l'accroissement de la population française* for his patronage of the "colonizing orphans."[14] The priest brought orphans with few prospects for the future to the abbey, where they were provided with a practical colonial education (farming techniques, carpentry, etc.) in preparation for a future in the colonies. In 1906 the Alliance nationale reported that Cros had forty-four boys under his tutelage who were almost old enough to go to the colonies and who had promised to send money back to the abbey as soon as they established themselves.[15] In response, one reader wrote a letter to the Alliance nationale praising the program, evoking the myth of the prolific settler on the grounds that "settlers, in a salubrious country with no shortage of space, have a birthrate that is much higher than in the *mère-patrie*."[16]

Though noteworthy because of the interest they elicited, Cros's organization and similar charitable endeavors involved relatively few individuals, and Chailley-Bert and other proponents of colonial emigration recognized the need to organize colonial emigration on a large scale. In 1900, Chailley-Bert explained that unlike France's first

RECRUITING COLONIAL SETTLERS

colonial empire, when Louis XIV or his minister Colbert could pursue colonial emigration endeavors without mass support, in Third Republic France successful colonial settlement depended entirely on the effectiveness of propaganda and information campaigns to sway public opinion.[17] Subsequently, each issue of *La quinzaine coloniale* included advertisements for both job seekers and employers in the empire, information about obtaining colonial land concessions, and advice on surviving in a different climate. Wishing to reach a larger audience, in 1895 the UCF contributed an article to the daily newspaper *Le petit journal* promoting colonial emigration as well as their new *Guide de l'émigrant* as an example of the kind of resources available for prospective emigrants.[18] On February 12 of that year the UCF leadership reported in one of their meetings that *Le petit journal* had sent out four thousand copies of the *Guide de l'émigrant* in response to requests from readers and that the UCF likewise sent out another five hundred copies of the guide in response to requests for information that they received.[19]

In addition to propagandizing, the UCF organized and promoted emigration to individual colonies, including New Caledonia, a group of islands close to New Zealand that had served as a French penal colony since 1864. Initial attempts at convict colonization had been largely unsuccessful, as only a small fraction of the convicts received land concessions and most of these convicts were ultimately unsuccessful in their endeavors.[20] The arrival in 1894 of Governor Paul Feillet marked a new phase in colonial settlement, as Feillet was determined to replace convict colonization with the settlement of "hard-working and honest" farmers.[21] This statement reflected the general opinion at this time that criminals made less-than-ideal candidates for establishing a settler colony. The UCF, in particular, played an important role in recruiting voluntary settlers for New Caledonia, assisting almost nine hundred of them between 1895 and 1900.[22] To inform prospective emigrants about the colony, the UCF published sixty-five newspaper articles, brochures, and promotional guides that drew on conversations with well-established settlers, letters from earlier emigrants they assisted, information from the minister of colonies, and published works.[23] Emphasizing that only those seeking agricultural employment should settle in New Caledonia, the guide provided a list of standard prices for goods in the colony to help the prospective emigrant decide what to bring and what to purchase upon arrival; it also warned them about the merchants who descended on the newly arrived with overpriced items. For example, sturdy work pants would cost 8 to 12 francs, a dairy cow 100 to 150 francs, and a liter of wine 0.80 to 1 franc. Every emigrant was guaranteed a concession from the government ranging from 10 to 18 hectares, at least 5 of which were designated for coffee production. Upon arrival, the emigrant would be greeted by the governor of the colony, could seek advice from the Union agricole calédonienne, and would receive free transportation to his or her concession.[24]

After having facilitated the emigration of a number of different groups of settlers to New Caledonia, the UCF asked them to write back with their personal accounts of the voyage, getting settled in the colony, and their success farming the land. Many letters described the emotional difficulties of the departure and the length of the voyage. Most settlers gave positive descriptions of life in the colony, emphasizing how warm the official welcome was upon their arrival and that the land they were allotted exceeded their expectations. However, one letter from a man named Dagrand, written in 1896, criticized the UCF for presenting too optimistic a picture of colonial settlement, something that had the unintended effect of attracting the wrong sorts of people. Dagrand apparently did not agree with the others in his emigration group, because he wrote his own letter instead of signing his name to the positive letter written collectively by his peers. He described settlers who devoted little energy to farming and refused to content themselves with a modest country life: "everyone is a merchant or a civil servant, or aspires to become one. Disdain of work is widespread."[25]

Letters like Dagrand's confirmed the fears of the UCF leadership about the preparedness and quality of many of their colonial emigrants. Although they wanted to attract as many settlers as possible, the UCF sought to promote colonial emigration in a cautious tone, because they knew that not everyone was likely to succeed in this type of endeavor. Chailley-Bert noted that unfortunately colonial emigration seemed to appeal to a type of individual he dubbed the *homme d'attaque*, a lazy man who never really tried or succeeded in his career or academic pursuits and yet somehow maintained a high opinion of his abilities. Having squandered whatever opportunities he had in France, and ready for a new adventure, the *homme d'attaque* believed he would succeed in whatever agricultural or commercial enterprise he might decide to undertake in the colonies.[26] Chailley-Bert and other UCF members feared that such men were unprepared for the challenges of colonial life, would soon give up, request to be repatriated, and from there generate negative publicity about colonial settlement. An even more dangerous possibility was that French people who failed to provide for themselves in the colony would undermine notions of racial superiority simply by looking poor or, worse yet, taking refuge among colonial subjects and living off of their charity.[27] The UCF had these types of concerns about many of the people who wrote to them, even those who did not seem as arrogant as the *homme d'attaque*. Of the hundreds of letters the UCF received annually, many expressed the unrealistic expectation that wealth and success would come easily for them in the empire. One such letter, received in 1899, was from a Mme Dardouillet inquiring about emigration to Senegal:

> In St. Louis or Dakar, could a woman, without any particular skills or funds, hope to make a living by working whatever jobs are possible in those two cities? Is the climate okay? Could a man, going there to start out on the railways, hope for a quick promotion, being educated but without any money? In short, are the conditions of life easier there than in France?[28]

The frank reply, written to dissuade Mme Dardouillet and her male companion from emigrating on a whim, reflected the organization's general frustration with such letters. They explained that no one should go to the colonies without sufficient funds and without having made prior arrangements for employment.[29] The UCF also received letters from working-class men who presumed that there was such an enormous demand for labor in the colonies that they would immediately find a lucrative job upon arrival.[30] In response to such letters the UCF had to stress continuously that the people most likely to succeed in the colonies would be those willing to run an agricultural enterprise or work on a farm. In most places, colonial subjects filled menial jobs, and Europeans with no skills or capital would find few opportunities.

Although the letters they received indicated that many people were not the serious emigrants the UCF was established to help, their casual and uninformed curiosity also suggested the general ignorance of the French public of the realities of colonial life. People lacked a real sense of how or if Europeans could survive in a different climate, what employment opportunities existed, and what life was really like. The fact that many of the letters the UCF received included simultaneous requests for information about dramatically different colonies, their writers apparently curious about moving to either Algeria or the Congo, suggests that people did not grasp fully the differences between life in a Mediterranean colony with a large European population and life in a tropical colony with few European residents. In an effort to address this problem, Chailley-Bert gave a number of conferences to schoolteachers emphasizing the great influence that they had over the next generation and the contribution that they could make to colonial emigration efforts by teaching their pupils about the geography, ethnography, and history of the colonies.[31] The UCF also sought to tone down the celebratory language used in some earlier propaganda that presented the colonies as a land of unlimited opportunities. They subsequently ran a second article in the *Petit journal* that stressed the realities of colonial life and promoted emigration in a more cautious tone.[32]

For its part, the French government made an effort to provide free transportation to the colonies only to emigrants of the highest quality by requiring prospective emigrants to write to the minister of colonies with a "certificate of good morals" from the mayor of the commune, a medical certificate, proof of capital of at least 5,000 francs (8,000 to 10,000 was recommended for a bourgeois emigrant), and a police record. Nevertheless, the Ministry of Colonies had no way to

RECRUITING COLONIAL SETTLERS

determine which emigrants were hardworking, ambitious individuals willing to live the simple life of a country farmer. They could only weed out those who would be likely to arrive in the colonies with few resources or who were too unhealthy to adjust to a rougher life.

In addition to being only partly successful in screening emigrants, these procedures represented yet another obstacle for people who wished to emigrate. Colonial-interest groups alleged that this had the unintended consequence of preventing the departure of individuals who were desirable candidates for colonial settlement. As an example of this, in 1898 a Mme Paul-Louis Courrier wrote to the colonial-interest newspaper the *Dépêche coloniale* about her ordeal with the French bureaucracy.[33] After the recent deaths of her brother and his wife, Mme Courrier took their son and daughter into her home, despite the family's tenuous financial situation. She planned to send the children to live and work with their uncle in New Caledonia. The family agreed that the children would have a better future in New Caledonia, because Jean-Martin, the son, would learn how to work the land and would eventually procure a concession of his own, and Louison, the daughter, would have no difficulty finding a husband once she was old enough to marry. Although these children were ideal candidates for emigration because they lacked a situation in France, would be unlikely to seek repatriation, and had family and a means of survival in New Caledonia, their aunt had great trouble navigating the French bureaucracy in order to procure free passage to New Caledonia for them. Courrier recounted her frustrating experiences acquiring and submitting the necessary documentation and forms only to have her application lost, then denied multiple times. It seemed that with each application submitted, additional requirements specific to her case were added, prompting her to wonder if she could ever assemble an application that would be approved. Courrier's letter is revealing of the frustration felt by many French citizens who were interested in colonial settlement but felt dissatisfied with the options with which their government presented them. In her letter to the *Dépêche coloniale*, Courrier concluded that she never would have imagined the complications involved in making arrangements for two French children to go live with their uncle in a French country. She surmised that if there were 250,000 British people who migrated to the British colonies each year, as opposed to the mere two hundred French colonial emigrants, it was probably because the British government did not hassle people who simply wanted to improve their lives by joining family members in the empire.[34]

An Absence of "Real Men"

In addition to bureaucratic red tape and government disinterest, UCF members cited France's population woes as a major obstacle to recruiting French settlers for the colonies. Like Charles Richet and other pronatalists, they were inclined to present colonial emigration and demographic growth as interrelated issues. First of all, drawing on pronatalist arguments, they were preoccupied with the idea that France lacked a "surplus population" to export abroad, something that distinguished it from neighboring countries whose domestic population pressures compelled large numbers of people to migrate. Pronatalist literature was replete with language likening populations to water and expressing fears that the growing populations of other countries represented rising tides poised to overflow into France and French colonies.[35] Many pronatalist studies asserted that France, on the other hand, was caught in a vicious cycle: although emigration to the colonies was a vital part of achieving a stronger birthrate, it was unlikely to occur without the kind of rapid population growth that would push people to emigrate.[36] Compounding the existing population shortage was the idea that the French, as a group, seemed to prefer not to emigrate, a "flaw" in the national character that could be traced to such factors as family size and the educational system, both of which played a role in the social development of French boys. Concerned about the quality of French men, members of the UCF expressed some of the same ideas that pronatalists did about the impact of modernity on French masculinity and how this affected both demographic growth and colonial emigration. Pronatalist ideas about the connections between migration and the birthrate in turn shaped how the UCF recruited men for colonial settlement. It was by evoking the myth of the prolific settler, therefore, that the UCF sought to promote settler colonialism in France and appeal to a larger audience amid widespread concerns about demographic decline.

In explaining why few Frenchmen migrated to the empire, the UCF expressed concerns about French masculinity that revealed the mixed feelings that many people at this time had about modern society. On the surface, the fin de siècle appeared to be a time of great stability for bourgeois men, who took pride in the scientific advancements of the age and the great prosperity and political power they had achieved as a social class. Yet, as scholars have shown, beneath the surface of this optimism lurked fears that normative masculinity was under attack from a variety of internal and external sources.[37] As we have seen, many late-nineteenth-century French people expressed concerns about feminists, "the new woman," and other women who simply appeared liberated or inclined to challenge the fragile gender order. Because male and female gender identities were conceived of as binary opposites, with both sexes being defined in terms of, and in contrast to, one another, changes in the status of women necessarily had an impact on masculinity.[38] According to this logic, if women appeared to become more masculine or assumed a more public role in society, men in turn would seem more effeminate and occupy a less dominant place in the public sphere. Consequently, people feared that the liberation of women, closely associated with modern and urban society, was contributing to this period's concerns about masculinity.[39]

These concerns about masculinity nevertheless extended beyond the status of women and were frequently traced to the behavior and physical state of men themselves, something that was itself understood in racial terms. The perception that modern society rendered men weak and effeminate and therefore unlikely or physically unable to produce strong offspring was symptomatic of what Christopher Forth calls the "double logic of modern civilization," the paradoxical idea that the signs of a great civilization—refined manners, education, culture, luxuries, and the attainment of an easier, more leisurely existence— simultaneously signified that civilization's potential undoing.[40] Many pronatalists argued that in order to understand the dangers of "overcivilization" one had only to look to ancient Rome for an example of how a people could attain a high level of civilization, become decadent and depopulated precisely because of their affluence and material comforts, and ultimately fall to the barbarians.[41] The modern-day barbarians that French pronatalists feared included both immigrants and foreign invaders who, unencumbered by the perils of overcivilization, would lay claim to French soil with their superior numbers. Moreover, this problem was not restricted to France; pronatalists were inclined to see the phenomenon in racial terms and believed that it was leaving its mark among civilized white men everywhere. In the United States, for example, many white men shared these fears and likewise evoked the concept of "overcivilization" when discussing the state of American masculinity. As in France, elite American white men expressed concerns about the debilitating effects of civilization on the white male body as evidenced by the growing cases of neurasthenia and the lack of virility and physical strength more generally among the American white elite.[42] Though taking pride in their status as a highly civilized people, white American men faced what they saw as a disturbing paradox: "only white male bodies had the capacity to be truly civilized. Yet, at the same time, civilization destroyed white male bodies."[43]

In late-nineteenth-century France, concerns about masculinity centered on this same paradox. For Frenchmen the deleterious effects of civilization on the male body could be traced to the modern, comfortable lifestyle and its impact on the health and sexuality of men. For instance, the growing number of desk jobs encouraged a sedentary lifestyle, technological advancements in the form of streetcars, coaches, and railroads minimized the need to walk, and greater prosperity produced a more comfortable existence that ultimately led to excess in the form of gluttony, overconsumption of material goods, and various urban vices.[44] These improvements in the quality of life also contributed to a variety of "modern" health problems, including obesity, constipation, and gout, maladies considered less prevalent in premodern times or among the lower classes and "uncivilized" races.[45] Besides causing a weakened, sickly, and generally less robust physique, contemporaries theorized, these aspects of modern life risked leading

RECRUITING COLONIAL SETTLERS

men to effeminacy, homosexuality, and a whole host of newly identified sexual ills that researchers, writers, and legislators studied and discussed extensively.

Adding to pronatalists' and doctors' alarm was the sense that these threats to French masculinity were becoming more pervasive and not merely the fate of a depraved minority. Not surprisingly, this fear was presented in biomedical terms, something that exemplified the growing prestige and influence of medicine in the nineteenth century.[46] For example, doctors began to diagnose hysteria, a feminine ailment, in growing numbers of men. Max Nordau, in his famous work on degeneration, linked male hysteria to modern life by blaming the vibrations of the railroad, otherwise considered a symbol of progress and modernity, for shattering men's nerves.[47] What made this trend even more disturbing is that not all of these male hysteria patients appeared to be weak and effeminate, as doctors would have expected. On the contrary, symptoms of hysteria and weakness were visible in men who ought to have been part of mainstream respectable society yet somehow failed to attain the masculine ideal.[48] The impact of this decline in normative masculinity on society as a whole was also visible in the decline in the male sex ratio. At the start of the nineteenth century the ratio of live male births to live female births stood at 107 to 100; by 1900 that ratio had dropped to 104 to 100.[49] By this point, scientists recognized male responsibility for the sex of the offspring and generally interpreted the declining proportion of male births as an indication of a lack of sexual vigor on the part of French fathers, and consequently another sign of degeneration in the male population as a whole.[50] Collectively these anxieties about the health, vigor, and manliness of French men explain the growing popularity of gymnastics and military associations promoting strength, discipline, and physical fitness in the late nineteenth century.[51] Proponents hoped that the ills of modern civilization could be counteracted by achieving an appropriate equilibrium between intellectual pursuits, a comfortable existence, and access to culinary delights, on the one hand, and adequate time spent exerting oneself outdoors and building stamina, on the other.[52] Given all these anxieties about masculinity, it is not surprising that it was during this period that the Boy Scouts became popular in countries such as France, Great Britain, and the United States; this organization was designed to reacquaint boys with the great outdoors, teach them survival skills, and transform them into men by enduring physical hardships.

Adding to concerns about the harmful effects of modern life on the physical quality of French men were anxieties about their social development and the impact that this had on efforts to both increase the birthrate and recruit men for colonial settlement. Many pronatalists argued not only that France lacked the excess population necessary to produce large numbers of emigrants but also that French families were often so small that they failed to produce sons with the right spirit of self-reliance. Pronatalists argued that Britain's empire was strong because of adventurous younger brothers who had nothing handed to them for free, were certain that they would not inherit, and were consequently obliged to go out into the world and create a situation for themselves.[53] After all, in Zola's pronatalist novel *Fécondité* it was the protagonist's youngest sons who felt the urge to migrate to Africa.[54] Pronatalists believed that France needed large families in order to produce the kind of sons who would want to emigrate.

Yet instead of producing large numbers of sons, the typical French family had only two children. Emphasizing that small families were common and that many men chose not to marry, Roger Debury described France as a "country of single men and only sons" and with this characterization made a lasting impression on pronatalists. Decades after the book's publication, authors continued to quote Debury when denouncing the trend toward small family sizes.[55] Not only did the parents of single children fail to contribute to France's population growth, but they raised their sons differently than did parents of large families, claimed Debury and other pronatalists. Boys growing up in small families had the undivided attention of their parents, were babied by their mothers, and never learned such qualities as responsibility and independence. Such a social development, they believed, was frequently self-perpetuating, because "only sons" were unlikely to have large numbers of children themselves.[56] Repre-

RECRUITING COLONIAL SETTLERS

senting their parents' only child and hopes for the future, only sons were also unlikely to leave their families and migrate to the empire.

In addition to familial influences, pronatalists argued, the French educational system had negative influences on the social development of boys and, by extension, the national birthrate and colonial endeavors. Many people asserted that the curriculum in French schools was antiquated and failed to prepare young men for life outside the classroom, let alone colonial careers. An example of this reasoning was Auguste Isaac, the longtime president of the Lyon Chamber of Commerce who, during World War I, would found the pronatalist and familialist organization La plus grande famille. In his capacity as president of the Lyon Chamber of Commerce, Isaac also presided over the city's colonial studies program, first established in 1899. Similar to the national École coloniale in Paris, this educational program prepared men (and a small number of women) for colonial careers with courses on history, geography, ethnography, legislation, economics, agriculture, and hygiene in the colonies as well as relevant languages such as Chinese and Arabic. Isaac explained that this program of study was necessary because the French educational system failed young people by emphasizing "theory" over "practice" and teaching dead languages like Greek and Latin.[57]

Another criticism of the educational system was that schooling created ambitions and aspirations that were frequently left unfulfilled by available careers. Victor Turquan, in his celebrated career guide, argued that academic success in childhood rendered the simple life of an agricultural worker unappealing to young men, who instead aspired to enter the liberal careers.[58] Delaying fatherhood as they invested years preparing for their exams, many young men would ultimately find that they were unable to get a position in their chosen professions. According to Turquan, in the year 1880, 2,021 men applied for only 43 teaching positions in Paris.[59] Rather than simply pursuing a different vocation, many would reapply in subsequent years. The problem of unrealized aspirations, pronatalists concluded, was that young men would postpone fatherhood and marriage as they spent years studying for exams and trying to obtain a position.

While pronatalists worried that the educational system created misguided ambitions that prevented Frenchmen from having children, they also contended that French pedagogy directed boys toward vocations that were insufficiently masculine, such as working as a clerk or a bureaucrat. To many French pronatalists, the German Dr. Rommel defined the influence of the educational system on male social development the best.[60] Rommel argued that the French educational system destroyed all initiative, trained the nation's youth to follow established procedures blindly, and created large numbers of bureaucrats and politicians, not men. After a young French man completed school, Rommel argued, the life of a bureaucrat was appealing because it did not require energy, imagination, physical activity, or initiative. Each person's task was simple, small, and easily mastered within a short period of time. The formation of such a male type, Rommel argued, had disastrous effects on France's efforts to establish viable settler colonies. The French man in the colonies, Rommel alleged, "always needs his mamma, that is the State," because migrating anywhere that did not have a prefect of police or other administrative agencies was inconceivable.[61] In Rommel's eyes, the French man lacked the spirit of enterprise and adventure necessary for colonial settlement.

Pronatalists begrudgingly agreed with Rommel's assessment of the bureaucrat, as it reflected their own ideas about the connections between degeneration, modern urban professions, and masculinity. Discussing nineteenth-century caricatures of clerks, for example, Forth explains that the men who worked such jobs were ridiculed for being effeminate or weak. In contrast to the jobs of many working-class and peasant men, a clerk's job was sedentary and did not require physical exertion; it also lacked the prestige or autonomy of other liberal careers like law or medicine. To make matters worse, as the nineteenth century progressed, increasing numbers of women began to enter this profession, competing with men for positions and by their very presence giving the work a more feminine image.[62] In their criticisms of such men, pronatalists frequently used the verb *vegetate*, evoking images of these men wasting away at their desks, neither dead nor fully alive. One of many scapegoats in pronatalist propaganda, the weak, pale, and effeminate bureaucrat or clerk was responsible for France's inability to overcome depopulation and produce large numbers of children to ensure the nation's future and settle the colonies.[63] Pronatalist propaganda debated the pros and cons of this career, acknowledging that the life of a childless bureaucrat meant material comforts and a life without risks. Simultaneously, it was not a man's life, because a bureaucrat was a slave to the established procedures, over which he had no influence, and the whims of his superiors, of which there would always be many, no matter how far he advanced in the hierarchy. Using the image of the bureaucrat as a way of describing many problematic traits in French society, pronatalists presented French men as cautious, preferring a secure job in the bureaucracy over the risks associated with a colonial enterprise, and too complacent to leave the familiarity of their surroundings.[64]

Sharing pronatalists' disdain for the metropolitan bureaucrat more generally, imperialists constructed the male colonial settler as the masculine ideal and a symbolically potent countertype to the complacent and weak metropolitan bureaucrat. On the one hand, imperialists imagined the metropolitan bureaucrat to be lacking in energy and displaying passive qualities in the workplace, both of which translated to a lack of virility when combined with the few children he produced. Unlike the metropolitan bureaucrat, the colonial settler, they argued, was truly a man, because he was free to take the initiative and make his own decisions. Owning and working a land concession in the colonies was full of risks and required hard, physical labor. Furthermore, imperialists argued, the colonial settler was useful to France. While bureaucrats failed to produce anything and often had one or no children, the colonial settler produced crops that added to the colonies' wealth and had large numbers of children who ensured France's future.[65]

These idealized visions of colonial masculinity reflect two late-nineteenth-century preoccupations that intersected with concerns about the impact of modern civilization on French masculinity: the "disappearance" of the peasantry, and class-based anxieties about social mobility. First, important comparisons can be made between the image of the settler in the empire and contemporaneous ideas about the peasantry in the French countryside. Throughout the Third Republic, observers described the provinces and rural society as the "true France," the repository of authentic, traditional French life.[66] As we have seen, statistics showing that the birthrate was higher in rural areas than in cities such as Paris affirmed their belief that there was a correlation between traditional agrarian societies and a strong birthrate. The "disappearance" of country life as peasants migrated to the cities over the course of the nineteenth century contributed to anxieties about the destabilizing influence of modern life. In fact, the low birthrate and corrupting influences of the French cities prompted Senator Edme Piot to write that French cities were "devourers of men" to which peasants were attracted "like moths to a flame."[67] In essence, young peasants in the countryside were first exposed to outside ways of thinking through primary education and then lured to the city, attracted by its excitement, glamour, and promise of a better life, while naively underestimating its danger. Elsewhere in his study, Piot expressed the widely held belief that the rural exodus was a consequence of modern society with its improved communications and desire for social mobility.[68] The consequence of this false allure of the cities was, according to another writer, Mgr Gibier, that France was losing its "supreme reserves," the peasantry: "by falling into urban conglomerations, in the slums of the city, the peasant quickly loses his pure blood, vigorous health, and he soon becomes unable to procreate except a few sickly, anemic beings, who are like the last drops of the stream of life that runs out and disappears."[69] Gibier conveyed the idea that the city itself deprived peasant men of their once robust, virile masculinity by sapping their strength and rendering them impotent. The sense that the migration of peasants to the cities deprived France of its life forces was evident in Charles Lambert's pronatalist book, *La France et les étrangers*, in which he described towns as having "tentacles" drawing people in, depriving the countryside of "those robust peasants who were our force and our pride."[70]

These types of anxieties about the demise of rural life prompted many pronatalists and other reformers to advocate back-to-the-land

RECRUITING COLONIAL SETTLERS

programs and envision "internal colonization."[71] Shanny Peer has shown that even as late as the 1930s there was a commitment, evident on both the left and the right, to maintain an appropriate balance between agriculture and industry, in other words, between rural France and its urban counterpart. Although many French people considered maintaining this equilibrium vital, French peasants were nevertheless subject to two contradictory images: "Whereas one set of negative images portrayed peasants as an uncivilized counter-model for the bourgeoisie, another positive set of images praised the peasant and the countryside in order to vilify the worker and the city."[72] Still, although reformers articulated their anxieties about urban growth and the working classes by painting an idealized image of the countryside, many continued to view rural areas as backward and potentially resistant to progress and advancement. Clearly, its ideological importance aside, rural France seemed to have little to offer the many young adults who continued to migrate to the cities each year.

In the late nineteenth century, imperialists and pronatalists envisioned the empire, on the other hand, as a land of opportunity, similar to the American West. Such arguments were premised on ideas of imperial manhood and the redemptive, masculinizing effects of living in a rough frontier environment. Similar ideas about imperial manhood have been well documented in the case of Australia, where contemporaries believed that settlers would bring civilization to the wilderness, regain the masculinity that had been compromised by overcivilization in Europe, and establish a stable gender order in the process.[73] Likewise, in the United States, President Teddy Roosevelt was well known for overcoming the image of effeminacy and weakness that plagued his early political career by establishing himself as a cowboy on a ranch in South Dakota. Later in life he was preoccupied with the interrelated threats of effeminacy, overcivilization, and racial decadence, concerns that made him a proponent of American imperialism as a "way to retain the race's frontier-forged manhood."[74] For the French, colonies likewise represented a frontier society essential for French masculinity. Colonial life embodied the desired equilibrium between tradition and modernity, rural and urban life. Their ideas about the advantages of settler societies also drew on older ideas about the redemptive qualities of colonial life. Earlier in the nineteenth century, social reformers had envisioned penal colonization as a means by which to both rehabilitate criminals and establish France's presence in the colonies. Accepting Rousseau's theories on the virtues of country life, reformers hoped that "convicts would be restored to an upright moral life by being close to nature and participating in an idealized vision of a rural France that no longer existed."[75] By the late nineteenth century, penal colonization had been all but abandoned, yet the romanticized visions of nature and the possibilities of redeeming problematic populations through deportation to the wild landscapes of the colonies had persisted. At this time, the colonies offered what the French countryside apparently no longer could: the health and virility that came with country living, in contrast to the decadence and sterility of cities, and greater opportunities than in the French countryside.

The contrasting images of the metropolitan bureaucrat and the colonial settler also reflected class-based anxieties about social mobility that were shared by elites in both imperialist and pronatalist circles but never explicitly stated. The fact that some men in French society lived in urban centers, had small muscles, and spent much of their days indoors, sitting down, and engaged in tasks requiring only mental energy was certainly not unique to the late nineteenth century. What was disturbing to pronatalists was the fact that the numbers of such men had grown considerably over the course of the century. From the pronatalist perspective, the growth of such a category of men reflected larger destabilizing transformations in French society, including the expectation of social mobility in the lower and middle classes, the dwindling peasantry, and the growing petit bourgeoisie. Expanded educational opportunities, particularly after the Ferry Laws of the 1880s made primary education universal, free, and secular, had created what many elites considered unrealistic or inappropriate expectations among the masses. Because nineteenth-century studies indicated that the working classes and petit bourgeoisie had on average higher birthrates than did the wealthy, and demographers positioned these groups as the main source of France's demographic growth, the growing numbers of men from modest backgrounds seeking social mobility was particularly worrisome. As depicted in Zola's *Fécondité*, for example, pronatalists feared that many of these men emulated the wealthier classes, limiting their family sizes in the hopes of becoming more bourgeois and securing a place for their only child in that social class. Although they believed that it was acceptable for exceptionally gifted men to father few children while advancing civilization through their careers, pronatalists lamented the fact that vast numbers of men were losing the masculine and reproductive qualities associated with their social class as they rejected their place in the hierarchy and sought career advancement. Because the colonial settler on the other hand embodied many of the same characteristics as did the peasant due to the nature of his work, his aspirations, his physical strength, and the number of children he generally produced, pronatalists viewed this masculine type as an ideal alternative to men from modest backgrounds seeking white-collar jobs in the city.

The pronatalist assessment of French masculinity and its settler counterpart shaped how the UCF sought to recruit men for settlement. For instance, the belief that the French were reluctant to leave their familiar surroundings prompted the UCF to solicit information from colonial governors about the composition of their settler populations so that they could better reassure potential colonial emigrants that they would adjust to their new lives in the empire. To assist the UCF's recruitment efforts for Madagascar, Governor Gallieni attempted to find out not only how many French people resided in each region of the colony but also from which part of France these settlers originated. He explained that French settlers were only comfortable settling in places where compatriots from the same region of France were already established; this would remind them of home and convince them that they would receive the guidance and assistance they needed when first arriving.[76]

The UCF also appealed to the fears that many French parents had about placing their sons in the liberal careers and advanced the idea that this was not an appropriate career choice for most middle-class families. They subsequently presented colonial emigration as a solution both to the shortage of white-collar jobs and to problems with French masculinity. For example, in a speech given in 1899, Chailley-Bert deplored the absence of "real men" in France and explained that the typical French man aspired to be a functionary, risked nothing, relied on his family, would only seek to increase his wealth through his wife's dowry, and finally, only had one child. This, Chailley-Bert maintained, was why France was a small country and foreigners alone exploited the natural resources of the French colonies. Chailley-Bert suggested further that parents deciding their sons' futures should "start by making men of them; that is to say, individuals with the will to do something and the energy to carry out what they have decided to do."[77] According to Chailley-Bert, it was through the life of a colonial settler, and not a metropolitan bureaucrat, that boys could become self-sufficient, productive men.

Other proponents of colonial settlement argued that those men who were useless in the metropole due to the nature of their work and the few, if any, children they produced were exactly the men who should be recruited for colonial settlement. In a book promoting colonial settlement, Jean-Baptiste Piolet, for example, suggested that the main problem with these men was that they simply had misguided ambitions. If, however, these ambitions and energies could be redirected to the colonies, the educated metropolitan man could be transformed, improve the birthrate, and strengthen the empire. In the colonies, Piolet maintained, men could find an outlet for their intelligence and energy and could succeed at something, raise a family, and contribute to the establishment of a new, prolific French race. Piolet asserted that it was in the emigration of such unproductive elements of the male population that France would find "the most practical remedy" to the depopulation crisis.[78] Appealing directly to these men, Piolet wrote: "emigrate, young men who do not know what to do; emigrate far away, go settle our colonies where you will become transformed men, men with energy and purpose, the future heroes of the *revanche*. Emigrate also to enrich our country, to restore the race's lost fecundity and stop the scourge of depopulation, all the while pro-

RECRUITING COLONIAL SETTLERS

curing for yourselves rewarding opportunities that you can no longer find in France."[79] As Piolet's and Chailley-Bert's arguments reveal, in the context of depopulation and colonial settlement, men who failed to reproduce adequately in France had a purpose: they could migrate to the empire and become productive French settlers. To promoters of colonial settlement, targeting these elements of the male population for colonial emigration was essential, because France lacked the excess population, characteristic of prolific nations, to send to the empire. Colonial propagandists like Piolet were therefore careful to situate their goals of recruiting men for emigration within the larger framework of French depopulation.

After the Great War, the qualities that the colonial settler supposedly held continued to present imperialists and pronatalists with a means by which to express their anxieties about modern French masculinity. For instance, in 1927 the Maréchal Lyautey described North Africa as a place where the French race could be reborn through the formation of a new kind of man. Unlike in the metropole, where men were constrained to follow established procedures and lacked the ability to take the initiative or be innovative, in the empire men could become energetic, self-made "men of action."[80] Imperialists and pronatalists shared Lyautey's vision that the empire represented France's future and could exert a positive influence on young French men. Their discussions of the colonial settler and the qualities he supposedly held enabled imperialists and pronatalists to articulate their class-based anxieties about modern life and French masculinity. Imperialists in the UCF believed that the functionary, or the man with otherwise misguided ambitions, could be transformed into a productive element of society through colonial emigration.

"The Indispensable Auxiliary of Colonialism"

As many people in the late nineteenth century recognized, settler populations could never be self-reproducing and demographically strong if they were composed predominantly of men who would die childless. Although European women were obviously an essential part of establishing permanent settlements, for much of the nineteenth cen-

tury they represented only a small percentage of the settler populations in the French empire. One reason for this was that many soldiers
remained in the colonies after completing their military service. Furthermore, it was more common and generally considered safer for men
to migrate to the empire, as was reflected in emigration statistics. For
instance, France's Emigration Service showed that 26,015 French people emigrated between 1875 and 1881, of whom 17,989 were men and
only 8,026 were women.[81] Finally, there was a general perception that
imperialism was a masculine enterprise, a view propagated by many
nineteenth-century administrators and settlers who feared that the
presence of white women created extra complications. Among other
disadvantages, it was believed that white women needed constant protection and vigilance, required more material comforts, adjusted poorly
to the climate, and criticized men's interactions with colonized women.
As historians of British and French imperialism have shown, it was
with these types of objections in mind that many nineteenth-century
men asserted that the empire was simply "no place for a woman."[82]

As the nineteenth century progressed, the image of the empire as a
rough frontier unsuitable for European women gradually gave way to
arguments that women were vital to the success of the colonial enterprise. Increasing numbers of administrators, propagandists, and settlers asserted that European women brought unique qualities to the
empire, qualities that were critical to establishing civilization and
maintaining order. As many scholars have shown, developing notions
of domesticity extended to European empires in the nineteenth century and shaped the process of maintaining colonial rule and managing colonial populations.[83] It was with ideas of domesticity in mind, in
fact, that colonial propagandist Charles Lemire described women as
"the indispensable auxiliary of colonialism. As wife and as mother . . .
a woman renders the settler's enterprise bearable and perpetuates it
after him."[84] In making this statement, Lemire evoked the notion of
separate, albeit complementary, spheres that was central to metropolitan bourgeois society: women emigrants were needed to both reproduce the race and create pleasant households for their husbands. In
addition to its emphasis on domesticity, Lemire's statement hints at

the role that French women would play at civilizing French men in the empire. This relates in part to the widely held belief that if unable to find a white woman, many settlers would choose colonized women as their concubines. Although such relationships were frowned upon in the metropole, they were commonplace in the empire and initially largely tolerated.[85] In fact, many young men viewed the empire as a place where they could "escape metropolitan social restraints and act out various fantasies of power."[86] Some men also argued that in the colonial context, colonized women made better companions than did European women because they were used to the climate and had modest expectations.[87] Yet, even if it was common in the empire, relations between white men and colonized women threatened the sustainability of French colonial rule by breaking down the barriers between "colonized" and "colonizer" as well as between "civilized" and "savage."[88] As Ann Laura Stoler has shown, the "intimate" and the "domestic arrangements" of Europeans were subject to significant scrutiny in the colonial context, as they were central to upholding the image of racial superiority that was a crucial part of maintaining colonial rule.[89]

It was also widely feared that relations between French men and colonized women would produce children who were not entirely French, something that both metropolitan pronatalists and colonial administrators opposed. Piolet, for example, wrote that "French women need to emigrate to our colonies, if we want to create in these colonies a race that is truly French; without that, we would have a mostly mixed population that would take from the French person and the native all of their vices without borrowing any of their qualities."[90] Piolet's assumption that *métis* children inherited the worst racial characteristics of both parents was consistent with the "findings" of contemporary anthropological studies and in turn reveals an important paradox in demographic arguments in favor of empire.[91] While pronatalists considered colonial settlement conducive to stronger demographic growth, *métissage* nevertheless incited fears that imperialism could further contribute to the degeneration of the French race.[92] To pronatalists, French men who had sexual relations with colonial subjects effectively removed themselves from the French gene pool, reneged on their duties to be good fathers (by abandoning their *métis* children), and became otherwise corrupted by colonial life.[93] Many of the pronatalists who advocated colonial settlement, including Richet, simultaneously expressed fears that the empire represented an additional hazard to strengthening the French population precisely because of the high incidence of *métissage*. In his book *La sélection humaine*, Richet admonished those who failed to see beyond "the boulevards of Paris and the hotels of Nice" to the threat that lay beyond in the colonies.[94] He therefore saw both opportunities and danger in French migration to the colonies.

It was with these concerns in mind that ultimately, by the late nineteenth century, colonial governments more actively discouraged such relationships and began to argue that the migration of French women to the colonies was especially important. The arrival of French women would give the male settler population a choice of partners, thereby directing them away from relationships with colonized women, and would make the establishment of traditional, large French families possible. Thus, the migration of women to the empire would simultaneously address metropolitan demographic concerns, by making colonial settlement endeavors possible, and also address colonial demographic concerns, by reducing the frequency of *métissage* and establishing future generations of French settlers. Pronatalists believed that women would put a stop to the corruption of French men in the empire by deterring them from promiscuity and interracial relationships and transforming them into good husbands and fathers. From this perspective, the arrival of women in the colonies would bring a moralizing and civilizing influence to colonial life more generally. As Piolet explained, "French women must emigrate to our colonies, to bring to them better manners, more decency, and better behavior. Nothing, in actuality, is more slovenly, shameless, barbaric, savage, and without restraint, than a society that lacks the presence of a woman."[95] Piolet went on to argue that one of the biggest obstacles missionaries faced in converting the colonial subjects was the horrible moral example set by the male European settler population. Consequently, the emigration of French women to the colonies and the subsequent establishment of pleasant French homes and families would serve a dual purpose: the birth of French children, who would make the colonial population permanent, and the arrival of civilization, order, and morality.

La Société Française d'Émigration des Femmes

It was with these concerns in mind that members of the UCF subsequently turned their attention to recruiting women for colonial settlement, a task they considered far more challenging than recruiting men. They believed that unless pushed to do so out of desperation, women would not be interested in migrating to the colonies. The UCF subsequently targeted women who were unmarried, educated, struggling to have a successful career, and were either middle class or aspired to be middle class. They believed that these women wanted to get married and were only pursuing careers because they could not find a suitable husband. In creating the Société française d'émigration des femmes (SFEF), France's only women's emigration organization, the UCF presented the empire as a land of opportunity for such women. In contrast to how the UCF appealed to prospective male settlers, they presented the SFEF as a quasi-charitable organization that would provide women, whom they generally depicted as victims, with a situation in the empire. Although their first priority was matching these women with jobs to ease their transition to colonial life, it was expected that their protégées would marry soon after arriving in the colonies and would not need to work for very long.

Although officially the UCF targeted unmarried women who were unemployed and educated because they were the ones most likely to be desperate enough to emigrate, the idea of sending them to the empire also responded to a number of gendered and class-based concerns in both the metropole and the colony. First of all, from the perspective of French authorities in the colonies, educated, middle-class women, unlike their working-class counterparts, were an essential part of bringing refinement, civilization, and morality to the colonies. Working-class and peasant women, on the other hand, could not fill this particular role and were not considered to be the best representatives of the race. In fact, colonial administrators considered the migration of working-class women, whose manners and morality were considered to be hardly better than those of colonized women, to be particularly unappealing, as their presence in the colony did little to sustain ideas of racial superiority.[96] Second, in the context of fears of decline and depopulation in fin de siècle France, unmarried or "surplus" women were a particularly troublesome category, their very existence inciting all kinds of fears. As an example of the connection between unmarried women and the sense of national decline, Andrea Mansker argues that the celibacy and voluntary sterility of such women was increasingly presented in pathological terms and linked to a wide array of disorders, including suicide and hysteria.[97] Moreover, contemporaries feared that this segment of the female population was growing larger due to urbanization, the increasing cost of living, and other changes in the economy. In 1900, for example, 12 percent of women between the ages of forty-five and forty-nine had never been married, and this percentage was significantly elevated among women professionals.[98] Pronatalists considered all unmarried women problematic, as they did not fulfill what was believed to be a woman's most important role in society: motherhood. However, unmarried middle-class women were especially worrisome. Such women represented something of an anomaly in metropolitan society, because they did not embody the domestic ideal, otherwise so central to a middle-class woman's gender identity. Moreover, they needed to work to support themselves, but because of their education and class origins they could not seek work in sectors of the economy that hired large numbers of women: domestic service, factories, and so forth. The sense that the class identity of such women was ambiguous, situated somewhere between the working classes and middle classes, was conveyed very clearly in the term used to designate them: *non-classée*.

One person who had a great deal to say about France's *non-classées* was Gabriel Paul Othenin de Cléron, most commonly known as the Comte d'Haussonville. The son of another well-known Comte d'Haussonville, who organized the emigration of French citizens from Alsace-Lorraine to Algeria following the Franco-Prussian War, the younger Comte d'Haussonville not only served in parliament but was a prolific writer who was elected to the Académie française in 1888. In particular, he was well known for his charity and concern for the plight of working women.[99] Though not initially in favor of colonialism and never a feminist, d'Haussonville nevertheless saw the colonies as a way to resolve various social problems in the metropole, including unemployment for women.[100] D'Haussonville's role in promoting colonial emigration illustrates how the issue of depopulation transcended metropolitan political divisions; even individuals who did not have a vested interest in colonial affairs agreed on the empire's utility in solving the metropolitan social questions with which they were concerned.

According to the Comte d'Haussonville in his 1900 study, *Salaires et misères de femmes*, the term *déclassées* referred simply to women who were born into a social position that they could not maintain; the term *non-classées*, by contrast, referred to women who were unsuccessful in their attempt to rise to a higher social position "and who oscillate, uncertain of their future, between the condition that they left and that which they have not yet managed to attain."[101] According to d'Haussonville, the emergence of this latter group was simply a consequence of modern society. While significant percentages of French women had always worked out of economic necessity, it was only later in the nineteenth century that France witnessed a rise in the numbers of women pursuing liberal careers. With the extension of educational opportunities and the entrance of women into careers hitherto exclusively male, young women could dream of having a future outside of marriage and motherhood, or at least pursuing a fulfilling career prior to marriage and motherhood. Girls who excelled in school, took their exams, and received their diploma often felt ambitious, wanted to put their skills to use, and dreamed of a better life. For these young women, teaching or working for the Administration des postes et télégraphes were desirable careers because they represented job security, steady pay, a pension, and entrance into the petit bourgeoisie.

Yet, the shortcoming of France's educational reforms was that they created ambitions that frequently went unfulfilled. In his career guide, Turquan made it clear that educated women faced even more severe competition than did men.[102] In January 1893, for example, there were 13,000 young women in France hoping to obtain a teaching position; 6,441 of these women wanted a position in Paris, where only 54 positions were available.[103] D'Haussonville drew heavily on Turquan's statistics to estimate that there were about fifteen to twenty thousand *non-classée* women in Paris alone, who accomplished nothing as they spent year after year searching for a position.[104] In addition to being bad for them personally, their unsuccessful career pursuits were detrimental to the nation, since these women did not do what pronatalists considered vital to France's well-being: getting married at a young age and becoming devoted mothers to large numbers of children. Similar to their criticism of French men pursuing a white-collar job and a bourgeois existence, pronatalist complaints about the *non-classées* reflected a combination of gendered and class-based concerns about the expansion of education and its impact on the birthrate.

While in the metropole pronatalists viewed these *non-classée* women as problematic and partly responsible for French depopulation, in the context of empire and colonial settlement such women could play a valuable role in national regeneration. Promoters of colonial emigration seemed to respect the ambition and intelligence that drove these women to pursue better opportunities and believed that if they could find an appropriate outlet for this misdirected ambition and intellectual energy, they could contribute to France's repopulation. They presented the empire as a solution to this dilemma, as it would give women options that perhaps did not exist for them in France. For instance, in her book promoting women's colonial emigration, Grace Corneau argued that ambitious, smart, and adventurous women who felt unfulfilled in France could find a better life in the colonies.[105] After describing the miserable plight of unmarried, educated women in the metropole, Corneau presented the French empire as a land of opportunity for exactly the kind of women who did not fit neatly into metropolitan society. Having lived in both Tonkin and Tunisia, Corneau felt particularly qualified to address the opportunities available for women in those parts of the empire. Concerning Tonkin, she stressed the need for more pastry and bread makers, dressmakers and florists.

In this respect, Tonkin was an ideal place for an ambitious and entrepreneurial woman wishing to open her own business. Furthermore, the government in Tonkin did give land concessions to women, who were, Corneau assured her readers, perfectly capable of directing a large agricultural enterprise without the guidance of a man.[106] With the rising European settler population, demand for educated women was great; the colony needed women professionals such as schoolteachers, nurses, and doctors. Nuns and military doctors were at that time the only people with medical expertise available to assist European women giving birth. A woman doctor who might face scorn and unemployment in France would find great opportunities in Tonkin. The growth of the European settler population in this colony would require both mothers and women professionals.

Likening North Africa to the American West, Corneau described the qualities of a new type of French woman shaped by the spirit of independence, enterprise, and adventure that colonial life in Tunisia represented. Corneau explained that French women had the necessary energy to work the land in Tunisia and direct agricultural enterprises, despite being perceived in France as simply refined, coquettish, and charming. Moreover, she advanced the idea, similar to what was seen in propaganda aimed at men, that the challenges and hardships of living in a rough, untamed environment would improve a woman, bringing out her "rare qualities of energy and endurance."[107] As an example of the kind of strength and leadership qualities that a woman could develop in this context, she provided a quaint depiction of the American West where cowboys took orders from the "cattle queens" directing ranches.[108] She maintained that the same was true in Tunisia, an extension of France where gender relations and society were undergoing rapid changes. Whereas in France, society had not yet caught up with educational reform and remained largely prejudiced against educated and ambitious women, in the empire French society was being born anew and influenced by the harsh conditions of life. In this nascent pioneer society, women could find opportunities that were virtually nonexistent in metropolitan France, where social prejudices remained almost impervious to reform.[109]

The belief that social conditions were different in colonial society and could therefore be conducive to restoring demographic growth prompted the UCF to create the SFEF in January 1897. At the society's inauguration, d'Haussonville explained that in the colonies there were essentially three types of French women: prostitutes, nuns, and the wives of the civil servants who did not want to be there and could not, therefore, be considered part of the permanent settlement.[110] By contrast, there were very few young women of marriageable age, and this demographic imbalance represented a serious obstacle to the development of the French colonial population. Simultaneously, in France there were many single working women struggling to survive and find a fulfilling career. While in France there were too few opportunities for career women, in the colonies there were too few women for the careers that were available. In Tonkin, New Caledonia, and Tunisia, women could find the employment they had been seeking unsuccessfully in France, as well as a husband. D'Haussonville concluded that marriage was, after all, a woman's true career; other labor represented simply a means of survival in the absence of a husband.[111]

The class-based anxieties about French masculinity also shaped the UCF's understanding of women's emigration. In his inaugural speech of the SFEF, Joseph Chailley-Bert explained that because French society had become so decadent and materialistic, many women were forced to work for a living because they lacked the dowry necessary to find a husband and subsequently could not get married. From this perspective, the problem clearly originated with men who had lost sight of the moral reasons for getting married and had instead adopted the attitude of the elites, namely, that marriage was a business transaction in which receiving a large dowry was of paramount importance. Again, unmarried middle-class women were portrayed as victims of male greed. Chailley-Bert emphasized that in the colonies, by contrast, French men's priorities were more simple, as they were less concerned with emulating the bourgeoisie and more interested in finding a wife who would be a partner in the familial enterprise. In the empire, from a prospective husband's perspective, it was more important for a woman to be smart, energetic, and hardworking than to have a large

RECRUITING COLONIAL SETTLERS

dowry. Furthermore, in the empire there were too many men who did not get married because of the absence of eligible partners. Chailley-Bert estimated that in some parts of the empire the ratio was one French woman for every ten Frenchmen.[112]

The founders of the SFEF believed that women's colonial emigration would benefit metropole and empire alike; the empire would have a self-reproducing settler population, and the metropole would be strengthened by redistributing its population to more fruitful ends. Chailley-Bert explained the pronatalist contributions of the SFEF in his inaugural speech. If the estimated 1,302,471 *non-classée* women in France between the ages of twenty-five and fifty were to migrate to the colonies, they could contribute to the growing numbers of colonial French families that were twice as prolific as their metropolitan counterparts.[113] Because such women were unlikely to find a stable means of support or become wives or mothers in the metropole, their emigration to the colonies would by no means represent a population loss to the metropole. By facilitating the emigration of this category of women to the empire, the SFEF would fulfill a mission "at once philanthropic and patriotic." Through colonial emigration they would end the suffering of women unlikely to contribute to France's repopulation by providing them with the opportunities they lacked in the metropole: employment and marriage prospects. In Chailley-Bert's speech it is clear that he was influenced by the myth of the prolific settler, as he stated that "as soon as French people are no longer on metropolitan soil, the natural fecundity of their race reappears."[114] As proof he pointed to Canada, citing the rapid growth of French settlers in the former colony despite the fact that many of them had ancestors from Normandy, a region in France with one of the lowest birthrates. A similar phenomenon was also evident in Algeria, where settlers' birthrates were twice as high as in France, despite the fact that many of them were from southern French departments with low birthrates. Similar to pronatalists, Chailley-Bert stated that this abundant population growth could one day be returned to France: "in a century or two, maybe it will be necessary to create societies that will have the opposite goal of that which we are pursuing today and that will return to the metropole the overly abundant population of the colonies."[115]

Whereas in the early modern era women, many of whom were orphans, were simply shipped to the empire against their will with no purpose other than to serve as wives to the large male population, the UCF presented the SFEF as primarily a career agency and only indirectly a matchmaking agency. Chailley-Bert emphasized that sending women to the colonies solely to find husbands would never work; it would lead to nothing more than hastily arranged and unhappy marriages, and could potentially reduce women to greater poverty and desperation than they faced in France. Consequently, the SFEF would send select women to the colonies, make employment arrangements for them, and then hope that with time these women would meet suitable men, get married, and have children. In this vein, the SFEF had four official objectives: to "develop a taste for life in the colonies among French women by way of brochures, conferences, and any appropriate propaganda methods; to provide those who wish to emigrate and who have what it takes to succeed, with employment appropriate to their skills; to ensure these individuals aid and protection during their trip, as well as upon their arrival in the colony; to stay in touch with them for at least the first months of their stay in the colony."[116]

The latter two objectives illustrate another way in which the SFEF differed from the UCF's other colonial emigration endeavors: in order to be respectable, its leaders needed to take responsibility for protecting and chaperoning the young women they assisted. The leadership of the organization was well aware of the potential dangers young women would face when traveling alone and living far away from their families. The greatest fear was that their clients would become prostitutes in the colony, either out of desperation if their employment arrangements fell through, or involuntarily after having been tricked by unscrupulous characters involved in the white slave trade. With any offer of employment they received, the SFEF sought to do a thorough investigation to determine that the job did in fact exist and that the person making the offer was of good moral character. Charged with this task was a committee in each colony, headed by the wife of the governor.[117] These committees were also responsible for staying in touch with the emigrant after her arrival and helping her with any problems that arose. The letters the SFEF received suggested that many of these emigrants appreciated the friendship of the older women assigned to look after them upon their arrival; these women often became almost like adopted family members who attended their weddings in the absence of their real families in France.[118]

Like these local committees, the central committee of the SFEF in France was staffed entirely by women. The SFEF was headed by Mme Pégard, a feminist with a long history of government service.[119] As a young woman, Pégard was awarded a medal for her assistance at the 1870 siege of Metz during the Franco-Prussian War.[120] Later she worked closely with the French government in a variety of capacities and became an important figure in the French feminist movement. For instance, as secretary-general of the decorative arts she fought for and secured the right of women to enroll at the École des beaux-arts.[121] In 1899 the government appointed her as their official representative to the Franco-Russian Exposition in Saint Petersburg and, upon her return, made her a Chevalier de la Légion d'honneur.[122] Moreover, she was an active member of the feminist organization the Conseil national des femmes françaises (CNFF) and served as the president of its labor section until her death in 1916. In this role she studied employment opportunities and working conditions for women in all areas of the economy, including unskilled labor, the trades, and the liberal careers. She was particularly vocal in condemning women's unequal pay, which, in all industries and professions, was lower than that of a man.[123] Fairly radical in some respects, she met with groups of women in every working-class district in Paris and encouraged them to form syndicates to defend their professional interests.[124] Generally speaking, Pégard considered unemployment, unequal opportunities, and the poor working conditions of women to be feminist issues that had larger demographic, as well as moral, repercussions in French society.

Although her primary motive for collaborating with the UCF was her feminist convictions about women's work, Pégard also expressed an interest in the issue of depopulation and, like men such as Bertillon and Chailley-Bert, presented colonial emigration as a solution to France's demographic decline. Her views on this matter came across most clearly at the Colonial Congress of 1906 in Marseilles, at which Pégard represented the SFEF and reported on women's colonial emigration. First of all, she dismissed out of hand any notion that for reasons of acclimatization or women's supposedly frail constitution, colonial emigration was dangerous for women. By contrast, she evoked the myth of the prolific settler, emphasizing that settler birthrates far surpassed those of the metropole, thereby testifying to French women's ability to thrive and reproduce in the colonies.[125] Moreover, she seemed to share many of the gendered assumptions behind this myth, emphasizing, as had Louis-Adolphe Bertillon many years earlier, that what restrained the birthrate in France was parents' fears about being able to situate their children in a career or the family enterprise.[126] Yet her early-twentieth century understanding of this issue differed slightly from that of Bertillon in that she asserted that it was parents' concerns about placing both sons and daughters in careers that influenced family planning.[127] She believed that many parents envisioned a future in which their daughters, whether married or not, would need to earn a living. Still, influenced by her own experience studying actual working conditions, as well as gender-based barriers to employment and educational opportunities in the metropole, Pégard saw young women's employment prospects as bleak. Because of this inequality in the economy, women migrated for reasons that were very different than those of men. Echoing Chailley-Bert's ideas on this issue, Pégard concluded that "it is the desire for wealth that sends men to the colonies; the lack of wealth is what sends young women there."[128] As confirmation of this desperation, Pégard explained that she received thousands of letters from young women, many of whom had children or elderly family members to support, explaining their dire financial situations and imploring her to help them find a position in the colonies.[129]

Although the SFEF was initially created with great enthusiasm and received warm support from the president, the minister of colonies, colonial officials, and settlers, its leaders encountered a number of problems during its existence. The first problem was that the SFEF was underfunded and could not afford to operate on a large scale. For example, in 1898 the society wanted to fund a woman emigrant but, lacking the 150 francs needed for her departure, turned to an English emigration society for support.[130] According to Mme Pégard, the British had eighteen emigration societies specifically for women at this time, many of which had large operating budgets enabling them to send thousands of women to the colonies.[131] In explaining the lack of support and funding for such endeavors in France, Pégard said that following the SFEF's creation they encountered some skepticism about the organization's chances of success and then, when they did continue to exist and operate, this skepticism turned into a general disinterest.[132]

Pégard's contention that colonial organizations and officials mostly ignored the SFEF can be confirmed by comparing the significant attention the organization received in its first years with the waning interest evident thereafter. Shortly after the creation of the SFEF, the minister of colonies gave the organization official sanction by addressing all the governors and residents-general in a letter dated July 31, 1897, in which he expressed support for the organization.[133] The president of the Republic, Félix Faure, and his wife became honorary members. The SFEF also sent a brochure to all of the colonial governors introducing the organization and emphasizing its philanthropic work in helping to address the problems of depopulation and *non-classées*.[134] In 1898 a group of male settlers in Madagascar wrote to the SFEF expressing their support for the organization and complaining that there were too many single men in the colony.[135] In 1897 and 1898 the UCF reported regularly on the activities of the SFEF in its journal *La quinzaine coloniale*. However, *La quinzaine coloniale* stopped reporting on the activities of the organization after 1899, which would seem to imply that it was no longer functioning or had ceased to be of interest to the UCF.[136] Still, the evidence shows that the SFEF continued to exist for a number of years after 1899, as it was affiliated with the CNFF from 1901 until at least 1908. Moreover, Mme Pégard continued to promote her organization in the first decade of the twentieth century, publishing an article about the SFEF in the *Revue coloniale* in 1901, reporting on the SFEF's status to the CNFF in 1902, and giving a presentation at the Colonial

Exposition in Marseille in 1906. Her efforts aside, the relative silence about the organization in the UCF's journal and elsewhere is consistent with her contention that despite fairly widespread acceptance of the idea that women's emigration to the colonies was essential, there was little real interest in fully supporting such endeavors.

The biggest challenge the SFEF faced, however, was that the realities of women's employment prospects in the colonies did not correspond with the mission statement and hopes of the organization's founders. Initially, the society seemed hopeful. In 1897 the SFEF reported proudly that following its creation they immediately received hundreds of letters, more than two hundred of which were from women asking to be placed in jobs. In the early months of its existence the SFEF sent two women to Algeria in response to the colonial government's request for midwives to care for women and children. The SFEF received requests for cooks and maids in Tunisia, a teacher in Tonkin, and laundry women for the French population in the Transvaal, although this was not a French colony. The SFEF also arranged for a young woman, who had been engaged for some time to a civil servant in Tonkin and whose requests to join her fiancé had been rejected by the colonial administration, to go to Tonkin and get married.[137]

In 1902, five years after the SFEF was established, Mme Pégard reported that the society had arranged the emigration of sixty women to the colonies: twenty to Indochina, seven to Madagascar, five to Tunisia, one to Senegal, seven to Algeria, fifteen to New Caledonia, one to Guyana, and four others who were about to depart.[138] Yet the letters the SFEF received suggested that many of the women they helped did not migrate to the colonies to work as dentists, doctors, and teachers, but rather to join fiancés who were already in the colonies serving in the army or working as civil servants.[139] Although uniting the engaged couples served the goal of encouraging people to marry and establish households in the colonies, the SFEF's patronage of these particular women deviated from the original goals of establishing women in careers that were highly competitive in the metropole and providing single men in the colonies with the possibility of meeting young, marriageable French women.

Mme Pégard and the other women of the SFEF soon learned that the empire was not quite the land of opportunity for ambitious French women that they had originally envisioned it to be. They found that colonial administrations did not hire very many women and generally reserved available positions for the widows and daughters of deceased civil servants.[140] Furthermore, most colonies had only a small European population and therefore had little need for European midwives and teachers. Moreover, European women could not work as cooks, maids, seamstresses or in other such professions, because these jobs were filled by colonized women who earned very low wages, lower than what any European woman would accept.[141] Because the number of colonial jobs available was considerably smaller than the number of women who appealed to the SFEF for help, Mme Pégard and her staff responded to thousands of letters with apologetic replies, informing women that there was nothing the SFEF could do to assist them.[142]

Mme Pégard explained in 1901 that the paucity of women's employment in the empire forced a shift in the SFEF's goals. "To our thinking, the women that we would send to the colonies were supposed to create a position for themselves, administrative, in public education, postal and telegraph services, customs, etc. or private, in various jobs, in private teachings, or the professions of mid-wives, fashion-designers, dress-makers, etc., and marriage was not supposed to arrive except as an after effect and be nothing but a consequence of their presence in the colonies."[143] Pégard surmised that once France established more European families in the empire, there would be greater demand for women teachers, nurses, and dressmakers, and the SFEF would then be better able to help France's *non-classée* women emigrate. Many colonial governments emphasized that the SFEF needed to shift its goals; the emigration of women to the colonies was of the utmost importance to them, but women qualified to work in agriculture would be much more desirable than teachers. General Gallieni, governor of Madagascar, expressed this sentiment to the SFEF when he explained that he envisioned a colony full of French people and not a race of *métis*. In his letter to the SFEF, Gallieni wrote: "I do not want a single woman teacher, I only want farm girls and no others."[144] Before single women could migrate to the colonies and find work in the liberal careers, the French would need to establish large communities of French families that would provide arriving women schoolteachers with pupils, dentists with patients, and dressmakers with customers.

Gallieni's statement reflected a fundamental tension in early-twentieth-century arguments in favor of women's colonial emigration. Educated middle-class women were considered the best candidates for reproducing the race and bringing French civilization and moral rectitude to the colonies. Nevertheless, as the SFEF's trials and tribulations indicate, a schoolteacher or governess was unlikely to find a situation in the colonies. This contradiction in the colonial propaganda was also evident in other European colonies, such as Australia. According to Rita Kranidis, British colonial emigration societies wanted to recruit women who were educated and bourgeois yet required that they also have skills in domestic labor and agriculture, skills that a woman of their class would not generally possess.[145] Although such incompatible requirements were not explicitly stated in the SFEF's literature, the SFEF's recruitment efforts were similar in that they did not correspond with the realities of colonial life. Once aware of this problem, the SFEF sought to shift its goals, but was ultimately unsuccessful in developing an approach to women's emigration that would respond to metropolitan concerns about *non-classées*, fulfill the needs of the colonies, and appeal to women interested in emigrating. For instance, Mme Pégard figured that peasant girls would make ideal candidates for colonial emigration as they had the skills necessary to thrive in the empire and contribute to colonial life. Yet, unlike the *non-classées*, peasant girls had a place in metropolitan society in that they could marry without a dowry, have children, and assist their husbands on the farm. Mme Pégard consequently turned the SFEF's attention to the young girls of the Assistance publique: poor girls with no family and few prospects for the future who could, with a small amount of training, develop the skills necessary to become farmers. Unfortunately, the Ministry of Agriculture charged five hundred francs for its training programs, and the SFEF lacked the resources necessary to pay for the girls to receive this training. Mme Pégard requested scholarships from the Ministry of Agriculture to help with this cost and funds from the Ministry of the Interior to help with the expense of placing the girls in the empire after they received this training.[146] These plans, however, do not appear to have been successful. In 1906 Mme Pégard concluded sadly that "a woman's role in the colonies seems well-defined: a man's companion, guardian of the home and of the race," a formula that excluded single, working women, the very women she was determined to help.[147]

Maternalism and Women's Colonial Emigration after the Great War

A number of recent studies have looked at the personal histories of women who traveled to European colonies in the nineteenth century hoping to find better opportunities and freedoms than awaited them in Europe.[148] In some cases women were indeed more successful than would have been the case in Europe. For instance, Rebecca Rogers has detailed how colonial Algeria offered a French schoolteacher named Eugénie Luce the opportunity to flee an unhappy marriage in France and pursue her ambitions of opening a school for Algerian girls. Even after the colonial government withdrew its financial support for her school, Mme Luce continued to work with Algerian girls by teaching them embroidery.[149] Despite the occasional success story, the challenges faced by the SFEF are an important reminder of the obstacles many women faced when seeking new opportunities in the empire. For most women the empire was not quite the land of opportunity that the propaganda suggested. For this reason, by the interwar years propagandists had begun to modify their optimistic tone and, in keeping with Mme Pégard's earlier conclusions, emphasized the paucity of employment opportunities for women and advised against arriving in the colonies without a husband. Still, colonial propaganda continued to stress that the colonies needed more French women and argued that educated women could find a different sort of life in the empire than in France. Clotilde Chivas-Baron, who wrote a book preparing women for colonial life and founded the organization Entr'aide coloniale féminine,[150] argued that most women's jobs were filled by colonial subjects and that women should avoid going to the colonies unless their husbands already had a job offer.[151] Chivas-Baron nevertheless emphasized that colonial life offered married women innumerable opportunities unavailable in France outside formal careers. Advocating a colonial version of maternalism, she argued that while remaining faithful wives, women could use their intelligence and skills to facilitate the colonial project by improving the lives of the colonial subjects and introducing hygiene.[152] Like the SFEF, Chivas-Baron emphasized that women who felt unfulfilled in France could find in colonial society an outlet for their ambitions and intellectual energy.

Formal career options were few, but the leadership qualities of educated and ambitious women could nevertheless further the colonial enterprise. Imperialism could offer women a third option between the two choices they faced in the metropole: postponing marriage and motherhood while hoping to enter a highly competitive career, or feeling unsatisfied in a marriage that offered few outlets for the skills and ambitions that their educations had inspired. Contributors to the *Bulletin de l'œuvre coloniale des femmes françaises* presented colonial emigration for women as the natural consequence of the social transformations French society had undergone; education had given women a sense of independence that only colonial life could fulfill.[153] The main goals of this colonial women's organization, created in 1900, were to provide moral and material assistance to French women migrating to, or already living in, the colonies and to organize conferences designed to promote colonial emigration for families.[154] The organization, which published a monthly journal containing articles on colonial life and women's activism on behalf of female colonial subjects, promoted the idea that educated women could find in colonial life precisely what they lacked in the metropole. In 1912, for example, Gaston Valran wrote that for women "the colonial idea has become a sentiment: it corresponds to her intense desire of devotion; it has discovered for her large fields of action; it has targeted the direction of her superior energies awoken by a more modern education and upbringing."[155]

Specifically, women could assume a position of leadership in colonial life by balancing their responsibilities as wives with their efforts to improve the lives of colonial subjects. In this respect, Alexandre Brou wrote, the female settler would continue the work initiated by nuns, the first French women who headed to the colonies to further the civilizing mission.[156] Brou explained, "Women settlers, you will have to civilize. You will have to undertake the education of the natives who will depend on you. You will have to uplift them."[157] In explaining why French women were ideally suited to this task, Brou mentioned that in Muslim countries especially, colonized women were inaccessible to French men. Demonstrating the European fascination with those closed, mysterious feminine spaces, he explained that French women were needed to enter the "jealously guarded" harems and use their female intuition and sensitivity to extend French influence to an otherwise hidden population.[158]

Brou's argument about the position of leadership that women would hold as they undertook the moral uplifting of colonial subjects converged with that of many feminists. An early example of this feminist activism was that of the radical feminist Hubertine Auclert, who lived in Algeria from 1888 and 1892. Auclert embraced France's position as an imperial power, as she saw in France's civilizing mission the potential to both liberate colonized women and claim a greater public role for French women. Still, she rejected the idea of imperialism as a largely male project and was highly critical of male colonial administrators who showed little interest in the plight of colonized Algerian women. For this reason, Auclert argued that French women were essential to the success of the civilizing mission and the strength of the empire.[159] Her activism on behalf of colonized Algerian women was emblematic of the ways in which France's position as an imperial power could and did influence feminists' understandings of the "woman question" in France as well as the strategies they chose to pursue their objectives.[160]

Although Auclert's feminist activism was unusual in the late nineteenth century, by the interwar years many feminists displayed an interest in the opportunities offered by colonial life.[161] Like Mme Pégard and Grace Corneau decades before, the interwar feminists of the CNFF presented the empire as a land of opportunity for women seeking to put their ambitions, intellectual energy, and skills to use. In 1931 the CNFF organized a congress devoted to the topic of empire and focused largely on the status of women colonial subjects and the ways in which French women could further the civilizing mission.[162] The permanent committee of honor included three prominent pronatalists of the period (Charles Richet, Adolphe Landry, and Paul Strauss), and the congress opened under the presidency of the feminist Ghénia Avril de Sainte-Croix. Included on the program were presentations by professional women working in the colonies as doctors and nurses, by representatives of Catholic, Jewish, and Protestant charitable organizations, by activists concerned about the status of women colonial subjects and *métis* children, and by *visiteuses* whose duties included overseeing the implementation of Western notions of hygiene and child care. One such *visiteuse*, a Mlle Girard, presented herself as a mother to the colonial subjects under her jurisdiction. Girard described her job as rewarding but challenging, because one had to have "the firmness of a mother to see that treatment be instituted in time and not interrupted too early."[163]

Conclusion

"Over there, there is a place for everyone, new lands, open air that none has breathed, and a task to be accomplished which will make all of you heroes, strong, sturdy men, happy to be alive!"[164] This line from *Fécondité* is consistent with the image that many late-nineteenth-century French people had of the empire: the struggles and exigencies of frontier life would exert a masculinizing influence on French settlers, transforming these languishing, weak, urban individuals into stronger, more virile men. Influenced by the myth of the prolific settler, the UCF presented the empire as a way to address not only persistent concerns about masculinity but also related problems such as the decline of rural life, the expectation of social mobility, and the low birthrate. Similar to Bertillon's earlier studies, the UCF's approach to recruiting male settlers rested on the assumption that men's ambitions and determination to find lucrative opportunities motivated their decision to migrate and informed their family-planning decisions. However, unlike what was seen in earlier studies by social scientists like

Bertillon and Ricoux, the UCF's propaganda directly acknowledged that colonial emigration could appeal to women who, like men, were struggling to find suitable opportunities in the metropole.

Although the UCF acknowledged a connection between financial well-being, the decision to migrate, and the number of children a woman produced, the way in which the society approached women's migration nevertheless differed in some fundamental ways from how they sought to appeal to men. Despite arguing that women could find in the colonies an outlet for ambitions left unfulfilled in the metropole, rhetoric that on the surface suggested more acceptance of the idea of women's work, UCF leadership persisted in casting women in traditional roles. Securing a job in the colonies was supposed to be merely a temporary solution to the problems these women faced in France, something that would enable them to support themselves prior to finding a husband. In addition, when considering the larger question of how migrating to the colonies could influence individuals' reproductive choices, the UCF tended to place women in a passive role. Concerning French society, the UCF depicted women as victims of modernity, struggling to survive after failing to find husbands, a predicament that would be remedied by relocating to the empire. On some level this assessment of the *non-classées* would seem to contrast significantly with the assertions often seen in pronatalist propaganda that women seeking careers acted out of selfish and reprehensible motives and were responsible for the low birthrate. That said, the UCF's apparent sympathy for the *non-classées* was not at odds with pronatalists' negative assessment of women pursuing careers. By presenting a woman's attempt to have a career as an unsustainable, desperate act, the UCF in its own way joined pronatalists in delegitimizing the idea of middle-class women's work. Like Ricoux and Bertillon, the UCF suggested that the impact of colonial settlement on the birthrate hinged more on men's choices than on those of women, despite recognizing that both men and women were needed to establish a prolific population. When recruiting men, the UCF recognized that a man would weigh his employment options and financial situation when deciding whether or not to start a family, and they sought to appeal to those impulses directly when recruiting male settlers; the goal was simply to direct men from one vocation in France to another in the colonies. With the *non-classées*, on the other hand, directing women to a colonial career was simply a first step toward marriage, a way of making colonial settlement initially appealing and feasible. The UCF preferred to think that the main reason why women's migration to the empire would generate a stronger birthrate is that they would be in a settler community where men were more inclined toward marriage and having a family; this in and of itself would be sufficient to transform single, middle-class women into married mothers.

Ultimately, the UCF's plans to respond to gendered anxieties in the metropole by recruiting women and men for colonial settlement fell short of expectations. As Mme Pégard explained, in the colonies, as in France, women faced enormous obstacles in securing jobs. Without legitimate employment opportunities to support themselves prior to finding husbands, women had little incentive to migrate. In practice, the thousands of "surplus" unmarried, middle-class women who were considered so problematic in the metropole could not simply be relocated to the colonies where future husbands awaited them. Similarly, the UCF's notions that urban and somewhat effeminate men in France could become more virile and masculine in the empire never fully developed. The letters that the UCF received from individuals interested in colonial settlement revealed that many French men were uninterested in renouncing their "overcivilized" existence in favor of the rough, challenging life of a settler. The UCF had to respond continuously to such letters by explaining that the life of a settler was not "easy." Moreover, as the kind of white-collar jobs sought by many men were scarce, any man going to the colonies needed to be willing to get his hands dirty and break a sweat while working the land, a willingness that these letters suggested was generally not present. Consequently, even if imperialists like Joseph Chailley-Bert believed that weak, soft urban men should aspire to become more masculine by undergoing the physical hardships required of the colonial settler, it seems that most men interested in migrating were not motivated by this same desire for self-improvement.

As the twentieth century progressed, the idea of addressing depopulation through migration to the colonies, whether it involved men or women, was advocated less frequently. This was consistent with an overall decline in French colonial migration. Nevertheless, settler colonies and populations continued to factor into pronatalists' ideas about the strength of the French population and to shape their proposed solutions to demographic decline. In particular, pronatalists drew inspiration from colonial initiatives in population policies designed to extend French influence and increase the birthrate simultaneously. In some colonies such policies were focused exclusively on the French settler populations. Elsewhere, as the next chapter will show, colonial experiments with pronatalism were focused on the colonized population, the growth of which was considered essential to French interests in the colony.

THREE

Creating a "Labor Reservoir"

Pronatalism, Medicine, and Motherhood in Madagascar

> Safeguarding the indigenous population, seeking to
> increase it by any methods, to diminish its physiological
> misery and at the same time ameliorate its moral condi-
> tion, this is the foremost duty of a colonizing people.
>
> —JOSEPH GALLIENI, *Madagascar de 1896 à 1905*

In the decades following Dr. Ricoux's publication, pronatalists projected their gendered anxieties about the French birthrate onto the empire, imagining Algeria and other settler colonies as ideal societies that lacked the decadence, sterility, and disorder of the metropole. In addition to envisioning utopic settler societies in the empire, pronatalists sought laws and programs in France that would decrease child mortality rates and encourage a higher birthrate. The perceived need to influence family-planning decisions became all the more acute at the end of the nineteenth century when the national census revealed that during four years in the 1890s (1890, 1891, 1892, and 1895) deaths outnumbered births. These grim statistics provided pronatalists with ample material to use in their propaganda depicting coffins outnumbering cradles and the French race simply dying off. The specter of depopulation, it seemed, loomed larger than ever. Responding to the perceived urgency of the situation, the pronatalist movement entered a new phase, becoming more organized and influential in political life. In 1896 Jacques Bertillon and three colleagues formed the Alliance nationale pour l'accroissement de la population française, an organization with the stated purpose of generating awareness about depopulation and lobbying the government for reforms intended to encourage population growth.[1] This organization worked closely with the government in a variety of capacities, including the Commission de la dépopulation (extra-parliamentary depopulation commission) established in 1902 to study the low birthrate and develop potential solutions. Many of the proposals that pronatalists urged the government to adopt in the two decades prior to World War I were focused on protecting children and eliminating some of the barriers to having and supporting a large family. Developed by male reformers with very little input from women, the majority of these proposals focused on child care and pregnancy. Stressing the social and national importance of motherhood, pronatalists justified increasing levels of scrutiny of, and outside intervention into, this aspect of women's lives.

As pronatalists developed their political agenda and worked with the government to devise reforms, a similar phenomenon was under way in the French colony of Madagascar. Concerned about the relatively small size of the colony's Malagasy population and the implications of an inadequate workforce for plans to make the colony profitable, Governor-General Gallieni introduced a series of measures to increase Malagasy population growth through propaganda, familial reforms, and European medicine. Similar to much of the proposed legislation in France, Gallieni's measures affected some of the most intimate areas of women's lives: pregnancy, childbirth, and child rearing. The measures in Madagascar can be contrasted with what was seen in some other colonial contexts, such as Australia, where the government considered aboriginal women racially unfit as mothers, a belief that inspired their child removal policy.[2] In Madagascar, by contrast, the colonial state encouraged Malagasy women to be mothers and sought to instruct them on how to fulfill and embrace this role. Although this approach to motherhood was similar to what was seen in France, racial ideas shaped how the colonial state understood Malagasy motherhood, informing both the propaganda and the types of intervention to which Malagasy mothers were subjected. Therefore, despite the similarities between pronatalism in France and in Madagascar, Gallieni's pronatalist measures should not be interpreted as a simple transmission of metropolitan ideas of reform to the empire; the decrees in Madagascar originated in response to the exigencies of colonial rule and were shaped by the unique conditions of the colony.

Gallieni's decision to undertake such a project reflected a larger development that was also under way in France at this time: a growing conviction that the state had a responsibility to intervene in private family-planning decisions and control population growth. The desire to bring reproduction and family formation under state control was also evident in other European colonies.[3] While some colonial governments concentrated their efforts almost exclusively on reducing mortality, by seeking to eradicate diseases or certain cultural practices, others were pronatalist in their orientation, focusing on prenatal care, childbirth, and infant welfare.[4] Madagascar was one of the few colonies in which the colonial government adopted both approaches to encouraging indigenous population growth. Like Gallieni, many of these other colonial administrators equated indigenous population growth with economic strength. Yet these types of steps were not taken until after the Great War in most colonies and were motivated as much by postwar concerns as they were by anxieties about the size of the labor force. For instance, colonial officials in British East Africa felt obliged to take steps to improve the health of their populations as colonial practices increasingly came under the scrutiny of the League of Nations.[5] Unlike postwar governments in other colonies, Gallieni in 1898 was not pressured by international scrutiny and displayed little concern for how his initiatives would be received in France.

Gallieni's pronatalist decrees in Madagascar are noteworthy not only in terms of their timing but also because of the attention they received in France. Because these measures were more comprehensive and far-reaching in scope than the sporadic legislation introduced in France at this time, French pronatalists were very interested in studying these initiatives, which they believed to be successful. The newly formed pronatalist movement observed how a determined government with a strong, masculine leader could trigger repopulation from above, what sorts of measures could be effective, and which of

CREATING A "LABOR RESERVOIR"

Gallieni's innovations should be applied in France. As editorials in pronatalist newspapers indicate, many pronatalists had only a general idea of what Gallieni actually did in Madagascar, seeing in his decrees mainly what they wished to see implemented in France. In this regard, the figure of Gallieni, and what he represented to pronatalists, was as important as the measures he actually devised. Still, among pronatalist leaders, particularly those involved with the depopulation commission, there was substantial interest in studying the specific policies that Gallieni implemented. Although these policies were designed to address the gendered and racial causes of depopulation in Madagascar, pronatalist leaders in France saw them as innovative and equally applicable to their own efforts to address French racial decline. Pronatalist leaders therefore presented these population policies in a positive light despite the fact that they were aimed at increasing a population that was not French, something that would seem to contradict pronatalist priorities of ensuring the demographic dominance of the French population. In order to understand this apparent contradiction, it is important to recognize that Gallieni intended Madagascar's population growth to be controlled by the colonial state and directed toward French interests. Consequently, these measures did not provoke the same hostility with pronatalists as did population growth elsewhere in the world. Pronatalist interest in Gallieni's population policies reveals that French pronatalism extended beyond simple efforts to increase numbers of French people. By working to create a larger Malagasy labor force in order to attract settlers to the colony, Gallieni contributed indirectly to future efforts at increasing and strengthening the French population.

Medicine, Motherhood, and Population Growth in France

Understanding Gallieni's pronatalist decrees on motherhood and infant welfare requires, first of all, an examination of social reformers' efforts in France in the two decades preceding World War I. Most pronatalist proposals in France at this time aimed to improve population growth in one of three ways: improving the health of the population, offering incentives to encourage people to have larger families, and protecting children. First of all, in terms of reducing mortality and improving the health of the population more generally, pronatalist reformers hoped to promote better sanitation and hygiene, extend the reach of medicine, and improve the French public health system. They built on the efforts of earlier generations of French legislators who, over the course of the nineteenth century, passed a series of measures establishing committees on public hygiene and introducing regulations concerning unsanitary housing, laws that were ultimately weakened by the fact that they were underfunded and reliant on voluntary compliance.[6] Hoping to make local authorities more serious about intervening in matters of public health, legislators passed a law in 1902 giving mayors the authority to disinfect unsanitary dwellings and ensure the quality of drinking water. This law also called for compulsory smallpox vaccinations and notification of contagious diseases.[7] Like earlier such initiatives, these measures also suffered from a lack of enforcement.[8]

Efforts to extend medical assistance to the poor proved equally discouraging to pronatalist reformers in France. As a general rule, large cities had more charitable and state-funded medical facilities than did small cities and rural communes. Though more numerous, urban hospitals also struggled to meet the needs of the population, as they were overcrowded, unable to accommodate the growing populations of the cities, and lacked isolation wards for patients suffering from contagious diseases.[9] A law passed in 1893 was designed to expand the reach of medicine by guaranteeing medical attention to the poor who were temporarily afflicted with an illness or injury. Though representing a step toward the establishment of a more comprehensive system of public health assistance, the law was weakened by the fact that it was subject to local application.[10] As for preventing outbreaks of disease, French reformers hoped to follow the lead of Germany, where vaccination campaigns had been under way as of the 1880s. Yet their efforts to make vaccinations in France obligatory were not achieved until 1902, and diseases such as smallpox and typhoid fever continued to kill large numbers of people on an annual basis.[11]

In light of the heightened concerns about French depopulation during this period, it may seem surprising that reformers in parliament

CREATING A "LABOR RESERVOIR"

struggled in their attempts to overhaul the public health system and make health care more accessible to the masses. The main reason why legislation in this area stalled is that many French leaders distrusted the idea of government intervention into the economy and public welfare. For instance, many members of parliament worried that legislation on unsanitary dwellings would infringe on the rights of property owners, that extended medical services would require higher taxes, and that governmental welfare agencies would compete with existing private charity and prevent the working classes from learning self-reliance. Consequently, they were faced with an almost insurmountable conflict of interest as they expressed a desire to improve population growth by reducing mortality rates but were nevertheless resolute in their commitment to protecting private property rights and other interests from government intervention.

A second approach to encouraging population growth in France was introducing measures that had a direct impact on family life, either by protecting mothers and children or offering incentives for having more children. Among the incentives proposed during this period were exemptions from military service for fathers of large families, housing subsidies for large families, and family allowances; yet few such measures came into existence prior to World War I. Pronatalists in the twenty years leading up to the war were far more successful in introducing measures intended to protect children and reduce infant mortality, measures that had a direct impact on women's lives. Their proposals in this area included placing a variety of restrictions on where and when women could work, creating nurseries and nursing rooms at factories, promoting maternal breast-feeding, assisting unmarried or indigent mothers, and mandating (unpaid) maternity leaves prior to and following childbirth. As the nature of these measures suggests, French pronatalists' approach to promoting infant welfare reflected preexisting anxieties about working women. Many social reformers linked the "problem" of women's work to the changes wrought by industrialization and urbanization, both of which were seen as highly destructive and detrimental to family life.[12] First of all, as women moved from the countryside to the cities, they no longer worked as part of a family unit, close to their husbands and with their children close at hand. Reformers worried that, lacking adequate supervision, women working away from their families would be corrupted by immoral women, seduced by men, or lured into prostitution. Even if women avoided such moral calamities, critics claimed, by working away from home women inevitably neglected domestic responsibilities and their families suffered as a result. With two wage earners, instead of a mother and a father, "there was no longer a family to return to at the end of the day, only a dirty lodging where children were abandoned and deprived of a mother's love."[13] To social reformers, it was the very young children who perhaps suffered the most from a lack of maternal supervision. For one thing, urban working women generally sent their babies away to nurse in the countryside, frequently not seeing them again for up to two years. The very idea of a woman sending her baby away, to be nursed by a stranger whom she might never meet in person, was abhorrent to social reformers, who often saw in these arrangements a lack of maternal feeling as opposed to simply a difficult set of circumstances that made maternal breast-feeding impossible. As we have seen, a more serious problem with this practice was that the rate of infant mortality among babies sent away to nurse was higher than that of the general population.[14] Second, social reformers saw the high rates of child abandonment in French cities as clear evidence of the problems that resulted from women's paid employment. Child abandonment was partly connected to the higher rates of illegitimacy in the cities and also to the poverty and desperation of many urban working-class women who could not rely on the kind of supportive family network presumed to exist in rural communities. For a combination of reasons, babies abandoned to the Assistance publique and religious charities faced an elevated mortality rate.[15] In light of all these factors, pronatalist reformers sought to introduce restrictions on women's work outside of the family unit.

Some of the aforementioned proposals on women's work faced the same kind of opposition seen with public health reforms. For instance, despite potentially making it easier for women to work and care for their children, policies requiring employers to establish day-care cen-

CREATING A "LABOR RESERVOIR"

ters and nursing rooms would ultimately infringe on the rights of business owners; measures extending financial assistance to indigent mothers, though potentially improving the child's odds of survival, would nevertheless require use of public funds. While pronatalists may have been reticent about telling employers how to run their corporations, they had fewer reservations about infringing on the rights of individual women with some of these other proposals. As scholars have pointed out, laws dictating how many hours per week a woman could work, forbidding nighttime employment for women, and mandating that pregnant women stop working in the final weeks of their pregnancies interfered with a woman's freedom to work and compromised her ability to support herself and her family. One reason why social reformers were mostly untroubled by the prospect of diminishing a woman's rights and freedoms was that they were generally bourgeois men and therefore unlikely to identify with the predominantly working-class women who were the subject of most of these proposals. Still, their ability to justify such legislation went well beyond differences of gender and class and is best explained by how pronatalist reformers understood motherhood as a social function. As Joshua Cole explains, with the new science of demography in the nineteenth century, experts interpreted rates of infant and child mortality as more than simply statistics indicating numbers of deaths for a particular age group. Louis-Adolphe Bertillon, for one, believed that when babies and children died, it was often not from factors intrinsic to the individual; most such deaths resulted from external, environmental factors and were therefore indicative of social health in general.[16] This meant that if large numbers of babies were dying from causes such as preventable illnesses, neglect, and malnutrition, their deaths exposed problems with society as a whole. Because mothers were primarily the ones responsible for the welfare of their young children, these mortality rates gave experts a means by which to assess motherhood in general.[17] Considering that the survival and health of babies was a matter of national importance, women's success or failure as mothers was therefore of public interest, and pronatalist reformers felt that state intervention into those areas of women's lives that had any kind of connection to their role as mothers was justified. It followed that because women were the ones who produced babies and were responsible for the welfare of children, they could not be considered autonomous individuals. To consider one example of this logic, doctors believed that when a woman worked during the final weeks of pregnancy she greatly increased the risk of childbirth complications and low birth weight. Consequently, in the name of public welfare, legislators and reformers felt justified in intervening in her working life (by mandating that she stop working) to ensure a successful outcome for her pregnancy.

Many of these pronatalist measures were purportedly passed with the interests of both mothers and babies in mind and were frequently described as "the protection of motherhood" or "the protection of the child." Yet scholars have emphasized that such measures were intrusive and potentially coercive, as they opened a woman's private life up to outside scrutiny and often unwanted intervention. For example, in 1903 the pronatalist Paul Strauss proposed offering a small amount of financial assistance to any indigent new mother who was willing to keep and breast-feed her child. One can assume that in many cases it would have been in the baby's best interest to be breast-fed and cared for by his or her mother, as opposed to being abandoned to the Assistance publique.[18] Still, it is important to recognize that because accepting this funding obligated a woman to hear expert advice on how to care for her child and agree to follow the recommendations about breast-feeding, it is clear that reformers used this valuable financial assistance as a means to intervene into a woman's life and promote their ideas about how to be a good mother. Another example is a law passed in 1917 mandating that establishments employing one hundred or more women have a nursing room and give breast-feeding mothers breaks for this purpose. Many firms also voluntarily opened nurseries as part of this reform, though this was not initially a requirement.[19] On the surface, these changes appear advantageous, as they would seem to make it easier for women to both work and have babies. However, at the Citroën plant, for instance, the company nursery was underutilized by its employees. The women disliked the rigid rules and strict hygiene, preferring instead the flexibility that came with making their

CREATING A "LABOR RESERVOIR"

own arrangements. As this example illustrates, this reform and others like it were designed by male experts who did not have the mother's convenience in mind; such facilities were created following expert advice about what was best for children, without any input from the mothers.[20]

Many of the earliest pronatalist measures in France targeted women's employment, something that necessarily meant that they focused more on working-class women than their bourgeois counterparts. Still, this is not meant to imply that bourgeois mothers escaped pronatalist scrutiny. Although it may have been more difficult for pronatalist reformers to intervene as directly in bourgeois women's lives during these early years, women of all backgrounds were subjected to a propaganda campaign that not only emphasized the social importance of having numerous children but also advocated that they breast-feed their babies and instructed them on the science of child care, known as *puériculture*. In addition to propaganda, women in the late nineteenth and early twentieth centuries were confronted with often contradictory expert advice from hygienists and doctors seeking to prepare and orient women toward the task of producing more babies by educating them on personal hygiene, marital sexuality, and pregnancy.[21] Moreover, like their working-class counterparts, bourgeois women were affected by growing calls to prevent women's access to, and increase penalties for, information about family planning, contraceptive devices, and abortion, lobbying that would culminate in the 1920 law. Finally, proposed laws on women's work in the twenty years leading up to World War I were part of a larger evolving process affecting women of all social classes that defined a woman's place in society in terms of her role as a mother. This in turn justified outside scrutiny of that role in the name of public welfare.

As the next section will show, pronatalist decrees in Madagascar were not by any means identical to those introduced in France. One important distinction is that Madagascar was not an industrialized society, and the nature of women's work did not become a primary focus of Gallieni's pronatalist policies. Still, as in France, colonial officials placed a strong emphasis on motherhood and interpreted high rates of infant mortality and an inadequate birthrate as means by which to assess Malagasy women's failures and success as mothers. Consequently, as in France, propaganda, familial reforms, and intervention into child care and pregnancy were central components of Gallieni's plans for improving population growth. One striking feature of these measures in Madagascar is that they were based on colonial officials' ideas about what women needed in order to have healthy pregnancies and provide for their children, as well as what kinds of incentives would persuade individuals of both sexes to marry and reproduce. Like pronatalist reformers in France who generally did not consult women when developing reforms for mothers, Gallieni introduced measures that in many cases did not correspond with what colonial subjects needed or were willing to accept.

Colonial Inspirations and Population Growth in Madagascar

Despite French claims dating back to the seventeenth century, Madagascar remained independent of French rule for much of the nineteenth century. Of the island's eighteen "official" ethnic groups, the dominant population in the nineteenth century was the Merina, who inhabited the central region of the island, known as Imerina, and to whom the French referred erroneously as the Hova.[22] While they maintained Madagascar's political independence, Merina monarchs in the eighteenth and nineteenth centuries gradually opened the island up to Western influences, including missionaries from France, Great Britain, Norway, and the United States.[23] The London Missionary Society enjoyed the closest relationship with the Merina government, as both Queen Ranavalona II and Prime Minister Rainilaiarivony converted to Congregationalism in 1869 and made it the state religion.[24]

The growing foreign presence in Madagascar was nevertheless a source of tension that culminated in the Merina government's adoption of a law in 1881 outlawing foreign property ownership. The French, already in control of the neighboring island of Réunion and seeking to extend their empire into Madagascar, responded by demanding that French citizens be compensated for lost property and that Madagascar become a French protectorate. The ensuing Franco-Malagasy War ended in 1885 with a treaty recognizing Queen Ranavalona III

CREATING A "LABOR RESERVOIR"

as the ruler of Madagascar (even though her empire had previously been confined to only the central parts of the island) and establishing Madagascar as a French protectorate. These two provisions of the treaty produced an uneasy truce culminating in a second French invasion of the island in 1895. The Merina queen and her government surrendered in October of that year, effectively signaling the collapse of the Merina empire and the establishment of direct French rule in the colony. Despite this French military victory, conquest of the colony remained incomplete. The Menelamba revolt began in November 1895 with the murders of a family of missionaries and was directed at the French invaders as well as the Merina government, Malagasy Christians, and missionaries, all of whom the rebels held responsible for the decline of traditional customs and of the Merina empire.[25] Although this revolt prompted the French to annex the entire island as a colony in 1896, France continued to lack effective control over much of Madagascar. The French military was not able to subdue the Menelamba revolt until 1898, and it continued to face other revolts in the southern regions of the island until 1904.

Because of the precarious nature of French rule in Madagascar, colonial officials in 1896 sought a strong military leader who could subdue the rebellions and bring the entire island under French control; they chose General Gallieni. Born in 1849, Gallieni is perhaps best remembered for saving Paris from the German advance while serving as military governor of Paris during World War I and then becoming minister of war in 1915. However, prior to his service in the Great War, Gallieni built his military career in the empire and was, according to his admirers, one of France's great colonial leaders.[26] Gallieni first gained recognition following his arrival in French West Africa in 1879 where he successfully extended French influence in the region by advancing into the Sudan. His success in this mission earned him a military promotion, and when he returned to Africa in 1886, after recuperating in Martinique, it was as governor of French Sudan.

Yet it was Gallieni's experiences in Tonkin, where he served from 1892 to 1896, that shaped his method of rule in Madagascar. Although Tonkin had been incorporated into French Indochina by this period, the French military had not managed to subdue the widespread revolts and gain complete control over the region. In response, Gallieni developed the *tâche d'huile* method of "pacification" for which he would become well known. *Tâche d'huile* (generally translated as "oil spot") involved bringing populations under French control through the use of military force followed by the extension of social services, such as schools and medicine. With this approach, Gallieni hoped to increase the standard of living just enough to convince the populations of the benefits of French rule and prevent further uprisings. When he arrived in Madagascar in 1896 as the newly appointed governor-general, Gallieni again used the *tâche d'huile* method to pursue his objectives of subduing the rebellions and extending French influence in the island.

Gallieni's decision to introduce schools and medical facilities extended beyond a simple desire to pacify the indigenous population, however. The governor also wanted to make the colony profitable for arriving French settlers, and he believed that the exploitation of the colony's natural resources could not proceed without a large indigenous workforce. While early explorers had estimated Madagascar's population to be somewhere between five and ten million, and initially described the island as a "labor reservoir" that would serve neighboring French possessions, experts at the end of the nineteenth century placed that number at a mere three million.[27] Gallieni believed that the existing population was too small to serve French interests, but he rejected any idea of relying on imported labor from other colonies, as his predecessors had done. Instead, he drew on nineteenth-century theories of acclimatization to argue that local colonial subjects would be the best labor force for the colony.[28] "Nothing equals in value, for the goal that we propose to ourselves, the populations of the country itself, those that have learned to adapt themselves to local conditions, especially the climate of each of the regions of the colony," Gallieni wrote.[29] He believed that the success of settler colonialism depended on having a large population of colonial subjects already adapted to the island's climate and ready to provide arriving settlers with a workforce. Consequently, he decided that the colonial government would need to take steps to increase the local colonized population.

In Gallieni's time, the most recent research suggested that Madagascar had once had a very large population that had recently dropped precipitously and would likely continue to decline. Influenced by these studies, Gallieni concluded not only that the island's population was too small but also that the Malagasy were facing a depopulation crisis that threatened French interests on the island. Local depopulation, he concluded, had resulted from such factors as political upheaval, decadence, cultural practices, and diseases such as smallpox, leprosy, tuberculosis, syphilis, and malaria. By declaring a preexisting depopulation problem in Madagascar and attributing it to the Merina government and cultural practices, Gallieni in effect used demographic arguments to justify French intervention and colonial rule. On June 15, 1898, he introduced a series of pronatalist measures aimed at increasing the population of the Merina people in the colony through the extension of European medicine, propaganda, and familial reforms.

The population policies introduced in Madagascar represented a selective form of pronatalism in that they were initially directed at the Merina population and only later extended to the rest of the island's population. This decision was inspired by notions of racial hierarchy based in the ethnographic studies of European explorers. In the precolonial period, explorers such as Alfred Grandidier established a racial typology for the island that positioned the Merina as the most civilized ethnic group due to their "respect for authority, the spirit of obedience, the habit of work, and, above all else the social organization characteristic of the races that grow out of the yellow trunk."[30] This classification led European writers to view the Merina with a certain ambivalence, considering them more civilized than other Malagasy but also tyrannical and treacherous.[31] Influenced both by Grandidier's work and his own experiences in Tonkin, Gallieni concluded that, of all the ethnic groups in Madagascar, the Merina would be the best suited to his goal of creating a prolific workforce. Gallieni described them as the "superior" race in Madagascar and, because of their purported work ethic and appreciation of monetary gain, the most likely to assimilate to European work practices. He therefore assigned the Merina high reproductive and economic values and presented them as a natural resource. Gallieni's discussions of the need to increase this population frequently included phrases such as "the development of the race" and "the development of large families."[32] The Merina would be "called upon to spread out over more and more of the entire island, to absorb the other peoples and to give our settlers intelligent and disciplined auxiliaries."[33] In this regard he likened the Merina to the Annamese population in Indochina.[34]

Like pronatalist reformers in France, Gallieni believed that population growth could be directed from above by introducing measures designed to address the medical, economic, and social factors deemed responsible for disappointing demographic trends. Though cognizant of contemporaneous efforts to increase the French population, he understood the limited success with which metropolitan pronatalists had met in extending medical assistance and encouraging a stronger birthrate. Specifically, he dismissed French efforts as being primarily focused on protecting newborns, citing the Roussel Law as one such example.[35] He sought therefore to depart significantly from the metropolitan model and tailor his population policies to the colonial context. A major component of Gallieni's pronatalism was establishing a public health care system whose goals included introducing medicalized childbirth and slowing the spread of infectious diseases.

The Colonial Public Health System in Madagascar

Although in his memoirs, *Neuf ans à Madagascar*, Gallieni frequently implied that he built Madagascar's public health system from the ground up, it is important to recognize that he was not the first person to express concerns about the health of the island's population. During the twenty years that preceded French rule, British and Norwegian missionaries established a small number of hospitals and a medical school, the Medical Mission Academy, which by 1896 had awarded diplomas to thirty-three students.[36] Also in the precolonial period, the government of Queen Ranavalona II issued decrees intended to isolate lepers, punish alcoholism, criminalize abortion, outlaw the sale of spoiled meat, and give local officials the authority to oversee public hygiene and the sale of medicine. Gallieni nevertheless dismissed

CREATING A "LABOR RESERVOIR"

the Merina government's efforts for coming only at the instigation of European missionaries and for being ineffective due to the weakness and disorder of the government.[37] As for the medical facilities established by European missionaries, Gallieni distrusted their efforts, believing that their larger purpose was to convert patients to Christianity; he also emphasized their limited reach, asserting that these facilities were few in number and restricted to the capital, Tananarive.[38]

Consequently, Gallieni's first course of action in developing a public health system and wresting control from the foreign missionaries was to acquire medical facilities from the missionaries and to create, in 1896, a French medical school in the capital. This was followed by a decree of February 16, 1897, requiring that military doctors give medications and consultations freely to all colonial subjects who requested them. Simultaneously, military doctors were charged with making hygiene inspections, giving vaccinations, and quarantining lepers. It was with the 1898 decree that Gallieni built on these health services by establishing an extensive public health system presided over by two administrative branches, the Assistance médicale indigène (AMI) and the Service de santé (SDS). This decree was bolstered by a series of subsequent decrees creating and organizing hospitals, leprosariums, maternity clinics, venereal disease treatment centers, and orphanages.[39]

As Nancy Rose Hunt has shown, colonial medicine was as much a site of negotiation as it was one of imposition.[40] One of the biggest challenges Gallieni faced was convincing colonial subjects to seek care from licensed health workers, get their children vaccinated, and give birth in European facilities. In his memoirs and reports Gallieni repeatedly stressed the importance of *frapper l'imagination* (striking the imagination) of the population, thereby convincing them that French medicine was superior to their own practices.[41] Despite establishing health facilities and, as early as 1896, requiring that military doctors treat anyone who came to see them, French authorities noticed that colonial subjects continued to seek medical care from people within their own communities.[42] Gallieni lamented the influence of witch doctors, as he called them, to whom people in the countryside "delivered themselves blindly" any time they were sick.[43] He presented the so-called witch doctors as unscrupulous individuals who took advantage of the trust and ignorance of the population with little concern for the consequences of their actions.[44]

Gallieni's greatest concern, though, was the preference of Malagasy women to have their babies delivered by unlicensed midwives within their own communities, not French doctors. Gallieni believed that these midwives were responsible for the deaths of untold numbers of expectant mothers and babies due to their ignorance and disregard for hygiene.[45] Officials hoped that by getting women to seek prenatal care from licensed health workers and give birth in hospitals and clinics, they could reduce the maternal and newborn mortality rates. Although officials' goal of making childbirth safer was admirable, the means they adopted illustrate how women's health care became a site of conflict in the early colonial state. On one side stood the state, embodied in the licensed practitioners to whose authority pronatalist-minded colonial officials hoped women would submit. On the other side were expectant mothers who were resistant to outside intervention and had their own preferences about where and with whose assistance they would give birth.

To bring the practice of medicine under state control and displace local practitioners, Gallieni decreed that only those licensed by the colonial state could practice medicine. He argued that the birthrate was certain to go up once babies were delivered by midwives "worthy of the name."[46] In the interest of making European medicine more appealing to the population, he paired this law with a series of decrees establishing corps of Malagasy doctors and midwives who would serve as intermediaries between the European medical establishment and the population.[47] These health care professionals, Gallieni maintained, would do what French doctors could not: communicate with the Malagasy people, convince them that French medical expertise was superior to their own practices, and persuade them to get their children vaccinated, give birth in European hospitals or maternity clinics, and seek care from licensed doctors and midwives.

The French medical school was funded by the city budget, and tuition was free for the young men training to be *médecins indigènes* (native

　　　　　　　　　　　CREATING A "LABOR RESERVOIR"

doctors) and the women training to be *sages-femmes indigènes* (native midwives).[48] While their title suggested that they were doctors, the *médecins indigènes* were really trained to be medical assistants.[49] In his report to the minister of colonies, Gallieni emphasized that their training would be relatively simple, as they would not need a wide range of knowledge to do their jobs. They were nothing more than "good health officers, who are intelligent and whose aptitudes have been perfected by specialized studies."[50] Consequently, the curriculum was not identical to that followed by medical students in France and focused more on training *médecins indigènes* to assist French doctors. In addition to taking courses on anatomy and hygiene, the students studied dissection, surgery, the dressing of wounds, pharmacology, veterinary science (in particular meat inspection), and "judicial and administrative medicine."[51] The training of *médecins indigènes* was less directed toward pregnancy and childbirth as they took only one course on obstetrics (in the fourth year). The midwives, not surprisingly, were trained primarily to work with pregnant women; they took courses on vaccination, hygiene during pregnancy and the postpartum period, and hygiene for newborns. Their curriculum focused heavily on the practice of normal childbirths, and it was only in the third and final year of study that they took an introductory course on dystocia (difficult labor or delivery). Although they learned about dystocia, they were not trained to perform complicated childbirths and were expected to defer to a doctor in these cases.[52] In 1913 the medical school had awarded degrees to 273 colonial doctors and 159 midwives and had 79 students currently enrolled.[53]

Although colonial officials considered the Merina the "superior" race in Madagascar and also, because of their "racial characteristics," the best suited to work as *médecins indigènes* and assist in Gallieni's efforts to the improve the health of the population, French officials sometimes saw these racial characteristics as an obstacle. One concern that arose repeatedly was whether the *médecins indigènes* could ever abandon the "prejudices of the race" and adopt the "European mentality." One example of this relates to the dissection classes that medical students took two of the five years that they were in school. As one *médecin indigène* explained, because the Merina believed in the existence of good and evil spirits, they felt it was essential to handle human corpses in a respectful manner in the case of a relative and, in the case of a stranger, to avoid handling the corpse at all. By extension, dissecting a corpse postmortem, as they were expected to do as part of their coursework, was considered a profanity.[54] However, French doctors were unable to understand the initial "superstitious" reluctance of Merina students to participate in autopsies and dissections.[55]

Other concerns raised by French doctors and colonial officials about the "prejudices of the race" reveal the tensions that resulted from their desire to educate Merina men so that they could serve the colonial state but simultaneously to ensure that these men did not forget their place within the colonial hierarchy. Although French doctors spoke with pride about the aptitude and progress of their medical students, there were concerns that once they had their degrees the Merina health workers would resist being relegated to a subordinate position in the public health system. For instance, some of the courses at the medical school were taught by Merina men, all of whom had completed their education in France and returned to Madagascar as full doctors, as opposed to *médecins indigènes*. In 1913, for example, three of the ten professors at the medical school were Merina.[56] The French head of the medical school, Dr. Fontoynont, however, described these professors as lacking the altruistic desire to share their knowledge with their students, being instead determined to monopolize their erudition. This problem, Fontoynont argued, was compounded by their tendency to try to showcase their expertise when, in fact, they were not as knowledgeable as they pretended to be. He described these two qualities as a prejudice of the race that only a select few were likely to overcome after many years of assimilating.[57] A letter written by Louis Hubert Lyautey to Gallieni in 1902, when Lyautey was engaged in suppressing rebellions in southern Madagascar, reflects a similar perception that once Merina men were trained to be *médecins indigènes* they would be too proud to accept their subordinate position.[58] Presenting the problem in racial terms, Lyautey described the Merina practitioners as ambitious and career-driven, instead of being content simply to serve the colonial regime as auxiliaries of European doctors.

These doctors have thus far been recruited and will continue to be recruited from the Hova [Merina] population. They have the qualities of that race, intelligence and the ability to assimilate as well as disadvantages, their pretentiousness and avarice. Spread out in the provinces, they resign themselves badly to the modest role of the European doctor's auxiliary. They seek to become true doctors, which they are not, and sometimes seek to shed their subaltern role to take on paying clients as much as possible.[59]

Lyautey went on to criticize Merina men for attempting operations and serious procedures better left to European doctors. Clearly uncomfortable with the idea of colonial subjects taking the initiative in this respect, he argued that more should be done to remind them of their humble position within the colonial hierarchy. This, he maintained, could be achieved by changing their uniforms (since he believed that *médecins indigènes* were excessively proud of the gold embroideries) and changing their title from *médecins indigènes de colonisation* to one more consistent with their "true role."[60]

Despite concerns raised by other colonial officials, Gallieni defended his decision to train Merina men to be health workers. In his official reports, he described the *médecins indigènes* as devoted civil servants who were respected by the population and by the administration and who represented the "kingpin" of the public health system. He even claimed officially that not one of these men had ever been subjected to disciplinary action, a claim that was actually inconsistent with regional reports.[61] As evidence of the program's success, Gallieni also affirmed that "the Europeans themselves do not hesitate to go to the *médecins indigènes* for advice and care."[62] However, this statement was likely an exaggeration, as evidence suggests that the European population had reservations about Merina health workers. For instance, any mistakes made by *médecins indigènes* tended to generate more criticism than those made by French doctors. In a 1904 annual report, Dr. Jourdan, head of the medical school in Tananarive, cited an incident involving a Merina doctor who injected a young girl with mercury instead of quinine; the resulting scandal made the local newspapers.[63] Jourdan complained, moreover, that the extra criticism to which Merina practitioners were subjected meant that they lacked any real authority, something that undermined their ability to do their jobs effectively. The fear of facing severe criticism, no matter how minor the mistake, discouraged them from intervening when necessary, and this in turn opened them up to accusations of being incompetent or unwilling to assist.[64]

Even more critical to extending the reach of European medicine in the colony was the establishment of corps of Merina midwives. Becoming state employees as a result of the July 1, 1903, decree, the *sages-femmes indigènes* earned an annual salary of 400–600 francs, considerably less than the 1,500–2,500 francs earned by *médecins indigènes*.[65] Although their salaries did not reflect it, Gallieni considered midwives essential to the colonial state's efforts to access some of the most intimate areas of Malagasy women's lives: pregnancy, childbirth, and infant welfare. Statistics provided by local health officials indicate that even when medical services became available, nearly half of all women giving birth with the assistance of a licensed health worker chose to do so at home. For instance, in the province of Fianarantsoa in 1904 the AMI recorded that there were 203 babies born in their facilities versus 192 babies delivered by licensed midwives outside a medical facility.[66] Training Merina women to be midwives thus represented an effective means by which colonial authorities could adapt women's preferences concerning childbirth to their goals of introducing Western medicine and encouraging population growth.

The significant influence wielded by the Merina midwives in their communities was nevertheless a source of frustration for Gallieni and other officials, who criticized these women for failing to support the colonial regime's demographic goals enthusiastically.[67] Similar to Lyautey's criticisms of Merina doctors, Gallieni's concerns about Merina midwives revealed a fundamental tension in his pronatalist policies. Bringing pregnancy and population growth under the colonial state's control required convincing the population of the benefits of European medicine, something that could not be done without the assistance of Merina health workers. The *sages-femmes indigènes* were particularly vital to such efforts because, as one regional medi-

CREATING A "LABOR RESERVOIR"

cal report stated, they were generally the ones who met with pregnant women and advised them about hygiene and child care. This report also stated that these midwives received many repeat visits from the same women, thereby demonstrating women's preference to seek medical advice from other Malagasy women rather than from French doctors.[68] Despite their status as low-ranking government employees, therefore, *sages-femmes indigènes* had more influence and authority among the women in the colony than did anyone else employed by the colonial state, a fact the colonial state was obliged to acknowledge. This reliance on colonial subjects, particularly female colonial subjects who were "doubly colonized," stood in stark contrast to the racial and gender hierarchy that officials considered essential to maintaining colonial rule.[69] While recognizing the need to train colonial subjects to work as health professionals, officials such as Gallieni and Lyautey felt that it was critical that these Merina men and women work exclusively for the colonial state, support the goals of the regime enthusiastically, and remain entirely under the control and guidance of French doctors. Still, it was clear that French officials had great difficulty convincing *médecins indigènes* and *sages-femmes indigènes* to devote themselves selflessly to the regime's objectives and abandon any self-interest that might otherwise influence their work.

Creating Families

Despite the importance he placed on establishing a public health system, Gallieni believed that this would not increase the population adequately unless he bolstered it with a series of measures intended to bring sexuality and family life under state control and transform colonial subjects into "good" mothers and fathers. While the stated objective of these measures was purely economic (the creation of a large workforce), their very nature illustrates how closely racial and gendered assumptions were intertwined with economic objectives. Among several factors, Gallieni attributed depopulation to the "loose morals" he thought to be a general feature of Malagasy society. Many of his statements about Malagasy cultural practices reflected Europeans' beliefs concerning the effects of warm climates on sexuality, particularly the prevalent nineteenth-century notion that African women had "primitive" sexual appetites.[70] For example, Gallieni described two customs that he considered detrimental to the health and morality of the population. One of these customs was the *Famadihana*, or "the turning of the dead," a custom of rewrapping the deceased person in new shrouds and celebrating with music, dancing, and feasts.[71] The other practice he condemned was what he described as "alcoholic and sexual orgies practiced, during the three or four consecutive days following the death of a relative or a friend, in the home of the deceased whose corpse remains exposed during that entire period of time."[72] This description not only reflects the late-nineteenth-century preoccupation with hygiene but also suggests that Gallieni saw Malagasy society as decadent, chaotic, and lacking in monogamous relationships. The general consequently emphasized the need to bring the "growth of the native population, its physical and moral development, [and] the constitution of the family" under French guidance in order to rescue the population from the moral depravity he considered to be an endemic feature of their society.[73]

The perception that there was an absence of stable family structures most likely originated in part in the observations of European travelers in the nineteenth century who reported that it was common for Malagasy women to have children before marriage and that some women had more than one husband.[74] The sense that the Malagasy family needed to be "organized" and "developed" by the colonial state was further reflected in a questionnaire that Gallieni sent to local commanders several months prior to issuing his 1898 decree. This questionnaire contained more than fifty questions relating to all aspects of Malagasy family life, including marriage, divorce, repudiation, adoption, inheritance, and child abandonment, and asked that commanders report on the local laws and customs within their jurisdiction pertaining to these questions. Some of the questions reflected an interest in determining the exact role of the father within the family as they inquired about paternal authority over minor children, the circumstances under which a man could repudiate his wife, and paternal recognition of illegitimate children.[75]

CREATING A "LABOR RESERVOIR"

In the interest of "ensuring the stability" of the Merina family, the 1898 decree mandated that couples register their marriages with the colonial government.[76] Not only did Gallieni expect this to reduce the numbers of children born outside of marriage, but he also believed it would enable the government to track individuals'—particularly men's—contributions to the larger repopulation efforts. It also addressed colonial officials' perception that relationships between male and female colonial subjects were poorly defined and lacking in commitment. Further solidifying this new model of marriage, the decree imposed harsh punishments for repudiation, which Gallieni considered a threat to the strength and integrity of marriage. This component of the decree actually built on an earlier law, introduced in 1881 during the precolonial period, illustrating that Gallieni was aware of older Malagasy laws and was willing to adapt them to his present objectives.[77]

Also included in the 1898 legislation were a number of measures intended to encourage couples to have more children. Ideas of race and gender permeated Gallieni's understanding of the reasons why Malagasy men and women did not have large enough families. For example, one decree criminalized abortion, a practice that, according to the colonial government, was common in Madagascar due to the absence of modern medical techniques and facilities. Officials emphasized that numbers of women dying in childbirth were so high that pregnancy was widely feared and many women terminated pregnancies in the interest of their own survival.[78] In France, by contrast, pronatalists provided a different set of explanations for why French women had abortions. They believed, mistakenly, that French women generally had abortions out of vanity or the "modern" desire to have a small family, thus minimizing expenses and responsibilities. Thinking that Malagasy women, on the other hand, were untainted by modern sensibilities and instead terminated their pregnancies primarily because they did not have access to Western medicine, officials believed that criminalizing abortion in Madagascar would go hand in hand with improving health care and dramatically reducing the number of women dying in childbirth. One medical officer wrote in 1904 that as growing numbers of women gave birth in maternity wards with the assistance of Western doctors, they would convince others that it was not necessary to have an abortion in order to survive pregnancy.[79]

Whereas Gallieni attributed women's reluctance to having children to fears of childbirth, he directed most of his administrative and fiscal measures at men and in this way made clear that being a provider was a man's main role within the family. Specifically naming fathers in this section of his decree, Gallieni introduced a series of incentives designed to encourage men to not only have children but to become good fathers, something that reflected an assumption that the role of the father in the Malagasy family was somewhat ambiguous. These incentives included exempting all fathers from military service and exempting fathers of five or more children from *prestation* (compulsory labor).[80] Furthermore, men with at least seven children were guaranteed that one of their children would be given a job in the colonial administration and would have his or her education expenses covered by the state. The decree also created a system of land concessions for large families; after three years of growing crops on the concession, the family could become owners.[81]

Finally, in addition to rewarding those colonial subjects who contributed to population growth, Gallieni sought to punish men and women who did not marry and raise children. He implemented an annual tax amounting to 15 francs for men over the age of twenty-five and 7.5 francs for women over the age of twenty-one.[82] In order to understand the magnitude of this tax, it is useful to compare it against some other taxes to which the Malagasy were subject. As these fines greatly exceeded the annual tax of 2.5 francs paid by Malagasy men to fund public services, it is likely that people would have considered it a great burden.[83] Gallieni hoped that given the prospect of such a fine, people would come to view marriage, on the other hand, as a financial necessity. Based on the age at which the penalties were assessed, it is clear that women were expected to marry and start families at an early age. Still, for women who failed to do this, the fine was lighter than it was for men who did not meet the requirements. It is possible that this was because the state was more inclined to blame men for choosing not to marry but to pity women who did not manage to

CREATING A "LABOR RESERVOIR"

find husbands, perhaps viewing them more as victims. The difference might also be explained by perceptions of the individual's capacity to pay the fine; a single woman presumably would have less income at her disposal than a single man. Regardless, it seems that individuals of both sexes struggled with the fine because ultimately the colonial state repealed this measure after concluding that it was beyond most people's means and its impact on the birthrate was minimal.[84]

The Fête des Enfants

Like metropolitan pronatalists, Gallieni realized that medicine and familial reforms would have only a limited effect on individuals who simply did not want a large family. Seeking to persuade the population to embrace his objectives, therefore, Gallieni embarked on a propaganda campaign by instituting an annual children's festival.[85] The Fête des enfants was an official pronatalism holiday unlike anything that existed in France during this period. This was because it was not French in origin; its roots were in the empire. While serving in Indochina, Gallieni had been amazed by a custom he witnessed in which children were honored with a holiday.[86] As he designed the 1898 decree, Gallieni recalled seeing the streets of Indochinese villages filled with children wearing new clothes, carrying toys that had been offered to them by parents and friends, and taking part in activities organized on their behalf. What he was most likely describing was the Vietnamese holiday Tết Trung Thu, which was appropriated by colonial authorities in Indochina as Gallieni would do in Madagascar.[87] Convinced that the secret of Indochina's large population was related to this appreciation for children and family life, Gallieni decided to bring the custom to Madagascar in 1898. The Fête des enfants in Madagascar demonstrates his determination to draw from the example of colonized populations in the empire who had the kind of demographic strength that he believed the Merina and French populations lacked. Years after Gallieni left Madagascar, the festival was still an annual event promoting family life as a civic virtue.[88]

The main purpose of the festival was to convey a strong political message to the Merina population by demonstrating "in what esteem we hold the heads of large families, the mothers who have had a large number of children and the interest that we take in those children themselves."[89] The statement is reminiscent of pronatalist and familialist propaganda in France that presented the father of many children as a distinguished citizen, respected and esteemed for being the head of the large household he represented in the public sphere, his role in actually producing the children being the less significant point. For women, on the other hand, the emphasis was on the private act of reproduction, with a woman's role bearing children being the critical contribution. To show the colonial government's pride in the colony's children and promote family life as a civic virtue, the festival included sports, games, children's contests, and awards for "good" mothers. At the 1903 festival, for example, 580 women received monetary awards for having large numbers of living children, and 100 schoolchildren received monetary awards for their ability to speak and write in French.[90] Gallieni intended for the propaganda to be educational; officials provided information on child care, and parents listened to speeches presenting the latest statistics detailing the rapid growth of the population. Parades of clean, healthy children wearing new clothing furthered this message by presenting an image of bourgeois respectability and the triumph of European hygiene and medicine.

Although the Fête des enfants was supposed to showcase the success of the French civilizing mission, photos of the event reveal that this message was incompletely embraced. One photo, for example, presents eight girls standing at the front of a crowd (fig. 2). At first glance their attire seems to be in line with the goals of the festival, as all eight of them are wearing smart white dresses, half of them are wearing large hats, and a tall girl in the middle is even carrying a parasol. Yet upon closer examination it becomes apparent that only two of the eight girls are wearing shoes. Not only did Europeans generally consider wearing shoes a marker of civilization, but in Madagascar medical officials considered shoes essential to the health of the population. Going barefoot, they believed, exposed the individual to dangerous parasites, particularly chigger fleas, which generally entered the body through the feet. Medical officials deplored how many Mal-

Fête des enfants, 7 Avril 1904, sur la place de Mahamasina.

Fig. 2. Photograph showing the Fête des enfants in Madagascar, 1904. Reproduced courtesy of Centre des archives d'outre mer.

agasy would go barefoot, exposing themselves to this risk, in defiance
of medical advice.[91] That these girls were photographed barefoot at an
event intended to display the achievements of France's civilizing mission is striking for its apparent rejection of the goals of the festival.

Malagasy Responses to French Pronatalism

After receiving their degrees at the medical school in Madagascar,
a select group of Merina graduates went to Montpellier and Paris to
complete their studies and return to the colony as full doctors. While
in France they most likely would have heard that the French faced a
depopulation crisis of their own and would have been in a position
to make comparisons between demographic concerns in the metropole and the colony. Furthermore, from having observed and studied
the practice of medicine in both cultures, these doctors were able to
question many of the assumptions behind the colonial state's efforts
to address depopulation in Madagascar. Although it is not clear what,

if any, influence these students had on their professors and colleagues in France, analyzing their medical theses offers a number of insights into the functioning of medicine in Madagascar. In particular, their theses reveal a number of blind spots in French officials' thinking on Malagasy depopulation.

Many of the Malagasy students who traveled to France wrote theses about the practice of medicine in Madagascar, the idea being that their unique perspective on a topic that was relatively unknown in Europe would be of great interest to the French medical establishment. Generally, their theses indicated that they supported Gallieni's attempts to improve the health of the Malagasy population through the introduction of modern medicine and that they were studying to be doctors because they wanted to be part of this process. Some of their comments suggest they had either adopted the "European mentality" referenced earlier or felt that it was in their best interest to express the accepted views. The most striking example of this is in Dr. Rabary's thesis on the chigger flea. In his introduction, Rabary thanks Gallieni for taking on the task of "regenerating" his country, an effort that was already yielding positive results due to Gallieni's "patient, yet firm and vigilant administration."[92] This statement evokes the commonly held view of colonial administrators that the populations under their rule were childlike and consequently needed to be governed with a mixture of strict discipline and patience.

Yet even if the theses expressed support and gratitude for Gallieni's initiatives, many of them also conveyed a desire to inform the medical community in France that the Malagasy were not as backward as Europeans assumed them to be. A good example of this is the thesis written by Dr. Ravelonahina on the subject of depopulation in France and Madagascar. By writing on such a topic, Ravelonahina was in the unusual position of being able to enter the depopulation debate under way in both Madagascar and the metropole. With this thesis, Ravelonahina sought not only to examine in great detail the causes of depopulation but also to inform the medical community about what had been achieved in Madagascar and to vindicate his own people. To many colonial officials and metropolitan reformers, depopulation in

Madagascar could be attributed to "primitive" cultural practices. Yet, Ravelonahina argued that not all the customs of his country were "contemptible."[93] In fact, he emphasized that some of the causes of French infant mortality were rare in his country precisely because of those cultural differences. As an example of this he pointed to the thousands of infant deaths that French pronatalists attributed to the decision of many French women to not breast-feed their own babies. Ravelonahina stated that in Madagascar, by contrast, every woman breast-fed her own child. He noted further that the wet-nursing industry was virtually nonexistent in Madagascar and that infant diarrhea, associated primarily with bottle feeding, was considerably less common in Madagascar than in France.[94] Ravelonahina also emphasized that from a purely statistical perspective, infant mortality was an equally serious problem in both places.[95]

Ravelonahina also reported on Gallieni's work in establishing medical services in Madagascar and addressing depopulation in the colony. After exploring various solutions proposed in France, Ravelonahina argued that they had already been implemented in Madagascar. For example, French pronatalists proposed educating women about *puériculture*; this had already been achieved in Madagascar through the newspaper *Vaovao*, which instructed women through both written text and pictures on how to care for their infants.[96] Fully supporting Gallieni's work and taking pride in the accomplishments of his own country, Ravelonahina boasted that in a mere four years Gallieni had created "establishments or institutions that would make many French towns envious of my country and that European countries, so proud of many centuries of civilization, will never possess."[97]

The medical theses of Drs. Ramisiray and Ranaivo reflect a similar desire to vindicate the Malagasy people by explaining traditional medical practices in the colony. Dr. Ramisiray's thesis, for example, was premised on the idea that the main problem with Malagasy medicine was that practitioners did not understand the causes of illnesses and subsequently blamed most health problems on either evil spirits or witchcraft. Yet, by explaining how the Malagasy treated illnesses, he sought to show that the "Malagasy, despite their ignorance and superstitions, are not devoid of logic and that quite frequently their approach to treating certain illnesses is similar to that of civilized countries."[98] Along these lines, he wrote with pride about how the Malagasy experimented with smallpox vaccines and achieved good results with this technique prior to Edward Jenner's discoveries in Europe.[99] Dr. Ranaivo, in his thesis on Malagasy beliefs and practices concerning childbirth and pregnancy, likewise emphasized that in order for the medical establishment to better serve the population and have a positive impact, it was important to understand Malagasy medical beliefs rather than simply dismissing them. Similar to Ramisiray, Ranaivo emphasized that the population generally blamed health problems on sorcery and that by extension, unlicensed midwives, who were held in great esteem by the population, addressed childbirth complications in this way. Reflecting on the competition between French-trained doctors and unlicensed Malagasy midwives for influence with expectant mothers, Ranaivo criticized these women for their general ignorance of anatomy, their inability to diagnose in advance how the baby is presenting, their lack of skill in addressing complications during deliveries, and their disregard for notions of hygiene and antisepsis. Still, despite these problems, he believed that the population was receptive to change and predicted that civilization, as he understood it, would soon take hold in the colony.[100]

Ranaivo's thesis on Malagasy beliefs concerning childbirth and pregnancy reveals that he was not in agreement with Gallieni and French officials about the causes of depopulation in Madagascar. In contrast to Gallieni's conclusion that the Malagasy needed a festival to persuade them of the virtues of having a large family, Ranaivo argued that this was already a well-established value in the colony. Probably overstating his case, he emphasized that every Malagasy woman wanted to be a mother and wrote about the shame that came with sterility. As an example of this, he described the great lengths to which some women would go, consulting both midwives and "witch doctors," as they sought fertility treatment. Men also were enthusiastic about becoming fathers and sometimes preferred to marry a woman who had had a child out of wedlock, and thus proven her fertility, as opposed to a younger, childless woman whose ability to conceive was unknown.[101] In contrast to Gallieni's view that Malagasy women frequently had abortions because they feared pregnancy and childbirth, Ranaivo asserted that abortion used to be entirely unknown in the colony because women viewed any pregnancy as a blessing. Its prevalence in the colony was entirely attributable to the cultural changes that followed the arrival of European influences.[102]

Another way in which Malagasy doctors disagreed with Gallieni's views about the causes of depopulation in Madagascar relates to the spread of disease. Although Gallieni blamed Malagasy depopulation on indigenous factors that predated the French occupation, many of these doctors challenged this idea by arguing that some diseases arrived in the colony with the Europeans. One example of this is the chigger flea that Dr. Rabary argued was brought to Madagascar by the *tirailleurs sénégalais* (Senegalese colonial soldiers). Despite making it clear that this was a consequence of French conquest of the island, Rabary did agree with European doctors that its virulence in the colony could be attributed to the lack of hygiene and proper use of clothing and shoes among the Malagasy population. In a similar vein, Dr. Ramisiray argued that syphilis used to be unknown in the colony and that it was only in recent years that it had become a devastating epidemic in Madagascar.[103] While he did not overtly say that Europeans were responsible for this, the implication of his work is that syphilis was not an indigenous cause of depopulation that predated the arrival of Europeans.

Syphilis was a major preoccupation for health officials in Madagascar, whether Malagasy or French. However, the medical theses of the Malagasy students illustrate that French doctors' views of the disease were not neutral but were, on the contrary, shaped by the doctors' racialized and gendered views of their patients. As in France, efforts to understand the disease's epidemiology focused on women.[104] Official statistics indicated that syphilis was a widespread problem in Madagascar that had particularly serious consequences for pregnant women and their unborn children. Because of the impact of syphilis on the unborn child, officials saw infected women as a cause of depopulation and ignored the role of infected men in contributing to problems such as sterility and infant mortality. In terms of the disease's prevalence, one report from the district of Ambositra indicated that of the 488 women who gave birth in the district that year, 294 (60 percent) had syphilis. Of the live births, about half of the newborns were infected.[105] In making sense of these numbers, officials and doctors alike came to the simplistic conclusion that it was the result of prostitution and the general lack of morality. On the one hand, doctors echoed Gallieni's assumptions that the general acceptance of promiscuity and venereal disease made syphilis more treatable in Madagascar than in France because people were not ashamed to go to a clinic and seek treatment.[106] On the other hand, they believed that preventing its transmission was difficult due to what they saw as permissive attitudes concerning prostitution.[107] Dr. Ravelonhina, in his medical thesis, nevertheless raised some doubts about the official numbers concerning syphilis in both France and Madagascar. He argued that statistics indicating that the disease was more prevalent in Madagascar were simply a reflection of the differences in the ways in which public health authorities reported the causes of death of French citizens and colonial subjects. He explained that in France,

> out of decency, out of respect for the deceased and to not offend the family, the state doctor, even if he knows or suspects the presence, on the person he examines post mortem, of a . . . syphilitic lesion that led to the death, he attributes it to a banal cause that, in this way, diminishes the mortality rate of syphilis in Europe. Thus, while recognizing the extreme frequency of syphilis in Madagascar, it should be taken into account the two different methods of compiling statistics in our colony and in Europe concerning that illness, methods that depend on the social context in which they are recorded.[108]

In this way Ravelonahina suggested that French medical authorities were working with faulty statistics and that French pronatalists therefore underestimated some of the causes of depopulation in their own country. He also engaged the colonial medical discourse that, as Megan Vaughan argues, contributed to the construction of "'the African' as an object of knowledge."[109] In his thesis, Ravelonahina revealed this to be the case by demonstrating that, as Vaughan states, disease in the colonial context did not "exist in the abstract"; ideas of race and gender shaped how colonial officials understood syphilis among the Malagasy.[110] By suggesting that syphilis was just as common and deadly in France as in Madagascar, Ravelonahina contested the conclusion that the Merina suffered from depopulation in part because of a general lack of morality.

Diverging Results and Interpretations

In France, social reformers watched developments in Madagascar with interest, hoping to emulate many of Gallieni's measures. For instance, members of the Société française de prophylaxie sanitaire et morale, an organization aimed at defending society from the perils of venereal disease, were especially interested in Gallieni's efforts to not only treat syphilis but also to prevent its transmission by educating the Malagasy about the disease.[111] French pronatalists were likewise intrigued by these and other measures designed to transform Madagascar into a profitable settler colony. Although colonial administrators would eventually introduce related measures in other French colonies, most notably in French West Africa, these initiatives received less press in metropolitan pronatalist circles.[112] Increasingly interested in learning from colonial initiatives, pronatalists saw in Gallieni's population policies proof that a sufficiently determined government could stimulate population growth, and they argued that similar steps should be undertaken in France. Responses to Gallieni's decrees in editorials also indicate that for many pronatalists, Gallieni himself attained almost a mythical status, his decisive action standing in stark contrast to government inertia in France. As Edward Berenson tells us, in light of French defeat in the Franco-Prussian War, demographic anxieties, and concerns about French masculinity, the French public during this period yearned for heroic, virile men who symbolized national strength and the masculine ideal. Consequently, people looked to the empire for "men of action" who exhibited these qualities, avidly reading about the exploits of military officers like Hubert

Lyautey and explorers like Pierre Savorgnan de Brazza.[113] To pronatalists, Gallieni was a similar type of "man of action" who inspired them at a time when their own government seemed intractable and slow to address the depopulation crisis. Ultimately, the heroic idea of Gallieni was as important as the actual measures that he implemented and that pronatalist leaders studied in an attempt to gain insights into how to improve France's population growth.

Pronatalist discussions of Gallieni's endeavors first began in the extra-parliamentary depopulation commission established in 1902. A number of senators and prominent pronatalist scholars took part in this commission, including Jacques Bertillon and Charles Richet, two of the founders of the Alliance nationale.[114] One report, presented by Senator Edme Piot, reveals the influence of Gallieni's pronatalist efforts in Madagascar on the newly formed depopulation commission.[115] In his report, Piot discussed his correspondence with prominent individuals, including Gallieni, whose letters proved especially useful. In these letters, Gallieni expressed support for Piot's attempts to propose similar measures in France and promised to send additional documents of interest to the depopulation commission.[116] Impressed by Gallieni's work, Piot argued that the general had patriotically implemented a series of pronatalist measures in Madagascar; France had only to learn from the results that Gallieni achieved, imitate his efforts in France, and make them the standard practice.[117]

Senator Piot made Gallieni's work well known to the French pronatalist movement. However, it is difficult to determine the impact of this information on proposed laws in France. One thing is nevertheless clear: the law that Piot proposed in the Senate on November 6, 1900, while he was in the midst of what appears to have been a lengthy correspondence with Gallieni, resembles a number of the policies that Gallieni introduced in Madagascar. Piot believed that by granting financial support to large families, facilitating colonial emigration, and providing the children of large families with greater employment opportunities, this law would be the first step toward boosting population growth.[118] Just as the June 15, 1898, decree in Madagascar had stipulated that unmarried men and women be taxed more harshly than married couples, Piot's proposed law stated that unmarried men and women over the age of thirty would be taxed an additional 15 percent. Childless couples who had been married for five or more years would pay an additional tax of 20 percent until the birth of their first child.[119] He estimated that this would affect over four million French people.[120] Similar to the 1898 decree in Madagascar, the proposed law also included provisions extending financial assistance to large families on an annual basis and guaranteeing that the children from such families benefit from scholarships and career opportunities in the colonies.[121] None of these proposals were entirely new ideas in France. Still, it seems likely that at the very least Gallieni's apparent success with similar such measures would have helped Piot make a compelling case for his proposal.

After about a year, the depopulation commission ceased to meet owing to a lack of funds and long-term governmental disinterest.[122] It was nevertheless revived briefly in 1905, 1908, and 1912.[123] The successes and failures of the commission are emblematic of those of the Alliance nationale during the same period. In the first decades of its existence, the Alliance nationale was very successful at publishing information concerning the causes and effects of depopulation, making the issue well known to the public through a propaganda campaign, influencing parliamentary debates about depopulation, and lobbying members of parliament to propose laws (most of which did not pass) and establishing depopulation commissions. During this period the success of organized pronatalism and the depopulation commission consisted mainly in generating discussion and awareness of France's slow demographic growth. Other than a handful of laws, including some passed in the name of protecting mothers and children, it was not until after World War I that this discussion and awareness of depopulation led to more pronatalist legislation.

Although its existence proved short-lived, the depopulation commission had made Gallieni's efforts well known to the French pronatalist movement through Senator Piot's reports. Jacques Bertillon, president of the Alliance nationale, expressed great enthusiasm for Gallieni's efforts, which he considered the realization of the political program that he and his colleagues had been developing over the last decades. To Bertillon, Gallieni's pronatalism demonstrated that repopulation could be initiated from above and that France had only to learn from this example. A number of the recommendations that Bertillon made his 1911 book, *La dépopulation de la France*, were similar to the measures Gallieni introduced in Madagascar and that Piot proposed. For example, Bertillon recommended that single men over the age of thirty and childless married couples be taxed heavily. Arguing that raising children should be regarded as a form of tax, Bertillon also proposed that families with three or more children be exempt from taxation.[124] He also advocated the establishment of a Fête des enfants in France, pointing to its creation in Madagascar.[125] In 1904 Bertillon wrote the following in the journal of the Alliance nationale:

> One must make the French people understand that every man has the duty to contribute to the perpetuity of his country (by raising at least three children), exactly as he has the duty to defend it. This is the goal to which all of the reforms that we demand converge. This program has already been adopted in its entirety in French territory. Unfortunately it is in Madagascar! General Gallieni proposed it, in his decree "favoring the growth of the Hova race"; we would prefer that the growth of the French race be favored by the same means![126]

This statement reflects a contradiction commonly seen in pronatalist thinking, as Bertillon says "every man," suggesting that men would rescue France from depopulation. Still, in France, as in Madagascar, most pronatalist measures were focused on motherhood and restricting women to that role in society. Bertillon's article also shows that, while clearly impressed by Gallieni's work, he would have preferred to see such measures enacted in France first. This bitterness was also evident in the journal *La famille française*, where one author pointed out that twenty years after Gallieni enacted his measures in Madagascar, "not one minister, not one legislature has deigned to treat French papas as Gallieni treats the Malagasy. It is still better to raise numerous children in Imerina or the Betsileo [region] than on the banks of the Seine and the Loire."[127]

CREATING A "LABOR RESERVOIR"

Of all of Gallieni's measures, pronatalists such as Bertillon appeared to have been most interested in the Fête des enfants. This festival not only demonstrated Gallieni's willingness to draw inspiration from colonial subjects but also intersected with French pronatalist demands that the government take an active interest in promoting and protecting French family life. By the beginning of the twentieth century, French pronatalists began to demand that the government honor the French family. Though they would never achieve anything resembling a national pronatalism day, after World War I the government did establish a national holiday to honor French mothers. Although Mother's Day was markedly different from Gallieni's Fête des enfants, it reflected a similar philosophy: French mothers performed a great service to society and the nation and deserved to be treated with respect and honor. While monetary prizes for mothers of large families in France did not exist at the time of Gallieni's 1898 decrees, in 1913 the French government expanded private initiatives with family allowances, and French pronatalists organized contests and awards for deserving families, including the *Médaille de la famille française* in 1920.

The educational component of Gallieni's Fête des enfants also anticipated French pronatalists' objectives of educating the population about the crisis of depopulation and reducing infant mortality by training women to be good mothers. The Alliance nationale had been created with the stated purpose of promoting awareness of the problem of depopulation, and in the twentieth century pronatalists would demand that *enseignement démographique* (lessons in demography) be included in school curriculums. However, it was not until 1939 that schoolchildren would learn about comparative birthrates and population densities as part of their geography classes in France. Because reducing infant mortality was a key objective of the metropolitan pronatalist movement, pronatalist propaganda was also intended to teach women how to be good mothers, how to introduce proper hygiene into the home, and how to care for their infants. Although *puériculture* classes were introduced into the girls' schools in France prior to 1898, France did not have any sort of a national pronatalism day in which the government instructed adult women on an annual basis about these issues, as was the case in Madagascar beginning in 1898.

Decades after Gallieni left Madagascar, French pronatalists continued to discuss and applaud his efforts to increase the Merina population in the colony. For instance, in 1923 a local section of the Ligue des familles nombreuses de France printed an article criticizing the French government for its inaction concerning the depopulation crisis and holding up Gallieni's work as a model for what a government ought to do. Interestingly, even though the bulk of the reforms in Madagascar focused on mothers, this author emphasized that Gallieni "looked to raise the birthrate by according real material and moral advantages to fathers of large families."[128] Because this statement summarized exactly what this organization was seeking in France, it exemplifies how the understanding that many metropolitan pronatalists had of Gallieni's pronatalist measures was less an accurate representation of what actually happened in Madagascar and more a reflection of what they hoped to achieve in France. The author went on to compare Gallieni's pronatalist achievements in Madagascar with the situation in France by presenting a series of statistics and asserting that France needed a similar "man of energy" to achieve the same results.[129] The figure of Gallieni and what he represented was as important as the actual decrees.

Fernand Auburtin, in his 1921 study of depopulation, likewise presented Gallieni as a great national hero who demonstrated his "enlightened" approach to colonial populations.[130] Auburtin further suggested that France could learn about addressing depopulation from its colonial leaders who had experience working with colonial subjects. Of particular interest to Auburtin was Gallieni's children's festival and how Gallieni's inspiration came from East Asia, where large families "have always been honored." Auburtin also asserted that following the 1898 decree, Madagascar's birthrate had surpassed that of France, indicating the success of Gallieni's measures. Again, pronatalists like Auburtin saw in Gallieni's reforms what they wanted to see: a hero who could solve the depopulation crisis.

A number of scholars have presented French colonies such as Madagascar as "social laboratories" in which scientists, theorists, and other reform-minded individuals could try out reforms that would later be applied in Europe.[131] While pronatalists clearly regarded Madagascar as a "social laboratory," Gallieni developed policies that were only partially influenced by French reform efforts. Like administrators in other colonies, Gallieni was often guided by local conditions more than by ideology and with only minimal involvement from metropolitan reformers.[132] Consequently, pronatalist policies in Madagascar can be distinguished from similar measures in the Belgian Congo, for example, that were introduced later in the twentieth century and came, in many instances, at the instigation of individuals who were also active in reform movements in Belgium.[133]

Although Gallieni's goals and those of the metropolitan pronatalist movement diverged in intent and purpose, both groups agreed that Gallieni's formula for stimulating population growth was a success. In his memoirs and official reports, Gallieni detailed the expansion of French medicine in the colony and the growth of the population. The expansion of medicine could be measured partly by looking at the operating budget of the AMI. In 1896, at the beginning of the colonial period, the state spent 12,000 francs on health care in the colony. By 1905 the operating budget of the AMI had risen to 1,220,000 francs. This was funded largely through taxation, which varied throughout the colony, with taxes ranging from a high of three francs annually in Imerina to a low of a half a franc in Fort Dauphin.[134] Gallieni explained that another indication of the growing success of European medicine in the colony was that increasing numbers of people went to French hospitals when they had health problems instead of to local healers, suggesting that colonial subjects readily embraced European medicine.[135] Whereas only 40,000 people had received European medical assistance in Madagascar in 1895, that number rose to 250,000 in 1899.[136] The number of people receiving medical care at hospitals and getting inoculations, Gallieni argued, would continue to grow as existing services were expanded. A Pasteur Institute, designed to dispense 30,000 vaccinations a month, was under construction in 1899 and opened in 1901.[137] The leprosarium in Ambohidratrimo opened in 1900 and received six hundred patients.[138] Although he recognized that it was too early to judge accurately the long-term effects of his measures to raise the Merina population, in 1901 Gallieni presented the statistics shown in table 1 regarding population growth.

Table 1. Population by age (per 1,000 people)
in Madagascar and France, 1900

Age in years	Madagascar	France
0–15	431	275
15–60	502	617
60+	67	108

Source: Centre des archives d'outre-mer, Gouverneur général de Madagascar, Service de santé, 5D5 1–25: Annual Report, 1900.

These statistics present no comparison with the precolonial period and therefore do not establish definitively that the population grew as a direct result of Gallieni's measures. They do, nevertheless, demonstrate that Madagascar's population was, overall, younger than that of France, a quality that pronatalists and demographers considered critical to future population growth. Madagascar, at this time, displayed a stronger birthrate: the birthrate per one thousand was thirty in Madagascar but only twenty-six in France. Gallieni concluded that if his administration could manage to overcome the high mortality rates, the population would grow as quickly as in England and Russia, the two states in Europe with the fastest population growth. Based on these figures, the sds predicted that in fifty years the population of Madagascar would exceed 4.4 million.[139] While in 1896 Madagascar had had a crisis of depopulation similar to that of France, in 1901 the trends appeared to be reversing in Madagascar, but not in France.

By the end of 1902, Gallieni considered medical assistance to be established in the central provinces of Imerina and Betsileo, with the total number of colonial subjects receiving this medical care at 900,000.[140] The number of dispensaries and medical posts had risen from one in 1897 to twenty-one in 1902, the number of hospitals from one to eighteen, and the number of maternity clinics from one to three.[141] In the following three years, Gallieni focused on extending the health care system in Imerina and Betsileo to the rest of the colony. By

CREATING A "LABOR RESERVOIR"

1905 there were fifty-six dispensaries and medical posts, thirty-eight hospitals, and thirty-five maternity clinics in the colony.[142] Between 1895 and 1905, the number of colonial subjects receiving European medical assistance had risen from 40,000 to 1.7 million.[143]

Providing the population with an effective health care system and establishing the Fête des enfants were the measures that Gallieni believed to be the most effective. In discussing the achievements of the public health system, he emphasized how much the population had grown. At the end of 1902 the population of the capital had grown to 57,635, an increase of 3,846 over the previous year. The birthrate per 1,000 people was 47.4 in 1902, an increase of 2.1 over the previous year and of 17.4 over the year before that (1900). The regional reports from the AMI led officials to conclude that the Fête des enfants and the newly formed public health service had had an impact on population growth. A 1904 medical assistance report from the province of Itasy, for example, boasted that of the 3,684 births that took place in the province in that year, 1,017 were administered by AMI doctors.[144] For this province, 1904 was the first year that births exceeded deaths (see table 2).

Table 2. Numbers of births over deaths (per 1,000 people)
in the province of Itasy, 1901–1904

Year	Number of births over deaths
1901	-109
1902	-116
1903	-34
1904	+17.22

Source: Centre des archives d'outre-mer, Fonds ministériels/Assistance médicale indigène, 5D6 1–27: Province of Itasy, Rapport de l'assistance médicale, 1904.

One of AMI's triumphs was a sharp reduction in maternal deaths and stillbirths. For example, in the four maternity clinics in the province of Ambositra in 1904, only 5 of the 1,498 women who gave birth died as a result.[145] This, the report stated, represented a mortality rate of 33 per 10,000 women, which was "inferior to the averages observed in the best maternity wards in France."[146] Yet according to the figures, this reduction in deaths did not appear to result from increased medical intervention in childbirth. Many of the annual reports stated that Malagasy women, particularly the Betsileo, tended to give birth easily and that their doctors encountered few complications, an assertion that seemed to be corroborated by the statistics they presented in their reports. For instance, in the province of Fianarandsoa, the medical official reported that out of 203 full-term deliveries in 1904, forceps were needed only 4 times: once when there was a breech birth, twice because of uterine inertia, and once because of fetal distress. In addition, there were only ten premature births, two stillbirths, and three maternal deaths. Considering how frequently complications can arise during childbirth, it is striking that doctors decided that 98 percent of these full-term deliveries were normal and did not require forceps or other types of medical intervention. On the one hand, it should be acknowledged that it was widely believed at the time that a society's level of civilization determined how easily a woman could give birth. French doctors claimed that civilization had rendered French women weak and subsequently prone to difficult and complicated deliveries; for African women, many Europeans believed, the opposite was true.[147] It is possible that this belief would have made a French doctor less inclined to intervene in difficult cases if the expectant mother were Malagasy as opposed to French. Yet, interestingly enough, the lack of medical intervention in Malagasy deliveries did not seem to lead to a greater incidence of stillbirths or maternal death, according to these statistics. In making sense of these surprisingly glowing statistics, it is also important to recognize that the officers writing these reports were working within a state bureaucracy and would have wanted to show their superiors in Tananarive that their doctors were achieving good results. In some cases this objective might have colored these reports and the numbers that they presented. Whether or not these figures are credible, it is clear that because medical officials believed that complicated deliveries were very unusual in Madagascar, they attributed their success in reducing the number of stillbirths and maternal deaths primarily to the treatment of venereal diseases, such as syphilis, and the introduction of better hygiene and antisepsis in the delivery room, which greatly reduced the incidence of puerperal fever.

Although Gallieni's numbers paint a picture of an extensive, fully functioning public health system, doctors at the local level continued to see a number of problems. The earliest reports, written by local health officials from 1899 to 1901, suggest that at this time medical services were still poorly organized; the most common complaints related to insufficient personnel, supplies, and facilities and the failure of colonial subjects to fully embrace the medical establishment. In 1901, for example, a doctor in the province of Manjakandriana wrote to the AMI that "native assistance for the province of Manjakandriana last April needed at the very least to be organized, if not created."[148] He went on to explain that his most immediate challenge was treating contagious diseases and that they lacked the resources necessary to treat other problems.[149] Most reports from this period reveal medical officials overwhelmed by the lack of resources and colonial subjects who only sought medical assistance in emergency situations, had not adopted European hygiene in their daily lives, and did not seek preventive medical care.

By 1903, however, a shift appears to have taken place. Reports began to indicate that increasingly large numbers of colonial subjects were voluntarily seeking preventive care and were requesting medication; this, the reports indicated, revealed the confidence that the population was beginning to have in the public health system. By 1904 the regional reports were much more positive and presented the achievements of the last few years in glowing terms. Yet despite this impression of progress, the reports reflected a sense of inadequacy, particularly in those regions of the colony that were furthest from Imerina; the doctors writing these reports apparently continued to feel that they had not reached the numbers of people they wished to help and stressed the need for more funding, additional qualified medical personnel, larger facilities, and more supplies. A report from the province of North Imerina in 1904 indicated that the budget was still inadequate and that the health officials needed three times as many medical personnel.[150] Another report from this same province indicated that hospital personnel were overwhelmed to the point that they turned away patients because they did not have enough beds.[151]

The reports seem to indicate that *médecins indigènes* had a mixture of success and failure in their efforts to convince the population to embrace European medicine and adopt bourgeois European concepts of hygiene. Some *médecins indigènes* emphasized their success in *frapper l'imagination*, as Gallieni had described it: convincing the population of the benefits of French medicine by achieving what traditional practitioners apparently could not. A *médecin indigène* named Ratsemba, for example, boasted that his successful delivery of a baby convinced an entire village of the benefits of European medicine. He described how he came across a woman who was suffering through a complicated delivery of twins. A very discouraged midwife had delivered one twin in the morning but, nine hours later, was still struggling to deliver the other one. Ratsemba walked in, performed a maneuver with apparent ease (he did not specify what exactly he did), and delivered the baby. The baby appeared to be dead, but, much to everyone's amazement, Ratsemba resuscitated him. Word soon spread in the community about the doctor who could do anything, even bring a dead child back to life.[152] Along similar lines, the benefits of vaccinations and medications for malaria and syphilis seemed to make an impression early on, and reports indicated that colonial subjects voluntarily went to hospitals to receive these treatments.[153] In fact, one outside inspector, reporting to the minister of colonies in 1918, was struck by what he considered to be a "superstitious" reverence for European medications.[154]

Perhaps the greatest challenge to French-trained health workers was advancing their ideas of hygiene and proper sanitation. In some regions, doctors emphasized that great progress was being made in these areas.[155] One report described how living conditions were becoming less cramped as extended families were agreeing to live apart in separate homes. Furthermore, it was becoming more common for children and adults to sleep in separate rooms and for each member of the family to eat off of his or her own plate, using his or her own spoon.[156] Another report spoke of the success that health officials had achieved in convincing people to build external structures to house their pigs and fowls, rather than letting the animals live inside with the family.[157] On the one hand, these statements betray a specifically colonial repugnance of filth and the sense that cleanliness was an important marker of civilization and racial superiority.[158] Yet it should be acknowledged that these descriptions of parents and children sleeping in the same room among animals and eating off of the same plates could just as easily be bourgeois criticisms of peasant or working-class families in France. Moreover, it is worth noting that modern medicine was far from definitively established in France during this period. Jack Ellis documents the frustrations of doctors practicing in the French countryside during this period who, in addition to deploring the general lack of hygiene in rural homes, complained about how often peasants preferred to seek medical care from the local priest, unlicensed practitioner or charlatan, instead of a real doctor.[159] In many ways, the civilizing mission in which French and Malagasy doctors believed they were engaged in Madagascar was similar to that which was under way in France, where notions of hygiene were by no means universally established at this time.

Another frustration related to the widely held belief that the Malagasy wore too little clothing, something that was seen as a shortcoming on the part of mothers. Again this criticism was grounded in medical concerns about keeping children sufficiently warm (in order to fight off illnesses more effectively) and in European notions of decency and civilization. One report emphasized that the efforts of the public health system to reduce infant mortality were continuously undermined by women's failure to care for their children properly. "In effect it is shameful to see children practically naked during the winter. Every year during the Children's Festival [the colonial regime] distributes many warm *lambas* which all disappear shortly thereafter."[160] When describing the Sakalave population, an official lamented how they "live pell-mell in badly ventilated straw huts and quite often in a lamentable filthiness. Not knowing either how to dress or to feed themselves, they become . . . easy prey for all kinds of contagions."[161]

Gallieni's measures to increase the Merina population in Madagascar ultimately fell short of the ten million he had envisioned in 1903. Colonial censuses revealed that the population was 2,701,081 in 1906 and 2,965,508 in 1909, a modest increase.[162] Although the vaccination campaigns, the establishment of hospitals, and the training of Malagasy doctors and midwives could boast many achievements in terms of improving the health of the population and increasing the birthrate, some contemporary studies revealed that the colonial regime was itself undermining the achievements of the public health system. For instance, colonial authorities admitted that the incidence of malaria rose markedly around the turn of the century because of increased population movements from the coastal regions to the central highlands that were facilitated by improved transportation.[163] Contemporary experts even acknowledged that forced labor and poverty played important roles in outbreaks of malaria.[164] A study presented by the prominent physician Dr. Kermorgant at the Académie de médecine in 1907 found that 18,000 of the 35,000 inhabitants of Tananarive were afflicted with malaria that year.[165] Kermorgant explained that the causes of the disease were poverty, overwork, and unsanitary conditions, all of which he linked to public works projects.[166]

In addition, Gallieni's larger plans to create a population composed of both French families (who would own and manage farms) and large numbers of colonial subjects working for them never achieved the level of success he initially envisioned. Throughout his tenure as governor-general of the colony, the French settler population remained relatively small, despite his efforts. His attempts suffered in part because French conquest of the island was not only prolonged but also costly and negatively portrayed in the metropolitan press. The fact that of the fifteen thousand French soldiers who took part in the military expedition, only thirteen died in battle but close to six thousand died of disease, suggested that the colony was insalubrious and ill-suited for large-scale European settlement.[167] Determined to overcome these obstacles to French settlement, Gallieni collaborated with the UCF and even wrote a *Guide de l'immigrant* to promote emigration to the island.[168] He also sought, unsuccessfully, to attract French farmers, industrialists, and merchants with promises of cheap land.[169] Yet by 1905, a mere 630 European farmers had arrived in the colony, and the vast majority of land grants had been disbursed to plantation owners or industrialists.[170]

Conclusion

When Gallieni devised a series of measures to increase the Merina population in Madagascar, he drew on his experiences as a colonial administrator and not solely his awareness of the pronatalist movement in France. His first efforts to establish medical facilities in the colony came as a response to the unique challenges of colonial rule: pacifying the colony and then establishing a large labor force. Dissatisfied with the limited success achieved by the metropolitan pronatalist movement at this point, Gallieni sought to establish a public health system that would surpass that of the metropole in terms of the number of patients benefiting from its extensive services. Yet Gallieni believed that providing women with safe births and treating their syphilis infections would have only a limited impact on population growth if nothing was done to change cultural practices and persuade people to have more children. Gallieni thus introduced policies such as financial incentives for having children and strong penalties for abortion, and he drew on his experiences in Indochina to develop a propaganda campaign distinct from what existed in France during this period. Like the French pronatalists, Gallieni placed a strong emphasis on women and motherhood. In Madagascar this meant propaganda stressing that it was through motherhood that a woman fulfilled her duty, decrees that in a variety of ways fell under the category of "protection of motherhood," and state intervention into pregnancy, childbirth, and child care.

Although it is difficult to quantify the extent to which Gallieni's pronatalist measures improved population growth in Madagascar, it is clear that European medicine became more widespread in the colony as a result of these initiatives. By 1918 the AMI comprised 51 regional hospitals, 108 medical posts, 38 maternity clinics, and 3 leprosy treatment centers.[171] Moreover, the Merina health workers trained by the colonial regime were indispensable to the success of these objectives. By 1918 the colony's 23 European doctors were working with 182 *médecins indigènes*, 108 *sages-femmes indigènes*, and 395 Malagasy nurses.[172]

What is also evident is that Gallieni's measures served as a source of inspiration to pronatalists working to improve population growth in France. Whereas pronatalist reformers in France faced numerous obstacles, the most serious of which they saw as government inertia, they believed that Gallieni successfully created an extensive and centralized bureaucracy within a couple of years. They consequently saw him as a "national hero" who could achieve what the French government could not. Certainly, his position as a colonial governor enabled him to introduce these decrees without having to contend with the same sort of opposition that reformers faced in France. Under the provisions of the decree of December 11, 1895, establishing the position, the resident-general of Madagascar had the authority to direct, organize, and control the various administrative branches and services of the colony.[173] He was also responsible for determining a budget for the colony and submitting it to the minister of colonies for approval.[174] Gallieni's efforts were therefore not delayed by parliamentary debate, like those of metropolitan pronatalists, and he was not obliged to take the private property interests of his subjects into account. He was therefore well positioned to both implement policies ahead of analogous metropolitan laws and to pursue measures that were of colonial inspiration. Pronatalists viewed Gallieni's experiments in population growth not only as an example of what a determined government could accomplish in directing population growth but also as a lesson that could prove effective as they began lobbying the government for similar policies in France. Pronatalists in France seem to have been particularly impressed by Gallieni's creation of the Fête des enfants, though the decrees on the family and expansion of European medicine in the colony also received significant attention. Ultimately, what Gallieni achieved through his 1898 decrees was less important to many pronatalist thinkers than the inspiration he provided as a leader and a "man of action." Similar to the myth of the prolific settler, Gallieni and his pronatalist measures took on a mythical quality that shaped metropolitan pronatalism. The perception that colonial governments were often more serious about encouraging population growth continued to influence how pronatalists thought about their own depopulation crisis. As the next chapter will show, the next colony to shape pronatalism in this way was Tunisia in the 1920s.

FOUR

Voting for the Family

The Fight for Familial Suffrage in France and North Africa

> If we do not want to be submerged by the rising tide
> of Asians, or even Russian and German populations,
> we need to modify our customs. The establishment of
> familial suffrage would be the first step in that direction.
>
> —CHARLES RICHET, "Le vote familial,"
> *Revue des deux mondes*, 1934

Writing on the eve of World War I, pronatalist Fernand Boverat deplored the apparent failure of the French public to take the demographic crisis seriously. Boverat wrote that to many French people, the idea that France could "lose her colonies and a large portion of her territory [and] that she could even, within the next forty years, completely cease to exist as an independent nation, seems like an unreasonable absurdity."[1] While France's declining demographic growth had been a source of considerable concern since the birth of the Third Republic in 1870, French pronatalists appeared powerless in their efforts to reverse the demographic trends. Even as they became more organized in the last years of the nineteenth century and established a base of support in the French parliament, birthrates continued to decline, and elected officials proved uncommitted to enacting pronatalist laws. Ultimately, it was the experience of more than four years of devastating world war, during which France endured partial occupation, civilian and military casualties surpassing a million, and a severe drop in the birthrate, that transformed the apathy of which Boverat had written in 1913. Near defeat coupled with substantial casualties suggested that pronatalists had been correct in their predictions that the low birthrate would render France vulnerable to invasion.

As the Great War ended, many pronatalists emphasized that the Allies' victory was not a true victory; depopulated France had emerged from the war weaker than ever and would likely be invaded again.[2] In response to such fears, the pronatalist movement expanded during the interwar years, attracting more members and becoming increasingly desperate to address depopulation. Their frustration with the slow pace at which the French government adopted their proposals led pronatalists to conclude that the demographic crisis could not be resolved without redefining French citizenship and rejecting universal manhood suffrage, the very foundation of the Republic. They thus positioned familial suffrage, a system in which parents would cast supplementary votes on behalf of their children, as a central part of their political program. Pronatalists asserted that if familial suffrage were established, parliament would prioritize laws favoring large families and demographic trends would then be reversed.

Although familial suffrage was not enacted in interwar France, it was introduced in Tunisia in 1922 and then Morocco in 1926. A combination of factors inspired this political development. Similar to France, both of these settler colonies experienced declining birthrates that left officials and patriotic French people concerned about the strength of the French population. However, the establishment of familial suffrage in Tunisia and Morocco also reflected demographic concerns of a specifically colonial nature; French settlers represented only a minority of the overall population, outnumbered not only by colonial subjects but also by Spanish and Italian settlers. To many concerned officials and imperialists, this numerical disparity weakened France's grasp over its protectorates. In this way, demographic concerns of a specifically colonial nature made familial suffrage more relevant and politically expedient, revealing the relative strength of pronatalist interests in the colonial context. The precedent set in France's North African protectorates in turn fueled metropolitan pronatalist demands for its establishment in France.

New Definitions of Citizenship

In 1916, a year marked by high French casualties at the battles of the Somme and Verdun, members of the Alliance nationale pour l'accroissement de la population française achieved an important victory: a majority in the Chamber of Deputies. Three hundred and forty-eight deputies signed on to the pronatalist cause by joining the parliamentary group known as the Protection des familles nombreuses (Protection of Large Families).[3] In addition to gaining this important foothold in parliament, the pronatalist movement grew more influential and better organized with the formation of new groups sharing many of the same objectives. Among the largest such organizations were the Ligue française, La plus grande famille, and the Ligue pour la vie. According to Joseph Spengler, by 1922 the organized pronatalist and familialist movements in France consisted of 8 national associations, 62 regional associations, and 11 federations of large families.[4] Their numbers continued to grow throughout the interwar period, with at least 250 familialist and pronatalist organizations operating within French territory in 1939.[5] In addition to meeting annually at the Congrès national de la natalité, the four largest familialist and pronatalist organizations formed the Comité central des ligues de familles nombreuses to lobby for something they all considered critical: familial suffrage.[6] Sometimes referred to as the plural vote or the family vote, familial suffrage was a system of voting in which parents of large families would cast extra votes on behalf of their dependent family members.[7]

The familialist model of politics advocated by pronatalists in the 1920s was not unique to this era. Jean-Yves Le Naour and Catherine Valenti have shown that although the Revolution of 1789 did lead to the establishment of the "individual-citizen," revolutionaries saw this individual-citizen in terms of social function, as a property owner or a head of household.[8] For this reason, Anne Verjus argues, revolutionaries never considered extending suffrage to servants, women, and children, whom they viewed as dependent members of the household.[9] In this respect, individuals voted on behalf of the family unit, in their capacities as heads of households or property owners, and not solely as individuals. This view of voters is similar to the one that pronatalists would promote in the twentieth century. However, as Le Naour, Valenti, and Verjus all argue, the year 1848 transformed perceptions of suffrage from a social "function" into an individual "right" decided not by social status or family but by sex: all men could vote equally.

The establishment of universal manhood suffrage in 1848 was followed by the first arguments in favor of familial suffrage, such as those made by Justin André and Alphonse de Lamartine.[10] In terms similar to those used by pronatalists seventy years later, André asserted that the family and all its members constituted the true citizen and that the family, not the individual, should therefore vote.[11] The fall of the Second Republic in 1851 temporarily silenced these debates about familial suffrage.[12] With the establishment of the Third Republic twenty years later, however, came renewed efforts at suffrage reform, most notably from the monarchist faction within parliament from 1871 to 1875.[13]

Whereas it was mostly monarchists advocating familial suffrage in the 1870s, by the early twentieth century this model of voting became an important part of the pronatalist platform and appeared on the agenda of a number of political parties.[14] Crucial to understanding why the idea of familial suffrage gained credibility in the 1920s is the impact of World War I on concepts of citizenship and rights. As many scholars have shown, reconstruction and recovery after the war entailed more than simply rebuilding damaged structures and roads. The devastation of the war went much deeper and seemed to weaken the national body. During the war, France's already low birthrate declined substantially as young men left for the front, and many couples chose to forego having children because of the uncertain times in which they lived. After the war, the weak birthrate showed little promise of a full recovery, given that over a million soldiers died at the front and many more returned home disabled.[15] Consequently, in the years after the war, France had a significant gender imbalance that left many young women struggling to find a suitable husband. In addition to these obstacles to restoring demographic health was the sense that the war had been an attack on French motherhood, masculinity, and the family. For instance, women who were raped and impregnated by German occupiers in the north symbolized the enemy's violent intrusion on French soil.[16] The existence of these "children of the barbarian" raised difficult questions about whether or not they could be absorbed into the French population by virtue of having a French mother and being raised with French values.[17] The inability of French men to protect these women from their German attackers also signified the weakened state of French masculinity.[18] Furthermore, the departure of so many men to the front required that women enter the workforce in greater numbers and in industries previously considered unsuitable for women. Though in many cases temporary, this employment destabilized the gender order and weakened the family by drawing more women out of the private sphere and away from their children. The effects of the war on family life persisted in the 1920s as conservatives feared that more and more women rejected their traditional roles as mothers and homemakers and instead sought a more independent life outside of the home.[19] The image of la garçonne, an independent girl from a good bourgeois family who sought sexual liberation and fulfillment like a man, immortalized in Victor Margueritte's novel of the same name, was a powerful symbol of these threats to France's recovery from the war.[20]

Postwar recovery in its fullest sense therefore comprised many different elements, including reconstruction, economic growth, the reintegration of men into the workplace (and concurrent departure of women from the workforce), the establishment of stable families, a proper gender order, and a robust birthrate. France's nascent welfare state developed amid these intersecting concerns and consequently advanced a new idea of citizenship. In the war's aftermath, the French state began to move toward "social citizenship," the idea that the state had a responsibility to ensure a particular standard of living to its citizens.[21] This developed through the initiatives of both employers, who introduced benefits like a family wage and family allowances (which granted a sum of money to each family with a certain number of children), and the state, which implemented legislation like tax incentives for families and assumed control of and generalized family allowances.

As Laura Levine Frader argues, it was because of the strong desire to reconstitute families and encourage a stronger birthrate that employers and the state no longer viewed workers as individuals but rather as members of families. Consequently, the aforementioned benefits, among others that they introduced in the aftermath of the war, were not allocated on an equal basis but were determined by one's employment, gender, and familial status.[22] For instance, at companies that had a family wage, men with children were paid more than their childless co-workers. Similarly, family allowances effectively differentiated between French citizens by granting state funds to those citizens who had children but not to those who were childless.

The notion that there were different types of citizens extended into the realm of political participation and was particularly evident in debates over familial suffrage in the 1920s. Many advocates of familial suffrage attributed the devastation of the Great War to the prewar government's failure to take decisive action to increase the birthrate. This lack of government action in turn revealed a weakness in the democratic system: elected officials appealed to the demands of the majority, not the minority. In France, men with few or no children represented the majority of voters and wielded the most electoral power, whereas fathers of large families were the minority of voters and subsequently had little influence on politics. Pronatalists were unanimous in their belief that a government, elected by precisely those individuals who lacked demonstrable commitment to reversing the demographic trends, could not be entrusted with the responsibility of implementing pronatalist legislation. As one article in the pronatalist journal *Natalité* explained, the government passed legislation with individual interests in mind, not those of the French family: "As long as our laws fail to address the needs of the family, the family will be unable to do anything except continue to perish."[23]

To proponents of familial suffrage, the injustices of the contemporary political system could be traced back to the French Revolution, an event that ushered in a new era of individualism. They pointed to the egalitarian spirit of the Revolution, which, by way of the Declaration of Rights of Man and Citizen and the Constitution, granted rights to individual men without instructing them on their civic or familial duties. The Napoleonic Code further privileged the rights of the male individual over those of the family by abolishing the practice of primogeniture and asserting the equal rights of children to the family inheritance.[24] As a result, Republican deputy Henri Roulleaux-Dugage argued, "selfishness practically single-handedly directs the life of each person; the principles of secular morality, with which one has tried to replace religious teaching, provide little defense against neo-Malthusianism, because they do not indicate, to the individual, rules of behavior other than the pursuit of his personal interest and immediate happiness."[25]

It is tempting to read pronatalists' criticisms of the French Revolution's egalitarian principles as an example of reactionary politics. However, as critical as many of them were of the legacy of the Revolution and the rise of individualism, pronatalists by and large did not outright reject the democratic system. In fact, like many French feminists, pronatalists simply emphasized its current failures and even evoked the principles of the Revolution as they criticized universal manhood suffrage.[26] For example, in his influential book on familial suffrage, André Toulemon argued that "universal suffrage," as it existed in France, was not truly universal, given that only ten out of forty million French people possessed the right to vote.[27] If all French people were to be "born and remain truly free and equal in rights, as indicated in the Declaration of Rights of Man and Citizen," the political system would have to be restructured to represent the interests of the thirty million women and children.[28] Thus, to Toulemon and other proponents of familial suffrage, the egalitarian principles of the French Revolution were less the cause of depopulation than was France's failure to fully realize those principles.

In their arguments in favor of familial suffrage, pronatalists contested the established definition of citizenship. They believed that the failure of the French Revolution had been its emphasis on individual rights and its tendency to treat citizens as individuals. In so doing, the government failed to acknowledge the distinctions between citizens; some contributed to the nation by assuming the burdens of parenthood, while others had few or no children. To pronatalists, the *père de famille* and the *célibataire* represented two distinct types of citizens, while in terms of voting and taxation the state treated them as equal individuals. Along these lines, Étienne Lamy argued that although the French Revolution was supposed to have done away with privileges, "there is one [privilege] that the Revolution did not foresee and which is significant: that of households who leave all the national burdens to other households."[29] From this perspective, the state perpetuated inequality and encouraged depopulation by failing to take into consideration such distinctions between citizens. In response to this perceived injustice, interwar pronatalists focused their efforts on elevating the *famille nombreuse* (large family) to a privileged and influential position in French society. As one advocate argued, with familial suffrage "the *père de famille* would thus become the master of France. The familial and plural vote is essentially democratic and would represent a truly universal suffrage."[30] Once familial suffrage was instituted, pronatalists believed, the population would truly be represented in its entirety. Elected officials would prioritize the needs of the *famille nombreuse*, and pronatalist organizations would see greater success in pushing their proposed laws through parliament.

One reason why pronatalists found familial suffrage so appealing is that they hoped that this model of voting would increase the authority of the *père de famille* within both the family and the French state. Similar to their criticism of the "individual citizen" that emerged after 1789, pronatalist discussions of the need to revive paternal authority within the family revealed some nostalgia for the Old Regime. Scholars have shown that the revolutionary era triggered a number of changes in family relations, particularly regarding the father's authority over the dependent members of his household. Under the Old Regime, the law endowed fathers with the responsibility of maintaining order at the family level, and to this end it granted them substantial legal authority over their dependent family members.[31] The father consequently ruled over his family just as the king ruled over the country, with the subordination of family members to the father being analogous to subjects' subordination to the monarch. When revolutionaries overthrew Louis XVI, the "father" of the country, they also envisioned a less patriarchal society more generally and introduced legislation that effectively dethroned French fathers at the familial level.[32] One of the main reasons for this was their belief that a citizen could not stand in full possession of his rights (and they envisioned autonomous citizens as male) if he was also subject to the tyrannical authority of his father.[33] The Napoleonic Code ultimately overturned some of this revolutionary legislation and reestablished some level of paternal authority within the family, but as Jacques Donzelot has argued, the Revolution did mark the end of the old "entanglement" of monarchical and paternal power and the birth of a "future state that would organize the citizens' welfare, dispensing assistance, work, education, and health to everyone without regard to outmoded family adherences."[34] Over the course of the nineteenth century, paternal authority within the family was increasingly displaced by that of the state.

In the late nineteenth and early twentieth centuries, legislators faced a dilemma as they sought to introduce laws to protect children and improve the birthrate. The enactment of such laws would mean intervening in family life and, by extension, reducing paternal authority within the family. Although legislators were often reluctant to pass pronatalist laws, in the last years of the Third Republic "the interests of the family, and most importantly those of children, consistently triumphed over considerations of the status and authority of fathers."[35] This occurred in a number of ways. Through the family allowance system, for instance, the state assumed some of the responsibility for providing for French families, thereby competing with the father's position as breadwinner. In the interest of protecting children, the state could also deprive a man of his paternal authority or, following the 1912 law on paternity suits, judge that he was the father of a child whom he did not wish to recognize as his own. Finally, through paternity suits and state support of motherhood, the state increasingly began to recognize the sexual independence of women and legitimate those families that lacked a strong male figurehead.[36] Unlike much of the existing pronatalist legislation, therefore, familial suffrage promoted population growth by strengthening paternal authority within the family. At a time when the French government increasingly intervened in family life to protect mothers and children, the institution of familial suffrage would effectively acknowledge a father's position as head of household, recognize his authority over his family members, and enable him to represent the interests of his family members in the public sphere. For this reason, the proposed reform held significant appeal to those pronatalists who believed that a stronger birthrate required first and foremost the reestablishment of stable, patriarchal families.

As they sought suffrage reform in the 1920s, pronatalists faced significant competition from feminists, who were also, albeit it in a different way, fighting to overturn the tradition of universal male suffrage. Even before the war, feminist organizations such as the Union française pour le suffrage des femmes, which had ten thousand members in 1912, actively sought the enfranchisement of women by publishing articles, organizing petitions and demonstrations, and refusing to pay taxes.[37] With the outbreak of the war, feminists were nevertheless expected to abandon their fight and rally behind the nation as part of the Union sacrée. Much to their disappointment, after the war women were not rewarded for their contributions with the vote, as were their counterparts in Great Britain, the United States, Germany, and a number of other Western states. Still, in the 1920s the feminist movement gained momentum when the public, as well as a number of well-placed political leaders, became increasingly receptive to the idea of women's suffrage.[38]

Because of the growing likelihood that women would receive the vote, pronatalists lobbying for familial suffrage in the interwar period could not disregard arguments in favor of women's political rights. An early example of pronatalists' attempts to engage feminism as part of their own lobbying for suffrage reform is an article that Jacques Bertillon published in 1910 likening the two proposed models of suffrage.[39] Bertillon critiqued the existing system of universal manhood suffrage because it excluded the representation of women and children. However, because there were more women than men in France and "never will a serious government consent to deliver the direction of a

VOTING FOR THE FAMILY

great country to a majority of women," Bertillon did not support full voting rights for women.[40] Despite his fears of the dangers of a "gynocracy," as he called it, Bertillon argued that without the representation of women in government, abuses such as alcoholism and child neglect would remain unaddressed. In this respect he agreed with the mainstream feminist view that women's participation in government was vitally important for the nation, as women were the most likely defenders of the French family. With these two considerations in mind, he advocated a system of voting that granted widows the right to vote on behalf of their families and in place of their deceased husbands. Women would therefore have a minor voice in government.

The question of whether familial suffrage should include any form of suffrage for women was divisive for pronatalists during and after the Great War. On the one side of the debate were the proposals of Henri Roulleaux-Dugage, Republican deputy of the Orne between 1910 and 1930, who made a series of attempts to introduce familial suffrage into parliamentary debate from 1916 until his retirement from public life in 1930. Although he modified his proposals repeatedly in order to gain supporters, the underlying principle of his model remained constant: every child should be represented individually with a vote. For example, in his October 1916 proposal, the father would receive a supplementary vote for each dependent member of his household (wife and children), and in the event of the father's death, the widowed mother would vote in his place. Single adult women would receive individual votes as well.[41] As feminists were quick to point out, though, for adult women one unfortunate consequence of getting married would be losing the right to vote. In 1920 Roulleaux-Dugage revised his proposal, stipulating that a married woman could cast her own vote.

Although pronatalists supported any form of suffrage that would give fathers greater electoral weight than single men, some were opposed to Roulleaux-Dugage's model of familial suffrage on the grounds that it promoted individualism. The idea that family members needed individual representation through individual votes contradicted the idea that the family unit should be represented in its entirety. To these pronatalists, the purpose of familial suffrage was not to extend political representation to women and children but rather to elevate the social status and electoral weight of the *père de famille* by giving him one or more supplementary votes in recognition of his social importance. These pronatalists preferred the model proposed by Jules Lemire, deputy from Hazebrouck between 1893 and 1928, who was also known as the *abbé démocrate*. Lemire proposed familial suffrage in the Chamber of Deputies in 1911 and again in 1920.[42] The system he proposed in 1920 stipulated that a single man would receive one vote, married men would receive two votes, and fathers with four or more children would receive three votes.[43] Under this system, women would not vote under any circumstances.

Pronatalists could only speculate on the impact that these opposing models of familial suffrage might have on elections and, by extension, the passage of pronatalist laws. Yet supporters of Roulleaux-Dugage could confidently assert that this proposal would more effectively minimize the political influence of single men than the one proposed by Lemire. In 1922, for example, comparisons between the models proposed by Lemire and Roulleaux-Dugage in 1920 appeared in the journal of the familialist organization La plus grande famille (see table 3).

Despite their ideological divisions, supporters of familial suffrage rallied around the Roulleaux-Dugage model in 1923. Proponents of Lemire's model gave their support to Roulleaux-Dugage mainly out of opportunism, wishing to see an initial victory in the fight for suffrage reform.[44] When the Chamber of Deputies met to debate Justin Godart's proposal for women's suffrage on December 6, 1923, Roulleaux-Dugage added his proposal for familial suffrage, declaring himself a supporter of women's suffrage.[45] Representing the most important victory for the cause of familial suffrage, the combined proposal was approved by 440 deputies, with only 135 dissenters. Despite this initial victory, which convinced many pronatalists that success was imminent, the measure ultimately failed after the Senate refused to take it under consideration.[46] According to Le Naour and Valenti, after this failure, supporters of Lemire's version of familial suffrage refused to lend their support to further efforts on behalf of the Roulleaux-Dugage model.[47] Many feminists were likewise disillusioned and felt

Table 3. Numbers of votes in three electoral systems
Total number of votes (including supplemental votes)

Familial categories	Current system	Roulleaux-Dugage model	Lemire model
Single men	3,450,000	3,450,000	3,450,000
Married men with no children	1,760,000	1,760,000	3,520,000
Men with one child	2,040,000	4,080,000	4,080,000
Men with two children	1,890,000	5,670,000	3,780,000
Men with three children	950,000	3,800,000	1,900,000
Men with four children	640,000	3,200,000	1,920,000
Men with five children	330,000	1,980,000	990,000
Men with six children	220,000	1,540,000	660,000
Men with seven or more children[1]	220,000	1,980,000	660,000
Total number of votes	11,500,000	27,460,000	20,960,000

Source: "Le vote familial," *Revue de la plus grande famille*, January 1922, 4–5.

[1]When calculating the number of votes for men with seven or more children, the authors of the study decided to give each man nine votes (eight for his children and one for himself) under the Roulleaux-Dugage model. Their calculations indicated that eight children was most likely the average for this category of men.

that the cause of women's suffrage had been weakened by Roulleaux-Dugage's proposal.[48]

Although proponents of familial suffrage would never again see the level of success witnessed in 1923, they continued their crusade until the outbreak of World War II. Increasingly, after witnessing the high level of support for women's suffrage in 1923, pronatalists sought to align their interests with those of feminists and to develop a model of familial suffrage that would be acceptable to feminists. Whereas nineteenth-century liberal feminists in France had been obliged to acknowledge the strength of pronatalist arguments, thus strategically choosing not to demand political rights amid heightened concerns about depopulation, by the 1920s the situation had changed considerably.[49] By then, arguments in favor of women's suffrage were so strong that pronatalists seeking familial suffrage were forced to acknowledge the strength of the feminist movement and subsequently revised their demands in order to meet the feminist challenge. In 1927, for example, the president of the Alliance nationale, Fernand Boverat, argued that familial suffrage was unlikely to be adopted unless it was combined with women's suffrage. He further expressed his fears that by alienating feminists, who refused any form of familial suffrage that placed women in an unequal position, pronatalists risked any possibility of seeing familial suffrage adopted. Thus, in order to align familial suffrage more effectively with feminist demands for women's suffrage, Boverat proposed a new model in which mothers and fathers would share equally their children's votes. In families with an odd number of children, the father would receive the extra vote. Recognizing that critics might interpret this version as another attempt to extend unequal voting rights to women, Boverat emphasized that in postwar France women outnumbered men and would as a group receive more votes on a national level.[50]

Despite this apparent concession on the part of the pronatalist movement, most feminist supporters of familial suffrage rejected the proposed model on principle, asserting that giving the husband greater electoral weight than his wife would create inequality within marriage. A prominent example of this thinking was Marguerite de Witt–Schlumberger, president of the Union française pour le suffrage des femmes. In addition to being a feminist leader and mother of six, de Witt–Schlumberger was one of the rare women who rose to a position of influence within the largely male-dominated pronatalist movement. She was one of the administrators of the Alliance nationale–produced journal La femme et l'enfant and was widely quoted in a number of pronatalist newspapers.[51] Very active in the French government, she was appointed to the Conseil supérieur de la natalité in 1920 and was awarded the cross of the Légion d'honneur that year. In 1924, the last year of her life, she represented the French government at an international conference on the trafficking of women and children and was appointed to the Consultative Committee on Commerce and Industry, where she was asked to draw on her experience as a mother to assist the committee in assessing the high cost of living.[52] Although she was a proponent of familial suffrage, de Witt–Schlumberger departed from her pronatalist colleagues by arguing that mothers and fathers should share equally the votes of their children. In the event of an odd number of children, she asserted, the mother should receive the extra vote, because she had given birth to the child in question.[53] In addition to rejecting any form of suffrage reform that was designed to simultaneously grant women suffrage and minimize its impact, de Witt–Schlumberger also defended the feminist view that women's suffrage and familial suffrage represented separate issues. Whereas most pronatalists viewed the extension of suffrage to women as part of the establishment of familial suffrage, feminists asserted that women deserved political rights for reasons that were entirely different from the need to represent the interests of children. Feminists such as de Witt–Schlumberger asserted that by conflating the two issues, pronatalists erroneously equated women's suffrage with the political representation of minors, an insulting notion.[54] Because of these differences of opinion, the alliance that pronatalists tried to forge with feminists after 1923 was destined to fail.

Pronatalists nevertheless continued to lobby for familial suffrage in the 1930s and under Vichy.[55] This included a number of proposed bills in parliament, including those of Georges Pernot in 1933 and Marcel Boucher in 1936. It also included André Toulemon's 1935 creation of a new organization (the Ligue pour le vote familial) uniting prominent pronatalists in the fight for familial suffrage.[56] Advocating that fathers of three or more children receive a supplementary vote, the group also urged that "if women are given the vote, that an extra vote be given to mothers of large families."[57] In 1935 the editors of the Alliance nationale's journal announced to their readership that they had gained the support of the Union nationale pour le vote des femmes as well as other feminist groups, a vague assertion that was most likely exaggerated.[58] Once again, pronatalists acknowledged the likelihood that women would eventually gain the right to vote and the need to attempt to reconcile their objectives with those of feminists seeking the vote. Pronatalists worried that if women gained the right to vote without the establishment of familial suffrage, their cause would lose considerable support, because few elected officials would be interested in undertaking suffrage reform a second time. After more than two decades of lobbying for familial suffrage, their worst fears were eventually realized; in 1944, Charles de Gaulle promised that women would gain the right to vote once the republic was restored, but he made no mention of familial suffrage.

Ultimately, the failure of the interwar campaign for familial suffrage can be attributed to a variety of factors. Pronatalists blamed feminists, asserting that feminists' efforts to revise voting laws competed with their own efforts to do precisely that, thereby complicating political debates by providing legislators with multiple models of suffrage from which to choose. This simplistic view of the debate ignored other factors, however. Pronatalists also encountered significant opposition from those who considered familial suffrage too complicated to implement or simply antithetical to the egalitarian principles of the French Republic.

Lucien Saint and Familial Suffrage in Tunisia

While French pronatalists lobbied unsuccessfully for familial suffrage in France, their arguments received serious consideration in France's North African protectorates. Beginning in Tunisia, a French protectorate since the Bardo Treaty of 1881, Resident-General Lucien Saint implemented familial suffrage with apparent ease in 1922 as part of larger political reforms aimed at curbing nationalist sentiments and addressing the demographic challenges of the colony's growing Italian and Spanish populations. Four years later, Resident-General Théodore Steeg introduced a nearly identical measure in Morocco. In both instances the colonial context exerted considerable influence on officials' decision to implement familial suffrage. Not only did French officials introduce this method of voting out of concern for France's numerical inferiority, but they also anticipated possible reactions among the colonial subjects and defined their decrees so as to minimize potential conflict.

Central to understanding the 1922 political reforms in Tunisia is the divisive issue of political representation that had for decades put the residency at odds with both the settler and colonized populations. This conflict first emerged in 1881, when Tunisia became a protectorate and French officials chose to rule indirectly in the interest of avoiding the types of conflict that the political assimilation of Algeria had engendered.[59] Subsequently, the preexisting system of government remained nominally intact, with the bey of Tunis retaining his title but lacking the power to act independently of French interests. The resident-minister (known as the resident-general after 1885) effectively administered through the bey on behalf of the Ministry of Foreign Affairs in Paris. Under this system of government, French settlers in Tunisia lacked the kind of political representation enjoyed by their compatriots in neighboring Algeria.[60]

Although they lacked direct political representation, French settlers in Tunisia did have a means by which to communicate their opinions and grievances to the residency: the Conférence consultative (Consultative Conference). Established in 1892, this elected body met biannually with the purpose of discussing problems in the protectorate, mainly of an economic nature, and making recommendations to the residency. To that end, its members were elected to represent their professional interests. Initially there were only two colleges, and these were derived from the settlers' chambers of agriculture and commerce; in 1896 a third college was added to represent government officials and the liberal professions.[61] The Conférence consultative had no legislative power, and the resident-general was by no means obliged to follow any of its recommendations; its role was merely advisory.[62] In 1907 the membership of the Conférence consultative was expanded to include sixteen Tunisians (out of fifty-two members in the conference); French members later consolidated the three chambers into a single chamber for French representatives and maintained a separate chamber of Tunisian representatives.[63] They argued that this was done not to marginalize the Tunisian representatives but rather to eliminate the language difficulties that arose out of having a combined chamber.

The issue of Tunisian representation within the Conférence consultative reflected a larger struggle under way between French authorities and Tunisian nationalists that ultimately led to the 1922 political reforms. Following World War I, economic problems, rising unemployment among Tunisians, and the French government's failure to follow through on promises made to Tunisian veterans who had fought in the French army gave strength to nationalist movements in existence since the nineteenth century. Of particular concern to French officials was the formation of the nationalist organization Destour, whose members demanded equal pay for equal work, a constitution, and a parliament to which French and Tunisian representatives would be elected by universal suffrage.[64] Tunisian nationalists also demanded equal representation within both the existing Conférence consultative and the parliament they hoped would eventually be established. This put them at odds with the many vocal French settlers who envisioned the formation of a representative government in which Tunisians would play little or no role.

It was in this context that Lucien Saint arrived in Tunisia to serve as the protectorate's new resident-general. Unlike earlier residents-general in Tunisia and Morocco, Saint was a civilian with no experience in colonial administration, though he did have colonial connections through his marriage to the daughter of former minister of colonies Georges Trouillot. Saint began his career in 1886 as a lawyer and went on to serve the French administration in a variety of capacities, including head of the cabinet of the Ministry of Commerce and a series of prefectural positions between 1906 and 1919.[65] Saint served as resident-general of Tunisia from 1921 to 1929, went on to be resident-general of Morocco between 1929 and 1932, and then returned to France, where he spent the remainder of his career as a *gauche-démocratique* senator for Haute-Garonne until his death in 1938.[66] Even before his departure for Tunisia in 1920, Saint made his position on political reforms abundantly clear by telling a delegation of Tunisian nationalists with whom he met in Paris that a constitution, an elected parliament, and a responsible government were by definition incompatible with the principle of a protectorate.[67] After his arrival in Tunisia, Saint immediately took a hard line against the nationalist struggle, refusing to make any concessions to nationalists, even after the bey threatened to abdicate in protest.[68] Instead, he sought to weaken the nationalist struggle by introducing small reforms intended to placate moderate

VOTING FOR THE FAMILY

nationalists and separate them from their more radical counterparts. He did this in July 1922 by introducing the Grand conseil (Grand Council), a representative body consisting of separate French and Tunisian sections and designed to replace the Conférence consultative. The French section was composed of twenty-one representatives of the colony's economic interests (agriculture, industry, and commerce) and twenty-three representatives of the French settler population; the Tunisian section, by contrast, contained only eighteen representatives.[69] Because of the disparity between the numbers of French and Tunisian representatives, the 1922 reform ultimately did little to undermine the nationalist movement.

Of the two sections of the Grand conseil, the Tunisian section generated the most controversy and as a result has received the most attention from historians studying the 1922 political reforms.[70] On one side of the debate were the French settlers, who objected to the very idea of Tunisian participation in government. The fact that there were more than twice as many French representatives as there were Tunisian representatives did little to mollify them. At the other end of the spectrum were Tunisian nationalists, who believed that their minority status within the Grand conseil weakened their voice. One telegram written by some nationalists, for example, expressed anger that the residency did not even consult the Tunisian representatives before proceeding with these reforms.[71] Because of the controversy surrounding the Tunisian section, historians have assessed the 1922 reforms as part of the larger trajectory of nationalist unrest in Tunisia that culminated in independence in 1956. The French section of the Grand conseil, however, has received less attention in historical studies, because its formation generated less controversy than its Tunisian counterpart and its history was therefore greatly overshadowed by the controversy surrounding the Tunisian section.

Though less controversial than the Tunisian section, the formation of the French section of the Grand conseil sparked some debate within the French population, dividing settlers between supporters and opponents of what became known as the *formule*. This conflict centered on the fact that within the French section there were two types of representatives: representatives of the French colony for whom any male citizen and resident could vote, and representatives of the economic interests elected solely by those citizens exercising the profession in question. The residency organized the French section this way because of some underlying frustrations with universal male suffrage as it existed in France. In a report to the Ministry of Foreign Affairs, French officials explained that universal male suffrage was more an expression of class rivalries than economic interests, something they wished to avoid in Tunisia.[72] To prioritize economic interests, therefore, the *formule* was designed to take into account the composition of the French population and give greater electoral weight to settlers working in professions of value to the residency. Of particular concern was the fact that bureaucrats represented 25.2 percent of the French population of Tunisia and greatly outnumbered agricultural workers, who represented only 12.3 percent of the population.[73] As "bureaucrats, railroad men, etc. represent the majority of people and [only] minority interests," the residency sought to give "settlers and shopkeepers a level of influence consistent with the large role that they take in the *mise en valeur* of the Protectorate."[74] What some members of the French community found objectionable was that in this system of representation voters were not all created equal; the opinions of those who contributed to the prosperity of the colony by working in agriculture or business were more important and valuable than the opinions of bureaucrats or those of the working class. The communists were among the most vocal opponents of the *formule*, arguing against the inequality they saw in this system that accorded greater influence to some voters and interests over others.[75] As the communists' criticisms of the *formule* suggest, French officials in Tunisia did not succeed fully in their attempts to establish a method of voting devoid of class rivalries.

By opening the door to limited female enfranchisement, the formation of the French section of the Grand conseil represented a departure from the metropole, where the right to vote was defined as a male prerogative. One place where some French women could vote was in elections for the twenty-one representatives of the economic chambers of the Grand conseil; this was provided that they met the same professional eligibility requirements as men.[76] To be eligible to vote in these elections, individuals had to be at least twenty-five years of age, have resided in the colony for at least six months, and had to practice one of the agricultural, mining, or business professions represented by the economic chambers. Though the possibility for women's political participation existed, relatively few women actually voted under these circumstances. For instance, in 1923, there were 371 people listed as registered voters for the agricultural chamber, but of these only 3 were women.[77] The most likely reason for this relates to the distinctions that were made between work recognized as a "profession" and other types of labor. In the case of elections to the chamber representing mining interests, for example, "exercising a profession" was defined as owning a mining operation, holding a permit for mining, or working as an engineer or administrator in a mining operation. Consequently, in the case of a family-owned enterprise, a married woman working with her husband in various capacities in the family business would not be officially recognized as actually exercising that particular profession. This is because the property would be in her husband's name, something that would give him the requisite professional identity that would be the basis of his political rights; the wife's labor, on the other hand, distinct from property ownership, generally unsalaried, and probably considered informal, would not qualify her as an "administrator" or another such profession linked with this particular economic interest. Because voting rights for these chambers were decided on the basis of work and profession, and because women's labor in Tunisia, as in France, was generally not recognized or understood in the same way as that of a man, relatively few women were able to vote in these elections, despite officials' statements granting women the right to vote on an equal basis with men. Furthermore, although women were able to elect representatives for the economic chambers under certain circumstances, they were not permitted to run for office.[78]

Elections to the chamber's twenty-three representatives of the settler population also enabled a small number of women to vote under limited circumstances. Elections for this chamber were by familial suffrage and in this way also represented a departure from the metropolitan tradition of universal male suffrage. Article thirty-two of the decree stipulated:

> In addition to his personal right, the head of the family exercises a right to a supplemental vote for his minor children of both sexes whether legitimate or illegitimate, if the number is at least equal to four. In the event of death, legal incapacity or the presumed or declared judicial absence of the head of the family, the complementary right of suffrage is exercised by the legal civil representative of the aforementioned minors. The right of supplementary vote is fixed each year at the moment at which electoral lists are established. These lists must mention the name and age of the minors for whom the supplemental vote exists.[79]

This version of familial suffrage combined aspects of both the Lemire and Roulleaux-Dugage models advocated by pronatalists in the metropole. On the one hand, familial suffrage in Tunisia was similar to Lemire's model in its stipulation that heads of households cast one supplemental vote on behalf of the family as opposed to multiple supplemental votes on a per-child basis. Yet in logic and purpose this version of familial suffrage resembled more closely the Roulleaux-Dugage model. In one document detailing the functioning of this elected body, the author explained that the right to a supplemental vote did not inherently belong to the father. Rather, the person exercising the supplemental vote was simply the head of household, which could just as easily be the mother or another legal guardian.[80] With this version of familial suffrage, therefore, the purpose was not solely to elevate the political status of the *père de famille*; the purpose was to extend greater representation to large families through the political participation of the head of household, whether male or female.

Even though women were by and large excluded from participating in the elections for the settler representatives, familial suffrage offered women the possibility of casting the supplemental vote as widows or legal representatives in the absence of a male head of household. The law made it clear that in these circumstances a woman was not vot-

VOTING FOR THE FAMILY

ing as an individual, thus casting a ballot with her own interests in mind, but rather as a representative, therefore casting a ballot to represent the children under her care. Yet such distinctions were merely symbolic; once given a ballot, a woman was free to vote in whatever manner she saw fit, whether with her own interests in mind or those of her children. The right of women to vote under these circumstances continued to be included in later decrees reforming the Grand conseil. Furthermore, the lists of registered voters for the protectorate reveal that a small number of women took advantage of the opportunity that familial suffrage represented and registered to vote. In 1928, for example, nine French women exercised this supplemental vote.[81] Five of these women were widowed mothers, and the other four women were legal guardians of the children on whose behalf they voted.[82] It should be pointed out that in these cases the woman only cast a single vote, representing her children, and did not receive a vote to represent herself as head of household. Because a man who was eligible for the family vote was allowed to cast two votes, one for himself and one for his children, there was an obvious inequality between those large families represented by a woman and those headed by a man.

The colonial context and French officials' perceptions of the Muslim family played an important role in their decision to adopt a model of familial suffrage that would offer only very limited political participation to women. Like many Europeans, French officials during this period viewed the status of women as indicative of a society's level of civilization.[83] This was particularly true in North Africa, where French visitors and officials displayed a mixture of disapproval of and fascination with Muslim cultural practices. French observers imagined Muslim women as oppressed, scorned by their husbands, and completely inaccessible, as they were either sequestered or veiled.[84] While this assessment was erroneous in a number of ways, it prompted some feminists to assert that French authorities should civilize gender relations in the empire by bringing the Muslim family under French law.[85] Colonial authorities, however, had no interest in attempting to abolish such practices as polygamy and child marriage, and they maintained a policy of nonintervention. Concerning French rule in Morocco, for example, Lyautey asserted that France should "respect the morals and private lives of the natives [and] also respect the existing hierarchies and powers."[86] This policy of nonintervention in North Africa stood in stark contrast to the policies of French officials in Madagascar and French West Africa, who sought to reform family life in order to raise the birthrate.[87] One factor that distinguished French policies in North Africa from those implemented elsewhere in the empire was the perception that North African families were prolific; officials lacked the same types of economic motivations for introducing pronatalist reforms as did their counterparts in Madagascar.[88] More significant was the French perception that Muslims were highly protective of their traditions and impervious to outside influences. Viewing Islam as immutable in this way, French officials believed that attempts to reform the Muslim family would have been not only futile but also dangerous. They did not want to alienate those Muslim elites who collaborated with colonial authorities and made indirect rule possible.

The belief that Islam defined cultural practices in Tunisia and that offending Muslim sensibilities could potentially weaken French rule in the protectorate made officials particularly sensitive about how the Muslim population viewed French women. This perception had an impact on whether it would be wise to extend voting rights to women as part of the family vote. Some archival evidence suggests that officials considered the possibility of adopting a version of familial suffrage that would enable women to vote on their own behalf, consistent with the model Roulleaux-Dugage proposed in 1920.[89] Because this model of suffrage would simultaneously augment the voting rights of some men, the extension of voting rights to women under this formula should not be misconstrued as equal voting rights for women, however. One document explained that ultimately the residency chose not to include women's suffrage as part of the family vote partly out of certain "prejudices" against the idea and partly because extending political rights to women, no matter how limited, could compromise French colonial rule. "In Tunisia, the natives would look unfavorably upon any interference, even indirectly, of the weaker French sex in the leadership of the country."[90]

In this way, officials expressed the fear that allowing women to participate actively in the government would make the French government appear weak, possibly even effeminate, and suggested that colonial subjects would resist its authority.[91] This same official went on to write that the "interference" of French women in political affairs would further confirm the colonial subjects in their belief that the French government was liable to being influenced by the devil, as opposed to "the clear and just inspirations of Allah."[92] It is unclear how officials thought the Tunisian population would react to the small number of women who were eligible to vote in elections for the economic section and those eligible to exercise the supplemental vote for representatives of the French colony. It is possible that because such women were few in number, authorities assumed that their participation would go largely unnoticed by the colonial subjects. What is clear, however, is that the residency either considered full voting rights for women to be too controversial in a colonial setting or was willing to use perceived Tunisian cultural norms as an excuse to refuse women the vote. It should be noted, moreover, that Tunisian women were specifically excluded from voting in the elections for the economic chambers.[93]

Although nationalist upheaval played a significant role in Saint's decision to pursue political reforms in 1922, a significant demographic imbalance between French and Italian settlers was also an important factor in the decision to introduce familial suffrage as part of these reforms. Unlike in Algeria, where the European population was composed of roughly equal numbers of French citizens and foreigners, in Tunisia French settlers were very much in the minority. For example, when Tunisia first became a French protectorate, in 1881, there were 1.5 million people, of whom 20,000 were European settlers.[94] This number included 11,000 Italians, 7,000 Maltese, and only 708 French settlers.[95] While the French population grew considerably after the establishment of the protectorate, French settlers remained in the minority. In 1911, for example, there were 88,000 Italian settlers compared to 46,000 French settlers.[96] French authorities alleged that the Great War added to this demographic imbalance as the French settlers enlisted in the army in far greater numbers than did the Italians. One consequence of this was that the Italian population continued to grow during the war years and began to encroach on French farmland and industries while French men were away fighting in the war.[97] In the aftermath of the war, therefore, the residency introduced the decree of November 8, 1921, mandating that children born in Tunisia to foreign citizens (with the exception of Italians) also born in Tunisia would have French citizenship.[98] This decree, which mimicked the law enacted in France in 1889, was specifically intended to increase the number of "French" settlers in order to counterbalance the Italian population. About 5,000 Maltese settlers immediately became naturalized as a result of this decree, much to the dismay of the British government.[99] Taking office shortly after the passage of this decree, Saint sought to build on his predecessor's efforts by exploring the possibility of recruiting Polish immigrants for settlement in Tunisia, plans that do not appear to have been put into action.[100] By 1931 the French population roughly equaled that of the Italians, due in large part to naturalization.[101] Yet even as the numbers began to improve, concerns about the size of the Italian population remained as poignant in the 1930s as in the 1920s.

Despite the growth of the French population, therefore, officials throughout the interwar period worried that the Italian population constituted a separate and unassimilated community. This was particularly worrisome given that French officials knew Italy had never fully relinquished its claims on the protectorate. It was not until 1896 that Italy recognized Tunisia as a French protectorate, and it only agreed to this in exchange for a series of privileges for Italian citizens residing in Tunisia.[102] These privileges included commercial advantages and the right to establish Italian schools and hospitals.[103] In response, French officials carefully monitored Italian newspapers, clergy, and other perceived disseminators of Italian nationalism.[104] When Benito Mussolini became prime minister of Italy in 1922, soon after Resident-General Saint's reforms, concerns about Italian nationalism and the potential expansion of Italy into North Africa appeared all the more pressing. Shortly after taking power, Mussolini made his imperial ambitions known, ambitions that included the ancient Roman colonies in North Africa and rejecting the treaty of 1896.[105] In response to these pressures, Saint carefully monitored numbers of Italian naturalizations and sought to encourage more Italians to become French citizens, using French schools as recruiting centers.[106] He proposed free tuition, books, and supplies as a way to draw students away from Italian schools, and he also suggested preferential employment treatment for Italians who agreed to become French citizens.[107] Despite all these efforts, the Italian population continued to be demographically strong in the 1920s, an advantage that, according to William Shorrock, the Italian government sought to exploit. Throughout this period, fascist leaders traveled to Tunisia and encouraged Italians to maintain their identities. This included lectures and newspapers for adults and literary clubs, free schoolbooks, and sponsored trips to Italy for children.[108] Rebellious youth wore fascist medals, and Italians clandestinely posted portraits of Il Duce in the streets, in defiance of French decrees forbidding the practice.[109]

Thus, while French pronatalists in the metropole and French officials in Tunisia shared similar concerns about French birthrates in the 1920s, the demographic situation appeared to be even more pressing in Tunisia than in France. As the French population continued to dominate in France and foreign immigrants remained a minority, the consequences of depopulation appeared to be mostly long-term, despite the heightened concern about immigration and low birthrates. By contrast, in Tunisia, demographic concerns were immediate and the threat of losing the protectorate to Italy was believed to be imminent. Therefore, the fact that the French of Tunisia were outnumbered by both Italians and colonial subjects further explains why familial suffrage was successfully implemented in Tunisia, despite its political failure in France. Along these lines, one French official wrote that it was essential that they establish in Tunisia a voting system that would "encourage French settlement."[110] This same official explained that the *famille nombreuse* was central to French settlement and the financial future of the colony: "In Tunisia, where there are so many pressing motives for wanting to increase the numbers of French people, large families deserve to be prominent, more than is the case anywhere else."[111] Hence it is clear that when making the decision to include familial suffrage in the 1922 reforms, the residency connected familial suffrage with concerns about the strength of the French settler population vis-à-vis other populations in Tunisia.

The fact that familial suffrage made its debut in Tunisia without ever being introduced in France can be partly explained by some fundamental differences between the political systems of the metropole and the protectorate. When Saint implemented familial suffrage in 1922, he was neither replacing an established tradition of universal manhood suffrage nor controversially redefining the democratic process. In France, by contrast, the suggestion that familial suffrage undermined the egalitarian principles on which the Republic was based was one of the main reasons why its opponents remained loyal to universal manhood suffrage and could not be swayed by pronatalists' arguments. Furthermore, despite gaining the support of some key members of the French government, familial suffrage ultimately failed in France because of parliamentary opposition. This particular obstacle was nonexistent in Tunisia because of the absence of a parliament or analogous elected body, and the resident-general did not need the support of the voting population in order to implement his reforms.

Although Lucien Saint was responsible for introducing familial suffrage in Tunisia, it is not entirely clear if he supported this method of voting prior to arriving in Tunisia or if his decision to introduce the reform was entirely motivated by the unique political and demographic situation of the protectorate. There is no evidence to suggest that he was either involved with the pronatalist movement or an outspoken proponent of familial suffrage prior to assuming the position of resident-general of Tunisia. It is clear, however, that upon arrival he demonstrated a strong commitment to encouraging French settlement, an objective that in Tunisia was considered to be closely connected to pronatalist policies. It is therefore likely that his decision to implement the reform was influenced largely by the demographic pressures in the colony. There is also evidence to suggest that Saint may have been influenced by the opinions of French settlers in Tunisia. Even prior to his arrival, there had been significant dissatisfaction with the method of

VOTING FOR THE FAMILY

voting and representation within the Conférence consultative, something that had compelled representatives of the conference to appeal to the Ministry of Foreign Affairs directly.[112] Amid this desire for political reform, a large contingent of settler familialists in the protectorate appealed to both Saint and his predecessors for the establishment of familial suffrage.[113] That Saint introduced the reform requested by settler familialists most likely resulted from the combination of pressing concerns that shaped Tunisian political life in 1922. The introduction of familial suffrage in Tunisia in 1922 was therefore the result of a combination of heightened postwar concerns about Tunisian nationalism and the size of the Italian population, preexisting frustrations with the method of representation within the Conférence consultative, and the belief that prioritizing the *famille nombreuse* was the only way to maintain French authority within the protectorate.

Théodore Steeg and Political Reform in Morocco

A late addition to the French empire, Morocco became a French protectorate in 1912 under the leadership of Resident-General Louis-Hubert Lyautey. Often regarded as a disciple of Gallieni, Lyautey served under the general in Indochina and Madagascar and was credited with completing the pacification of southern Madagascar in 1902. As resident-general of Morocco between 1912 and 1925, Lyautey demonstrated his commitment to indirect rule, believing that French influence would be strengthened by respecting the local conditions and maintaining preexisting hierarchies.[114] Like the Tunisian bey, therefore, the Moroccan sultan remained nominally in power as the sovereign of the Moroccan state, and the preexisting bureaucracy likewise remained intact. However, in practice the sultan was reduced to the status of a figurehead and lost much of his original influence. French officials gradually extended their authority over the Moroccan bureaucracy, reducing the importance of the Moroccan officials left in place.[115]

Unlike colonial administrators in other parts of the empire, Lyautey was ambivalent about large-scale French migration to Morocco, believing that large businesses, as opposed to small farmers, were more likely to cooperate with the government of the protectorate.[116] Despite this lack of encouragement, European settlers migrated to the protectorate in large numbers and became increasingly vocal in demanding political representation.[117] In response, Lyautey created a Conseil du gouvernement (Council of Government) in 1919 that closely resembled the Conférence consultative in Tunisia at that time. The Conseil du gouvernement was composed of representatives from the chambers of commerce and agriculture as well as the municipalities. Like the Conférence consultative in Tunisia, the Moroccan Conseil du gouvernement lacked the ability to enact legislation or make budgetary decisions; its role was solely advisory.[118]

Ultimately, France's intervention in the Rif War, a joint Franco-Spanish operation to pacify their respective protectorates in Morocco and end Mohammed Abd el-Krim el Khattabi's rebellion, led to Lyautey's resignation as resident-general of Morocco.[119] Of the colonial conflicts in which France was engaged during the interwar period, the Rif War was perhaps the most demanding, requiring 100,000 French and Algerian soldiers, of whom 2,500 were killed defending the northern boundary of France's Moroccan protectorate.[120] Because this military operation occurred in 1925, only a few years after the conclusion of World War I, France's participation was very unpopular in the metropole, and the French government made clear that the residency was to avoid such military entanglements in the future. In such a political climate, Théodore Steeg, a civilian, was an ideal choice as Lyautey's successor. Born into a political family, Steeg began his career as a philosophy professor before entering public life and being elected to parliament as a radical socialist.[121] From there he went on to have a number of cabinet positions in France, including minister of public education and minister of the interior, before serving as governor-general of Algeria from 1921 to 1925.[122] Unlike Lyautey, who often ignored directions from Paris and acted on his own instincts, Steeg showed little inclination for military expansion during his term as resident-general of Morocco from 1925 to 1929.[123]

The transition from Lyautey to Steeg signified a major shift in priorities that ultimately led to the establishment of familial suffrage in Morocco. Steeg emphasized that the military phase of French Morocco was over and sought to maintain an image of stability in the interest of attracting investors and settlers.[124] One major distinction between Steeg and Lyautey is that Steeg wanted to attract settlers to the protectorate and demonstrated far greater support for their demands.[125] In 1926 he added a third chamber to the Conseil du gouvernement to represent those French citizens who were not farmers, businessmen, or industrialists and who had been previously unrepresented.[126] This was a slightly controversial move, as some representatives of the colony's economic interests did not feel that the views of other French settlers were as important as their own and worried that their addition to political life would complicate the work of the assembly. Steeg responded to this criticism in 1928 by stating that "the life of a State does not reside in this or that social category; it resides in the harmony of the forces that each category represents."[127] Representatives to this third chamber of the Conseil du gouvernement were elected by familial suffrage. In many ways, this form of familial suffrage resembled that enacted by Lucien Saint in Tunisia. The language of the two decrees is virtually identical, suggesting that Steeg was not only aware of what Saint had initiated but was sufficiently satisfied with how familial suffrage had functioned in Tunisia to implement similar legislation in Morocco. Article 22 of chapter 5 of the October 13, 1926, residential decree stipulated:

> In addition to his personal right, the head of the family exercises the right to a supplemental vote for his minor children of both sexes, legitimate or recognized illegitimate, if the number of these minor children is at least equal to four. In the event of death, legal incapacity or the presumed or declared judicial absence of the head of household, the complementary right of suffrage is exercised by the legal representative of the aforementioned minors. The right to the supplemental vote is fixed each year at the moment at which electoral lists are established. The lists, established as stipulated in chapter three of this document, must include the name and age of the minors giving the right to a supplemental vote.[128]

One key difference between the 1922 decree in Tunisia and that of 1926 in Morocco is that women were specifically excluded from voting rights in Morocco. Although article 22 of chapter 5 does not indicate whether or not a woman could exercise the supplemental vote as a legal representative of the children following the death of the father, article 3 of chapter 2 clearly states that voters must be "French citizens at least 21 years of age, of masculine sex."[129] By contrast Tunisia's 1922 decree did not specifically exclude women, and subsequent interpretations of it allowed for the limited women's voting rights outlined earlier. In accounting for this distinction between the two protectorates, it is important to recognize that Steeg's decision to design the reform in a way that excluded women is not surprising, as it was consistent with the tradition of male suffrage in France.

Steeg's reasons for implementing familial suffrage as part of his reforms of the Conseil du gouvernement in 1926 remain somewhat unclear. Like Tunisia, Morocco had a large population of European foreigners. According to Deputy André Fribourg, for example, in 1921 the city of Casablanca had 35,283 Europeans, of which 19,098 were French settlers; the Spanish were the second-largest settler population, with 8,121.[130] While the demographic imbalance between French settlers and European foreigners was by no means as extreme in Morocco as it was in Tunisia, the presence of a large Spanish population did generate concerns about the strength of French influence. Moreover, as was the case in both Algeria and Tunisia, the European settlers as a group represented only a small minority of the total population of the protectorate. Even though the number of European settlers rose by 42 percent under Steeg's leadership, they still only amounted to 4 percent of the total population in 1937.[131] Like French officials in Tunisia and Algeria, officials in Morocco equated the future of French rule with the success of colonial settlement endeavors.[132] Attempting to increase the birthrate with familial suffrage was consistent with the larger goals of establishing a large French population that would surpass that of the Spanish settlers and the colonized Moroccans.

The fact that Steeg had established himself as a supporter of the pronatalist movement prior to his arrival in Morocco suggests that his decision to implement familial suffrage was as much a response to the demographic situation in the metropole as it was a response to the exigencies of colonial rule. While a radical socialist member of the Chamber of Deputies in 1909, Steeg published an article titled "Against Depopulation: Assistance to Large Families," in which he outlined the causes of depopulation and argued that the most significant factor was poverty.[133] Steeg emphasized that the task facing the French government was addressing poverty and making it genuinely possible to support multiple children on a modest income. He detailed, further, a series of proposed laws on assistance to needy and large families that had been debated in parliament between 1905 and 1909 and argued that none of these debates had led to any real reforms. Responding to these legislative failures, Steeg expressed his frustration with the parliamentary process and the slow pace with which legislators introduced measures that would help large families and encourage population growth.

It is also evident that Steeg was in direct contact with the pronatalist movement prior to his departure to North Africa. While minister of the interior in 1920, Steeg approved the creation of a national mother's day in France, a holiday that had been functioning on a local and private level for a number of years. This decision came as a result of his correspondence with Jacques Bertillon, president of the Alliance nationale, who requested the creation of this holiday. Fully supporting their objectives, Steeg authorized the Alliance nationale to organize the event.[134]

These two examples indicate that when Steeg became resident-general of Morocco in 1926 he was already sympathetic to the pronatalist cause and that his concerns about French depopulation were not specific to the demographic issues of the protectorate; in fact, these concerns had already been shaped by his political career in the metropole. It is likely that a politician who in 1909 was interested in improving the welfare of large families, concerned about depopulation, and frustrated with the failure of the French parliament to move quickly enough to address these concerns would have been exactly the sort of politician who would have been receptive to the alternative solution that pronatalists presented with familial suffrage in the 1920s. Becoming resident-general of Morocco presented Steeg with the opportunity to implement familial suffrage without being reliant on parliamentary support, something that was impossible in the metropole at this time for the reasons Steeg outlined in his 1909 article. Implementing familial suffrage therefore addressed Steeg's preexisting concerns about the demographic strength of the French population generally as well as his objective of extending French influence in Morocco through large-scale French settlement.

The Metropolitan Response

Colonial officials and metropolitan pronatalists were unanimous in their belief that the establishment of familial suffrage in Tunisia and Morocco was a sign of progress that put the protectorates ahead of the metropole in the fight against depopulation. In Tunisia, colonial officials were well aware of pronatalist campaigns in the metropole and, believing that they had surpassed the metropole in this regard, boasted about their achievements. One official wrote that by adopting familial suffrage, Tunisia had "moved ahead of France."[135] Another official, explaining the purpose of familial suffrage in Tunisia, emphasized that in matters of innovation Tunisia had the honor of "showing the Metropole the way."[136] Although pronatalists in the metropole applauded the establishment of familial suffrage in both Tunisia and Morocco, they showed more interest in the Tunisian example; this was due mostly to the fact that the Tunisian example predated that of Morocco.

The metropolitan response to developments in Tunisia was immediate. Auguste Isaac, president of the familialist organization La plus grande famille and president of the Comité permanent de la natalité, immediately wrote to Lucien Saint praising his initiative; this letter was later published in a Tunisian newspaper, Dépêche tunisienne, on July 28, 1922, two weeks after the passage of the decree.[137] French pronatalist organizations, both national and regional, announced in their journals the success of their political platform in Tunisia, explaining to their readers exactly how familial suffrage would function in

Tunisia.[138] Metropolitan pronatalists expressed hope that the colonial precedent would strengthen their own attempts at suffrage reform in France. Others communicated their resentment that a protectorate should be more progressive than metropolitan France. One article, for example, asserted that what was good enough for the protectorate should also have been good enough for the metropole.[139] Along similar lines, pronatalist André Toulemon expressed his hopes "that the French family in France will soon be treated as well as that in Tunisia."[140] He concluded that the metropolitan idea of familial suffrage was so popular in France that it had made its way to North Africa, thus suggesting that Saint had drawn on French political debates.

Pronatalists frequently cited the adoption of familial suffrage in Tunisia and Morocco in order to bolster their own arguments for its establishment in France. They emphasized, somewhat vaguely, that familial suffrage was functioning well in Tunisia and producing good results.[141] While familial suffrage did function well enough to be upheld by decrees following that of July 1922, it is clear that its introduction complicated the voting process in Tunisia. The names of individuals entitled to a supplemental vote appeared twice on the election registers along with the ages of the children on whose behalf they would cast the second vote. Although this was clearly laid out in the election registers and affected a large number of people, some election officials were nevertheless confused when individuals cast more than one ballot. For example, after the April 15, 1928, elections, at the meeting of the committee in charge of voting procedures, there was some confusion as to why the number of votes cast exceeded the number of registered voters.[142] After some telephone calls, the commission discovered that those extra votes were most likely supplemental familial votes. There were also problems with voters wanting to cast a second vote without realizing that they needed to be preregistered for two votes. For example, a father of four voted twice even though there was only one line listed for him on the register of voters. The commission decided in this case to subtract one vote from the total number and to also take away one vote from each of the elected candidates; this did not affect the outcome of the election.[143]

French pronatalists corresponded regularly with settler representatives in the Grand conseil, staying apprised of developments in the protectorate. For instance, when the Grand conseil in 1923 discussed their success in continuing the family allowance for the orphans of deceased functionaries, representative Jean Paoli made reference to what the metropolitan familialists had to say on the matter: "We admire with what wisdom and decisiveness M. Lucien Saint is building a family policy for the French colony in Tunisia, something that we have hardly instituted in France, and we hope that it won't be much longer before this legislation is introduced in the Metropole."[144] Pronatalists in France were particularly interested in any pronatalist legislation introduced in the colony, seeing each new policy relating to family life in Tunisia as evidence that numerous pronatalist measures inevitably followed the introduction of familial suffrage. For example, one article in the *Revue de la plus grande famille* discussed a decree of October 25, 1922, that granted discounts on school tuition to large French families in the protectorate.[145] The author of this article argued that there was nothing coincidental about the timing of this development; "the French of Tunisia, who were the first to benefit from plural suffrage for fathers, are also the first to have obtained regular exonerations from school fees."[146] Consistent with this idea, at the December 30, 1922, meeting the Grand conseil discussed ten proposals relating to the *famille nombreuse*.[147] While it is difficult to determine whether or not the institution of familial suffrage made the Grand conseil more inclined to pursue pronatalist reforms, metropolitan pronatalists chose to conclude that a major shift had taken place in Tunisian political life. Elected by familial suffrage, representatives in the Grand conseil were now more inclined to prioritize large families and fathers. To pronatalists, this change needed to take place in France with the adoption of familial suffrage before they could reasonably expect to see success in implementing pronatalist legislation.

Based on the Tunisian and Moroccan examples, metropolitan pronatalists concluded that they would see little progress in this regard unless French leaders set aside political differences and recognized that depopulation was an issue of national importance that transcended political divisions. In 1939 pronatalist Paul Haury wrote that Lucien Saint and Théodore Steeg approached the issue of familial suffrage from two very different political orientations.[148] Steeg was a radical and Saint was somewhat conservative.[149] Yet as these two residents-general had demonstrated, political divisions became irrelevant when faced with a national crisis. Both men had done what was necessary to protect French interests and support large French families by implementing virtually identical versions of familial suffrage. To pronatalists, therefore, the example set in North Africa revealed that addressing depopulation through suffrage reform transcended the political divisions and debates to which it was subjected in the metropole. Pronatalists hoped that the example set by Saint and Steeg in the empire would strengthen their campaign in France.

In contrast to what was seen in the pronatalist press, among feminists the establishment of familial suffrage in Tunisia and Morocco appears to have gone unnoticed. Although French feminists were certainly aware of pronatalist support for familial suffrage, and in some cases linked this reform to their own demands for women's suffrage, events in North Africa did not seem to influence their stance on this issue. For instance, when arguing for a form of the familial vote that would include a provision for women's suffrage, Marguerite de Witt–Schlumberger did not mention North Africa or demonstrate any awareness that familial suffrage existed in Tunisia.[150] Even more striking is the apparent absence of this topic in French women's and feminist publications in Algeria. One such publication, *La femme algérienne*, a 1930s journal published by the group Aide familiale de l'union féminine civique et sociale d'Algérie, had a number of articles on the topic of women's suffrage and made clear their support for familial suffrage.[151] In contrast to de Witt–Schlumberger, this organization was more firmly committed to this reform, as evidenced by their willingness to concede greater representation to the husband within the family in cases where there were an uneven number of votes.[152] Still, articles addressing this topic in *La femme algérienne* made no mention of the precedent set in Tunisia and Morocco. It is possible that the reason for feminists' silence on this topic is that to feminists, whether in Algeria or in France, obtaining suffrage for women was the primary consideration. Although some of them may have been inclined to accept familial suffrage as part of such a reform, it was of secondary importance to their larger objectives of obtaining voting rights for all French women. As we have seen, the reform in Morocco included no provision for women's suffrage and that in Tunisia only enabled a small number of women to vote, something that fell very short of these feminists' goal of equal voting rights. For these reasons, feminists probably did not consider the form of familial suffrage introduced in these protectorates particularly noteworthy. Pronatalists, on the other hand, approached suffrage reform from a different perspective than feminists and generally rejected any idea of women's suffrage separate from familial suffrage. As women's suffrage was of secondary importance to pronatalists, therefore, they embraced developments in Tunisia and Morocco despite the fact that this was a form of familial suffrage that denied voting rights to most French women in the protectorates.

Conclusion

The death and destruction of the Great War appeared to confirm pronatalists' worst fears; France's declining birthrate prior to the war had left the nation vulnerable to invasion, and the disappearance of an entire generation of young men crippled the nation's ability to reestablish a healthy birthrate in the 1920s. The increasingly desperate tone of pronatalist propaganda in the 1920s revealed a sense of urgency to resolve the depopulation crisis by whatever means possible, including redefining the democratic process through the introduction of familial suffrage. Pronatalists insisted that if individualism continued to define elections, and by extension parliamentary debate, the *famille nombreuse* would remain an abnormality in French society and birthrates would continue to decline.

Pronatalists' campaigns to replace universal manhood suffrage with familial suffrage in the 1920s met with mixed success. On the one hand, the idea of familial suffrage prior to the twentieth century was fairly obscure and primarily associated with reactionary political factions, such as the monarchist faction in parliament in the 1870s. Yet by the 1920s pronatalists had successfully moved this idea into the mainstream and convinced many prominent politicians of its national importance by tapping into the general hysteria concerning the birthrate that characterized this period. The effectiveness of the pronatalist movement in convincing the French parliament of the need for suffrage reform was particularly evident when, in December 1923, the Chamber of Deputies approved Roulleaux-Dugage's proposal to institute familial suffrage.

Yet this initial success proved short-lived. Familial suffrage was never adopted in France, despite the influence of pronatalists' campaigns and propaganda. Though sympathetic to pronatalist concerns, many people believed that familial suffrage would undermine the egalitarian ideals on which the Republic was based; or they believed that it was possible to address depopulation by working through the existing political system; or they simply emphasized that the idea of plural suffrage was too complicated to implement effectively. The familial suffrage campaign also emerged at a time when demands for women's suffrage were more powerful than ever before; in this context, the failure of pronatalists to align the familial suffrage campaign with that of women's suffrage ultimately made their own arguments less compelling.

Though metropolitan in origin, the idea of familial suffrage ultimately saw far greater success in France's North African protectorates than in France. The fact that familial suffrage was adopted in Tunisia and Morocco but not in France can be attributed in large part to the political organization of the protectorates. Like Gallieni in Madagascar, Residents-General Saint and Steeg were free to implement decrees as they saw fit without being slowed by parliamentary debate or the need to address criticisms that familial suffrage undermined the democratic process. Furthermore, demographic concerns were different in the protectorates than in France. In Tunisia, the issue of the French birthrate and its impact on colonial settlement endeavors was seen as particularly acute given the large Italian population and Italy's imperial ambitions. French officials in Tunisia saw depopulation as an immediate problem; French pronatalists in France had difficulty convincing the French government that the threat of depopulation had short-term consequences requiring their immediate attention. In Morocco the demographic situation resembled more closely that of Algeria than that of Tunisia. The French population constituted a slight majority of European settlers, and therefore, while significant, concerns about the assimilation of the foreign population were therefore less severe than was the case in Tunisia. In this case it is evident that when adopting familial suffrage, Resident-General Steeg was influenced both by the demographic situation in the metropole and that of North Africa. Steeg had arrived in Morocco already a partisan of pronatalist ideas, having supported and corresponded with the Alliance nationale while minister of the interior and expressed dissatisfaction with parliament's failure to implement pronatalist reforms. His sympathies with pronatalist demands as well as his objective of encouraging settler colonialism made Steeg particularly interested in introducing familial suffrage in Morocco.

The introduction of familial suffrage in Morocco and Tunisia reveals how pronatalist objectives could be more powerful and politically expedient in the colonial context. It was for this reason that events in North Africa were relevant to metropolitan pronatalists who studied the transformations under way in Tunisia and Morocco. On the one hand they expressed some frustration that a metropolitan idea would see greater success in North Africa than in France and resentment that French families in the protectorates received better treatment than in France. Simultaneously, they viewed the establishment of familial suffrage in North Africa as the realization of their political campaign and a powerful precedent. Similar to their responses to Gallieni's reforms in Madagascar, therefore, pronatalists interpreted the introduction of familial suffrage in North Africa uncritically and overemphasized its impact. The causal link that they tried to establish between this new method of voting and the familialist reforms that soon followed is questionable given the short time frame between these events. However, the actual impact of these reforms on the priorities of the residency and, ultimately, the French settler birthrate in Tunisia and Morocco was ultimately less important to metropolitan observers than their symbolic value. Metropolitan pronatalists viewed these reforms as the realization of the political agenda they sought in France: a political system in which the state distinguished between male citizens on the basis of their contributions to population growth, bestowed political rights not on individuals but on family units generally headed by men, and accorded privileges to the *père de famille nombreuse* in recognition of his social importance.

FIVE

A Colonial Fountain of Youth

Family Rights, Pronatalism, and Settler Politics in North Africa

French social life must be organized in such a way that
it be very advantageous to have many children and
extremely costly to have hardly any.

—LA LIGUE DES FAMILLES NOMBREUSES
FRANÇAISES D'ALGÉRIE, 1927

In a speech he gave in Algeria in 1907, Lyautey described North
Africa as a vast domain offering France what the "*le Far West*" had
offered Americans: energy, youthfulness, and fecundity.[1] His optimism, rarely seen in contemporary assessments of the metropolitan
population, echoed the views of French pronatalists, who, beginning in
the late nineteenth century, believed that establishing and maintaining
settler colonies would aid their efforts to reduce demographic decline.
Following the Great War, however, pronatalists became increasingly
concerned that the settler population in North Africa had ceased to
be as prolific as before and was in the throes of a depopulation crisis not unlike the metropole's. It was in the context of North Africa's
"French depopulation crisis" that French settlers in Algeria, Morocco,
and Tunisia established familialist organizations with the express
purpose of securing state support for the settler *famille nombreuse*.

On the one hand, the existence of such a movement represented
the extension of metropolitan familialist and pronatalist ideologies
into the empire. However, most of these settler organizations oper-
ated independently of their metropolitan counterparts and evolved

out of specifically colonial concerns and influences. Although both groups identified many of the same obstacles to achieving adequate population growth, settlers asserted that their crisis was more pressing than that faced by the metropolitan French. First, settlers feared that their population was growing too slowly relative to that of other European settlers and colonial subjects. In the context of rising nationalism among colonial subjects, the French population's failure to compete demographically with rival populations appeared all the more acute. Second, while the French government after the Great War was increasingly willing to accept the idea that the family, as a unit, had rights distinct from those of individuals and to grant financial support accordingly, these newly acquired benefits, which familialists in both France and the empire considered fundamental rights, were not always extended to the empire. Settler familialists consequently presented the French government's failure to support and uphold the rights of the settler *famille nombreuse* as a major cause of demographic decline and a threat to the future of colonial rule.

This chapter explores the emergence of familialist organizations in the North African settler communities during the interwar period. Surviving archival records and collections of newspapers are incomplete, thus making a comprehensive study of this movement impossible. Despite the fragmented nature of existing sources, however, there is clear evidence of collaboration between metropolitan pronatalists and settler familialists. Settlers attended pronatalist congresses in France, and their metropolitan colleagues wrote editorials in North African newspapers and held a congress in Algeria in 1930. Pronatalist issues unique to North Africa became part of the metropolitan pronatalist agenda, and the Groupe parlementaire de protection de familles nombreuses represented the interests of settler populations in parliament.

This collaboration marked a shift in metropolitan pronatalist visions of empire. Whereas earlier pronatalist arguments in favor of colonial settlement had been premised on the idea that France had only to export population to the empire in order for it to grow, by the interwar years pronatalists had come to believe that the growth of the settler population required state support. Although the settler depopulation crisis would seem to suggest the demise of the myth of the prolific settler that had followed Ricoux's research decades earlier, settlers and pronatalists alike continued to assert that North Africa was essential to France's demographic strength. That the settler population was exhibiting a birthrate only slightly higher than that of the metropole could be attributed, they believed, to the French government's failure to develop this demographic resource adequately.

The North African Depopulation Crisis

Following World War I, settlers and colonial officials alike expressed fears that French settlers in Algeria were facing a depopulation crisis that in many ways resembled that of France. The roots of this perceived demographic crisis extended back into the nineteenth century. Despite the hope that Ricoux's study inspired in the 1880s, concerns about the size of the French population relative to other European populations and the colonial subjects persisted throughout the colonial period. As emigration from France tapered off around the turn of the century and the French population ceased to be as "youthful" as before, anxieties about the size and growth of the French settler population grew even more intense. Though stronger than that of the metropole, the settler birthrate appeared inadequate in light of the growth of rival populations in Algeria.

At the time of Ricoux's study, the French population in Algeria was greatly outnumbered by the colony's three million colonial subjects and barely constituted a majority of the colony's European population. In 1881, French settlers numbered 227,000, while European foreigners, mainly Spanish, Italian, and Maltese settlers, numbered 189,600.[2] Without the transient military population, the civilian French population numbered only 184,400 and was therefore smaller than that of the other Europeans.[3] On the one hand, officials watched the arrival of immigrants from other European countries nervously, worrying that they could challenge and jeopardize French influence in the colony. Simultaneously, as Jonathan Gosnell explains, officials saw the cultural differences between the French and other European settlers as "insignificant when compared to the greater and menacing differences between them and the Muslim populations."[4] Cultural differences aside, they clearly perceived a common white, racial identity with these other settlers. Because they were more concerned about the colonized Algerian population, therefore, officials hoped that if settlers from other European countries could be assimilated into the French population, they could strengthen France's position in the colony numerically.

The first formal efforts to absorb other European settlers into the French population were undertaken with a number of naturalization laws. Particularly effective in tipping the statistical balance was a law of 1889 that made French citizenship accessible to foreigners and automatic for children born in Algeria of foreign parents.[5] Consequently, the number of European Algerians legally defined as French grew rapidly and provided officials and experts with promising numbers with which to assess French population growth in the colony. Supporters hoped that in addition to gaining French citizenship, this population would also become "French," both culturally and linguistically. The most optimistic observers held up the United States as an example of the ease with which immigrant populations could be assimilated. The political economist Paul-Leroy Beaulieu argued in 1891 that the United States had managed to absorb its large Irish and German immigrant populations without losing its own national character, something that he believed would be equally true for French Algeria. Leroy-Beaulieu went on to argue that the process of assimilation would be furthered by such institutions as French schools, which would teach students the language, in his mind a necessary step toward making them French.[6]

In this respect, foreign settlers' assimilation in Algeria would resemble the process of cultural integration that Eugen Weber describes in France at this same time, but with one notable difference: in France the task of creating "Frenchmen" was conceived in secular terms, but in Algeria, French priests were considered an essential part of the process because they could reach the Catholic settlers from Italy and Spain.[7] Like Cardinal Lavigerie, Leroy-Beaulieu emphasized the power of French priests to unify and assimilate their devout Italian, Maltese, and Spanish parishioners by giving homilies in the French language and uniting them under one banner.[8] Ultimately, however, French priests faced competition from their Spanish counterparts who arrived in large numbers to serve the Spanish population. As one letter from a French bishop in the department of Oran makes clear, the Roman Catholic leadership in Algeria faced great difficulties in recruiting sufficient numbers of French priests to serve the entire Catholic population, both French and foreign in origin. Consequently, there were many Spanish priests in Algeria who communicated with their parishioners in Spanish and effectively hindered efforts to use Catholicism to create a unified French population.[9]

In the twentieth century, therefore, the integration of European foreigners into French-Algerian society remained incomplete. Statistician Victor Demontès, for example, took the position that the creation of additional "French" people by way of naturalization belied the demographic reality and masked a growing danger. Demontès explained that while the naturalization law could have positive benefits in France, where European foreigners represented only a small minority, in Algeria this law did nothing to make these foreigners more loyal to French rule. Demontès asserted that Algeria's foreign population was too large to assimilate and that the naturalization law of 1889 had created too many "pseudo-French" people.[10] Of all the settlers of Algeria, it was the Spanish that Demontès believed to be the greatest obstacle to the creation of a unified French population. In an 1899 article he described the Spanish population as "illiterate, lacking in foresight, destitute, the population also has crude and brutal manners. . . . They fight for the most petty reasons, see red and their anger is only satisfied by blood."[11] Their anti-Semitism and opposition to the Crémieux decree, Demontès argued, was greater than that of the French settlers, thus showing how much "they are still foreigners to our liberal and tolerant spirit and how much it is dangerous to allow them to meddle in our political life."[12] While marriages between French and Spanish citizens were fairly common, and contributed to the "fusion of Latin races," Demontès argued that the most problematic elements of the Spanish population remained outside the assimilating influence of intermarriage. Demontès analyzed Ricoux's statistics concerning the number of marriage certificates containing two signatures and found that the French generally only married those Spanish settlers with enough education to sign their names.[13] The illiterate and uneducated Spanish settlers, on the other hand, generally did not marry French settlers and had less exposure to French culture. Demontès was not alone in questioning whether naturalized settlers were "really" French. Even after World War I, officials distinguished between the "real French" and the "phony French."[14] The residents of Algeria used terms such as "Français de souche" to designate the "true French" and phrases like "fifty percent French" or "néo-Français" to designate those who were not truly French.[15] Clearly, ideas about what it meant to be French were challenged and redefined in a variety of contexts.

In addition to declaring naturalization laws to be largely a failure, Demontès produced the first study that gave a statistical validation to the more general concerns about the relative strength of the French settler population. Published in 1906, *Le peuple algérien* was both a continuation of and a response to Ricoux's 1880 study.[16] Demontès showed that, though still healthy and growing, the birthrate of the French settlers had declined over the last three decades from 37 per thousand to roughly 29.[17] This trend, Demontès argued, was only natural considering that mortality and immigration rates had also declined. The decline in mortality rates meant that elderly people now accounted for a greater proportion of the population than ever before. Because most immigrants arrived in Algeria as young adults, a decline in immigration meant a slight reduction in the number of individuals likely to have children.[18] Despite these factors, Demontès argued, the birthrate of 29 per thousand was still comparatively strong, because it placed Algeria's population ahead of the populations of France and Belgium and on equal footing with those of Britain. Demontès nevertheless questioned whether a birthrate surpassing that of the metropole was sufficient when the settler population of Algeria had such a large foreign minority with a higher birthrate than that of the French settlers.

Like Demontès, many settler familialists considered immigration from France, particularly the settlement of French families in the *bled* (the Algerian countryside), to be essential to triggering population growth. In terms that were identical to pronatalists' arguments about France's rural exodus, familialist L. Barthelet asserted that rural Algeria was losing population to the cities, where the birthrate was lower than in the rural areas.[19] Attracting settlers to the rural regions had been a persistent problem throughout the colonial period, as most arriving immigrants preferred to settle in towns and cities in the coastal areas.[20] In fact, following World War I only about 10 percent of settlers lived in rural areas.[21] In the 1920s and 1930s, when few immigrants arrived from France, there were concerns that this problem was getting worse as increasing numbers of settlers abandoned their concessions and headed to the cities. Colonial censuses confirmed this trend by revealing that between 1930 and 1950 the settler population in a number of rural regions had declined by more than 50 percent.[22] Familialists in Tunisia and Morocco expressed similar concerns as the European populations of the largest cities increased at the expense of the countryside. In the 1930s, for example, 50 percent of Tunisia's European population lived in Tunis, and in 1926, 42 percent of Morocco's European population lived in Casablanca.[23]

As settlers flocked to the coastal cities, abandoning the vast interior regions of French North Africa to the colonized populations, colonial officials demanded that the French government encourage additional French emigration.[24] The seriousness with which colonial authorities treated the issue demonstrates a significant distinction between the rural exodus in French North Africa and similar migratory trends under way in the metropole. In essence, the absence of a large settler population in the countryside working the land and generating agricultural wealth compromised French influence and, by extension, the permanence of French rule in these regions. This demographic reality, of which French settlers were well aware, stands in stark contrast to the visions of empire conveyed in pronatalist publications in the nineteenth century. Novels such as Zola's *Fécondité* presented the empire as a vast territory, practically uninhabited and simply waiting for French settlers to arrive. Inherent in this imagery was the idea that the empire held abundant untapped resources that the French settler would put to profitable use as well as large quantities of available land into which

A COLONIAL FOUNTAIN OF YOUTH

this prolific population could grow. Yet the reality, Peter Dunwoodie shows, is that the image of the virile and energetic French farmer in the Algerian frontier was continuously undermined by the fact that the European settlers had not reduced the colonized population to a small minority of the overall population, as had been the case in the United States.[25] Dunwoodie shows that Franco-Algerian literature throughout the colonial period reflected a sense of European demographic vulnerability that led to feelings of paranoia and acts of violence.[26]

This sense of demographic vulnerability intensified in the years after the Great War, with data showing that the population of colonized Algerians was growing much more rapidly than that of the settlers. For example, between 1921 and 1925 the European population had a birthrate of 26, while the colonized Algerians had, during the same period, an estimated birthrate between 37.2 and 38.[27] In the following decade, French officials recorded a birthrate of 23 for the European population; demographers later estimated that of the colonial subjects to be between 43.4 and 44.[28] Many French officials saw the growth of the colonized population as simultaneously evidence of the success of the French civilizing mission and the seeds of its own destruction. The success of French health care, they maintained, had reduced infant mortality and the spread of infectious diseases, thereby facilitating the growth of the very population that would contest colonial rule.[29] While few contemporary demographers dissented from this view, Kamal Kateb cites one 1937 study indicating that this population growth was not solely the consequence of French influences. By comparing birthrates in different regions of the colony, these demographers concluded that the colonized population's growth was the strongest in rural regions of the colony, where French social and economic infrastructures were the least developed.[30] As effective as inoculation campaigns may have been in reducing the mortality rate, this particular study revealed that the regions experiencing the strongest population growth were precisely those in which people had the least access to French medicine. Regardless of why it was happening, however, the growth of the colonized population in Algeria intensified fears about the decline in the settler birthrate.

By the twentieth century, French immigration to Algeria, Morocco, and Tunisia had declined substantially, and as a result, few French immigrants arrived to replace those settlers who migrated to the cities. With little expectation that immigration would help the French settler population continue to grow, settlers worried about the future of French colonial rule. Barthelet, for one, expressed concern that the birthrate would continue to decline and that the growth of the settler colonies would then be fueled solely by foreigners. In 1927 he wrote that "if the birthrate crisis does not cripple Algeria with the same acuteness as in France, the Colony owes it to the Latin immigrants who bring the aptitude of their race to create large families."[31] He went on to state that in 1921 the average French household in Algeria had fewer than two children, whereas the average non-French European household had more than two children. Barthelet nevertheless emphasized that the tendency of other European settlers to have larger families was unlikely to be maintained in the long term, as their birthrate "seems to diminish as their material well-being improves."[32] By the 1920s, therefore, it was clear that the French would not be able to rely on the high birthrate of the other European settlers whom they hoped would assimilate into French society and strengthen the French presence numerically.

Upholding the Rights of the Settler *Famille Nombreuse*

This sense of demographic vulnerability converged with a growing conviction that the state had an obligation to protect the rights of the family; these factors prompted French settlers in Algeria and elsewhere in the empire to create familialist organizations. Some of these organizations represented the interests of bureaucrats stationed overseas and were colonial branches of Achille Glorieux's Ligue des fonctionnaires pères de famille nombreuse, founded in France during World War I. For instance, in Madagascar a local schoolteacher headed a branch of this organization that represented 181 members in 1919.[33] Indochina had multiple such sections, including one representing Cochinchine and another representing Saigon.[34] These organizations presented their arguments in favor of familial rights within the general context of French depopulation, expressing less concern about the demographic situation of the colony in which they were stationed. Foremost among their concerns was the idea that relocating overseas to serve the state was an underappreciated sacrifice that generated expenses unknown to bureaucrats in France, such as sending one's children back to France to be educated. They phrased their demands for greater state support in pronatalist terms by asserting that without governmental assistance it was harder for them to fulfill their national duty of producing a minimum of three children. In addition to these organizations representing French bureaucrats, other groups focused more on the interests of the permanent settler colony. Some of these groups were likewise local sections of metropolitan-based organizations. The Ligue pour la vie, founded in France in 1916 by Paul Bureau, had a section in Madagascar as well as a North African section representing Algeria and Tunisia. Many of the members of the Ligue pour la vie also belonged to other organizations. Most members of Madagascar's section, for example, were also members of the Ligue des fonctionnaires pères de famille nombreuse.[35]

The vast majority of settler familialists lived in North Africa and belonged to organizations that originated as local branches of the Ligue populaire des pères et mères de familles nombreuses, established in France in 1908 by Captain Simon Maire. By the end of World War I, however, most of these groups had broken away from Maire's organization and had begun to pursue an agenda that was geared toward the specific needs of French settlers in North Africa. With its large French settler population, Algeria not surprisingly had the largest familialist movement. The main organization, representing all the Algerian leagues, was founded in 1911 as a colonial section of Maire's organization. This group split off in 1914 and became the Ligue des familles nombreuses françaises d'Algérie.[36] By 1925 the organization was headed by L. Barthelet and represented twelve thousand families.[37] Within this confederation there were three departmental federations and numerous local sections, representing either a commune or a city. The department of Constantine, for example, had a particularly active membership with at least twenty local branches.

In Tunisia at least twenty-two hundred families were represented by the Ligue française des pères et mères de familles nombreuses, headed by French-born Henri Lacoux, who had relocated to Tunisia in 1895.[38] This organization had at least thirteen local sections. Because Morocco was a new addition to the French empire and had a relatively small French population, the familialist movement in this protectorate was significantly smaller than in Algeria and Tunisia. The main organization in Morocco was the Union des familles françaises nombreuses du Maroc (UFFNM), headed by Gaston Bernaudat and representing about a thousand members. There were fifteen local sections, the most active of which represented 115 families in Marrakech.[39] The familialist organizations in Algeria, Morocco, and Tunisia were loosely united in a federation called the Ligue des familles nombreuses françaises de l'Afrique du Nord, which expressed itself through a journal called *La voix des familles nombreuses françaises de l'Afrique du Nord*. Its first issue appeared in 1924 under the editorship of a man named Attali in Algeria. This journal presented articles addressing demographic issues specific to each colony as well as reports detailing decisions made at familialist congresses all over North Africa.

As we will see later in this chapter, the Alliance nationale took an active interest in the situation of the French settler family and worked closely with these North African organizations, even though they were more familialist in their orientation than pronatalist. Despite this collaboration, the Alliance nationale never created any local sections in North Africa, although they did, by the time of World War II, establish a readership in Algeria.[40] In fact, all of the settler organizations were familialist in that they restricted their membership to families with at least three children. This was something that distinguished them from the Alliance nationale, which counted many childless individuals among its members. Settler familialist organizations also differed from the Alliance nationale in their main agenda, as they were organized primarily to improve the material and moral situation of French families in North Africa.[41] As will be shown in this chapter, this entailed securing financial benefits for settler families and fighting against what they considered immoral influences in society at odds with the family values they promoted. Yet even if their main raison d'être was different from that of the Alliance nationale, North African familialists had much in common with their metropolitan pronatalist colleagues. For example, one of the main goals of the Ligue des familles nombreuses françaises d'Algérie (LFNFA) was "to provoke and associate with any action that will fight against *dénatalité* [the declining birthrate] and to favor the development of the French family in Algeria."[42] North African familialist organizations often presented their pursuit of rights for French settler families and efforts to raise the birthrate in Algeria as part of a larger struggle against depopulation within greater France. In this regard they made the same arguments about the place of North Africa in French efforts to combat depopulation that metropolitan pronatalists had been making since the late nineteenth century. For instance, the main objective sought by the LFNFA was an "expanded pronatalist policy [in Algeria] ensuring the development of the North African population, development that is indispensable to the life of the mère-patrie."[43] In a similar vein, the North African section of the Ligue pour la vie asserted that North Africa "must be at the forefront of national strength upon which France should count" in efforts to raise its birthrate; it was in the colonies that France would find "living examples of the virile virtue by which races last and rejuvenate themselves."[44] Settler familialists presented their status and numerical strength as integral parts of France's demographic stability.

In addition to asserting the importance of the colonies in French regeneration, settler familialists drew on the language of family rights to demand financial benefits for their members. The idea that the family, as a unit, had rights distinct from those of the individual and deserved state support was an integral feature of both pronatalist and familialist organizations from the very beginning, though not always articulated as such. As the first such organization to achieve political influence, the Alliance nationale was at the forefront of lobbying the government to introduce laws that would help increase population growth by making it easier for French families to support and raise their children. In so doing they argued that bestowing certain financial benefits on French families was essential to the survival of the nation. After World War I, pronatalist and familialist demands for family benefits were increasingly presented as fundamental rights as well as financial incentives that would encourage population growth. This concept of family rights coalesced in 1920 at a familialist congress held in Lille at which Eugène Duthoit, president of the Semaines sociales, presented a Declaration of the Rights of the Family. In this document Duthoit sought to replace the individual as bearer of rights, as seen in the 1789 Declaration of Rights of Man and Citizen, with the family as the bearer of rights. The declaration asserts that the family is endowed with inalienable rights that exist prior to and above the law.[45] Many of the articles within the declaration focus on the right of the family to grow and exist (which meant being protected against nefarious influences such as divorce and alcoholism). Article one spells out many of the problems in French society that hurt the family: propaganda, taxes, poor distribution of profits, and the disorganization of work. Elsewhere in the document, Duthoit positions the main goals of the family movement as fundamental rights of the family, including the right to a salary sufficient to support one's family, the right to a decent home, the right to taxes and benefits calculated not on an individual basis but on a family basis, and the right to the family vote.[46]

It was also after World War I that the French government began to legitimize the concept of familial rights by introducing legislation designed to extend financial benefits and assistance to families. One example of this was a 1922 law that built on previous laws giving state subsidies to companies constructing low-cost housing reserved for large families.[47] There were laws in 1920 and 1921 mandating that the central government help finance birth incentives distributed at the local level to families with three or more children.[48] Many of the laws introduced during this period built on private initiatives that predate World War I. For example, there were employers who established *caisses de compensation* giving workers a family bonus, if they had children, in lieu of across-the-board raises. As Susan Pedersen argues, some employers introduced the *caisses* for philanthropic reasons, while others had more pragmatic motivations, such as minimizing the influence of the labor movement.[49] In 1932 the French government took this private initiative and made it mandatory for all French employers. Also noteworthy is the 1923 Loi d'encouragement national aux familles nombreuses, which expanded the system of family allowances introduced in 1913 and established family allowances for French families who pay no income tax.[50] For the purposes of the family-rights movement, the significance of laws such as those of 1923 and 1932 is that they transformed what was once a small initiative undertaken voluntarily by certain employers into a right guaranteed by the state and extended to all eligible families.

A source of great frustration to settler familialists, however, was that laws enacted in the metropole did not automatically extend to Algeria or other parts of the empire unless the colonies and protectorates were specifically named in the legislation. Subsequently, as metropolitan legislators passed new laws granting benefits or rights to French families, they failed to extend these laws to North Africa. At times this may have happened simply because French legislators did not think to add a clause extending the legislation into greater France; frequently, however, it was because legislators believed that many French laws could not be applied effectively in such a different political, racial, and demographic context.[51] The idea that the colonies and their French populations should be administered differently and be subject to a separate body of laws was not unique to the early twentieth century. During the French Revolution, for example, the question of whether or to what extent revolutionary changes could be brought to colonies such as Saint Domingue and Guadeloupe produced heated debates and ultimately was among the causes of the Haitian Revolution.[52] However, to settler familialists who defined themselves as French, both racially and in terms of citizenship, and therefore deserving of the same rights and benefits as any other French citizen, the failure of the French government to extend advantageous laws to North Africa was a source of bitterness and a sign that the metropole did not recognize the settlers as part of the French population. As one settler familialist wrote, "the French person of Algeria, who has the same financial burdens as the French person in the metropole, should have the same advantages: he should not be a diminished citizen, a second-class French person."[53]

Settler familialists presented the application of these laws in North Africa as a fundamental right owed to them as French citizens. The statute of the main Algerian organization stated that "large families do not seek acts of pity or charity. They seek the full application of their rights, rights that must be recognized."[54] In the interest of upholding the rights of the settler family, the number-one objective listed in the political program of the Ligue des familles nombreuses de l'Afrique du Nord was "the application of protective metropolitan laws to large French families in North Africa."[55] Settlers continuously linked the metropolitan government's failure to uphold such rights in North Africa with colonial authorities' inability to recruit adequate numbers of French people for colonial settlement. Barthelet, for one, insisted that it was impossible to attract immigrants to Algeria, not only because life was more difficult in North Africa than in the metropole, but also because salaries were lower, benefits to large families were virtually nonexistent, and taxes were high. Consequently, instead of recruiting large numbers of immigrants from France, the colony lost population as working-class settlers migrated to France in search of a higher standard of living.[56]

Occasionally, the French government did respond to this criticism and agree to apply metropolitan pronatalist legislation in North Africa. For example, the *médaille de la famille française*, an annual award given to "deserving" mothers and created by decree in 1920, was not initially extended to the protectorates. However, the Direction des affaires politiques et commerciales in Tunisia wrote letters to the Ministry of Foreign Affairs in 1921 requesting the award on behalf of two women living in the protectorate: a widow Penciolelli and a madame Mosnier (née Marie Josephine Vachet).[57] In 1923 the ministry wrote two letters approving that these women be awarded the medals despite the fact that the award was not supposed to be applicable in the protectorates.[58] The case of these two women was, however, exceptional and did not convince the French government to make the prize available to all French citizens in the empire.

A COLONIAL FOUNTAIN OF YOUTH

Such examples of the French government implementing pronatalist legislation in North Africa, either in individual cases or generally, were unusual. Issues of *La voix des familles nombreuses française
de l'Afrique du Nord* were replete with articles detailing the ways in
which large French families were treated better in the metropole than
in the empire. The author of one such article examined laws concerning family allowances, financial assistance to impoverished large
families, allowances to women giving birth, financial incentives to
breast-feeding women, and birth incentives and emphasized that these
benefits only applied to French citizens who lived in France, not the
empire.[59] In the absence of beneficial metropolitan legislation, such as
the *loi d'encouragement national* of 1923 or the birth incentives, settler
familialists used their limited resources to support families within their
own ranks. For instance, the Algerian leagues functioned as mutual-
assistance organizations, giving their members 200 francs to cover
funeral expenses in the event of the death of one of the parents, 100
francs for the birth of each child, and warm clothing for needy children in large families.[60] Similarly, as an example of the prominence
of his organization, Henri Lacoux boasted that his organization was
the second-largest mutual-aid organization operating in Tunisia.[61]

"We Must Act Alone"

Frustrated with the metropolitan government, Barthelet asserted that
addressing depopulation required that settler familialists relinquish
any hope that their problems would be solved in Paris and should
instead take matters into their own hands.[62] This assertion reflected
an independent spirit that characterized Franco-Algerian attitudes
toward the metropole in many ways. On the one hand, Barthelet and
other settler familialists resented what they considered metropolitan
disinterest and neglect, clearly sought the application of metropolitan
pronatalist legislation to North Africa, and wanted the government to
encourage increased French colonial settlement. Simultaneously, they
asserted that they neither needed nor wanted metropolitan meddling
in their affairs. Barthelet even maintained that metropolitan efforts
to boost the birthrate in France were hardly inspiring and were not

responsive to the uniquely colonial context in which French settlers' demographic troubles developed. He argued that in order to address depopulation, settlers would have to count

> not on the miracle that the French wish to see happen every time current difficulties appear to be insurmountable, but solely on a colonial policy taking into account all the different elements that constitute the population and drive them to develop, in quantity and quality, in the interest of France. We must act alone; France, on the brink of disaster [and] lacking children, counts on the colonies to ensure her own rebirth and she cannot give us the necessary aid.[63]

This statement makes it clear not only that settler familialists could not expect assistance from France, but also, due to the specific racial composition of the North African colonies, that their governments could not simply import metropolitan pronatalist policies. Rather, they needed to develop different methods for improving French settler population growth, something that could not be achieved without considering French settlers as part of a larger, racially diverse population.

French settlers did sometimes benefit from the largely decentralized nature of the French empire, which enabled colonial governments to implement pronatalist reforms that were well suited to the unique conditions of individual colonies. One report issued by the Ministry of Colonies on this topic stated that it was difficult to draw conclusions concerning the existing benefits for large families in the empire, as these benefits had all been enacted at the local level and varied significantly from one colony to the next.[64] In New Caledonia, for example, benefits for large families were fairly generous in the 1930s. A decree enacted in 1938 stipulated that any woman who was a French citizen and had resided in the colony for at least ten years was entitled to 500 francs upon the birth of her fifth child, 250 francs for the sixth child, 300 francs for the seventh child, and 400 francs for each subsequent child.[65] The decree indicated that the Kanak population was excluded from these monetary awards on the grounds that they were not French nationals.[66]

Because decisions about family benefits in the empire were made by individual colonies, familialists in North Africa depended largely on the sympathy of their respective colonial governors or residents-general. If a particular colonial governor happened to be particularly interested in this cause, large settler families might acquire benefits that did not even exist in France. Conversely, a disinterested colonial governor could paralyze settlers' efforts to introduce such reforms. In Algeria, familialists worked well with General-Governor Théodore Steeg (in office 1921–25) and considered him a "collaborator" in their efforts to establish financial advantages for large settler families.[67] For example, *La voix des familles nombreuses françaises de l'Afrique du Nord* reprinted many of the letters Steeg wrote expressing support for the organization. Steeg's support extended beyond written statements, and familialists applauded a number of his efforts to support settler families, despite the neglectful attitude of the metropolitan government. For example, Steeg introduced family allowances for impoverished French families, though for budgetary reasons these allowances were less substantial than in France.[68] Steeg also decreed that in the village of Berriche, a *centre de colonisation*, free plots of land would be reserved for large families.[69] Although it received support in familialist and pronatalist circles, the Berriche experiment was mostly a failure. Initially, twenty-five families, mostly immigrants from France, settled the village in 1919 but were unable to make ends meet and could not grow crops.[70] According to the familialist Paul Bénos, the main reason why Berriche failed was that the land concessions were too small; familialists subsequently demanded larger concessions for the families in the *bled*.[71] In contrast to what familialists argued, though, the colonial administration's records indicate that families abandoned their land in Berriche for a variety of reasons. For instance, the Lacrampe family decided to move away because of health problems. Philémon Noé and his wife and four children left because it was a remote location and his children could not attend school.[72]

In Morocco, familialists were initially disappointed with the residency's apparent lack of resolve in supporting their cause. Morocco did not become part of the French empire until 1912, so the familialist movement was still new and relatively small in the 1920s. After taking office in 1912, Resident-General Lyautey demonstrated some interest in the organization's objectives, and familialists commended him for his awareness of the demographic issues. It was under Lyautey that the residency wrote to the Ministry of Foreign Affairs to ask that the 1923 *loi d'encouragement national*, which extended children's allowances to qualifying families, be applied in Morocco.[73] Lyautey even expressed some interest in working to address familialist concerns by assigning a member of the civil cabinet to meet with the UFFNM and address their demands. Ultimately, however, very little came of these decisions, and by the time of his departure, familialists in Morocco had come to view Lyautey as more of an obstacle to achieving their aims than a collaborator. For example, after familial suffrage was established in Tunisia, the UFFNM asked for an identical reform in Morocco, but Lyautey refused.[74]

In 1926 the situation for familialists in Morocco changed with the arrival of Steeg as the new resident-general. Like their counterparts in Algeria, familialists in Morocco found Steeg sympathetic to their cause and a welcome change from Lyautey. One member of a local group, the Union des familles françaises nombreuses de Marrakech, argued in 1926 that "large families . . . have obtained more since the arrival of Monsieur Steeg in Morocco, than in six years of lobbying under the Lyautey regime."[75] One of Steeg's first actions as resident-general was to officially recognize the Fédération marocaine des familles nombreuses, giving them a subsidy of 6,000 francs.[76] He also mandated a series of discounts for large families, promised medical inspections in schools, and improved municipal health-care services. Most importantly, in the fall of 1926, Steeg implemented familial suffrage.[77] Although the UFFNM would have preferred that the family vote be accorded to fathers of at least three children (as opposed to four, as Steeg decided), they were pleased to have a resident-general who was willing to implement many of their proposed reforms.[78]

In 1928 Steeg consolidated these efforts by creating the Office des familles nombreuses in Rabat.[79] Connected closely with the government, this office was run by an administrative council comprising a

A COLONIAL FOUNTAIN OF YOUTH

number of top government officials including, the secretary-general of the protectorate, the health and public hygiene director, and the general director of finances, among others.[80] One of the office's primary functions was devising ways to increase the population; this entailed studying pronatalist reforms that existed in the metropole, lobbying for the application of these reforms in Morocco, and devising local solutions. The office was also organized to assist large families by providing them with information and advice about the benefits for which they were eligible, guaranteeing that the heads of large families would receive governmental assistance with housing, and building affordable housing for large families.[81]

Similar to Steeg in Morocco, Resident-General Lucien Saint's support for the familialist cause in Tunisia extended beyond his decision to enact familial suffrage. Shortly after taking office in 1921, Saint began working with the Ligue des familles nombreuses, an organization founded in 1912 by Henri Lacoux.[82] Saint first showed his support for the group by giving it a subsidy of 2,000 francs.[83] He then sought to work around the fact that metropolitan pronatalist legislation was not extended to Tunisia by introducing some forms of financial assistance for large families. For example, he gave the Ligue des familles nombreuses a 6,000-franc subvention so that they could distribute birth incentives to their members.[84] He also introduced a credit of 120,000 francs into the state budget for assistance to large families with demonstrable need.[85] He further indicated his support by writing to the Ministry of Foreign Affairs and recommending that Lacoux receive the *croix de chevalier de la légion d'honneur*. In his letter, Saint highlighted the importance of settler familialists by explaining that Lacoux's work with the Ligue des familles nombreuses was a patriotic act connected directly to strengthening French interests abroad.[86]

Despite his sympathy for the familialist cause, Saint faced a number of obstacles to implementing the measures proposed by Lacoux and other members of the Tunisian settler familialist lobby. Budgetary considerations weighed heavily on Saint, as they did on his counterparts in Algeria and Morocco, and usually were the main reason colonial leaders gave for not meeting settlers' expectations. For example, when responding to Lacoux's request that large families be given discounts on basic necessities like oil and bread, Saint expressed sympathy for needy families but stated that such a reform would be impossible for purely budgetary reasons.[87]

Budgetary considerations also frustrated Steeg's desire to introduce family allowances in Algeria in a manner similar to what existed in France during this period. In France, family allowances began as a private initiative, with some businesses—starting with the engineering firm of Régis Joya in 1916—giving allowances to employees who had children.[88] This practice expanded in subsequent years, with four million workers receiving such allowances by the end of the 1920s, and ultimately it came under state control in 1932.[89] The amount of the allowance varied considerably by occupation and *département*, but Joseph Spengler provides the following amounts that an average recipient would have received each month in 1925: 19 francs for one child, 48 francs for two, 90 francs for three, and 140 francs for four.[90] According to Algerian familialists, Steeg's attempts to establish a similar system of family allowances for impoverished families in Algeria failed to help settler families to the same degree. Bénos stated that in Algeria these allowances ranged from 20 to 50 francs, an amount he knew to be greatly inferior to that of the metropole.[91]

While budgetary constraints were the stated reason why colonial governments were reluctant to extend certain benefits to settler families, it is evident that other factors also informed their decisions. The racial diversity of the population in North Africa presented colonial governments with unique challenges in meeting the demands of familialist organizations. All three North African governments expressed concerns about according financial benefits to both French citizens and colonial subjects. For example, in Tunisia, the residency told the Ligue des familles nombreuses that even in the absence of budgetary problems, it would have been impossible to organize bread discounts for large French families in the protectorate in the same way that such discounts were given to large French families in France. This was due to "the difficulties one would encounter in determining the composition of Muslim families and the impossibility of applying to the French element a measure that would not be extended to the natives and foreigners."[92] Likewise, the Tunisian general director of public works wrote to the resident-general in 1920 explaining why it would not be feasible to give large families in Tunisia discount cards for public transportation, as existed in France at the time. While these discount cards worked well in France, in Tunisia it would be impossible because of "the existence of populations of different races and the abuses that would inevitably result."[93]

In some cases, settler familialists sought to devise ways by which to improve benefits for French families without extending the same level of assistance to colonial subjects. For instance, in Tunisia the Grand conseil in 1922 debated whether or not Tunisians working for the colonial administration should receive the same family allowance as their French colleagues. One French representative in the Grand conseil, Paul Omessa, argued against an equal allowance on the grounds that the cost of living for French families in the protectorate was considerably higher than it was for Tunisia's colonial subjects, who could easily make do with less. Perhaps getting more to the point, he explained further that the real purpose of this allowance was to "increase the French birthrate in the country" and that there was subsequently no need to subsidize the Tunisian population when Tunisians already had a robust birthrate: "Examining the statistics shows, in effect, that the indigenous population is increasing extremely quickly; bestowing on it a birth incentive would be tantamount to sprinkling [water] on a street on which the rain has already fallen in abundance."[94] Although some representatives agreed with this view, a number of counterarguments came from the French and Tunisian sections of the Grand conseil. One Tunisian representative, Si Amor Baccouche, emphasized that if Tunisians managed to make do with less it was only because many of them were already very poor, not because they needed fewer resources than French families. Ultimately, arguments like the latter carried the day, and the Grand conseil voted to give equal allowances to French and Tunisian functionaries.[95] Still, this debate illustrates that the diversity of North Africa's population made the introduction of pronatalist and familialist laws more complicated than in France. French officials and settlers wanted to strengthen the French population through such financial incentives but worried that by doing so they could simultaneously encourage population growth among rival populations, namely, the colonized Tunisians, whom many settlers and officials believed to be already very numerous. They subsequently attempted, with limited success, to introduce racially exclusive pronatalist reforms. This frequently entailed interpreting poverty in a racially specific way, presenting low standards of living as normal and natural for colonial subjects while deeming such conditions unacceptable and intolerable for white French settlers.[96]

The challenges that Barthelet, Bernadaut, and Lacoux faced in the 1920s frustrated their successors in the 1930s. In 1939, correspondence between the French government and General Laignelot, at this time president of the Ligue des pères et mères de familles nombreuses en Tunisie, was particularly revealing of such frustrations. Laignelot emphasized that the French government's refusal to invest money in large French settler families would undermine French influence in Tunisia and had the potential to strengthen Italian claims on the protectorate.[97] In particular, Laignelot argued that as a result of the government's refusal to extend benefits to French citizens without also extending them to the Muslim population, many French settlers were returning to France where it was less expensive for the government to support large families. The Italian population, which by contrast was supported and financed by its government, would continue to grow in Tunisia and would take over the land and industries abandoned by departing French settlers.[98]

Familialist Strategies

The belief that French families in North Africa were denied family rights simply because they happened to reside in a racially diverse colony, and not France, prompted settler familialists in Algeria to change their membership requirements and reevaluate their notions of which individuals could contribute to their goals. From the very beginning, settler familialist organizations in this colony reflected the diverse composition of the population. Many of the names on their membership lists were Spanish or Italian, for instance.[99] While some of these individuals may have been French citizens and a product of the "fusion of races" of which Demontès had written earlier in the twentieth century, others may have been foreign residents of Algeria. French citizenship was not a requirement for admission into one of the Algerian organizations; membership was open to European foreigners provided only that their children had French status.[100] As this policy indicates, the nationality of the parents was less important than their decision to raise their child as French and in this way contribute to the growth of the French population.

By creating a separate Muslim section and effectively expanding their Muslim membership, at least one familialist organization went a step further in forging alliances to strengthen their cause. The Fédération des ligues des pères et mères de familles nombreuses françaises du département de Constantine was a departmental organization in Algeria headed by Paul Bénos and claiming 4,197 members in 1927.[101] In 1924, members of the federation voted to allow the membership of Muslim Algerian fathers, in a separate section, and approved the addition of a small number of Muslim Algerian members to the federation's central leadership.[102] Four Muslim Algerian members would join the thirty-six French representatives of the Administrative Council; one of these Muslim Algerian members would also serve as one of four vice-presidents of the organization. Of more than 4,000 members in the organization, 150 were listed as Muslims. This decision to admit Muslim members was not unusual for a Franco-Algerian organization during this period. The Algerian section of the nationalist Croix de feu, for example, was open to Muslim veterans in recognition of their service to the nation in World War I. Few Muslims, however, were interested in joining that organization.[103]

The federation's decision to admit Muslim members, on the other hand, came at the instigation of the Muslim section's first leaders, who were all from the educated elite.[104] With the exception of a teacher, all of these men worked within the colonial administration. One was a clerk at the Prefectural Council, another was a judicial city councilman, and a third was an interpreter at the prefecture. The level of assimilation into French society was a critical factor behind the federation's decision to accept the Muslim men, who would only be admitted under certain conditions. In order to join, a Muslim father had to be considered sufficiently assimilated and needed to adhere to French definitions of responsible fatherhood. Reflecting French perceptions of Muslim masculinity, the federation's new statute stipulated that a Muslim member could not be polygamous and that he could join only if "his role as father is not limited to having children, but to inspiring in children the best conditions of moral and public hygiene, love of work, of integrity and awareness of their duties to France."[105] The language of the statute also touched on the widespread belief that girls occupied an inferior position within the Muslim family; a Muslim man could therefore only join the organization if "his male, as well as female, school-age children attend French schools."[106]

A speech written by Ben Mouffock, the Muslim man who led the effort to create the Muslim section, indicates why settler familialists in the city of Constantine supported the creation of the Muslim section.[107] At the 1925 congress of the department of Constantine's familialist federation, one of the topics under discussion was whether or not all the leagues in this department should follow the city of Constantine's example and create a Muslim section. Ben Mouffock argued in his speech that such a move would be advantageous not only for Muslim families but also for the settler movement in its attempts to negotiate the application of metropolitan laws in Algeria. This could only be achieved through their solidarity, he argued, because "for some time one has made a pompous show of our so-called special condition in order to refuse French North Africa the benefits of assistance laws. It has even been claimed that social legislation has not been applied in Algeria precisely because of the natives."[108] He went on to explain that even in the absence of these laws, considerable work had been done to help the Muslim family and that building on these efforts requires closer collaboration between the administration and "qualified representatives of these miserable natives." Bénos added to these comments by arguing that the creation of the Muslim section enabled them to achieve better results in working toward the "emancipation of the native family" and bringing progress to the native family.[109] These comments suggest that these settler familialists considered themselves to be engaged in a civilizing mission; they also appear to have been attempting to strengthen their political influence and demands for the application of metropolitan pronatalist legislation by presenting themselves as representatives of "the *famille nombreuse*" in North Africa, whether French or Muslim. It is a tactic that recalls British feminists' efforts to strengthen their demands for political rights by positioning themselves as the best-qualified representatives of Indian women.[110]

The suggestion that all of the leagues in the department of Constantine should likewise create Muslim sections was controversial, however. In the discussion that followed Ben Mouffock's speech, the representative from Bône, Dr. Quintard, stated that his league had given him an "imperative mandate" to reject any such idea, a view that was quickly seconded by the representative from Philippeville. Other representatives, including a Lecomte from Batna, said that his league would go forward with this plan. After Dr. Quintard reiterated his strong opposition to this idea, a representative from the city of Constantine argued that at the Monument aux morts the names of "native" and French soldiers who died for the country were presented together, without the kinds of differences and barriers that his colleagues insisted on maintaining between French and Muslim families. Ultimately, the representatives decided to vote for this measure at the local level, thereby enabling local sections to make their own decisions. Some local sections, such as that in Guelma, did follow Constantine's example and create a Muslim section.[111]

In a variety of ways, the Algerian familialists sought to represent the Muslim *famille nombreuse* by lobbying for benefits for both French and Muslim families. For instance, in 1929 the Algerian federation's general assembly adopted a resolution stating that they would try to create a prize for large families for which colonial subjects and Europeans would both be eligible.[112] Also, the familialist leagues were involved in the decisions regarding the Médaille de la famille française, some of which were awarded to women who were not French citizens and whose applications listed their status as "Muslim subject." In some cases their applications contained a certificate, signed by the president of the Ligue des pères et mères de familles nombreuses de l'arrondissement de Batna, indicating that the information about the size and morality of the family were in fact correct.[113] This demonstrates that in Batna, at least, settler familialists recommended certain Muslim families for the award.

It is clear that the goal of strengthening the French presence in North Africa through the establishment and protection of large families pushed settler familialists to think about who could further their cause in new ways. By raising his children to support the colonial regime, a Muslim could contribute to the maintenance of French colonial rule. The fact that some settler familialist organizations welcomed the membership of Muslims whom they considered sufficiently assimilated, as well as settlers with Italian and Spanish heritage, demonstrates that they thought about the demographic issue differently than did their metropolitan counterparts. This was in large part a consequence of the French government's refusal to extend a number of pronatalist laws to North Africa and the determination of settler familialists to present themselves as representatives of all families in Algeria in order to strengthen their cause.

The membership requirements also raise important questions about the role of race in shaping settler familialism. On the one hand, settlers' racially based fears about being a minority population in the protectorate and possessing a birthrate inferior to that of the rapidly growing Algerian Muslim population were at the core of their arguments for family rights. Still, although race was an essential part of why settlers formed familialist organizations, the fact that eligibility was not restricted to individuals possessing European heritage indicates that settler familialists did not conceive of the task of strengthening the French population in solely racial terms. There was instead a degree of openness to supporting select Algerian Muslim families, something that makes it difficult to interpret settlers' demands as an entirely racially based pronatalism. Clearly, there was a rupture between reforms envisioned in racial terms and the development of an actual political movement, shaped and determined by pragmatic considerations and negotiations with the metropolitan government.

Pronatalist-Familialist Alliances

As settler familialists formed organizations in the twentieth century and sought the application of pronatalist legislation in the empire, they found metropolitan organizations such as the Alliance nationale and La plus grande famille to be particularly important allies. Metropolitan pronatalists, who had long been supportive of settler colonialism, developed a better understanding of the situation in North Africa as a result of their collaboration with their settler counterparts. This greater awareness of colonial demographic issues was instrumental in moving metropolitan pronatalists away from the earlier optimism that Dr. Ricoux's study had inspired. Armed with more realistic ideas about the demographic situation in North Africa, metropolitan pronatalists were more assertive than ever about the importance of maintaining a strong French presence in North Africa. They therefore positioned large French settler families as essential to the realization of such objectives and lobbied for settler rights in Paris.

Prior to the foundation of these settler organizations during the interwar years, metropolitan pronatalists received much of their information on North Africa from either the colonial lobby or colleagues who had visited North Africa. Consequently, metropolitan pronatalist articles typically discussed the settler population in abstract terms, referring to them mainly in terms of statistics. For example, an article published in the bulletin of the Alliance nationale in 1907 described the large numbers of European foreigners in Algeria and how the superior birthrate of foreign women was likely to reduce the French population to a minority within the colony.[114] This and similar articles from this period conveyed no information about settler perceptions of the demographic issue or any sense of whether settlers were working to address depopulation independently of metropolitan discussions.

By the 1920s, however, a shift had taken place in metropolitan pronatalists' discussions of settler demographics. By this period, many of the articles about North Africa revealed that metropolitan pronatalists were in correspondence with settler familialists and were receiving their information about North Africa primarily from these sources. For example, in the July 1925 issue of the *Revue de la plus grande famille*, the editors reprinted a letter written by the president of the Ligue des familles nombreuses françaises d'Algérie to the governor-general of Algeria.[115] In the letter, he outlined Algerian familialists' main grievances and indicated their desire to see metropolitan pronatalist legislation enacted in Algeria. By reprinting this letter, leaders of La plus grande famille demonstrated their solidarity with the Algerian familialist movement and informed their readers of the challenges faced by their compatriots in North Africa.

Showing that pronatalists recognized and supported settler efforts to address the colonial demographic concerns, other articles in metropolitan journals detailed the achievements of settler organizations. For example, a 1927 article in the *Revue de la plus grande famille* contained information sent by Henri Lacoux regarding the many accomplishments of the Ligue des familles nombreuses françaises de Tunisie since its inception in 1912.[116] Among the accomplishments listed were the introduction of the family vote, the establishment of family allowances, and the representation of the league in every governmental council and commission in the protectorate. Articles of this nature demonstrated that metropolitan pronatalists recognized the strength of the colonial movement.

Not only were metropolitan pronatalists well aware of the unique challenges that French settlers in North Africa faced, but settler familialists demonstrated a strong awareness of France's depopulation crisis and presented North Africa as a central part of addressing France's demographic woes. For instance, the Algerian federation suggested that organizing the migration of Berbers to France might provide a solution to France's rural exodus and the shortage of agricultural labor in the countryside.[117] While it is not clear what metropolitan pronatalists thought of this particular suggestion, it is unlikely that they would have been receptive to such an idea given their larger concerns about racial purity in France.

A COLONIAL FOUNTAIN OF YOUTH

The alliances forged between pronatalists and settler familialists were further evidenced by the appearance of articles written by metropolitan pronatalists for settler journals. In 1927, for example, both Fernand Boverat, president of the Alliance nationale, and Charles Richet, one of the co-founders of the Alliance nationale, wrote articles for *La voix des familles nombreuses françaises de l'Afrique du Nord*.[118] Both of these articles addressed topics relating to depopulation that were relevant to metropolitan pronatalists and settler familialists alike: expanding existing birth incentives and encouraging young people to have large families. In this way, pronatalists such as Boverat and Richet demonstrated not only that they collaborated with settlers in the interest of strengthening French influence abroad but that they also saw settler familialist journals as an important forum in which they could express their views.

In addition to collaborating with their metropolitan counterparts through newspapers and letters, settlers traveled to France to meet with their metropolitan allies in person at the national pronatalist congresses. Beginning with the 1919 Congrès national de la natalité, held in the French city of Nancy,[119] representatives from the three major pronatalist and familialist organizations—La plus grande famille, the Alliance nationale, and Pour la vie—met annually to discuss issues pertinent to all three organizations and to agree on a common agenda. As early as 1921, settler familialist organizations also sent representatives to these congresses to present on issues specific to colonial life. The participation of French settlers at these congresses was instrumental for two reasons: settlers educated their metropolitan allies about pronatalist issues specific to colonial life, and, despite their minority status, they were able to integrate their proposals into the larger metropolitan pronatalist agenda. For example, in 1921 the president of the Union des familles nombreuses du Maroc, Bernaudat, represented Tunisian and Moroccan settlers at the third annual congress, in Bordeaux.[120] At the legislative section of the congress, Bernaudat presented information concerning the situation of French families in the protectorates and voiced concern about the future of French influence in the empire.[121] In response, the legislative committee adopted two resolutions concerning the French protectorates directly: a demand that metropolitan laws favoring fathers of large families be applied in Tunisia and Morocco, and a request that French citizens of the protectorates be specifically mentioned in legislation concerning national assistance to large families under debate in the Chamber of Deputies.[122]

This gradual integration of settler familialism into the larger metropolitan movement was further solidified at the twelfth annual congress, held in Constantine, Algeria, in 1930. The choice of Algeria was largely symbolic; 1930 was the centennial of France's conquest of Algeria and the formation of the second colonial empire. In the metropole, the centennial was marked with great celebration and larger efforts to educate the French public about France's vast colonial empire. For example, French officials organized a colonial exhibition in 1931 at which organizers displayed colonial subjects in zoo-like exhibits and presented the public with information intended to showcase the success of France's civilizing mission in the colonies.[123] A feminist congress specifically about colonialism was held that same year and also reflected a desire to celebrate France's achievements in the empire.[124]

Metropolitan pronatalists' decision to hold the annual congress in Algeria represented more than a simple desire to join other political organizations in celebrating the French empire; they also sought to strengthen the empire by further integrating pronatalist issues specific to colonial life into their larger agenda. In an article explaining why the congress would be held outside France, Auguste Isaac told readers that it was essential that France establish itself more definitively in North Africa by strengthening the settler population.[125] Isaac emphasized that earlier pronatalist congresses were not organized with this particular objective in mind but had focused instead on strengthening the French population in urban, metropolitan centers rather than in the empire. With the twelfth congress, Isaac hoped that the metropolitan movement would focus on addressing issues of depopulation in North Africa on an equal basis with those of the metropole.[126]

Isaac's slightly defensive tone indicated that he recognized that some pronatalists might not embrace the decision to have the congress outside France. In fact, the question of whether pronatalist issues

A COLONIAL FOUNTAIN OF YOUTH

of a specifically colonial nature should dominate the metropolitan agenda became a source of division within the metropolitan movement. For example, one reader of the pronatalist journal *La femme et l'enfant* wrote a letter to the journal to complain (anonymously) about the choice of location for the congress.[127] Foremost among the objections was that the congress would be dominated largely by settlers, as many metropolitan pronatalists had been discouraged from attending due to the expense of traveling to Algeria. Furthermore, because the congress was held in Algeria, it would receive a lot of publicity in Algerian newspapers but less coverage by metropolitan newspapers. The writer went on to explain that despite supporting the empire in principle, he or she believed that saving France's population in France was of considerably greater importance and resented the degree to which local (Algerian) pronatalist issues figured on the agenda at the congress.[128] It is clear, therefore, that while pronatalist leaders such as Isaac viewed settler familialists as part of the larger French pronatalist movement and considered their demographic concerns highly relevant to those of the metropolitan movement, other pronatalists insisted that metropolitan issues should come first.

Nevertheless, pronatalist leaders lauded the 1930 congress as a success. According to the printed report of the congress, metropolitan attendees stated that "if the task accomplished by France is great, there is still a lot to be done in order that this vast, beautiful and fertile country take . . . its place in national rebirth."[129] The predominant theme of the congress was depopulation in Algeria and its connections to the future of French rule in the colony. The willingness of metropolitan pronatalist leaders and congress attendees to devote an entire congress to the subject of depopulation in Algeria, with little discussion of metropolitan issues, reveals how closely pronatalist leaders connected the future of French settlement with their own depopulation crisis. Among the resolutions they adopted, therefore, were the establishment in Algeria of a Commission de la natalité similar to that in France, the extension of metropolitan legislation to Algeria, and the creation of additional support for large agricultural families in order to ensure their success and that of French colonial rule.[130] Other resolutions were as pertinent to metropolitan pronatalists as they were to their settler counterparts. For example, representatives from Tunisia and Morocco presented on familial suffrage and emphasized its effectiveness in producing beneficial political reforms in the protectorates; attendees thus adopted the resolution that familial suffrage be adopted in both Algeria and France.[131]

The collaboration with settler familialists and the integration of settler issues into the metropolitan pronatalist agenda had important implications for the metropolitan movement. As a direct result of this collaboration, pronatalist leaders and the pronatalist lobby within parliament, the Groupe parlementaire de protection des familles nombreuses, became the unofficial political representatives of the French settler population. Although the pronatalist lobby existed primarily to represent the interests of metropolitan pronatalists and to encourage the passage of laws designed to increase the population, the pronatalist movement was transformed into a colonial lobby through its representation of the interests of French settlers.

The issue of political representation had long been a source of bitterness for French settlers in North Africa. Because Algeria was politically assimilated, its three departments were considered as much a part of France as any of the metropolitan departments, and French citizens of Algeria were represented in the French parliament. However, many Franco-Algerians felt that the number of settler representatives in parliament was too small to serve the unique needs of the colony. Constituting only a minority of deputies and senators within parliament, Algerian representatives had little influence as a group. It was for this reason, many settler familialists claimed, that pronatalist legislation passed in France did not extend to Algeria; the Algerian settlers were simply overlooked. In Tunisia and Morocco issues of political representation were arguably even worse than in Algeria, as French citizens lacked political representatives in Paris entirely. The complaint that by emigrating from France to one of the protectorates a French person effectively lost his or her citizenship rights and ceased to matter in the eyes of the French government was common in settler familialist literature. One such settler wrote that "we

A COLONIAL FOUNTAIN OF YOUTH

no longer want to be treated like pariahs, we are the sons of the *mère-patrie*, we want her [France] to recognize us as her children and not abandon those who in the distant *bled* of North Africa work for the future and prosperity of greater France."[132]

Settler familialists thus appealed to their influential metropolitan allies to do precisely what the French parliament had failed to accomplish: represent their interests and ensure that pronatalist legislation was applied in North Africa. For example, an article in *La voix des familles nombreuses françaises de l'Afrique du Nord* detailed a number of reforms pursued unsuccessfully by the Union de familles françaises nombreuses du Maroc and how this organization subsequently appealed to the pronatalist lobby in parliament, asking that they represent Morocco in parliament and pursue reform on their behalf.[133] The author explained that this approach had been partially successful in the past: "Once already, at the request of Monsieur Bernaudat, Monsieur Isaac obtained for us the status of Frenchmen. It is necessary that this manner of thinking be adopted once and for all and that the laws from which large families in France benefit be applicable without modification in the colonies and protectorates."[134] Although the writer was not specific about how Isaac had accomplished this task, the article shows that settler familialists believed their metropolitan counterparts would be effective at addressing their needs.

Evidence also suggests that metropolitan pronatalists were persistent in their efforts to fight for settler rights, even if they were not entirely successful. In 1920, for example, Jacques Bertillon wrote a series of letters to the Ministry of Foreign Affairs demanding that official Mother's Day celebrations be extended to the colonies and the protectorates in order to show how strongly France valued its population, whether at home or abroad.[135] Bertillon ultimately met with a mixture of success and failure. Concerning this issue, the residency in Tunisia wrote to the Ministry of Foreign Affairs explaining that local familialist organizations were already sufficiently active in addressing issues of depopulation and that Bertillon's request was unnecessary.[136] In Morocco, the French delegate wrote to the Ministry of Foreign Affairs explaining that while interested in this event, he wanted French officials in Morocco to organize the event in their own way.[137] Like Bertillon, Fernand Boverat also represented the settler familialists and fought on their behalf. In 1939, Boverat wrote to the minister of foreign affairs, on behalf of the Alliance nationale, asking that the government establish birth incentives for French citizens residing in Tunisia.[138]

Conclusion

Pronatalists' interactions with their North African settler counterparts during the interwar period transformed their perceptions of the colonial "fountain of youth."[139] Strengthening French influence in the empire, establishing densely populated settler colonies, and drawing demographic strength from settler colonialism remained pronatalist priorities during this period. However, in the 1920s and 1930s pronatalists witnessed what they perceived to be a burgeoning French depopulation crisis in North Africa that threatened the future of French colonial rule and jeopardized the demographic possibilities that empire offered the metropole. Though still "youthful" and displaying a stronger birthrate than the "old" metropolitan population, the French settlers in North Africa feared that reduced immigration from France, declining birthrates, and French abandonment of the vast North African farmland left them vulnerable to being overwhelmed by the growing indigenous population.

The developing settler familialist movement in North Africa was consequently shaped by French settlers' perceptions of how their population growth compared with that of other populations in their respective colony and protectorates. The image of a prolific Muslim population in North Africa and its implications for the future of French settler colonialism produced pronatalist policies that stood in stark contrast to what was seen in Madagascar two decades earlier. As we saw, Gallieni and other colonial officials in Madagascar concluded that the Malagasy population was dying off, something that would ultimately hinder French settlers' efforts to develop the island's resources. The sense that there were too few colonial subjects led to reforms designed to reverse these trends and bring Malagasy population growth under state control. In North Africa, by contrast, French settlers believed that the colonized population was growing quickly and feared the consequences of their own modest demographic growth. The sense of numerical inferiority produced pronatalist policies designed to extend family rights to French settler families, something that was considered a necessary step toward maintaining French colonial rule. Moreover, officials developed these policies with the specific racial composition of their respective colonies in mind, hoping to increase French settler population growth without simultaneously encouraging population growth among the colonial subjects. Introducing a racially exclusive form of pronatalism nevertheless proved difficult, as the challenges of denying colonial subjects the same material advantages extended to French settler families was frequently presented as a reason why French settlers could not obtain the very family rights they believed to be so essential to increasing their birthrate. Due to this dilemma, concepts of who could contribute to French population growth in Algeria and the protectorates were not as straightforward as they would seem. Some settler familialists welcomed foreign settlers and Algerian Muslims into their ranks, seeing these members as valuable allies in their quest to obtain pronatalist legislation and family rights for "French" families in the colonies.

Settler familialists' interactions with the metropole involved resentment and a sense of fierce independence on the one hand and a desire to forge alliances in the pursuit of a common objective on the other. They saw their efforts hindered by the metropolitan government's lack of concern for the welfare of the settler family, an attitude evidenced by the government's failure to extend pronatalist laws and family rights to the empire. Settler familialists asserted that they would work to resolve their own depopulation crisis instead of waiting for metropolitan "miracles." The notion that settler familialists could undertake such a task was never questioned by their metropolitan counterparts, who soon became valuable allies to the newly formed North African familialist movement. Through this alliance, metropolitan pronatalist leaders became an unofficial colonial lobby and, with their many connections in parliament, worked to represent settler interests in Paris. As a result of this collaboration, metropolitan pronatalists developed a deeper understanding of settler colonialism; this, in turn, moved them further away from the initial euphoria about empire that Dr. Ricoux had generated half a century earlier, but more determined than ever to protect the demographic resource that empire represented.

Conclusion

The last two years of the Third Republic were marked by a flurry of pronatalist initiatives introduced by the new government of Édouard Daladier. With a series of decrees in 1938,[1] Daladier made inheritance laws more flexible, expanded the family allowance system, and introduced the *allocation de la mère au foyer*.[2] Building on the existing family allowance system, this provision for stay-at-home mothers was designed to encourage women to leave the workforce and devote themselves to their families. The following year saw the creation of the Haut comité de la population, a governmental committee uniting representatives from various ministries with outside experts, such as pronatalist leaders Adolphe Landry and Fernand Boverat. The work of the committee led to the decree law of July 29, 1939, better known as the Code de la famille.[3] Although the Code did not include familial suffrage among its provisions, as pronatalists had hoped, it did incorporate many of their proposals, including more substantial family allowances, the teaching of demography in schools, and harsher penalties for abortion, pornography, and "public immorality."[4] Dissatisfied with the sporadic nature of prior state efforts to address depopulation, pronatalists hailed the Code de la famille as an important step forward. No longer, it seemed, would pronatalist reforms fall victim to governmental inertia; the Code represented a systematic approach to safeguarding the French family and improving the birthrate.

Their immense support for the Code notwithstanding, French pronatalists' celebration of its passage was sober, reflecting the dark, uncertain times in which they lived. They watched Hitler's growing power with concern, worrying that Nazi Germany would seek to reclaim its former colonies, some of which had been added to France's empire as League of Nations mandates.[5] Within Europe's borders, Nazi Germany had already begun its expansion east, absorbing Austria and Czechoslovakia into its empire. With the German invasion of Poland less than two months after the passage of the Code de la famille, France was drawn into another world war, one that few French people wanted to fight. As Maréchal Pétain, the hero of Verdun, would later declare, France had "too few children" to successfully fight such a war.[6] More than a million French soldiers had died in World War I and did not return to produce the sons who, by 1939, would have been of age to serve in the army. Historians have for many years contested this assessment of the French army, citing non-demographic factors that weakened French defenses.[7] Nevertheless, to pronatalists, France's devastating defeat at the hands of the Germans in 1940 constituted the crisis of which they had tried, for decades, to warn the public.

Following France's surrender in June 1940, the nation was divided into seven zones, the two most important of which were the German occupied zone, encompassing both the north (including Paris) and west (including Bordeaux), and the "free" zone in the south, where the French government took up residence in the town of Vichy.[8] In July of that year, what remained of the French parliament voted full powers to Pétain, now head of state, thereby dealing the definitive blow to the Third Republic. Surprisingly, it was the realization of pronatalists' worst fears (military defeat) and the demise of the Republic that ultimately facilitated the adoption of much of the political platform they had long sought.

Blaming the French defeat on the weak birthrate, which purportedly stemmed from the decadence, disorder, and corruption of the interwar years, Vichy embarked on a Révolution nationale intended to restore France to its former glory by improving the birthrate and resurrecting the family. Validating the kinds of arguments long made by pronatalists and familialists, Pétain asserted that "a people is a hierarchy of families." Emphasizing that the family, not the individual,

238

is "the very foundation of the social edifice," Pétain explained that "in the new order we are instituting, the family will be honored, protected, aided."[9] As Cheryl Koos, Miranda Pollard, and Kristen Stromberg Childers have demonstrated, the Révolution nationale placed a strong emphasis on restoring "natural" gender identities by discouraging women's employment outside the home, limiting women's sexual freedoms, strengthening a man's role as *chef de famille*, and disseminating propaganda promoting these ideals.[10] These reforms all had their roots in the Third Republic, as we have seen. Further symbolizing this continuity between Vichy and the Third Republic was the work of pronatalist organizations such as the Alliance nationale, which continued to operate and had considerable influence in the government. Vichy's decision to create a special "antiabortion police unit," for example, came at the initiative of Fernand Boverat.[11] The new regime further gained the support of pronatalists by creating, in September 1941, the Commissariat général à la famille, which represented the interests of the family in the government, had the authority to develop laws pertaining to the family, and was in charge of all propaganda related to encouraging family values in the population.[12] Similar to French defeat in the Franco-Prussian War and near defeat in World War I, therefore, the debacle in 1940 propelled the pronatalist movement forward, rendering its program more urgent and compelling to the nation's leaders.

Along similar lines, the French empire stood as a symbol of hope to the humiliated nation in 1940, just as it had in 1871.[13] Although Vichy officials blamed French defeat on the corruption and weakness of the Third Republic as well as the moral decay of metropolitan society, they saw settlers and colonial life in a different light. From their perspective, colonial settlers were untainted by the decadence that characterized the metropole and, with their supposed virility and superior health, represented key elements in the anticipated national regeneration.[14] This construction of the prolific settler and the reforming potential of imperialism, was not, however, specific to the Vichy period, as we have seen. During the Third Republic, pronatalists and members of the Union coloniale française distinguished between metropolitan and colonial societies by emphasizing the purity of colonial life and positioning settler colonialism as essential to the survival of the nation. Thus, while Vichy officials believed themselves to be departing from the "old regime" that was the Third Republic, many of their ideas drew heavily on arguments first advanced in the nineteenth century.

The idea that empire would play an important role in national regeneration gained greater poignancy under Vichy. While France was invaded, defeated, and partly occupied, the colonies remained under French control and, for this reason alone, stood as a symbol of French power. Yet despite their loyalty to "France," the colonies were a contested space, divided between two different French governments, each purporting to be the true, legitimate French government: Vichy France and the Free French movement. When Charles de Gaulle rejected the armistice that was signed "as if France did not have an empire," he hoped that all of France's colonies would do the same and join the Free French forces in liberating France.[15] French Equatorial Africa, the New Hebrides, and French outposts in India were the only colonies to do so in 1940. Allied victories in 1941 and 1942 would later bring Syria, Madagascar, and North and West Africa over to the Free French side.

Prior to Allied "reconquests" of the French empire, however, the vast majority of French colonies were loyal to the Vichy regime. According to Eric Jennings, one way to understand this loyalty was that Vichy's paternalist ideology held considerably more appeal to colonial governments and French settlers than did the democratic notions of liberty, equality, and fraternity that were, they believed, incompatible with the realities of colonial rule.[16] As the empire already represented "paternalism, authoritarianism, tradition, and hierarchy," some colonials even asserted that the metropole was following the empire's lead, having found its salvation in the colonial example.[17] In Algeria, in particular, the ideology of the Révolution nationale responded to preexisting political concerns. One contentious issue during the interwar period, for instance, had been the proposed Blum-Viollette bill, which would have extended citizenship rights to some colonized Algerians without requiring them to abandon their legal status as Muslims.[18] According

CONCLUSION

to Jacques Cantier, settlers who had vehemently opposed this metropolitan proposal viewed Vichy's emphasis on hierarchy to be conducive to defending colonial society against Algerian nationalism.[19] In Madagascar, Vichy's ideology about returning to the land and reestablishing "natural" hierarchies also represented a move away from the Third Republic's brand of colonialism. Vichy officials sought to "retribalize" the Malagasy population by replacing republican education with technical and agricultural courses, revoking citizenship rights from recently naturalized Malagasy, and actively reducing the number of Malagasy bureaucrats.[20] Such measures stood in marked contrast to Gallieni's earlier decisions to train colonial doctors and introduce civic education through the Fête des enfants.

To understand settler support for Vichy's Révolution nationale, it is also important to remember that the French government had failed to win the support of many colonial settlers in the final decades of the Third Republic. Settlers had long considered the survival of their way of life to be dependent on governmental support for large families, whether in the form of familial suffrage or financial incentives. Despite appeals on their behalf by such pronatalists as Fernand Boverat and Jacques Bertillon, the governments of the Third Republic generally considered extending pronatalist measures and family rights to the settler populations a low priority, as this book has demonstrated. Consequently, pronatalist measures enacted in the settler colonies resulted from local initiative rather than from the intervention of the metropolitan French government. Dissatisfied with the Third Republic, settlers hoped that the Vichy government would usher in a new era and new policies vis-à-vis settler colonies. The history of colonial pronatalism and its interaction with that of the metropole thus sheds considerable light on why many French pronatalists and settler familialists initially embraced Vichy's Révolution nationale. The Révolution nationale built on pronatalist measures developed in both the metropole and the settler colonies prior to World War II and appealed to settlers and metropolitan pronatalists long frustrated by government inertia or disinterest.

Yet settler familialist organizations never lost their raison d'être and, like pronatalists in France, continued to operate and demand additional reforms in the 1940s and beyond. Despite settlers' initial hopes that the Vichy regime would validate and support their objectives, these hopes were quickly dashed when the 1939 Code de la famille and subsequent pronatalist laws introduced in France under Pétain were not extended to the empire in their entirety.[21] In this respect, there is remarkable continuity in the types of demands made by settler familialists in the 1920s and 1930s and those made by their successor organizations after 1940. For instance, one of the main objectives of the three hundred families represented by the Association des chefs de familles françaises à Madagascar in the 1940s was the full application of the Code in the colony.[22] In particular, settlers were frustrated that state employees in Madagascar were the only ones to receive family allowances and demanded that this benefit be extended to all French citizens, as was the practice in France. Following their colony's "liberation" in 1942, these familialists then hoped that de Gaulle's government would be sympathetic to their demands. In 1943, the president of the association, Dr. Fontoynont, appealed to the governor-general of the colony asking that this inequality between state employees and other French citizens in the colony, "incompatible with the new and republican spirit of tomorrow's France," be suppressed in keeping with de Gaulle's stated goal of supporting all French families. Fontoynont explicitly linked the financial support of large French families with the maintenance of French rule, presenting colonialism as a pronatalist question at its core. Although he asserted that the extension of the Code in Madagascar was conducive to upholding "white prestige" on the island, something that was essential to the future of the colony, this idea was more broadly defined than his words would seem to suggest; consistent with many other such organizations in the French empire, naturalized Malagasy were active in Madagascar's familialist movement, and the association demanded financial familial benefits for all French citizens, whether of European or Malagasy origin.

Regeneration through Empire: The Legacy of the Third Republic

Settler arguments linking the full application of the Révolution nationale in their colonies with maintaining colonial rule and improving

French population growth overall represent the final chapter in a long history, stretching back to the early Third Republic, of French efforts to address depopulation by drawing on the full resources and opportunities of the empire. While the pronatalist movement initially emerged in response to France's poor performance in the Franco-Prussian War, pronatalists' perceptions of the depopulation crisis quickly evolved beyond the European context to include empire. Pronatalists' support for settler colonialism, as well as their role as advocates for settler interest groups, demonstrates the impact of imperialism on French political movements. Consequently, as this book has shown, the influence of empire on French life extended beyond mass culture, transforming political movements organized to address specifically metropolitan concerns.

Initially, pronatalists' interest in empire was linked to their objective of establishing an outlet for French migration and influencing individuals' reproductive choices. In their propaganda, pronatalists rejected family planning, depicting the idea of choosing when or if to have a baby as an immoral act that had dire consequences for the nation as a whole. Such assertions aside, many of the reforms they proposed implicitly acknowledged that they would be far more effective at shaping individuals'—especially men's—choices than trying to eliminate the idea of family planning altogether.[23] Consequently, they became interested in colonial settlement because they hoped that migrating to the empire would have a positive influence on men's family-planning decisions. In this regard, they drew on the conclusions of expert statisticians and demographers who, in the 1860s and 1870s, distinguished between what they considered healthy and unhealthy patterns of migration. Peasants abandoned the countryside, their traditional way of life, and high birthrates in order to migrate to Paris and other large cities, where they lived in cramped, disease-ridden quarters and produced few children. Louis-Adolphe Bertillon's dire warnings about the dangers of such migratory trends led him to advance a demographic argument in favor of colonial expansion and settlement. Bertillon posited that the French population required additional territory into which it could expand so as to avoid remaining confined to growing within narrow, suffocating borders. As persuasive as Bertillon's theories were to his colleagues, however, demographic experts initially hesitated to recommend that more French people be recruited for colonial emigration. Existing efforts at establishing colonial settlements in Algeria and elsewhere had produced discouraging results. France, it seemed, lacked the right sort of colonies with which to test Bertillon's theory of reviving the birthrate through colonial settlement.

The year 1880, however, transformed pronatalists' perceptions of the demographic crisis; from this point forward, settler colonialism was on the pronatalist agenda, shaping pronatalists' discussions of how to strengthen the birthrate and which individuals could contribute to such efforts. Pronatalists were inspired by the results of Ricoux's demographic study showing that French settlers in Algeria had a higher birthrate than their compatriots in the metropole. This conclusion led to the myth of the prolific settler. One of many myths that shaped French imperialism, this myth was premised on the idea that French people exhibited a higher birthrate once established in the colonies. Gender was an essential part of how the prolific settler was imagined, as pronatalists and prominent social scientists believed that the demographic benefits of colonial settlement stemmed primarily from the impact that migration and colonial life had on men's choices about marrying, reproducing, and raising children.

The existence of settler colonies and the apparent comparisons between colonial and metropolitan life offered pronatalists new ways to articulate and understand their anxieties about modern life and its effects on familial values, gender identities, and individuals' reproductive choices. Organizations committed to the cause of encouraging colonial settlement, such as the Union coloniale française, appropriated and expanded pronatalists' arguments concerning which types of women and men contributed to depopulation, thus demonstrating the pervasiveness of such ideas. Although women were notably absent from the earliest depictions of the prolific settler, recruiting women for colonial emigration and settlement was essential to establishing a self-reproducing and racially "French" population in the colonies. Out of such discussions emerged organizations such as the Société française d'emigration des femmes, created to address the metropolitan problem of "the surplus woman" and to establish prolific French populations in the settler colonies.

Discussions about French depopulation and empire were thus closely connected, with members of both pronatalist organizations and the colonial lobby emphasizing the demographic need for large settler colonies. Despite such discussions, all colonial governments faced one common challenge, albeit to varying degrees: making settler colonialism both viable and permanent. It was with the objective of establishing a large labor force for arriving settlers in mind, therefore, that Joseph Gallieni introduced a series of colonial pronatalist measures intended to increase Madagascar's Merina population. These measures constituted an important precedent to related measures introduced at later dates in other European colonies. Gallieni's initiatives also demonstrated that French pronatalism was not always limited to increasing the French population. Rather, he believed it necessary to work with a select group of colonial subjects in the interest of establishing a strong, growing French settler population. The value that French pronatalists saw in Gallieni's initiatives transcended the demographic importance they attached to colonial settlement endeavors, however. Gallieni's initiatives coincided with a critical phase in French pronatalism: the birth of the Alliance nationale, the creation of the Commission de la dépopulation, and the beginnings of the movement's push to lobby for legislative reforms. Like pronatalists in France, Gallieni focused much of his reform agenda on women, placing an emphasis on expert intervention into pregnancy, childbirth, and childcare. In part because of Gallieni's status as a great leader and a "man of action," pronatalists were eager to learn from his initiatives, most of which were inspired in one way or another by his experiences as a colonial administrator.

Pronatalists' willingness to draw from the colonial example and their astonishment that colonial governments would precede them in introducing important reforms continued during the interwar period. At this time, a defining feature of the French pronatalist movement was the effort to redefine the democratic process by replacing universal male suffrage with familial suffrage. This, pronatalists believed, would elevate the *famille nombreuse* to its rightful place in French society and give the family man greater electoral weight, thus redirecting elected officials' attention away from the interests of single men. Throughout the 1920s and into the 1930s, pronatalists struggled to garner sufficient support in parliament and were ultimately unsuccessful. Yet across the Mediterranean, in France's protectorates of Tunisia and Morocco, Residents-General Lucien Saint and Théodore Steeg supported the idea of familial suffrage and introduced the reform with little difficulty. Not only did this development embolden pronatalists in their efforts to introduce familial suffrage in France, but it also enabled them to draw conclusions about the kind of impact such a reform could have on the birthrate. They pointed to various pronatalist reforms introduced in Tunisia following the establishment of familial suffrage, seeing in these reforms the direct result of the residency's decision to redefine citizenship in a way that prioritized French fathers above all other settlers in the protectorate.

The high birthrates among French settlers and the introduction of pronatalist reforms in settler colonies combined to confirm French pronatalists in their belief that the French settler colonies represented a "fountain of youth" that would aid France in the fight against depopulation. Yet the creation, during the interwar years, of a settler familialist movement, predominantly in North Africa, suggested that French settlers faced a depopulation crisis of their own. Fully supporting their settler counterparts, metropolitan pronatalists asserted that this demographic crisis stemmed from the metropolitan government's refusal to extend family rights to settlers, a North African rural exodus, reduced immigration from France, and declining French birthrates that failed to keep pace with those of the growing colonized population. Reflecting the multiethnic composition of the North African colonies, settler pronatalist organizations sought racially exclusive pronatalist measures that would prioritize "French" settler population growth and that would not be extended to the colonial subjects. Still, these plans were not as straightforward as they would seem. Although the familialist organizations existed to secure family rights for specifically French families, they included members with a mixture of French, Spanish, and Italian heritage as well as a number of Muslims. In this way, settlers contributed to metropolitan pronatalists' evolving notions of which individuals could contribute to French efforts to address depopulation; in the colonial context, strengthening the French birthrate required working with other populations who had either assimilated into French society or supported French colonial rule.

Throughout the Third Republic, French pronatalists joined the colonial lobby in asserting the importance of an empire that would make France one hundred million strong. Yet in expanding their vision beyond Europe's borders, pronatalists were more careful in asserting the demographic potential of imperialism. Of greatest importance to pronatalists were developments in Algeria, Tunisia, Morocco, and Madagascar, where the growth of the settler populations, the activities of settler familialist organizations, and the introduction of colonial pronatalist measures combined to transform the metropolitan pronatalist movement. The idea that France could overcome depopulation by establishing young colonies overseas, in natural environments untainted by metropolitan life, inspired great hope in pronatalists struggling to come to terms with the vast transformations under way in Europe. By witnessing uniquely colonial pronatalist reforms that were distinct from what existed in France at this time, pronatalists gained insight into how they might address depopulation in the metropole. Finally, their study of colonial pronatalism and their interaction with settler familialists transformed metropolitan pronatalists' notions of which individuals could contribute to strengthening the French population. Consequently, in the struggle to overcome depopulation, the French empire offered pronatalists more than a simple population reservoir that could come to the metropole's aid in times of war and crisis. It was through the establishment and maintenance of settler colonies that pronatalists believed they could work to reverse the demographic trends and return France to its former glory.

Fears of depopulation influenced French politics greatly, as evidenced by the numbers of pronatalists who worked to generate public awareness about the birthrate and lobbied the government for reforms. Yet in the end, did these efforts produce results? The simple answer to such a question would be that pronatalists ultimately failed in their efforts to create the kind of society they considered essential to stable population growth. As the twentieth century progressed, the French population became increasingly urban, the average French family continued to have fewer than the desired four children, and while women gained the vote following World War II, the family did not. Yet these developments did not have the destructive impact on the birthrate that pronatalists had feared. For example, concerning the consequences of women's political participation, scholars have shown that many of the first women to enter the French parliament supported reforms relating to child care and the family, reforms that were central components of the pronatalist agenda.[24] More importantly, France in the second half of the twentieth century never experienced the much-anticipated "true depopulation," or overall population decline, that many pronatalists had expected would occur by century's end. In fact, France experienced greater population growth following World War II than pronatalists had predicted, beginning with "le baby boom" that began in the late 1940s and continued into the 1960s.

These were, nevertheless, the decades during which France lost most of its colonies, including Morocco and Tunisia in 1956, Madagascar in 1960, and Algeria in 1962. Decolonization initiated waves of postcolonial migrations, including the "return" of French settlers, many of whom had never been to France before and in some cases lacked French ancestry, and the migration of former colonial subjects and their descendants, who continue to migrate to France today.[25] While the latter migration has provoked many debates within French society about national identity and cultural assimilation, the arrival of immigrants has contributed to France's overall population growth and provided the nation with additional workers to help support the welfare state.

France's continued population growth is not, however, due to immigration alone. As the 2006 census revealed, France currently has a cumulative birthrate of 2.1.[26] Although this would not have seemed impressive to Third Republic pronatalists, it is presently the highest cumulative birthrate in Europe. The French government proudly reported in 2006 that France is now one of only two European states to have a birthrate above the replacement rate (birthrates in Germany and Italy, by contrast, are currently well below the replacement rate). This reveals pronatalism's enduring impact on French politics in the twentieth and twenty-first centuries. While no one can say with absolute certainty why one country has a higher birthrate than another, experts have pointed to the vast array of support mechanisms for working mothers and financial incentives for families that exist in France to a greater degree than in many other European states. For example, in France, where up to 80 percent of women work, there is state-subsidized child care.[27] This recalls early pronatalist efforts to establish nurseries in factories to accommodate working women and ease the financial burden of caring for a young child. The continuity between early pronatalism and the present day is also seen in the *carte de la famille nombreuse* (a discount-card for large families), family allowances, paid maternity leaves, and many other forms of state assistance.

Pronatalist concerns about racial purity and migration continue to be felt in France today, particularly in view of controversies surrounding Muslim headscarves and growing support for the far right. One example of this is the scandal that engulfed the French town of Vitrolles in 1998 when the mayor, Catherine Mégret, instituted a *prime de naissance* (birth incentive). Under this offer, 5,000 francs would be given to the mother of each baby born in the commune, but with one stipulation; to be eligible a new mother had to either be French or European in origin. Amid accusations of racism and discrimination, Mégret defended her actions by stating that the birth incentive would alleviate "the threat to the renewal of the French population that foreign families pose by way of the numbers of their family members and their fertility."[28] Mégret's proposal recalls the efforts of settler familialists in the 1920s to introduce a racially exclusive form of pronatalism in North Africa in order to encourage the growth of the settler population, considered to be too few in number, without simultaneously encouraging the growth of the colonized population. Ultimately, Mégret was fined, sentenced to three years in prison, and made ineligible for office for two years as a result of her discriminatory policy.

While the birth incentive was short-lived and only a small number of women received their rewards, its very existence is emblematic of France's struggle to adjust to recent waves of immigration and a post-colonial order. The scandal also reveals the persistence into the present day of racial anxieties surrounding the national birthrate that originated during the Third Republic.

Abbreviations

AD	Archives diplomatiques
AMAE	Archives du ministère des affaires étrangères
BMD	Bibliothèque Marguerite Durand
CAOM	Centre des archives d'outre-mer
GGM	Gouverneur général de Madagascar
GGM/AMI	Gouverneur général de Madagascar, Assistance médicale indigène
GGM/SS	Gouverneur général de Madagascar, Service de santé

Introduction

1. Spengler, *France Faces Depopulation*, 22. The statistic for the United Kingdom includes Ireland.

2. Levasseur, *La population française*, 2:253. The birthrate is measured as the number of births per thousand people per year.

3. Examples of this approach include Betts, *France and Decolonization*; and Ageron, *La décolonisation*.

4. For example, this is the argument made by Thomas August in *The Selling of the Empire*.

5. Wilder, *The French Imperial Nation-State*, 25. Another example of this approach can be seen in Ann Laura Stoler and Frederick Cooper, "Between Metropole and Colony: Rethinking a Research Agenda," in Stoler and Cooper, *Tensions of Empire*, 1–56.

6. Studies analyzing colonial imagery in metropolitan film, advertisements, and the press include Ezra, *The Colonial Unconscious*; Hale, *Races on Display*; Slavin, *Colonial Cinema and Imperial France*; Schneider, *An Empire for the Masses*.

7. On colonial exhibitions see, Lynn E. Palermo, "Identity under Construction: Representing the Colonies at the Paris Exposition Universelle of 1889," in Peabody and Stovall, *The Color of Liberty*, 285–300; Hale, *Races on Display*.

8. On colonial migration to France see, among others, MacMaster, *Colonial Migrants and Racism*; Fletcher, "Unsettling Settlers"; Boittin, *Colonial Metropolis*; Stovall, *Paris and the Spirit of 1919*; Wilder, *The French Imperial Nation-State*.

9. Some recent scholarship has examined French feminist interest in the empire, particularly the status of colonized women. See Boittin, *Colonial Metropolis*; Eichner, "*La Citoyenne* in the World"; Kimble, "Emancipation through Secularization."

10. M. Thomas, *The French Empire between the Wars*.

11. M. Thomas, *The French Empire between the Wars*, 5–6.

12. Spengler, *France Faces Depopulation*.

13. Spengler, *France Faces Depopulation*, 3.

14. For pronatalism in the Third Republic see Camiscioli, *Reproducing the French Race*; Joshua Cole, *The Power of Large Numbers*; Frader, *Breadwinners and Citizens*; McLaren, *Sexuality and Social Order*; Offen, "Depopulation, Nationalism and Feminism"; S. Pedersen, *Family, Dependence*; and Schneider, *Quality and Quantity*. For pronatalism in the Third Republic and Vichy see Childers, *Fathers, Families, and the State*; Le Bras, *Marianne et les lapins*; and Pollard, *Reign of Virtue*.

15. According to Sophia Quine, this was especially the case in Italy. See Quine, *Population Politics*, 9.

16. Davin, "Imperialism and Motherhood."

17. Weinbaum, *Wayward Reproductions*.

18. Weinbaum, *Wayward Reproductions*, 4.

19. See Renan, "What Is a Nation?" For an analysis of the influence of Renan's essay on French ideas of race see Jackson, *France*, 108.

20. On the idea of "the French race" see Cohen, *The French Encounter with Africans*; the essays in Peabody and Stovall, *The Color of Liberty*; and the essays in Chapman and Frader, *Race in France*.

21. Harp, *Marketing Michelin*, 149.

22. The naturalization law of 1889 combined both *jus soli* and *jus sanguinis* by making citizenship accessible to the children of foreigners, provided that the children were born in France and had lived there for a minimum of five years. The latter requirement was intended to ensure that such children would be sufficiently assimilated after five years of exposure to French language and customs.

23. Camiscioli, *Reproducing the French Race*.

24. Camiscioli, *Reproducing the French Race*, 35–36.

25. Stovall, *Paris and the Spirit of 1919*, 130 n. 56.

26. On concerns about both "quality and quantity" see Schneider, *Quality and Quantity*.

27. On eugenics and pronatalism in Germany and Great Britain see Gisela Bock, "Antinatalism, Maternity and Paternity in National Socialist Racism," in Bock and Thane, *Maternity and Gender Policies*, 233–52; Koonz, *Mothers in the Fatherland*; Jane Lewis, "Models of Equality for Women: The Case of State Support for Children in Twentieth-Century Britain," in Bock and Thane, *Maternity and Gender Policies*, 73–92.

28. On pronatalism in Italy and Spain see De Grazia, *How Fascism Ruled Women*; Quine, *Population Politics*; Chiara Saraceno, "Redefining Maternity and Paternity: Gender, Pronatalism and Social Policies in Fascist Italy," in Bock and Thane, *Maternity and Gender Policies*, 196–212; Mary Nash, "Pronatalism and Motherhood in Franco's Spain," in Bock and Thane, *Maternity and Gender Policies*, 160–77.

29. Quine, *Population Politics*, 131.

30. One well-known book about the "yellow peril" that uses this type of imagery is Dennery, *Foules d'Asie*.

31. This was particularly evident in the *Revue des deux mondes* beginning in 1889. A number of contributors, including Alfred Fouillé and the political economist Paul Leroy-Beaulieu, contributed articles expressing concern over French depopulation and the concurrent growth of East Asian populations. Also see Zola's 1899 pronatalist novel, *Fécondité*.

32. On pronatalist concerns about Japan, see J. Bertillon, *La dépopulation de la France*.

33. See Lake and Reynolds, *Drawing the Global Colour Line*.

34. A review of this pamphlet appeared in the journal of the Alliance nationale. See "'La race blanche en danger de mort': Une nouvelle brochure de l'alliance nationale," *Revue de l'alliance nationale pour l'accroissement de la population française*, September 1933, 255–60.

35. "'La race blanche en danger de mort,'" 255–60. Another good example would be the articles that appeared in the journal of the Alliance nationale in 1927 and 1928. These were written by the organization's president Fernand Boverat and titled "The Scourge of the White Race." Each month the article in this series discussed depopulation in a different western European country. The countries assessed in these articles were as follows (in order of appearance): Sweden, Norway, Denmark, Switzerland, Holland, Germany, and Great Britain. See *Revue de l'alliance nationale pour l'accroissement de la population française*, December 1927–June 1928.

36. "Le péril jaune: Excédents des naissances sur les décès en 1926," *Revue de l'alliance nationale contre la dépopulation*, July 1928, 208.

37. Many theorists in the Third Republic thought of France and the empire as a single unified entity of one hundred million people. One notable example is Albert Sarraut, who served both as minister of colonies and as the governor-general of Indochina. See Wilder, *The French Imperial Nation-State*, chapter 4.

38. Mangin, *La force noire*. West Africa's population was not nearly as abundant as Mangin believed, and colonial officials were already at this time complaining of a labor shortage in the region. His argument was also premised on the faulty premise that Africans made tough, fearless soldiers who did not feel pain the same way that Europeans did and for this reason would also make ideal recruits. See Echenberg, *Colonial Conscripts*, 28–29.

39. On the participation of colonial soldiers in World War I see Echenberg, *Colonial Conscripts*; Lunn, *Memoirs of the Maelstrom*; Michel, *L'appel à l'Afrique*.

40. On colonial workers in France during World War I, see MacMaster, *Colonial Migrants and Racism*. Although it deals more with the interwar period, also see Rosenberg, *Policing Paris*.

41. Gosnell, *The Politics of Frenchness*; Lorcin, "Rome and France in Africa"; Lorcin, *Imperial Identities*.

42. For example, Debury, *Un pays de célibataires*, 22; and Gonnard, *La dépopulation en France*, 63.

43. On the comparisons pronatalists made with Rome see Jacques Bertillon, "Comment Auguste sauva Rome de la dépopulation," *Bulletin de l'alliance nationale pour l'accroissement de la population française*, January 15, 1911, 106–11; and Debury, *Un pays de célibataires*.

44. These reform movements expressed their views in periodicals such as *Le relèvement social* and *La réforme sociale*. On the subject of prostitution in nineteenth-century France more generally, see Harsin, *Policing Prostitution*; and Corbin, *Les filles de noce*.

45. For instance, a 1912 article in the feminist newspaper *La française* reported that the government had formed a new commission to study depopulation and make recommendations. The commission was composed of a very long list of prominent men but not a single woman. Pauline Rebour, the author of this article, pointed out that feminists were very used to hearing that women did not need political rights because their true influence was in the home and that their real authority was in matters concerning children and family life. Yet their exclusion from the commission, with its emphasis on motherhood and children, would seem to expose the flaw in that particular argument against women's political rights. Rebour, "Les lois d'intérêt féminin au parlement: Pas une femme à la commission contre la dépopulation!," *La française*, November 30, 1912, 1.

46. In particular, there was significant interaction between the organized pro-natalist movement and the feminists of the Conseil national des femmes françaises and the Union française pour le suffrage des femmes.

47. For more on the intersection of pronatalism and feminism see, in particular, Offen, "Depopulation, Nationalism and Feminism."

48. On French missionaries abroad see the articles in White and Daughton, *In God's Empire*; and Foster, *Faith in Empire*.

49. Koos, "Engendering Reaction."

50. P. Smith, *Feminism and the Third Republic*, 217.

51. As scholars have argued, condoms' exemption from the 1920 legislation indicated that legislators were primarily concerned with limiting women's reproductive choices, not men's sexual freedoms. At the time, condoms were mostly used to protect against venereal disease and were not generally used as a contraceptive device by married couples. Because the products banned under the law were contraceptive in nature, the law was clearly intended to prevent women from taking precautions against pregnancy. The continued legality of condoms, on the other hand, indicates that legislators had no desire to place constraints on the freedom of men to have

sexual relations outside of marriage but still protect themselves from venereal disease. See, e.g., J. E. Pedersen, "Regulating Abortion and Birth Control."

52. Koos, "Engendering Reaction," 39.

53. The École coloniale was founded in 1889 and the Ministry of Colonies in 1894. Wilder, *The French Imperial Nation-State*, 308 n. 2.

54. See, e.g., Jennings, *Vichy in the Tropics*; Daughton, *An Empire Divided*; Jennings, *Curing the Colonizers*.

55. On pronatalist policies introduced in French West Africa see Conklin, "Faire Naître v. Faire du Noir."

1. France's "Supreme Chance"

1. For French ideas on "white" identity during the Third Republic, see Chapman and Frader's introduction to Chapman and Frader, *Race in France*, 5; and Camiscioli, *Reproducing the French Race*, 12. For ideas of "whiteness" in French slaveholding societies prior to this period see Schloss, *Sweet Liberty*; and Cohen, *The French Encounter with Africans*.

2. In particular this comes up in Ricoux's 1874 study, *Contribution à l'étude de l'acclimatement*.

3. For more on the demographic transition see Blum, *Strength in Numbers*; and Joshua Cole, *The Power of Large Numbers*.

4. Blum, *Strength in Numbers*, 6.

5. Blum, *Strength in Numbers*, chapter 2.

6. On the collection of statistical data in the eighteenth century see Joshua Cole, *The Power of Large Numbers*, chapter 1.

7. Blum, *Strength in Numbers*, 2.

8. See Tuttle, *Conceiving the Old Regime*.

9. Joshua Cole, *The Power of Large Numbers*, 25.

10. Spengler, *France Faces Depopulation*, 107.

11. Blum, *Strength in Numbers*, 6–7.

12. Blum, *Strength in Numbers*, 18. Blum points out that in opposition to Montesquieu, many eighteenth-century thinkers, among them Thomas Malthus, believed that people multiplied in countries where there was plenty of space and food.

13. Joshua Cole, *The Power of Large Numbers*, 1.

14. On the image of the "dangerous classes" see Chevalier, *Classes laborieuses et classes dangereuses*.

15. Chevalier, *Classes laborieuses et classes dangereuses*.

16. Hecht, *The End of the Soul*, 153.

17. On French plans for Algeria during this period, see Sessions, *By Sword and Plow*.

18. Spengler, *France Faces Depopulation*, 112.

19. Prévost-Paradol, *La France nouvelle*, 415.

20. France's defeat in 1870 cost Legoyt his job as director of the Statistique générale. Hecht, *The End of the Soul*, 153.

21. Schneider, *Quality and Quantity*, 12.

22. Pick, *Faces of Degeneration*, 100–101. Also see Schneider, *Quality and Quantity*, 87–88.

23. Schneider, *Quality and Quantity*, 16.

24. On concepts of masculinity and honor in French society see Nye, *Masculinity and Male Codes of Honor*.

25. "Concours de familles nombreuses," *Bulletin de l'alliance nationale pour l'accroissement de la population française*, October 1904, 598–600.

26. J. E. Pedersen, "Regulating Abortion and Birth Control," 673–74. Pedersen explains that Royer's statement, as well as some of her proposed solutions to depopulation, were too radical to appear in the published proceedings of this meeting.

27. See, in particular, Riley, *Am I That Name?*, 1–2.

28. Joshua Cole, "There Are Only Good Mothers."

29. Roberts, *Disruptive Acts*, 22.

30. The Naquet Law of 1884 made it easier for couples to obtain a divorce. Although it did not treat husbands and wives equally, the law increased the number of circumstances under which wives could seek a divorce and was in this regard a great improvement over the restrictive Napoleonic Code. Some proponents of the law argued that facilitating divorce would actually improve demographic growth, as it would enable an unhappy and presumably unproductive couple to part ways, remarry, and reproduce with their new spouses. On the other hand, many opponents of the law feared that divorce under any circumstances weakened patriarchal authority and undermined the institution of marriage and that its general availability encouraged people to lose sight of their familial duties.

31. It is impossible to make a blanket statement about what French feminists in the late nineteenth century believed, given that there were so many different organizations with divergent agendas. Radical feminists generally supported voting rights for women, and in some cases they sought reproductive rights such as expanded access to birth control. Liberal feminists steered clear of the most controversial issues, like voting and contraception, and instead sought legal equality, focusing in particular on reforming a woman's subordinate, childlike status within marriage. For an overview see Offen, *European Feminisms*.

32. Roberts, *Disruptive Acts*, 8.

33. See, e.g., Mangin, *La force noire*, 54.

34. On the health "risks" of bearing few or no children, see Joshua Cole, *The Power of Large Numbers*, 181–83.

35. Joshua Cole, *The Power of Large Numbers*, 187–88.

36. Joshua Cole, *The Power of Large Numbers*, 11; and Schweber, *Disciplining Statistics*, 3.

37. Schweber, *Disciplining Statistics*, 4.

38. Joshua Cole, *The Power of Large Numbers*.

39. "La vie et les œuvres du Docteur L.-A. Bertillon, professeur de démographie à l'école d'anthropologie, chef des travaux de la statistique municipale de la ville de Paris," *Annales de démographie internationale* (1883): 6–46.

40. Hecht, *The End of the Soul*, 147–48.

41. Schweber, *Disciplining Statistics*, 36.

42. The Bertillon family included a number of well-known individuals. Louis-Adolphe Bertillon's oldest son, Jacques, would continue the work of his father and his grandfather, Achille Guillard, by becoming a respected demographer in his own right and founding the Alliance nationale pour l'accroissement de la population française. Each of these three men is remembered as the most prominent demographer of his respective generation. One of Jacques Bertillon's daughters, Jacqueline, became a lawyer, worked to educate women about their legal rights, and collaborated with her father on various natalist projects. Another of Louis-Adolphe Bertillon's sons, Alphonse Bertillon, invented a system of criminal classification used by police forces in France and in other European states and North America. For more on the Bertillon family, see Hecht, *The End of the Soul*.

43. Louis-Adolphe Bertillon, "Mouvements de la population dans les divers états de l'Europe et notamment en France: Leurs relations et leurs causes," *Annales de démographie internationale* (1877): 3–206.

44. Joshua Cole, *The Power of Large Numbers*, 151, 149.

45. "La vie et les œuvres du Docteur L.-A. Bertillon," 106.

46. Louis-Adolphe Bertillon, "Études nouvelles sur la population," *Journal de la société de statistique de Paris* 18, no. 8 (August 1877): 199–209; L.-A. Bertillon, "Migration"; L.-A. Bertillon, "Mouvements de la population," 202.

47. L.-A. Bertillon, "Études nouvelles sur la population," 202.

48. J. Bertillon, *La statistique humaine de la France*, 150.

49. On the connections between statistical data and metropolitan reform movements, see Joshua Cole, *The Power of Large Numbers*.

50. On French migration to Canada, see Choquette, *Frenchmen into Peasants*.

51. On the nation's *esprit de clocher* (love for their native land) see Sessions, *By Sword and Plow*, 292.

52. Sessions, *By Sword and Plow*, 290.

53. L.-A. Bertillon, "Migration," 661.

54. L.-A.Bertillon, "Migration," 663. Victoria was part of Britain's Australian colony.

55. See, e.g., A. Legoyt, "Des conséquences de l'émigration au point de vue de l'acclimatement," *Journal de la société de statistique de Paris* 6, no. 1 (January 1865): 7–13, 93–105.

56. For more on the impact of acclimatization on French imperialism, see Jennings, *Curing the Colonizers*; and Michael G. Vann, "Of *Le Cafard* and Other Tropical Threats: Disease and White Colonial Culture in Indochina," in Robson and Yee, *France and Indochina*, 95–106.

57. Legoyt, "Des conséquences de l'émigration."

58. L. A. Bertillon, "Mouvements de la population," 203.

59. Legoyt, "Des conséquences de l'émigration."

60. "Procès-verbal de la séance du 5 juillet 1873," *Journal de la société de statistique de Paris* 13, no. 8 (August 1873): 197–200, quote on 198.

61. Louis-Adolphe Bertillon, "Dénombrement de l'Algérie depuis 1856: Algérie et Victoria comparées," *Bulletins de la société d'anthropologie de Paris* 2, no. 8 (1873): 597–603.

62. For more information on the "foundation myth" and how it shaped French colonialism in Algeria, see, in particular, Lorcin, "Rome and France in Africa"; also see Lorcin, *Imperial Identities*; and Gosnell, *The Politics of Frenchness*; A similar foundation myth existed in Tunisia after it was incorporated into the French empire in 1881, though this subject has received less attention from scholars.

63. Lorcin, "Rome and France in Africa." As Diana Davis shows, this historical narrative also shaped French ideas about the environment in North Africa and their role in returning it to its "natural" state. Land-tenure policies were in part predicated on the idea that nomadic Arab populations in the precolonial period were responsible for deforestation and desertification in the region. Davis, *Resurrecting the Granary of Rome*.

64. Louis-Adolphe Bertillon, introduction in Ricoux, *La démographie figurée de l'Algérie*.

65. Dr. E. Bertherand, "La longévité romaine dans le nord de l'Afrique," *Annales de démographie internationale* (1882): 204–5. Also see Jean-Pierre Bonnafont, "De l'acclimatement des Européens et de l'existence d'une population civile romaine, en Algérie, démontrée par l'histoire," *Bulletins de la société d'anthropologie de Paris* 2, no. 7 (1872): 122–25.

66. Ricoux, *Contribution à l'étude de l'acclimatement*. For more information on the academic debates concerning the ethnological origins of the Kabyle populations see Lorcin, *Imperial Identities*, chapter 7.

67. J. Bertillon, "Les Français en Algérie," 456.

68. Ricoux, *Contribution à l'étude de l'acclimatement*. For instance, Jacques Bertillon wrote a review of this study. Bertillon, "Les Français en Algérie."

69. Ricoux, *Contribution à l'étude de l'acclimatement*, i.

70. For information on important precursors to Ricoux's racial theory see Lorcin, *Imperial Identities*, chapter 7.

71. Ricoux, *Contribution à l'étude de l'acclimatement*, 105.

72. Ricoux, *Contribution à l'étude de l'acclimatement*, 93.

73. J. Bertillon, "Les Français en Algérie," 460.

74. Jennings, *Curing the Colonizers*, 12–14.

75. Some earlier studies, such as Baudicour's *La colonisation de l'Algérie*, provided some population figures, including the overall size of the population (broken down by sex) and the total number of births between 1830 and 1854. However, because studies such as these lacked details such as the annual mortality and birth rates, demographers like Louis-Adolphe Bertillon did not consider them sufficient for drawing conclusions about the growth of the French population.

76. Ricoux, *La démographie figurée de l'Algérie*.

77. Ricoux, *La démographie figurée de l'Algérie*, xix.

78. Kateb, *Européens, "indigènes" et juifs en Algérie*, 98–99.

79. For an example of the reception that Ricoux's work received in the Annales de démographie internationale, see J. B., "La démographie de l'Algérie," *Annales de démographie internationale* (1880): 227–29.

80. Paul Leroy-Beaulieu, "La colonisation de l'Algérie," *Revue des deux mondes*, September 1, 1882, 762.

81. C. Buloz, "Essais et notices," *Revue des deux mondes*, September 1, 1880, 240.

82. Ricoux, *La démographie figurée de l'Algérie*, 302.

83. J. Bertillon, *La statistique humaine de la France*, 158.

84. V. Turquan, "Contribution à l'étude de la population et de la dépopulation," 157.

85. Ponsolle, *La dépopulation*, 58.

86. Rommel, *Au pays de la revanche*. According to LeNaour and Valenti, Dr. Rommel was the nom de plume of a Frenchman. See Le Naour and Valenti, *La famille doit voter*, 51. Yet it appears that few pronatalists at the time were aware of this distinction. They widely cited *Au pays de la revanche* in their own works and deplored the idea that a German had assessed French society so accurately.

87. One pronatalist, in particular, who agreed with Rommel was Paul Gemähling. See Gemähling, *Vers la vie*.

88. *Bulletin de l'alliance nationale pour l'accroissement de la population française*, January 15, 1900.

89. Lovett, *Pronatalism, Reproduction, and the Family*, 8. On American pronatalism and Roosevelt also see Bederman, *Manliness and Civilization*.

90. Debury, *Un pays de célibataires*.

91. Charles Richet, "L'accroissement de la population française," *Revue des deux mondes*, June 1, 1882, 610. Richet was referring to France's former settler colony in Canada. Despite becoming part of the British empire in the eighteenth century, the French colony and its French-speaking population remained an important symbol of French influence abroad in the nineteenth century.

92. J. Bertillon, *La statistique humaine de la France*, 151.

93. Poiré, *L'émigration française aux colonies*, 43. A number of members of the Alliance nationale also presented the demographic strength of Franco-Canadians as proof that depopulation in France resulted not from racial degeneration but rather from a desire in France to not have children. See, e.g., Ledoux, *Le problème de la population française*, 6.

94. Poiré, *L'émigration française aux colonies*, 43. Whereas Poiré asserts that there were two million French people in Canada in the 1880s, Edme Piot goes a step further and says that the number rose from 60,000 to three million. Piot, *La dépopulation en France*, 66–67.

95. Debury, *Un pays de célibataires et de fils uniques*.

96. It should be noted that when France fell to the Germans during World War II, the North African colonies served as an important base of operations for Charles de Gaulle and the Free French. In this respect, the scenario envisioned by Debury in 1896 became a reality; France was defeated, but the French family survived, and some of the French "children," most notably Algeria, aided in the Allied liberation of the *mère-patrie*.

97. For an example of this view see Gonnard, *La dépopulation en France*, 124.

98. Moch, *Paths to the City*, 19.

99. For example, Moch argues that because most migrations during this period occurred within regions, rural migrations were not the destabilizing force that many believed them to be. Moch, *Paths to the City*, 22–23.

100. J. Bertillon, *De la dépopulation de la France*, 9.

101. Bazin, *La terre qui meurt*.

102. For instance, an 1895 article presented figures showing that in Saint-Lazare Prison in Paris in 1882 there were 5,763 provincial women incarcerated, compared to 1,988 Parisian women. Henri Lannes, "L'influence de l'émigration des campagnes sur la natalité française," *Revue politique et parlementaire* 8 (February 1895): 309–29.

103. Lannes, "L'influence de l'émigration," 317.

104. A minority of pronatalists argued that colonial emigration was simply impossible, despite their agreement with the notion that it would be conducive to demographic growth. Arsène Dumont was the most prominent member of this faction. One important example of his thinking on the issue can be found in a series of articles that he wrote in the journal of the Société de statistique de Paris in 1900. Dumont, "Aptitude de la France." In July 1900, L.-L. Vauthier, in response to Dumont's article, agreed that France was demographically ill but criticized Dumont's argument on the grounds that it was akin to a doctor allowing a disease to progress without making an effort to find a cure. L.-L. Vauthier, "Note de M. L.-L. Vauthier sur le travail de M. Arsène Dumont: Aptitude de la France à fournir des colons," *Journal de la société de statistique de Paris* 41, no. 7 (July 1900): 226–34.

105. Piolet, *La France hors de France*, 316.

106. Gonnard, *La dépopulation en France*, 79–80.

107. Piolet, *La France hors de France*, 7.

108. The idea of a "colonial mind" attracted significant interest recently with the publication of a two-volume collection of essays devoted to this topic. See M. Thomas, *The French Colonial Mind*.

109. The term "matrimonial migration" comes from Nancy Green, who urges historians of migration to consider gender in their studies. See Green, "Changing Paradigms in Migration Studies," 791.

110. Zola, *Fécondité*, 742.

111. Zola, *Fécondité*, 743.

112. See Fuchs, *Poor and Pregnant in Paris*.

113. Ricoux, *La démographie figurée de l'Algérie*, 139. According to Ricoux, the statistics concerning infant mortality in France during the period 1841–70 were as follows (per 1,000): 43.82 legitimate male births, 78 illegitimate male births, 31.3 legitimate female births, and 66.52 illegitimate female births. In Algeria during roughly the same period, 1838–78, the statistics were as follows: 26.5 legitimate male births, 13.8 illegitimate male births, 16 legitimate female births, and 11.7 illegitimate female births.

114. Guiard, *Des Européennes en situation coloniale*, 93. For the period that Ricoux was studying, Guiard found that 54 percent of illegitimate children were recognized by their fathers, a figure that was much higher than in Paris.

115. Ricoux, *La démographie figurée de l'Algérie*, 138. For attitudes about illegitimacy in Algeria earlier in the nineteenth century see Rogers, *A Frenchwoman's Imperial Story*, 46–47.

116. L.-A. Bertillon, preface, in Ricoux, *La démographie figurée de l'Algérie*, x–xi.

117. This was reported by Charles Lemire in "Question du jour: La France et les colonies," *La dépêche coloniale*, August 25, 1898.

118. Gonnard, *La dépopulation en France*, 124.

119. CAOM: Algérie, gouvernement GI Algérie (10H/58): Notes sur la natalité européenne en Algérie.

2. Recruiting Colonial Settlers

1. See the quote by Charles Richet at the beginning of chapter 1.

2. Poiré, *L'émigration française aux colonies*, 241.

3. Persell, *The French Colonial Lobby*, 3.

4. Persell, *The French Colonial Lobby*, 28.

5. Persell, *The French Colonial Lobby*, 27.

6. Persell, *The French Colonial Lobby*, 3.

7. Persell, *The French Colonial Lobby*, 83–96.

8. "L'émigration française et l'union coloniale," *La quinzaine coloniale* 7 (May 1895): 67.

9. Daughton, "When Argentina Was 'French,'" 843–44. The size of the French population and the influence of French culture in Argentina led Daughton to argue that scholars need to move beyond France's formal empire when studying the French civilizing mission and assessing France's position in the world.

10. "L'émigration française et l'union coloniale," 67.

11. Direction de l'agriculture et du commerce, *Notice sur la Tunisie*, ii.

12. CAOM: 100 APOM 105–8: Archives du comité central français pour l'outre-mer: Encouragement à l'émigration.

13. For instance, in 1905 the UCF received one such letter from a settler in Argentina and worked with the Algerian government to get him a concession in Algeria. CAOM: Gouvernement général d'Algérie, 32L/15–16: Encouragements, indemnités, subventions à des œuvres, 1888–1915.

14. "Les colons de demain à Saint-Michel de Frigolet," *L'expansion coloniale*, March 1, 1909, 327; and "Travaux du conseil de direction," *Bulletin de l'alliance nationale pour l'accroissement de la population française*, April 15, 1906, 194–96.

15. "Travaux du conseil de direction," 196.

16. "Travaux du conseil de direction," 196.

17. Chailley-Bert, *La colonisation française au XIXe siècle*.

18. "L'émigration française et l'union coloniale," 67.

19. CAOM: 100 APOM 2: Archives du comité central français pour l'outre-mer: Comité de direction et assemblées générales, procès-verbaux, séance du 12 Février 1895.

20. Merle, *Expériences coloniales*, 144–45.

21. Merle, *Expériences coloniales*, 278.

22. Union coloniale française, *But, moyens d'actions, résultats*, 65.

23. Union coloniale française, *But, moyens d'actions, résultats*, 19–20. See, e.g., Union coloniale française, *Guide de l'émigrant en Nouvelle-Calédonie*. This guide also built on an earlier guide written by Dr. Davillé, titled *Conseils à ceux qui veulent s'établir aux colonies*. It had a fairly wide readership, and the UCF distributed ten thousand copies to the general public.

24. Union coloniale française, *But, moyens d'actions, résultats*, 19–20.

25. CAOM: 100 APOM 107–8: Archives du comité central français pour l'outre-mer: Encouragement à l'émigration.

26. Chailley-Bert, *Dix années de politique coloniale*, 111–12.

27. *La quinzaine coloniale* ran an article about this problem in Indochina, pointing to specific cases of impoverished Frenchmen living among the Annamese and Chinese and the danger this posed for French "prestige" in the colony. "L'émigration dans les colonies," *La quinzaine coloniale*, January 25, 1905, 47–48.

28. CAOM: 100 APOM 105: Archives du comité central français pour l'outre-mer: Encouragement à l'émigration.

29. CAOM: 100 APOM 105: Archives du comité central français pour l'outre-mer: Encouragement à l'émigration.

30. CAOM: 100 APOM 105: Archives du comité central français pour l'outre-mer: Encouragement à l'émigration.

31. Chailley-Bert, *La colonisation française au XIXe siècle*.

32. CAOM: 100 APOM 2: Archives du comité central français pour l'outre-mer: Comité de direction et assemblées générales, procès-verbaux, séance du 12 Février 1895.

33. Femme Paul-Louis Courrier, letter to the editor, *Dépêche coloniale*, June 3, 1898.

34. Courrier, letter to the editor.

35. See, e.g., Blaise, *La dépopulation de la France*, 4.

36. For example, Ponsolle, *La dépopulation*, 60.

37. Mosse, *The Image of Man*, 78. Also see McLaren, *The Trials of Masculinity*; and Forth, *The Dreyfus Affair*.

38. Nye, *Masculinity and Male Codes of Honor*, 7.

39. As scholars have pointed out, the notion that masculinity was in crisis was not unique to the late nineteenth century; hence I shy away from the label "crisis of masculinity." Recognizing that concerns about masculinity can be found in any period of history, some scholars have argued that we should refer to the phenomenon in the plural and acknowledge that this crisis of masculinity responded to anxieties specific to this period. For instance, see Forth, *Masculinity in the Modern West*, 3. Other scholars have argued that we should avoid using the word *crisis* altogether. Bederman, e.g., explains that although elite American men were worried about the state of manhood at the turn of the century, they did not question the belief that "people with male bodies naturally possessed both a man's identity and a man's right to wield power." She argues that we should distinguish between expressed

concerns about masculinity and an actual crisis of masculinity. See Bederman, *Manliness and Civilization*, 11.

40. Forth, *Masculinity in the Modern West*, 5.

41. See, e.g., Debury, *Un pays de célibataires*, 22; and Gonnard, *La dépopulation en France*, 63.

42. Bederman, *Manliness and Civilization*, 14.

43. Bederman, *Manliness and Civilization*, 88.

44. Forth, *The Dreyfus Affair*, 8.

45. Forth, *Masculinity in the Modern West*.

46. On how degeneration was understood in biomedical terms, see Nye, *Crime, Madness, and Politics*.

47. Mosse, *The Image of Man*, 82.

48. Mosse, *The Image of Man*, 83–85.

49. Nye, *Masculinity and Male Codes of Honor*, 83.

50. Nye, *Masculinity and Male Codes of Honor*, 86.

51. On the introduction of gymnastics in French schools during this period see Mosse, *The Image of Man*. On shooting associations and gymnastics see Chrastil, *Organizing for War*, 112–26. On the popularity of football/soccer in France and Algeria during this period see Dine, "Shaping the Colonial Body."

52. Forth, *Masculinity in the Modern West*.

53. Poiré, *L'émigration française aux colonies*, 35.

54. Zola, *Fécondité*.

55. Debury, *Un pays de célibataires*. See also Dumont, *Natalité et démocratie*, 35–36. For instance, Henry Bouscaren quoted Debury in his 1936 book on depopulation. See Bouscaren, *La dépopulation de la France*, 8.

56. For example, Dumont, *Dépopulation et civilisation*, 35.

57. CAOM: Algérie, Gouvernement G1 Algérie, 32L/16: Encouragements, indemnités, subventions à des œuvres, 1888–1915: newspaper clipping: "L'enseignement colonial de la Chambre de Commerce de Lyon," *La dépêche coloniale illustrée*, July 15, 1903, 173–76. For more information on debates about modernizing curriculum in the late nineteenth century see Surkis, *Sexing the Citizen*.

58. V. Turquan, *Guide pratique*.

59. V. Turquan, *Guide pratique*, 3.

60. Rommel, *Au pays de la revanche*.

61. Rommel, *Au pays de la revanche*, 62.

62. Forth, *Masculinity in the Modern West*, 155.

63. See, e.g., Raisin, *La dépopulation de la France*, 68–69. For more on why clerks and functionaries were seen as weak and responsible for depopulation see Surkis, *Sexing the Citizen*.

64. See, e.g., the findings of the 1902 depopulation commission. *Commission de la dépopulation: Sous-commission de la natalité, séance du 5 février 1902 sous la présidence de M. Bernard*.

65. See, e.g., Saurin, *L'œuvre française en Tunisie*.

66. Lebovics, *True France*.

67. Piot, *La dépopulation en France*, 30.

68. Piot, *La dépopulation en France*, 26–27.

69. Gibier, *Les berceaux vides*, 37.

70. Lambert, *La France et les étrangers*, 19. The depiction of cities as "mangeuses d'hommes" or "tentaculaires" was common during the Third Republic. See also the natalist novel by Jacques Péricard, *J'ai huit enfants*, 18, and the article by Émile Cheysson (one of the founding directing council members of the Alliance Nationale), "La question de la population en France," *Revue politique et parlementaire* 28 (October 1896): 18–44.

71. One of the classic works dealing with responses to urban growth in the nineteenth century is Chevalier's *Classes laborieuses et classes dangereuses*, which details the perception among French elites that French cities were "sick." A number of scholars have also explored how criminality was generally considered a more serious problem in the cities than in the countryside, where crime was considered infrequent and benign by comparison. See, e.g., Toth, *Beyond Papillon*.

72. Peer, *France on Display*, 103.

73. See Forth, *Masculinity in the Modern West*, 158–59.

74. Bederman, *Manliness and Civilization*, 186.

75. Toth, *Beyond Papillon*, 37. Also see Bullard, *Exile to Paradise*.

76. CAOM: GGM 3A/3 Circulaires, September 26, 1898: Notice from Gallieni to the administrators and commanders of the district.

77. Quoted in Adolphe Samson, "Que faire de nos fils?," *La dépêche coloniale*, March 15, 1899.

78. Piolet, *La France hors de France*, 7.

79. Piolet, *La France hors de France*, 85.

80. Lyautey, *Paroles d'action*, 52.

81. Lagneau, *L'émigration de France*, 22. These numbers represent all people who officially emigrated and would include both those who went to the colonies (a small percentage) and those who went to foreign countries or colonies (the majority). Official numbers of emigrants were always inaccurate, because they only took into account those emigrants who requested passports. Experts estimated that an even larger number of people left the country each year clandestinely, including young men who wanted to avoid military service and people who did not meet the necessary requirements and therefore found it easier to purchase a fake passport.

82. On this view of women in the empire see, e.g., Strobel, *European Women*; and Clancy-Smith and Gouda, *Domesticating the Empire*.

83. For the British empire see McClintock, *Imperial Leather*; Collingham, *Imperial Bodies*; the articles in Levine, *Gender and Empire*; and the articles in Chaudhuri and Strobel, *Western Women and Imperialism*. For France, see Clancy-Smith and Gouda, *Domesticating the Empire*.

84. Lemire, *Les colonies et la question sociale*, 11.

85. White, *Miscegenation and Colonial Society*. On this topic also see Saada, *Les enfants de la colonie*.

86. White, *Miscegenation and Colonial Society*, 23.

87. White, *Miscegenation and Colonial Society*, 23.

88. White, *Miscegenation and Colonial Society*, 182.

89. Stoler, *Carnal Knowledge and Imperial Power*.

90. Piolet, *La France hors de France*, 412.

91. On anthropologists' conclusions about *métissage*, see, e.g., a 1916 article in *Revue anthropologique* by T.-V. Holbé that detailed the frequency of, and perceived problems associated with, racial mixing in Cochin-China by examining various different types of mixed-race individuals, including "Franco-Annamites" and "Arabo-Anamites." He concluded that racial mixing would become increasingly common in all the regions of the world. "This is the first consequence of the growing communications among peoples that increasingly brings people of diverse races into contact." T.-V. Holbé, "Métis de Cochinchine," *Revue anthropologique* 26 (1916): 466.

92. In the text I use the same French terms, *métis* and *métissage*, that are used in my sources. *Métissage* is generally translated into English as "miscegenation," and a *métis* would simply be an individual with a mixed racial background. As Camiscioli and others point out, the translation of *métissage* as "miscegenation" is problematic, as the latter was coined in the American South, a specific historical and racial context distinct from that of the French colonies. Following her example, I have elected to not use the term *miscegenation*. See Camiscioli, *Reproducing the French Race*, 175 n. 1.

93. While exact figures concerning abandonment do not exist, one 1916 report did estimate that French men in Afrique occidentale française abandoned their *métis* children nine times out of ten. See White, *Miscegenation and Colonial Society*, 37. A more qualitative way to assess the extent of the problem is to look at the work of colonial governments in establishing orphanages to care for abandoned métis children. In Madagascar, e.g., general governor Gallieni considered abandoned métis children to be such a destabilizing force that he allocated funds to support the Société de protection et d'assistance aux enfants métis directed by Dr. Fontoynont.

94. Richet, *La sélection humaine*, 93.

95. Piolet, *La France hors de France*, 414.

96. On this topic, in the 1920s and 1930s, see Cooper, "Gendering the Colonial Enterprise."

97. Mansker, *Sex, Honor, and Citizenship*, chapter 2.

98. Mansker, *Sex, Honor, and Citizenship*, 68–71.

99. Goutalier and Knibiehler, *La femme au temps des colonies*, 88.

100. Goutalier and Knibiehler, *La femme au temps des colonies*, 88.

101. D'Haussonville, *Salaires et misères de femmes*, 128.

102. V. Turquan, *Guide pratique*. On the issue of women's secondary education and career aspirations see Margadant, *Madame le professeur*.

103. V. Turquan, *Guide pratique*, 3.

104. D'Haussonville, *Salaires et misères de femmes*, 133.

105. Corneau, *La femme aux colonies*. Corneau was the pseudonym for Mme Joliaud-Barral. See Goutalier and Knibhieler, *La femme au temps des colonies*, 324.

106. Corneau, *La femme aux colonies*, 13.

107. Corneau, *La femme aux colonies*, 52.

108. Corneau, *La femme aux colonies*, 52.

109. Other works of colonial propaganda echoed Corneau's assertion that women would find greater liberation and opportunities than in France. See, e.g., Poiré, *L'emigration française aux colonies*, 206.

110. *Questions du temps présent.*

111. *Questions du temps présent*, 7.

112. *Questions du temps présent*, 24.

113. Mme Pégard, president of the SFEF, presented this statistic at a feminist congress in 1902. See *Deuxième congrès international des œuvres et institutions féminines tenu au palais des congrès de l'exposition universelle de 1900*, 237.

114. *Questions du temps présent*, 58.

115. *Questions du temps présent*, 58–59.

116. "Société française d'émigration des femmes," *La quinzaine coloniale*, April 1897, 224.

117. Hélia, "L'émigration féminine."

118. "Société française d'émigration des femmes," *La quinzaine coloniale*, December 10, 1898, 734–35; and "Société française d'émigration des femmes," *La quinzaine coloniale*, January 25, 1899, 64.

119. Within feminist and imperialist circles she was always referred to simply as Mme Pégard, or occasionally Mme Léon Pégard, and no mention of her first name was ever made. The catalog of the Bibliothèque nationale de France lists her first name as Marie. In all other articles, including her own publications as well as in obituaries celebrating her life, she is referred to simply as Mme Pégard.

120. "Les disparus: Mme Pégard," *La française*, April 15, 1916, 1.

121. Julie Siegfried, "Madame Léon Pégard," *L'action féminine* 43 (May 1916): 22–24.

122. Siegfried, "Madame Léon Pégard," 22–24.

123. See, e.g., BMD: Assemblée générale du Conseil national des femmes françaises (1906): 60–66.

124. BMD: Assemblée générale du Conseil national des femmes françaises (1907): 16.

125. Depincé, *Exposition coloniale de Marseille*, 314.

126. Here she repeated pronatalist criticisms of the abolition of primogeniture and the division of property among heirs.

127. Depincé, *Exposition coloniale de Marseille*, 317.

128. Depincé, *Exposition coloniale de Marseille*, 320.

129. Depincé, *Exposition coloniale de Marseille*, 321.

130. "La société française d'émigration des femmes: Une année d'existence," *La quinzaine coloniale*, January 25, 1898, 42.

131. Pégard discussed the United British Women's Emigration Association in particular. According to Poiré, this organization sent 353 young women to South Africa and Australia in 1896. Poiré, *L'émigration française aux colonies*, 205.

132. Depincé, *Exposition coloniale de Marseille*, 321.

133. "Société française d'émigration des femmes," *La quinzaine coloniale*, January 25, 1898, 40–44.

134. CAOM: 44 PA8 Papiers d'Agents, Gallieni, Joseph: "Société française d'émigration des femmes."

135. "Société française d'émigration des femmes," *La quinzaine coloniale*, November 25, 1898, 702–3.

136. In 1905 the UCF did report that Mme Pégard attended one of their events.

137. "Société française d'émigration des femmes," *La quinzaine coloniale*, March 1897, 189.

138. This statistic was presented by Mme Pégard at a feminist congress in 1902. *Deuxième congrès international des œuvres et institutions féminines tenu au palais des congrès de l'exposition universelle de 1900*, 242–43.

139. "Société française d'émigration des femmes," *La quinzaine coloniale*, January 25, 1899, 64.

140. On this subject see Marie-Paule Ha, "French Women and the Empire," in Robson and Yee, *France and Indochina*, 107–20.

141. Depincé, *Exposition coloniale de Marseille*, 327. Though not given as a reason, administrators and settlers generally did not want to see white women performing menial labor in the colonies, as this could compromise the delicate image of white prestige they were determined to construct and maintain.

142. Depincé, *Exposition coloniale de Marseille*, 321.

143. Pégard, "L'émigration des femmes aux colonies," 253.

144. *Deuxième congrès international des œuvres et institutions féminines tenu au palais des congrès de l'exposition universelle de 1900*, 240.

145. Kranidis, *The Victorian Spinster*.

146. Pégard, "L'émigration des femmes aux colonies," 253.

147. Depincé, *Exposition coloniale de Marseille*, 327.

148. See, e.g., Gilles de Gantès, "Migration to Indochina: Proof of the Popularity of Colonial Empire?," in Chafer and Sackur, *Promoting the Colonial Idea*, 15–28; and Dea Birkett, "The 'White Woman's Burden' in the 'White Man's Grave': The Introduction of British Nurses in Colonial West Africa," in Chaudhuri and Strobel, *Western Women and Imperialism*, 177–88.

149. Rogers, *A Frenchwoman's Imperial Story*. For another example of a French woman who found greater success in the empire than in France see de Gantès, "Migration to Indochina."

150. CAOM: Fonds Ministériels, Affaires Politiques 843, Colonial Associations.

151. Clotilde Chivas-Baron, introduction to Faure, *La vie aux colonies*, 33.

152. Chivas-Baron, *La femme française aux colonies*, 134.

153. "Le rôle colonial de la femme," *Bulletin de l'œuvre coloniale des femmes françaises*, March 1913, 730.

154. *Bulletin de l'œuvre coloniale des femmes françaises*, January 1914.

155. Gaston Valran, "Le rôle colonial de la femme," *Bulletin de l'œuvre coloniale des femmes françaises*, December 1912, 701–3.

156. Alexandre Brou, "La femme française dans la société coloniale," in Faure, *La vie aux colonies*, 218.

157. Brou, "La femme française," 220.

158. Brou, "La femme française," 220–21.

159. On Auclert's feminist imperialism see Eichner, "*La Citoyenne* in the World."

160. Auclert, *Les femmes arabes en Algérie*.

161. Another important example for the nineteenth century is the feminist journal *Le droit des femmes*, edited by Léon Richer. Though focused, for the most part, on metropolitan issues, this journal contained a number of articles discussing the status of women in non-Western countries, including the French colonies. These articles reflected an interest in global women's issues, positioned French feminists in a leadership role in the resolution of these problems, and presented colonial rule as a means by which to institute feminist policies on behalf of women in these regions of the world. For information on the intersection of empire and French feminism in the twentieth century see, e.g., Kimble, "Emancipation through Secularization."

162. Conseil national des femmes françaises, *États généraux du féminisme* (1931).

163. Conseil national des femmes françaises, *États généraux du féminisme* (1931), 63.

164. Zola, *Fécondité*, 743.

3. Creating a "Labor Reservoir"

1. *Bulletin de l'alliance nationale pour l'accroissement de la population française*, January 15, 1899.

2. Jacobs, *White Mother to a Dark Race*.

3. Another example, predating World War I, occurred in the British Malayan colonies in 1905. See Alison Bashford, "Medicine, Gender, and Empire," in Levine, *Gender and Empire*, 112–33. Most such reforms appeared following the war, however. For the Dutch colonies see Ann Stoler and Frederick Cooper, introduction, in Stoler and Cooper, *Tensions of Empire*, 29. For the Belgian Congo, see Nancy Rose Hunt, "Le Bébé en Brousse: European Women, African Birth Spacing, and Colonial Intervention in Breast Feeding in the Belgian Congo," in Stoler and Cooper, *Tensions of Empire*, 287–321. For French West Africa see Conklin, "Faire Naître v. Faire du Noir." For British East Africa see L. Thomas, *Politics of the Womb*.

4. In British East Africa the emphasis was more on eradicating disease and certain cultural practices. See L. Thomas, *Politics of the Womb*. In the Belgian Congo, reformers were pronatalist in their approach. See N. R. Hunt, *A Colonial Lexicon*.

5. L. Thomas, *Politics of the Womb*, 23.

6. Ellis, *The Physician-Legislators of France*, 183.

7. Ellis, *The Physician-Legislators of France*, 189.

8. Ellis, *The Physician-Legislators of France*, 189–90.

9. Mitchell, *The Divided Path*, 120.

10. Mitchell, *The Divided Path*, 158. According to Mitchell, the majority of communes applied for an exemption from this law.

11. Mitchell, *The Divided Path*, 132. According to Mitchell, French proponents of obligatory vaccination frequently cited its success in reducing mortality rates in Germany. For example, in 1886 there were 15,000 deaths in France attributed to smallpox but only 225 such deaths in Germany. *The Divided Path*, 130.

12. Scott, "'L'ouvrière!'"

13. Scott, "'L'ouvrière!,'" 135.

14. On the expansion of the wet-nursing trade in nineteenth-century France see Sussman, *Selling Mothers' Milk*. For a discussion of why reformers criticized this business also see Joshua Cole, *The Power of Large Numbers*.

15. On the topic of child abandonment see Fuchs, *Poor and Pregnant in Paris*.

16. Joshua Cole, *The Power of Large Numbers*, 152.

17. Joshua Cole, *The Power of Large Numbers*, 152–53.

18. It is worth pointing out that by this period bottle-feeding was no longer as risky as it had been a couple decades earlier. As of the 1890s, a greater understanding of germ theory, improvements in the production and sale of cow's milk, knowledge of how to sterilize milk, and the availability of modern baby bottles with rubber nipples all combined to make bottle-feeding a reasonably safe alternative to maternal breast-feeding. Sussman, *Selling Mothers' Milk*, 11.

19. See Reynolds, *France between the Wars*, 33–34. This law is an example of how the prior objections to intervening in the workplace became less persuasive by World War I.

20. Reynolds, *France between the Wars*, 33–34.

21. As Mary Lynn Stewart points out in *For Health and Beauty*, many of the sex-education manuals emphasized women's maternal and reproductive duties but kept women in the dark about their bodies, sexuality, pregnancy, and childbirth.

22. Officially there are eighteen separate ethnic groups in Madagascar, but a number of problems are associated with dividing up the population in this manner. As Maureen Covell explains, many of these official ethnic groups can be subdivided into smaller, regional groups; others are of colonial creation; and still others never had a common political unit at all. See Covell, *Historical Dictionary of Madagascar*, 3–4; and Wesseling, *Divide and Rule*, 165. *Hova* is the word colonial officials used to refer to the Merina people in Madagascar. In Merina society, *Hova* was a term used to designate a particular social stratum. At the time of the French conquest this particular group was politically dominant, and the French mistakenly used the term to designate the entire ethnic group. See Wesseling, *Divide and Rule*, 165; and Jennifer Cole, *Forget Colonialism?*, 329. In this chapter I will use the term *Merina*, except when quoting colonial sources in which the word *Hova* is used.

23. Covell argues that the Merina monarchs viewed westernization to be politically expedient. It gave them a degree of "international respectability" which they hoped would help protect their independence from European domination. Covell, *Historical Dictionary of Madagascar*, 6.

24. Covell, *Historical Dictionary of Madagascar*, 131. On the topic of British missionaries in precolonial Madagascar see Gow, *Madagascar and the Protestant Impact*. According to Gow, the prime minister chose Congregationalism because it lacked

the kind of hierarchy that the Anglican, Lutheran, and Roman Catholic Churches possessed. By making it the state religion he could head the church without being subordinated to foreign church officials. As Daughton demonstrates in *An Empire Divided*, the significant influence that this British organization enjoyed in Madagascar became a source of tension during the colonial period.

25. *Menelamba* translates loosely as "red shawls" and refers to the clothing worn by the insurgents. Covell, *Historical Dictionary of Madagascar*, 141.

26. See, e.g., the book Guillaume Grandidier published in the Grandes figures coloniales series, *Gallieni*. Grandidier and his father, Alfred Grandidier, were the foremost French ethnologists on Madagascar in France during the Third Republic.

27. Gallieni, *Madagascar de 1896 à 1905*, 509.

28. Gallieni, "Instructions relatives aux mesures à prendre pour favoriser l'accroissement de la population en Emyrne," *Bulletin officiel de Madagascar et de ses dépendances*, June 15, 1898, 249. Hereafter cited as Gallieni, "Mesures à prendre pour favoriser l'accroissement de la population."

29. Gallieni, "Mesures à prendre pour favoriser l'accroissement de la population," 249.

30. Rabinow, *French Modern*, 154.

31. Rabinow, *French Modern*, 154.

32. Gallieni, "Instructions sur l'organisation de l'assistance médicale et de l'hygiène publique indigènes à Madagascar," *Bulletin officiel de Madagascar et de ses dépendances*, March 15, 1901, 169; Gallieni, "Arrêté édictant diverses mesures en vue de favoriser l'accroissement de la population en Imerina," *Bulletin officiel de Madagascar et de ses dépendances*, June 15, 1898, 259. Hereafter cited as Gallieni, "Mesures en vue de favoriser l'accroissement de la population."

33. Gallieni, "Mesures à prendre pour favoriser l'accroissement de la population," 251.

34. Gallieni, "Mesures à prendre pour favoriser l'accroissement de la population," 251.

35. Gallieni, "Mesures à prendre pour favoriser l'accroissement de la population," 255.

36. Gallieni, *Madagascar de 1896 à 1905*, 278–79.

37. Gallieni, *Madagascar de 1896 à 1905*, 278.

38. For more information on Gallieni's efforts to reduce the influence of foreign missionaries in Madagascar, see Daughton, *An Empire Divided*.

39. The decrees creating, organizing, and funding medical facilities are too numerous to list here. However, some of the more prominent such decrees are listed in Gallieni, *Madagascar de 1896 à 1905*, 281–88.

40. N. R. Hunt, *A Colonial Lexicon*.

41. Gallieni, *Madagascar de 1896 à 1905*, 282–83.

42. Gallieni, *Madagascar de 1896 à 1905*, 282–83. Reports from the Assistance médicale indigène also highlighted this problem, especially prior to 1903. See CAOM: GGM/AMI 5D6, 1–27.

43. Gallieni, *Madagascar de 1896 à 1905*, 279.

44. Gallieni, *Madagascar de 1896 à 1905*, 279.

45. Gallieni, *Madagascar de 1896 à 1905*, 294.

46. Gallieni, *Madagascar de 1896 à 1905*, 284.

47. The most important decrees concerning the creation of a corps of *sages-femmes indigènes* in the AMI were those of January 24, 1902, July 1, 1903, and March 29, 1905. The most important decrees concerning the organization of *médecins indigènes* were those of December 11 and 16, 1896, April 20, 1899, and October 15, 1900.

48. Gallieni, *Madagascar de 1896 à 1905*, 290. Because the term "native" is problematic, I will use the French titles hereafter.

49. CAOM: GGM/SS 5D5, 4: Annual Report, 1904, École de médecine de Tananarive; and CAOM: GGM/AMI 5D6, 24: Annual Report to the Assistance médicale indigène, 1904, province of Valinankaratra.

50. Gallieni, *Madagascar de 1896 à 1905*, 290.

51. CAOM: GGM 5D20, 10: Annual Report, École de médecine de Tananarive, 1913.

52. Annual Report, École de médecine de Tananarive, 1913.

53. Annual Report, École de médecine de Tananarive, 1913.

54. Ramisiray, "Pratiques et croyances médicales des Malgaches," 12.

55. Brau, *Trois siècles de médecine coloniale française*, 184. This also comes up in Gallieni, *Neuf ans à Madagascar*, 208.

56. CAOM: GGM 5D20, 10: Annual Report, École de médecine de Tananarive, 1913.

57. CAOM: GGM/SS 5D5, 4: Annual Report, École de médecine de Tananarive, 1904.

58. Lyautey, *Lettres du sud de Madagascar*.

59. Lyautey, *Lettres du sud de Madagascar*, 288.

60. Lyautey, *Lettres du sud de Madagascar*, 288.

61. *Médecins indigènes* in Fianarantsoa and Angavo-Mangoro-Alaotra were relieved of duty. CAOM: GGM/AMI 5D6, 14: Annual Report, 1904, province of Fianarantsoa; CAOM: GGM/AMI 5D6, 11: Annual Report, 1904, province of Angavo-Mangoro-Alaotra.

62. Gallieni, *Madagascar de 1896 à 1905*, 291.

63. CAOM: GGM/SS 5D5, 4: Annual Report, École de Médecine de Tananarive, 1904.

64. Annual Report, École de Médecine de Tananarive, 1904.

65. "Arrêté organisant un corps de sages-femmes indigènes de l'assistance médicale à Madagascar," *Bulletin officiel de Madagascar et de ses dépendances*, July 1, 1903, 686; "Création d'un corps de médecins indigènes de colonisation," *Bulletin officiel de Madagascar et de ses dépendances*, October 15, 1900, 174.

66. CAOM: GGM/AMI 5D6, 14: Annual Report, 1904, province of Fianarantsoa. These numbers would not include babies delivered by unlicensed midwives. It was difficult for the colonial state to track how many babies were delivered in that manner.

67. Gallieni, *Madagascar de 1896 à 1905*, 292.

68. CAOM: GGM/AMI 5D6, 24: Annual Report, 1904, province of Valinankaratra.

69. See Spivak, *The Postcolonial Critic*, 50–58.

70. On the connections between climate, race, and sexuality, see, e.g., Jennings, *Curing the Colonizers*; McClintock, *Imperial Leather*; and Clancy-Smith, "Islam, Gender, and Identities."

71. Gallieni, *Madagascar de 1896 à 1905*, 278.

72. Gallieni, *Madagascar de 1896 à 1905*, 278.

73. Gallieni, "Mesures en vue de favoriser l'accroissement de la population," 246.

74. J. E. Pedersen, "'Special Customs,'" 55.

75. CAOM: GGM 3A/4 Circulaires, January 28, 1898, Notice 303: "Envoi d'un questionnaire sur le droit coutumier malgache."

76. Gallieni, "Mesures en vue de favoriser l'accroissement de la population," 246.

77. The section of his 1898 decree dealing with abortion also drew on the 1881 law. CAOM: GGM 3A/3 Circulaires, a draft of a notice dated June 1898.

78. CAOM: GGM/AMI 5D6, 20: Annual Report, 1904, province of Mandritsara.

79. Annual Report, 1904, province of Mandritsara.

80. *Prestation* was a form of compulsory construction labor for Malagasy men between the ages of sixteen and sixty. It was abolished in 1901 and replaced by increased taxes. Brown, *A History of Madagascar*, 239. On the decree, see Gallieni, "Mesures à prendre pour favoriser l'accroissement de la population," 255.

81. Section B, article 5 of the June 15, 1898, decree.

82. Gallieni, "Mesures en vue de favoriser l'accroissement de la population," 247.

83. CAOM: GGM 3A/1 Circulaires, 1896, Notice 163: "Instruction relative à l'établissement de la taux provisionelle et de l'impôt des rizières."

84. Gallieni, *Madagascar de 1896 à 1905*, 522.

85. Gallieni, *Neuf ans à Madagascar*, 209.

86. Gallieni, "Mesures à prendre pour favoriser l'accroissement de la population," 259.

87. I would like to thank Christina Firpo for calling this holiday to my attention. For more information see her forthcoming book, *"Abandoned" Children: Crises in Racial Patriarchy and Eurasian Children in Colonial Indochina, 1890–1956*.

88. See, e.g., "A Madagascar, fête des enfants à Tananarive," *Bulletin de l'œuvre coloniale des femmes françaises*, May 1912, 663–64.

89. Gallieni, "Mesures à prendre pour favoriser l'accroissement de la population," 259.

90. "Documents et informations," *Revue de Madagascar*, April 15, 1903, 519.

91. Rabary, "La chique à Madagascar."

92. Rabary, "La chique à Madagascar," 3.

93. Ravelonahina, "Des causes de dépopulation," 132.

94. Ravelonahina, "Des causes de dépopulation," 128.

95. Ravelonahina, "Des causes de dépopulation," 104.

96. Ravelonahina, "Des causes de dépopulation," 105.

97. Ravelonahina, "Des causes de dépopulation," 106.

98. Ramisiray, "Pratiques et croyances médicales des Malgaches," 109.

99. Ramisiray, "Pratiques et croyances médicales des Malgaches," 47.

100. Ranaivo, "Pratiques et croyances des Malgaches," 11.

101. Ranaivo, "Pratiques et croyances des Malgaches," 13.

102. Ranaivo, "Pratiques et croyances des Malgaches," 58.

103. Ramisiray, "Pratiques et croyances médicales des Malgaches," 57.

104. Studies of regulated prostitution in France, e.g., have detailed how prostitutes were required to undergo regular venereal disease screenings in order to protect the health of their male clients. Male clients were generally not viewed as the source of the contagion and therefore were not screened for venereal disease or in any way prevented from infecting prostitutes. Not surprisingly, this approach to preventing the spread of syphilis and other venereal diseases was not effective. See, e.g., Harsin, *Policing Prostitution.*

105. CAOM: GGM/AMI 5D6, 9: Annual Report, 1904, province of Ambositra.

106. CAOM: GGM/AMI 5D6, 7: Annual Report, 1904, province of Imerina Nord; Gallieni, *Madagascar de 1896 à 1905*, 304.

107. CAOM: GGM/AMI 5D6, 14: Annual Report, 1904, province of Fianarantsoa.

108. Ravelonahina, "Des causes de dépopulation," 56.

109. Vaughan, *Curing Their Ills*, 8.

110. Vaughan, *Curing Their Ills*, 8.

111. Surkis, *Sexing the Citizen*, 227–29.

112. See Conklin, "Faire Naître v. Faire du Noir."

113. Berenson, *Heroes of Empire*. In addition to colonial heroes, many historical and literary heroes, like Napoleon and Cyrano de Bergerac, shaped late-nineteenth-century ideas of national identity and masculinity. See Datta, *Heroes and Legends.*

114. *Commission de la dépopulation: Sous-commission de la natalité, séance du 5 février 1902 sous la présidence de M. Bernard.*

115. This report was later published as a book. See Piot, *La dépopulation.*

116. Piot, *La dépopulation*, 154–55.

117. Piot, *La dépopulation*, 89.

118. Piot, *La dépopulation*, 94–95.

119. Article 1; Piot, *La dépopulation*, 101.

120. Piot, *La dépopulation*, 98.

121. Articles 2 through 6; Piot, *La dépopulation*, 101–2.

122. Spengler, *France Faces Depopulation*, 126.

123. Spengler, *France Faces Depopulation*, 127.

124. J. Bertillon, *La dépopulation de la France*, 267.

125. J. Bertillon, *La dépopulation de la France*, 289.

126. "Concours de familles nombreuses," *Bulletin de l'alliance nationale pour l'accroissement de la population française*, October 1904, 598–600.

127. Vitalis, "Petits papas malgaches," *La famille française* 7 (July 1919): 7. *La famille française* was the official journal of the Ligue des droits de la famille.

128. "La ligue des familles nombreuses de France, section de Marseille et arrondissement," *Bulletin de la ligue des familles nombreuses de France, section de l'Indochine*, November 1923, 20. This was an editorial originally printed in the bulletin of the Marseille section of the organization and then reprinted in the bulletin of the Indochinese section.

129. "La ligue des familles nombreuses de France, section de Marseille," 20.

130. Auburtin, *La patrie en danger*, 322.

131. See, e.g., Janet R. Horne, "In Pursuit of Greater France: Visions of Empire among Musée Social Reformers, 1894–1931," in Clancy-Smith and Gouda, *Domesticating the Empire*, 21–42; and Wright, *The Politics of Design*.

132. Daughton, *An Empire Divided*, 13.

133. N. R. Hunt, *A Colonial Lexicon*.

134. Gallieni, *Madagascar de 1896 à 1905*, 289.

135. Gallieni, *Neuf ans à Madagascar*, 50.

136. Gallieni, *Madagascar de 1896 à 1905*, 282.

137. "Instructions sur l'organisation de l'assistance médicale et de l'hygiène publique indigènes à Madagascar," *Bulletin officiel de Madagascar et de ses dépendances*, March 15, 1901, 174.

138. "Instructions sur l'organization de l'assistance médicale," 174.

139. CAOM: GGM/SS 5D5, 2: Annual Report, 1900, Service de santé.

140. Gallieni, *Madagascar de 1896 à 1905*, 286.

141. Gallieni, *Madagascar de 1896 à 1905*, 292.

142. Gallieni, *Madagascar de 1896 à 1905*, 292.

143. Gallieni, *Madagascar de 1896 à 1905*, 282.

144. CAOM: GGM/AMI 5D6, 16: Annual Report, 1904, province of Itasy.

145. Annual Report, 1904, province of Itasy.

146. Annual Report, 1904, province of Itasy.

147. For views on childbirth in France see Accampo, *Blessed Motherhood, Bitter Fruit*.

148. CAOM: GGM/AMI 5D6, 2: Annual Report, 1901, province of Manjakandriana.

149. Annual Report, 1901, province of Manjakandriana.

150. CAOM: GGM/AMI 5D6, 7: Annual Report, 1904, province of Imerina Nord.

151. Annual Report, 1904, province of Imerina Nord.

152. CAOM: GGM/AMI 5D6, 11: Annual Report, 1904, province de l'Angavo-Mangoro-Alaotra.

153. CAOM: GGM/AMI 5D6, 14: Annual Report, 1904, province of Fianarantsoa; CAOM: GGM/AMI 5D6, 18: Annual Report, 1904, district of Maevatanana, 1904.

154. CAOM: GGM 3D/5. General inspector V. Fillon report to the minister of colonies, dated April 30, 1918: "Situation financière: Budget annexe de l'assistance médicale indigène."

155. Examples of positive reports that emphasized all the progress that had been made along these lines came from the provinces of Nossi-Bé and Imerina Nord. CAOM: GGM/AMI 5D6, 23: Annual Report, 1904, province of Nossi-Bé; CAOM: GGM/AMI 5D6, 7: Annual Report, 1904, province of Imerina Nord.

156. CAOM: GGM/AMI 5D6, 11: Annual Report, 1904, province of Angavo-Mangoro-Alaotra.

157. CAOM: GGM/AMI 5D6, 14: Annual Report, 1904, province de Fianarantsoa.

158. On cleanliness, race, and imperialism, see Stoler, *Carnal Knowledge and Imperial Power*; and Burke, *Lifebuoy Men, Luxe Women*.

159. See Ellis, *The Physician-Legislators of France*.

160. CAOM: GGM/AMI 5D6, 26: Proceedings of the Commission de l'assistance médicale indigène, in the province of Vakinankaratra, February 6, 1905. A lamba is a type of shawl.

161. CAOM: GGM/AMI 5D6, 18: Annual Report, 1904, district of Maevatanana.

162. "La population de Madagascar," *L'expansion coloniale*, July 1, 1910, 117.

163. Jennings, *Curing the Colonizers*, 128.

164. Charles Joyeux, "Le paludisme à Madagascar," *Revue de Madagascar*, February 10, 1907, 116–17.

165. Joyeux, "Le paludisme à Madagascar," 116–17.

166. Joyeux, "Le paludisme à Madagascar," 117.

167. Jennings, *Curing the Colonizers*, 129.

168. See the letter he wrote to Joseph Chailley-Bert on April 27, 1898, reprinted in Gallieni, *Lettres de Madagascar*, 27–31.

169. Wright, *The Politics of Design*, 253.

170. Wright, *The Politics of Design*, 253.

171. CAOM: GGM 3D/5. General inspector V. Fillon report to the minister of colonies, April 30, 1918: "Situation financière: budget annexe de l'assistance médicale indigène."

172. Fillon to the minister of colonies, April 30, 1918: "Situation financière: budget annexe de l'assistance médicale indigène."

173. The position of resident-general was transformed into that of governor-general by decree on July 30, 1897. The position itself remained unchanged. You, *Madagascar*, 200.

174. You, *Madagascar*, 200–202.

4. Voting for the Family

1. Boverat, *Patriotisme et paternité*, 65.

2. See, e.g., Jacques Bertillon, "Le problème reste le même," *Bulletin de l'alliance nationale pour l'accroissement de la population française*, January 1919, 1–2.

3. *Bulletin de l'alliance nationale pour l'accroissement de la population française*, April 1916, 45.

4. Spengler, *France Faces Depopulation*, 128.

5. Boverat, *La résurrection par la natalité*, 473. Although Boverat does not specify what he means by "French territory," he was most likely thinking in terms of greater France and including colonial organizations in his figures.

6. The first Congrès national de la natalité took place in 1919.

7. As this chapter will show, in the twentieth century there were many different ideas about how familial suffrage should function in practice.

8. Le Naour and Valenti, *La famille doit voter*, 18–19.

9. Verjus, *Le cens de la famille*.

10. Le Naour and Valenti, *La famille doit voter*, 23.

11. André, *Le suffrage universel*, 9.

12. The Second Republic (1848–51) fell after three years following Louis-Napoléon Bonaparte's coup d'état.

13. Le Naour and Valenti, *La famille doit voter*, 30–34.

14. Le Naour and Valenti, *La famille doit voter*, 41.

15. In fact, in the years after the war, France's population growth was due entirely to immigration.

16. See, in particular, Grayzel, *Women's Identities at War*; Harris, "The 'Child of the Barbarian.'"

17. Harris, "The 'Child of the Barbarian.'" Interestingly, a similar kind of question arose following World War II, this time involving French fathers. There were thousands of cases where French POWs and French occupation soldiers had fathered children with German women. These half-French children came to be imagined as "spoils of war" by French occupation authorities, who hoped that they could become fully French after having been removed from their German mothers and then raised by French families. This plan represented a form of what Tara Zahra calls "demographic restitution for Nazi war crimes." See Zahra, *The Lost Children*, 157.

18. See Audoin-Rouzeau, *L'enfant de l'ennemi*.

19. For more on women's employment during the war and gendered anxieties after the war see Darrow, *French Women and the First World War*; Roberts, *Civilization without Sexes*; and Perrot, "The New Eve and the Old Adam."

20. When *La garçonne* was first published, in 1922, the pronatalist press decried the "scandalous" ideas about gender and sexuality that it seemed to promote. For a discussion of this novel's reception in French society more generally, see Roberts, *Civilization without Sexes*; and Bard, *Les garçonnes*.

21. The best discussion of the concept of "social citizenship" in interwar France is Frader, *Breadwinners and Citizens*.

22. Frader, *Breadwinners and Citizens*. On the development of the welfare state in interwar France, also see S. Pedersen, *Family, Dependence*; and Talmy, *Histoire du mouvement familial en France*.

23. "Pour vaincre la dépopulation . . . instituons le vote familial," *Natalité*, April 1925, 3.

24. According to pronatalists, a father's lack of *pouvoir testamentaire*, or ability to will his property as he saw fit, was one of the major causes of depopulation. Whereas in the eighteenth century a patriarch might have left his business or farm to one of many children (a son), the Napoleonic Code dictated that the property be divided equally among all children. Pronatalists believed that, as a result, bourgeois parents preferred to have small numbers of children in order to avoid the subdivision of property. They also emphasized the Napoleonic Code's detrimental effects on the countryside. Farmland became subdivided so many times that individual portions ceased to be large enough to support families. This, they believed, was one factor behind the rural exodus. In addition to discouraging parents from having large numbers of children, pronatalists alleged, the Napoleonic Code destroyed traditional family values. Households gradually ceased to be composed of extended family members working cooperatively together. Instead, young people lost sight

of their duties to their family members and felt a sense of entitlement to take what was rightfully their property and leave.

25. Henri Roulleaux-Dugage, "Natalité et léglisation," *Revue politique et parlementaire*, March 10, 1918, 283.

26. On how feminists responded to the legacy of the French Revolution as they developed arguments in favor of women's rights see Scott, *Only Paradoxes to Offer*.

27. Toulemon, *Le suffrage familial*, 18.

28. Toulemon, *Le suffrage familial*, 59.

29. Lamy, *La flamme qui ne doit pas s'éteindre*, 17–18.

30. Gibier, *Les berceaux vides*, 122–23.

31. Desan, *The Family on Trial*; Donzelot, *The Policing of Families*; Tuttle, *Conceiving the Old Regime*.

32. See L. Hunt, *The Family Romance*.

33. Desan, *The Family on Trial*, 61.

34. Donzelot, *The Policing of Families*, 52.

35. Childers, *Fathers, Families, and the State*, 38.

36. Fuchs, *Contested Paternity*.

37. Perrot, "The New Eve and the Old Adam," 54.

38. On interwar feminism see Bard, *Les filles de Marianne*.

39. Jacques Bertillon, "Il faut que le père de famille devienne le grand électeur," *Bulletin de l'alliance nationale pour l'accroissement de la population française*, October 15, 1910, 89–94. This article was also published in the *Écho de Paris* in August 1910.

40. J. Bertillon, "Le grand électeur," 91.

41. Le Naour and Valenti, *La famille doit voter*, 83.

42. Le Naour and Valenti, *La famille doit voter*, 67.

43. Le Naour and Valenti, *La famille doit voter*, 99.

44. Le Naour and Valenti, *La famille doit voter*, 99.

45. Le Naour and Valenti, *La famille doit voter*, 104.

46. "Pour le vote familial," *Bulletin de l'alliance nationale pour l'accroissement de la population française*, February 1924, 44–46.

47. Le Naour and Valenti, *La famille doit voter*, 110.

48. Bard, *Les filles de Marianne*.

49. On the intersection of fin de siècle feminism and pronatalism see Offen, "Depopulation, Nationalism and Feminism."

50. Fernand Boverat, "Une nouvelle formule de vote familial: Le partage des voix des enfants entre le père et la mère," *Revue de l'alliance nationale pour l'accroissement de la population*, April 1927, 107.

51. For example, her statement that "the single man is a debtor who does not pay his debts" was quoted in *Bulletin de l'alliance nationale pour l'accroissement de la population française* as well as *La voix des familles nombreuses de l'Afrique du Nord*. For more information on de Witt–Schlumberger, see her obituary in the *Revue de la plus grande famille*, January 1925, 791–92.

52. BMD: Dossier Marguerite de Witt–Schlumberger, "Une grande figure du féminisme," *Illustration*, November 8, 1924.

53. "Le vote familial: Action du comité central des ligues de familles nombreuses et de repopulation," *Revue de la plus grande famille*, April 1919, 366.

54. Marguerite de Witt–Schlumberger, "À propos du suffrage féminin," *La femme et l'enfant*, February 15, 1924, 256.

55. Under Vichy, Boverat continued to be an outspoken advocate of the family vote. See, e.g., Boverat, *Une doctrine de natalité*, 38; Boverat, *Famille et natalité*, 15; and Boverat, *La résurrection par la natalité*, 424–26.

56. P. Smith, *Feminism and the Third Republic*, 241.

57. P. Smith, *Feminism and the Third Republic*, 242.

58. "L'activité de la ligue pour le vote familial," *Bulletin de l'alliance nationale pour l'accroissement de la population française*, August 1935, 235–36. According to Paul Smith, very few feminist organizations supported familial suffrage, despite pronatalist claims to the contrary. Among the organizations that did support familial suffrage were the Union féminine civique et sociale, the Ligue patriotique des françaises, and the women's branch of Action populaire. Smith, *Feminism and the Third Republic*, 233.

59. Perkins, *A History of Modern Tunisia*, 40.

60. Algeria was considered another region of France, administratively and politically. Thus, just like French people in the metropole, French citizens in Algeria voted for senators and deputies who represented their interests in parliament. Tunisia was not represented in parliament.

61. Perkins, *A History of Modern Tunisia*, 67.

62. Ling, *Tunisia*, 56.

63. Perkins, *A History of Modern Tunisia*, 68.

64. Perkins, *A History of Modern Tunisia*, 79.

65. Arnoulet, *Résidents généraux de France en Tunisie*, 111.

66. *Dictionnaire des parlementaires français*, 2940.

67. Arnoulet, *Résidents généraux de France en Tunisie*, 113.

68. Perkins, *A History of Modern Tunisia*, 80.

69. "Décret du 12 juillet 1922," *Journal officiel tunisien*, July 12, 1922, 807–10. A decree of March 19, 1927, increased the size of the Grand conseil. Subsequently there were in the French section twenty-two representatives of the economic interests and thirty representatives of the colony; in the Tunisian section there were twenty-six members (one of whom was from the Jewish community). Rectenwald, *Les assemblées élues*, 29, 40.

70. See, e.g., Perkins, *A History of Modern Tunisia*; and Ling, *Tunisia*.

71. AD, Protectorat français de Tunisie, résidence générale, classement Bernard, 2189, "Réformes tunisiennes: projets de réformes de 1922, réformes de la conférence consultative et conseils de région 1920–1926."

72. Ministère des affaires étrangères, *Rapport au président de la république . . . 1922*, 11–12.

73. Balekm, *La Tunisie après la guerre*, 143.

74. Ministère des affaires étrangères, *Rapport au président de la république* . . . *1922*, 11–12.

75. Eventually, opponents persuaded the residency to revisit this system of voting. A decree in 1945 eliminated the representation of economic interests within the Grand conseil and mandated that all representatives be elected by direct universal suffrage. Sghair, "La fédération républicaine," 106.

76. AD, Protectorat français de Tunisie, résidence générale, classement Bernard, 1725, "Des assemblées élues du protectorat."

77. "Liste provisoire des électeurs de la chambre d'agriculture du nord," *Journal officiel tunisien*, February 28, 1923, 224–26.

78. AD, Protectorat français de Tunisie, résidence générale, classement Bernard, 1725, "Des assemblées élues du protectorat."

79. "Décret du 12 juillet 1922," *Journal officiel tunisien*, July 12, 1922, 807–10.

80. AD, Protectorat français de Tunisie, résidence générale, classement Bernard, 1725, "Des assemblées élues du protectorat."

81. AD, Protectorat français de Tunisie, résidence générale, classement Bernard, 1727, Grand conseil: état des électeurs (contrôles civils de Tunis, Bizerte, Le Kef) 1928.

82. AD, Grand conseil: état des électeurs.

83. In the context of French Algeria see Clancy-Smith, "Islam, Gender, and Identities."

84. Clancy-Smith, "Islam, Gender, and Identities"; also see Knibiehler and Goutalier, *La femme au temps des colonies*.

85. According to Souad Bakalti, polygamy was fairly rare in Tunisian society during the colonial period. Bakalti, *La femme tunisienne*, 239.

86. Quoted in Knibiehler and Goutalier, *La femme au temps des colonies*, 147. For more on Lyautey's views of colonial rule see Rabinow, *French Modern*; and Segalla, *The Moroccan Soul*.

87. See chapter 3.

88. According to Patricia Lorcin, some writers viewed the high birthrate among colonial subjects in North Africa as something that could potentially improve the French birthrate. Lorcin, *Imperial Identities*, 198.

89. AMAE, Direction politique et commerciale, Tunisie, 5, résidence générale, 1920–29: Administration générale, conférence consultative, 1920–24, 36: "Note sur le vote plural." Hereafter cited as AMAE: "Note sur le vote plural." This archival document appears to be an earlier draft of a part of a book published by Charles Monchicourt under the pseudonym Rod Balekm. See Balekm, *La Tunisie après la guerre*.

90. AMAE: "Note sur le vote plural."

91. Colonial officials' need to convey a particularly strong image of masculinity in the colonial context has been studied by a number of historians. See, e.g., Stoler, *Carnal Knowledge and Imperial Power*, 65.

92. AMAE: "Note sur le vote plural."

93. AD, Protectorat français de Tunisie, résidence générale, classement Bernard, 1725, "Des assemblées élues du protectorat."

94. Shorrock, "The Tunisian Question," 633.

95. Shorrock, "The Tunisian Question," 633.

96. AMAE, Direction politique et commerciale, Tunisie, 5, résidence générale, 1920–29: Administration générale, conférence consultative, 1925–29, 37.

97. Balekm, *La Tunisie après la guerre*, 6–11.

98. Barthelet, "Natalité et peuplement," 490.

99. Arnoulet, *Résidents généraux de France en Tunisie*, 115. Malta was part of the British Empire and Maltese settlers therefore were British nationals.

100. Arnoulet, *Résidents généraux de France en Tunisie*, 116.

101. The 1931 census indicated that there were 91,427 French settlers versus 91,178 Italians. Sghair, *La droite française en Tunisie*, 17.

102. Shorrock, "The Tunisian Question," 633.

103. Shorrock, "The Tunisian Question," 633.

104. See, e.g., AMAE, Direction politique et commerciale, Tunisie, 5, résidence générale, 1920–29: Étrangers en Tunisie, 1917–25, 26.

105. Arnoulet, *Résidents généraux de France en Tunisie*, 143.

106. Shorrock, "The Tunisian Question," 638.

107. Shorrock, "The Tunisian Question," 638.

108. Shorrock, "The Tunisian Question," 643.

109. Arnoulet, *Résidents généraux de France en Tunisie*, 145.

110. AMAE: "Note sur le vote plural."

111. AMAE: "Note sur le vote plural."

112. Balek, *La Tunisie après la guerre*, 257–58.

113. Balek, *La Tunisie après la guerre*, 260.

114. Gershovich, *French Military Rule in Morocco*, 64. According to Gershovich, this approach to colonial rule was consistent with Lyautey's aristocratic beliefs. This no doubt stemmed from the fact that Lyautey's family had aristocratic connections and royalist sympathies, as William Hoisington explains in his study of Lyautey's career. Hoisington, *Lyautey and the French Conquest of Morocco*, 1. For more biographical information on Lyautey, see also Berenson, *Heroes of Empire*.

115. Gershovich, *French Military Rule in Morocco*, 67.

116. Pennell, *Morocco since 1830*, 171.

117. Pennell, *Morocco since 1830*, 182. Pennell states that twenty-nine thousand European settlers arrived in the first year of the protectorate (171).

118. Pennell, *Morocco since 1830*, 182.

119. Gershovich, "The Ait Ya'Qub Incident," 66.

120. Gershovich, "The Ait Ya'Qub Incident," 67.

121. His father, Jules Steeg, represented Gironde in the French parliament from 1881 to 1889. *Dictionnaire des parlementaires français*, 3033.

122. Steeg was elected to the Chamber of Deputies in 1904 as a radical socialist and would later become a senator, minister of education, minister of the interior,

minister of justice, and, for six weeks from December 1930 to January 1931, prime minister. "Steeg, Théodore Jules Joseph (1868–1950)," in Bell, Johnson, and Morris, *Bibliographical Dictionary*.

123. Gershovich, "The Ait Ya'Qub Incident," 67.

124. Gershovich, "The Ait Ya'Qub Incident," 68.

125. Pennell, *Morocco since 1830*, 199.

126. Scham, *Lyautey in Morocco*, 75.

127. *Discours de M. Th. Steeg*, 13.

128. "Décision résidentielle du 13 octobre 1926 modifiant la composition de la section française du conseil du gouvernement," *Bulletin officiel de l'empire chérifien, protectorat de la république française au Maroc*, October 19, 1926, 1979–84.

129. "Décision résidentielle du 13 octobre 1926."

130. Fribourg, *L'Afrique latine*, 24.

131. Slavin, *Colonial Cinema and Imperial France*, 86–87.

132. On these types of demographic concerns in Algeria, see chapter 5.

133. T. Steeg, "Contre la dépopulation: L'assistance aux familles nombreuses," *L'aide sociale, prévoyance, hygiène, travail*, December 31, 1909, 670–80.

134. Jacques Bertillon, "La journée nationale des mères de familles nombreuses," *La femme et l'enfant*, March 1, 1920, 839–40.

135. AD, Protectorat français de Tunisie, résidence générale, classement Bernard, 1725, "Des assemblées élues du protectorat."

136. AMAE: "Note sur le vote plural."

137. AMAE, Direction politique et commerciale, Tunisie, 5, résidence générale, 1920–29. Administration générale, conférence consultative, 1920–24, 36: newspaper clippings on Tunisia.

138. See, e.g., *Revue de l'alliance nationale pour l'accroissement de la population française*, January 1923, 2; "Commission de législation: Le vote familial en Tunisie," *Revue de la plus grande famille*, October 1922, 227; "Vote familial à Tunis," *Bulletin de la ligue roussillonnaise des familles nombreuses* 9 (1923): 5–6.

139. "Vote familial à Tunis," 5–6. This article appeared in the newspaper of a regional branch of the familialist movement.

140. Toulemon, *Le suffrage familial*, 122.

141. Toulemon, *Le suffrage familial*, 122.

142. Specifically, this committee was called the Commission chargée de la centralisation des votes de la vérification des dépouillements. AD, Protectorat français de Tunisie, résidence générale, classement Bernard, 1725, "Des Assemblées élues du protectorat": "Élections au grand conseil de la Tunisie, scrutin du 15 avril 1928."

143. AD: "Élections au grand conseil de la Tunisie, scrutin du 15 avril 1928."

144. CAOM: BIB AOM 50433 "Procès-Verbaux du grand conseil de la Tunisie, 1922–1926," Second Session, November–December 1923, of the French section, 210. Specifically, he was referring to the Fédération nationale des associations de familles nombreuses.

145. "Dégrèvements scolaires en Tunisie," *Revue de la plus grande famille*, April 1923, 341.

146. "Dégrèvements scolaires en Tunisie."

147. "Grand conseil de la Tunisie, procès verbal," *Journal officiel tunisien*, April 14, 1923, 522–25.

148. Paul Haury, "Le vote familial s'impose," *Revue de l'alliance nationale contre la dépopulation*, September 1939, 321–26.

149. In his article Haury described Saint as a radical socialist and Steeg as a reactionary. This was not in fact the case, as noted in the text.

150. De Witt–Schlumberger died in 1924, two years after the reform in Tunisia and prior to the 1926 reform in Morocco.

151. See, e.g., "Ce que nous a dit Mme Pagniez," *La femme algérienne*, March–April 1934, 1.

152. "Ce que nous a dit Mme Pagniez," 1. On the feminist press in 1930s Algeria see Guiard, "Une presse féministe."

5. A Colonial Fountain of Youth

1. Lyautey, *Paroles d'action*, 52.

2. Levasseur, *La population française*, 3:426.

3. Levasseur, *La population française*, 3:426.

4. Gosnell, *The Politics of Frenchness*, 219.

5. This law originated in the metropole and was applied in Algeria.

6. Leroy-Beaulieu, *De la colonisation chez les peuples modernes*, 349.

7. On the process of cultural integration in late-nineteenth-century France see Weber, *Peasants into Frenchmen*, 349.

8. Concerning the potential role of French priests in assimilating Italian and Spanish settlers in Algeria see Lavigerie, *Conférence donnée dans l'église de la Madeleine*. Originally from Alsace, Lavigerie was a French cardinal in North Africa. He was well known for creating colonial orders of nuns (the *sœurs blanches*) and priests (the *pères blancs*). Lavigerie was also a strong supporter of French imperialism and considered French North Africa as a base from which he could work to end the practice of slavery in Sub-Saharan Africa.

9. AMAE: série K. Afrique, 1918–40 Algérie 28. Letter from the Bishop of Oran, Christophe Louis, to the minister of foreign affairs in Paris, August 8, 1919. On the importance of the Roman Catholic Church in making colonies "French," see Daughton, *An Empire Divided*. Daughton uses Madagascar, French Polynesia, and Indochina as his case studies.

10. Demontès, "Les étrangers en Algérie," 221.

11. Demontès, "La colonie espagnol en Algérie," 171.

12. Demontès, "La colonie espagnol en Algérie," 175. The Crémieux Decree, of October 24, 1870, gave the Algerian Jews French citizenship. In making this statement Demontès was clearly overlooking the anti-Semitism that also existed among French settlers. See, e.g., Joshua Cole, "Anti-Semitism and the Colonial Situation

in Interwar Algeria: The Anti-Jewish Riots in Constantine, August, 1934," in M. Thomas, *The French Colonial Mind*, 2:77–111.

13. Demontès, "Les étrangers en Algérie," 223. According to Demontès, in this article, the statistics concerning mixed marriages in the European population were as follows: in 1894, 817 out of 3,512 marriages; in 1895, 910 out of 3,880 marriages; in 1896, 968 out of 3,895 marriages. In his 1906 book *Le peuple algérien*, Demontès emphasized that intermarriage was an essential part of assimilating naturalized settlers into the French population.

14. Gosnell, *The Politics of Frenchness*, chapter 5.

15. Gosnell, *The Politics of Frenchness*, chapter 5.

16. Demontès, *Le peuple algérien*.

17. Demontès, *Le peuple algérien*, 251.

18. Demontès, *Le peuple algérien*, 279–81.

19. Barthelet, "Natalité et peuplement," 487–88.

20. For the nineteenth century see Sessions, *By Sword and Plow*, 216.

21. Lorcin, *Historicizing Colonial Nostalgia*, 76.

22. Gosnell, *The Politics of Frenchness*, 34.

23. Rivet, *Le Maghreb à l'épreuve de la colonisation*, 276.

24. Gosnell, *The Politics of Frenchness*, 35.

25. Dunwoodie, *Writing French Algeria*, 117–18.

26. Dunwoodie, *Writing French Algeria*, 117–18.

27. Based on those births that were officially registered with the colonial government, the birthrate for colonized Algerians (indigènes) was listed in 1921–25 as 26 and therefore equal to the European settler birthrate. However, it was widely recognized that colonized Algerians underreported their births. In 1954, J. Breil estimated the actual birthrate to be 38, and in 1969, J.-N. Biraben estimated it to be 37.2, estimates which Kateb says are generally recognized to be correct. Kateb, *Européens, "indigènes" et juifs en Algérie*, 246.

28. For the years 1931 to 1935, the birthrate for colonized Algerians based on officially registered births was 36. In 1954, Breil estimated the actual birthrate to be 44, and in 1969, Biraben estimated it to be 43.4. Kateb, *Européens, "indigènes" et juifs en Algérie*, 246.

29. Rivet, *Le Maghreb à l'épreuve de la colonisation*, 276. Gosnell states that settlers attributed this population growth not only to French medicine but also to cultural differences, such as polygamy. Gosnell, *The Politics of Frenchness*, 35. On colonial medicine in the North African context see also Keller, *Colonial Madness*.

30. Kateb, *Européens, "indigènes" et juifs en Algérie*, 242–43.

31. Barthelet, "Natalité et peuplement," 487–88.

32. Barthelet, "Natalité et peuplement," 487–88.

33. *Bulletin trimestriel de la section pour Madagascar de la ligue des fonctionnaires pères et mères de famille nombreuse*, June 1919.

34. *Bulletin de la ligue des fonctionnaires pères de famille nombreuse, section de Cochinchine*, May 1915.

35. *Bulletin trimestriel de la section pour Madagascar de la ligue des fonctionnaires pères et mères de famille nombreuse,* June 1919.

36. CAOM: BIB AOM B3622 Les cahiers de la ligue des familles nombreuses françaises d'Algérie.

37. "L'assistance aux familles nombreuses par la colonie: Création de la confédération des ligues d'Algérie groupant 12.000 familles nombreuses," *La voix des familles nombreuses françaises de l'Afrique du Nord,* July 1, 1925, 1.

38. "Tunisie," *La voix des familles nombreuses françaises de l'Afrique du Nord,* October 1, 1924, 2.

39. "Lettre de G. Bernaudat, président de la fédération des unions de familles françaises nombreuses au Maroc," *La voix des familles nombreuses françaises de l'Afrique du Nord,* November 1, 1924, 3; and "Union des familles françaises nombreuses de Marrakech," *La voix des familles nombreuses françaises de l'Afrique du Nord,* November–December 1926, 1–2.

40. During World War II the Alliance nationale came to an agreement with the Office algérien d'action familiale, a familialist organization, that members of the latter would automatically become members of the Alliance nationale and receive its newspaper, which at this time was called *Revue de l'alliance nationale contre la dépopulation.* CAOM: BIB AOM B1416 L'Office Algérien d'Action Familiale, 1945.

41. "Material and moral situation" were the exact words used in the statutes of the Algerian league. CAOM: BIB AOM B3622 Les cahiers de la ligue des familles nombreuses françaises d'Algérie, 1. Hereafter cited as CAOM: Familles nombreuses françaises d'Algérie.

42. CAOM: Familles nombreuses françaises d'Algérie, 1.

43. CAOM: Familles nombreuses françaises d'Algérie, 1.

44. "À l'œuvre," *Pour la vie: Bulletin de la section de l'Afrique du Nord,* October–December 1918, 1.

45. The entire text of the declaration is reproduced in Talmy, *Histoire du mouvement familial en France,* 1:236–37.

46. Talmy, *Histoire du mouvement familial en France,* 1:236–37.

47. Talmy, *Histoire du mouvement familial en France,* 2:32.

48. Talmy, *Histoire du mouvement familial en France,* 2:19.

49. S. Pedersen, *Family, Dependence,* 270–71.

50. Spengler, *France Faces Depopulation,* 246. Also see Talmy, *Histoire du mouvement familial en France,* 2:25.

51. As an example of this, see J. E. Pedersen, "'Special Customs.'"

52. On this question see, especially, Dubois, *A Colony of Citizens.*

53. "Ligue des familles nombreuses françaises d'Algérie," *La voix des familles nombreuses françaises de l'Afrique du Nord,* April 1, 1927, 1.

54. CAOM: BIB AOM B3622 Les cahiers de la ligue des familles nombreuses françaises d'Algérie.

55. "Notre programme," *La voix des familles nombreuses françaises de l'Afrique du Nord,* August 10, 1924, 2.

56. Barthelet, "Natalité et peuplement," 503.

57. AMAE, Direction politique et commerciale, Tunisie, 5, résidence générale, 1920–29: Étrangers en Tunisie, 1917–25, 26: Correspondence, médaille de la famille française. Because this was a French award that the residency was requesting for these women, it seems reasonable to assume that they were both French citizens. However, the archival collection in which these letters were preserved is titled "foreigners in Tunisia," which suggests that the women in question were not French citizens.

58. AMAE: Correspondence, médaille de la famille française.

59. "L'aide à la famille nombreuse en France et en Algérie," *La voix des familles nombreuses françaises de l'Afrique du Nord*, August–October 1927, 1.

60. CAOM: BIB AOM B3622 Les cahiers de la ligue des familles nombreuses françaises d'Algérie, 2–3.

61. "Tunisie," *La voix des familles nombreuses françaises de l'Afrique du Nord*, October 1, 1924, 2.

62. Barthelet, "Natalité et peuplement," 505.

63. Barthelet, "Natalité et peuplement," 505–6.

64. CAOM, Fonds ministériels, affaires politiques 1AFFPOL/2555: "Mésures prises aux colonies en faveur des familles nombreuses et des familles nécessiteuses," 3–6. This ministerial report dealt only with those colonies under the jurisdiction of the Ministry of Colonies and did not specifically address what existed in North Africa. Tunisia and Morocco were under the jurisdiction of the Ministry of Foreign Affairs, and Algeria was considered an administrative part of France.

65. "Mésures prises aux colonies en faveur des familles nombreuses et des familles nécessiteuses," 10.

66. "Mésures prises aux colonies en faveur des familles nombreuses et des familles nécessiteuses," 10.

67. Paul Bénos, "Congrès de la natalité tenu à Strasbourg les 24, 25, et 26 septembre 1924: Rapport sur les familles nombreuses d'Algérie," *La voix des familles nombreuses françaises de l'Afrique du Nord*, October 1924, 4.

68. Bénos, "Congrès de la natalité," 4.

69. CAOM, Algérie, Département d'Oran 1M/51: "Commission du relèvement des anciens centres de colonisation: rapport de la sous-commission du département de Constantine, présenté par M. Vallet."

70. "Le 5ème Congrès de la fédération des ligues des familles nombreuses, tenu à Souk-Ahras, les 7 et 8 mars 1925," *La voix des familles nombreuses françaises de l'Afrique du Nord*, August 1925, 4.

71. Paul Bénos, "Terres de colonisation," *La voix des familles nombreuses françaises de l'Afrique du Nord*, December 1924, 3.

72. CAOM: Algérie préfecture de Constantine FR CAOM 93/1989: Centres de colonisation: Berriche.

73. AMAE: Maroc, série M: 592, législation, 1921–29: Letter dated October 3, 1923, from the delegate of the residency in Morocco to the minister of foreign affairs concerning the "application of the law of July 22, 1923, on incentives to large families."

74. G. Bernaudat, "Ce qu'on a fait au Maroc pour les familles nombreuses," *La voix des familles nombreuses françaises de l'Afrique du Nord*, October 1, 1924, 3.

75. "Union des familles françaises nombreuses de Marrakech," *La voix des familles nombreuses françaises de l'Afrique du Nord*, November–December 1926, 1–2.

76. "Union des familles françaises nombreuses de Marrakech," 1–2.

77. See chapter 4.

78. "Union des familles françaises nombreuses de Marrakech," 1–2.

79. "Création d'un office des familles nombreuses au Maroc," *Revue de la plus grande famille*, October 1928, 1638–40.

80. "Création d'un office des familles nombreuses au Maroc," 1638–40.

81. "Création d'un office des familles nombreuses au Maroc," 1638–40.

82. AMAE, série K, Afrique, questions générales, 26: familles nombreuses. Letter dated September 19, 1925, from the resident-general in Tunis to the minister of foreign affairs in Paris.

83. AD, Protectorat français de Tunisie, résidence générale, classement Vallon, 1532-2: Sociétés et Associations, 1920–22. Letter dated July 7, 1921, from the resident-general to the general director of finances in Tunis.

84. "Tunisie," *La voix des familles nombreuses françaises de l'Afrique du Nord*, October 1, 1924, 2. The subvention was increased to 10,000 francs in 1924.

85. "Tunisie," 2.

86. AD, Protectorat français de Tunisie, résidence générale, classement Vallon, 1532-2: Sociétés et associations, 1920–22.

87. AD: Sociétés et associations, 1920–22.

88. S. Pedersen, *Family, Dependence*, 227–28.

89. S. Pedersen, *Family, Dependence*, 357–58.

90. Spengler, *France Faces Depopulation*, 244.

91. The presentation that Paul Bénos gave was called "Mésures à prendre pour faire bénéficier les familles françaises d'Algérie des lois protectrices de la métropole." See "VIème congrès de la natalité de Strasbourg" *La voix des familles nombreuses françaises de l'Afrique du Nord*, October 1924, 1.

92. AD, Protectorat français de Tunisie, résidence générale, classement Vallon, 1532–2: Sociétés et associations, 1920–22.

93. AD: Sociétés et associations, 1920-22. Algeria, however, was apparently able to work around this problem. In 1927 the Alliance nationale reported that large French families in Algeria would receive discounts on train fare. "Algérie," *Bulletin de l'alliance nationale pour l'accroissement de la population française*, September 1927, 281.

94. "Grand conseil de la Tunisie: Commission arbitrale, séance du samedi 6 janvier 1923," *Journal officiel tunisien*, May 5, 1923.

95. "Grand Conseil de la Tunisie."

96. Racial interpretations of poverty continued to shape policy on family benefits later in the twentieth century also. For Réunion, see Finch-Boyer, "'The Idea of the Nation.'"

97. AMAE, série K, Afrique, questions générales, 26: familles nombreuses.

98. AMAE, série K, Afrique, questions générales, 26: familles nombreuses.

99. The names listed as officers in Oran, e.g., illustrate that this is the case. "Oran, association des familles nombreuses," *La voix des familles nombreuses françaises de l'Afrique du Nord*, March 1, 1925, 2.

100. CAOM: BIB AOM B3622 Les cahiers de la ligue des familles nombreuses françaises d'Algérie.

101. Fédération des ligues des pères et mères de familles nombreuses françaises du département de Constantine, *Compte rendu du VIIème congrès*.

102. P. Bénos, "Constantine," *La voix des familles nombreuses françaises de l'Afrique du Nord*, August 10, 1924.

103. See Campbell, "Women and Men in French Authoritarianism," chapter 4; and Kalman, "Fascism and Algérianité."

104. Bénos, "Constantine," 3.

105. Bénos, "Constantine," 3.

106. Bénos, "Constantine," 3.

107. The speech was actually presented by a different man: Ben Diab.

108. "Le cinquième congrès de la fédération des ligues des familles nombreuses, tenu à Souk-Ahras, les 7 et 8 Mars 1925," *La voix des familles nombreuses françaises de l'Afrique du Nord*, April 1, 1925, 1.

109. "Le cinquième congrès," 1.

110. See Burton, *Burdens of History*.

111. "Guelma, ligue des familles nombreuses, réunion générale du 12 Mai 1927," *La voix des familles nombreuses françaises de l'Afrique du Nord*, May 1, 1927, 2.

112. CAOM: BIB AOM B3622 Les cahiers de la ligue des familles nombreuses françaises d'Algérie, adoptés à l'unanimité par l'assemblée générale du 17 mars 1929.

113. FR CAOM 93/6682: Algérie, Préfecture de Constantine: Médaille de la Famille Française 1934–38.

114. "Du mouvement de la population française dans ses rapports avec l'extension du commerce extérieur: Rapport présenté au comité du commerce extérieur par M. Jules Jacob, membre de ce comité," *Bulletin de l'alliance nationale pour l'accroissement de la population française*, July 1907, 299–309.

115. "L'aide à la famille en Algérie," *Revue de la plus grande famille*, July 1925, 923.

116. "Commission des avantages matériels: Ce qui a été fait pour les familles nombreuses en Tunisie," *Revue de la plus grande famille*, September 1927, 1436.

117. CAOM: BIB AOM B3622 Les cahiers de la ligue des familles nombreuses françaises d'Algérie, 8.

118. Charles Richet, "Pour que la France vive? Il faut mettre à la mode la création de familles nombreuses," *La voix des familles nombreuses françaises de l'Afrique du Nord*, March 1, 1927, 4; Fernand Boverat, "Il faut généraliser les primes à la natalité," *La voix des familles nombreuses françaises de l'Afrique du Nord*, March 1, 1927, 4.

119. As part of the 1919 Paris Peace Conference following World War I, Germany ceded Alsace and Lorraine to France. Located in Lorraine, Nancy was a highly symbolic choice for the first pronatalist congress.

120. AMAE, série K, Afrique, questions générales; 26: familles nombreuses.

121. AD, Protectorat français de Tunisie, résidence générale, classement Vallon, 1532-2: Sociétés et associations, 1920–22. Letter dated October 19, 1921.

122. AD: Classement Vallon, 1532-2: Sociétés et associations. Letter dated October 19, 1921.

123. Ezra, *The Colonial Unconscious*, 14.

124 Conseil national des femmes françaises, *États généraux du féminisme* (1931).

125. Auguste Isaac, "XIIe congrès nationale de la natalité et des familles nombreuses," *La femme et l'enfant*, March 1, 1930, 155.

126. Isaac, "XII congrès nationale," 155.

127. "Tribune libre: Le congrès de la natalité d'Alger-Constantine," *La femme et l'enfant*, May 15, 1930, 295–96.

128. "Tribune libre," 295–96.

129. *Douzième congrès national de la natalité et des familles nombreuses, compte rendu, Constantine, Algérie.*

130. *Douzième congrès national.*

131. L. Borie, "Le XIIe congrès de la natalité, Constantine-Alger, 4–8 avril 1930," *Revue de l'alliance nationale pour l'accroissement de la population française*, May 1930, 137–42.

132. "Ce qu'on a fait au Maroc pour les familles nombreuses," *La voix des familles nombreuses de l'Afrique du Nord*, November 1, 1924, 3.

133. "Ce qu'on a fait au Maroc pour les familles nombreuses," 3.

134. "Ce qu'on a fait au Maroc pour les familles nombreuses," 3.

135. AMAE, série K, Afrique, questions générales; 26, familles nombreuses.

136. AMAE, série K, Afrique, questions générales; 26, familles nombreuses.

137. AMAE, série K, Afrique, questions générales; 26, familles nombreuses.

138. AMAE, série K, Afrique, questions générales; 26, familles nombreuses.

139. See chapter 1. Following Ricoux's study of Algerian demographics, Algeria was described as a "fountain of youth" in the French press.

Conclusion

1. Following the German invasion of Czechoslovakia in 1938, Daladier gained the authority to govern by decree. Sowerwine, *France since 1870*, 184.

2. Childers, *Fathers, Families, and the State*, 40.

3. Pollard, *Reign of Virtue*, 21.

4. Childers, *Fathers, Families and the State*, 40. For a more complete assessment of pronatalist leaders' responses to the Code see Koos, "Engendering Reaction," 207.

5. See, e.g., Fernand Boverat, "La dénatalité française et les revendications coloniales du Reich," *Revue de l'alliance nationale contre la dépopulation*, December 1938.

6. Quoted in Pollard, *Reign of Virtue*, 9.

7. See, e.g., Sowerwine, *France since 1870*, 189. Sowerwine states that collectively the British and French outnumbered the Germans. In their explanations of French defeat, most historians point to the French High Command, emphasizing not only

their initial unwillingness to take decisive action but also their failure to understand or prepare for the type of war they would eventually face.

8. This situation changed in November 1942. Following Allied landings in North Africa, the free zone became part of the German occupied zone and the Italian zone (also in the south) was expanded.

9. Fishman, "Waiting for the Captive Sons of France," 184–85.

10. See Pollard, *Reign of Virtue*; Koos, "Engendering Reaction"; and Childers, *Fathers, Families, and the State*.

11. Pollard, *Reign of Virtue*, 175; Koos, "Engendering Reaction," 200.

12. Childers, *Fathers, Families, and the State*, 158.

13. Jennings, *Vichy in the Tropics*.

14. Jennings, *Vichy in the Tropics*, 40–41.

15. Jennings, *Vichy in the Tropics*, 40–41.

16. Jennings, *Vichy in the Tropics*, 11. Also see Ginio, *French Colonialism Unmasked*.

17. Jennings, *Vichy in the Tropics*, 44.

18. This proposal ultimately failed. For more information on how right-wing settlers responded to this proposal see Kalman, "Le Combat par Tous les Moyens"; and Kalman, "Fascism and Algérianité."

19. Cantier, *L'Algérie sous le régime de vichy*, 58.

20. Jennings, *Vichy in the Tropics*.

21. For example, this is seen in the statutes of the Ligue des familles françaises du Tonkin, which included a demand that more of Pétain's familialist measures be applied in Indochina. Article 3 of the statutes, printed in the *Bulletin de la ligue des familles françaises du Tonkin*, March 1942, 1.

22. CAOM: Fonds ministériels: 1 Affaires politiques 2412, dossier 8: Association des chefs de familles françaises à Madagascar.

23. As explained earlier, the idea of women restricting their fertility was far more controversial than men's decisions in this area and did lead to some punitive legislation intended to eliminate women's choices. The 1920 law strengthening penalties for abortion, contraception, and distribution of family-planning information is a prominent example of such a punitive measure affecting women. Still, many pronatalist reforms, including a variety of financial incentives introduced during the Third Republic, were designed to make having additional children seem more appealing and feasible. These reforms indicate that, even if they considered it immoral, pronatalists must have on some level resigned themselves to the fact that people were making reproductive choices and would continue to do so. As many scholars have pointed out, many of the prominent pronatalist leaders themselves had relatively small families and were clearly choosing to restrict their fertility.

24. Footitt, "The First Women Députés."

25. On the "return" of Maltese settlers to France see A. Smith, *Colonial Memory and Postcolonial Europe*. On postcolonial Algerian migration to France see Silverstein, *Algeria in France*.

26. "The cumulative birthrate is the average number of children a generation of women would give birth to all throughout their fertile life if their mortality is not taken into account. This is the sum of the fertility rates per age of a generation." Lucille Richet-Mastain, "Demographic Balance Sheet 2006: A Record Natural Increase" (Institut National de la statistique et des études économiques) INSEE Prémier #1118, January 2007, http://www.insee.fr/en/themes/document.asp ?ref_id=ipl118.

27. Russel Shorto, "No Babies?," *New York Times*, June 29, 2008, http://www .nytimes.com/2008/06/29/magazine/29Birth-t.html?pagewanted=all.

28. See, e.g., Luc Leroux, "Catherine Mégret défend, en appel, la 'prime de naissance' réservée aux français," *Le monde*, April 10, 2001.

BIBLIOGRAPHY

Unpublished Primary Sources

Archives diplomatiques, Nantes, France
    Classement Bernard
    Classement Vallon
    Protectorat français au Maroc, secrétariat général du protectorat
    Protectorat français de Tunisie, résidence générale
Archives du ministère des affaires étrangères, Paris, France
    Afrique, série K
    Maroc, série M
    Tunisie, série P
Archives nationales, Paris, France
    Série F7 13955. Police: Néo-Malthusianisme
    Série F7 3226. Ministère de l'intérieur, sûreté générale: Féminisme
Bibliothèque Marguerite Durand, Paris, France
    Assemblée générale du Conseil national des femmes françaises, 1903–8, 1917–27
    Dossier Cécile Brunschvicg
    Dossier Marguerite de Witt–Schlumberger
Centre des archives d'outre-mer, Aix-en-Provence, France
    3M20 Colonisation: Berriche, Berteaux
    100 APOM, Archives du comité central français pour l'outre-mer
    Algérie, département de Constantine
    Algérie, departement d'Oran
    Algérie, préfecture de Constantine
    BIB AOM B3622
    BIB AOM B1416
    BIB AOM 50433
    Fonds ministériels
    Gouvernement général d'Algérie
    Gouverneur général de Madagascar
    Papiers d'agents: Dossier Galliéni, Joseph, 44PA

Published Sources

Accampo, Elinor. *Blessed Motherhood, Bitter Fruit: Nelly Roussel and the Politics of Female Pain in Third Republic France.* Baltimore: Johns Hopkins University Press, 2006.

Agathon. *Les jeunes gens d'aujourd'hui: Le goût de l'action, foi patriotique–une renaissance catholique, le réalisme politique.* Paris: Plon, 1913.

Ageron, Charles Robert. *La décolonisation française.* Paris: Armand Colin, 1991.

Alliance nationale contre la dépopulation. *Comment enrayer la dépopulation de la France.* Angoulême: Coquemard, 1943.

Alliance nationale pour l'accroissement de la population française. *Comment sauver la France: Si j'ai des enfants, l'avenir est à moi!.* Paris: E. Pigelet, n.d.

Amster, Ellen. "Medicine and Sainthood: Islamic Science, French Colonialism and the Politics of Healing in Morocco, 1877–1935." PhD diss., University of Pennsylvania, 2003.

Andersen, Margaret Cook. "Creating French Settlements Overseas: Pronatalism and Colonial Medicine in Madagascar." *French Historical Studies* 33, no. 3 (Summer 2010): 417–44.

———. "French Settlers, Familial Suffrage, and Citizenship in 1920s Tunisia." *Journal of Family History* 37, no. 2 (April 2012): 213–31.

André, Justin. *Le suffrage universel dédié à la famille représentée par son chef le père de famille.* Paris: Garnier Frères, 1850.

Appy, F. *Pour la France: Sa repopulation et son relèvement.* Nice: Établissement Littéraire et de Beaux-Arts, Maison Visconti, 1899.

Arnoulet, François. *Résidents généraux de France en Tunisie . . . ces mal-aimés.* Marseille: Narration, 1995.

Auburtin, Fernand. *En péril de mort.* Paris: Éditions Spes, 1929.

———. *La patrie en danger! La natalité.* Paris: Éditions G. Cres & Cie, 1921.

Auclert, Hubertine. *Le droit politique des femmes: Question qui n'est pas traitée au congrès international des femmes.* Paris: L. Hugonis, 1878.

———. *Les femmes arabes en Algérie.* Paris: Société d'Éditions Littéraires, 1900.

———. *Le vote des femmes.* Paris: V. Giard et E. Brière, 1908.

Audoin-Rouzeau, Stéphane. *L'enfant de l'ennemi (1914–1918): Viol, avortement, infanticide pendant la grande guerre.* Paris: Aubier, 1995.

August, Thomas. *The Selling of the Empire: British and French Imperialist Propaganda, 1890–1940.* Westport CT: Greenwood Press, 1985.

Bakalti, Souad. *La femme tunisienne au temps de la colonisation, 1881–1956.* Paris: L'Harmattan, 1996.

Balek, Rodd. *La Tunisie après la guerre (1919–1921): Problèmes politiques.* Paris: Comité de l'Afrique Française, 1922.

Bard, Christine. *Les filles de Marianne: Histoire des féminismes, 1914–1940.* Paris: Fayard, 1995.

———. *Les garçonnes: Modes et fantasmes des années folles.* Paris: Flammarion, 1998.

Barnes, David. *The Great Stink of Paris and the Nineteenth-Century Struggle against Filth and Germs*. Baltimore: Johns Hopkins University Press, 2006.

Baroli, Marc. *Algérie, terre d'espérances: Colons et immigrants, 1830–1914*. Paris: l'Harmattan, 1992.

Barthélemy, Georges. *Les colonies françaises: Ce qu'elles sont, ou elles sont ce qui y fait, comment on y vit*. N.p., 1928.

Barthélemy, Joseph. *La crise de la démocratie contemporaine*. Paris: Recueil Sirey, 1931.

Barthélemy, Pascale. "Sages-femmes africaines diplômées en AOF des années 1920 aux années 1960: Une redéfinition des rapports sociaux de sexe en contexte colonial." In *Histoire des femmes en situation coloniale: Afrique et Asie, XXe siècle*, ed. Anne Hugon, 119–44. Paris: Karthala, 2004.

Barthelet, L. "Natalité et peuplement en Afrique du Nord." *Bulletin de la société de géographie d'Alger* 112 (1927): 478–508.

Baudicour, Louis de. *La colonisation de l'Algérie, ses éléments*. Paris: J. Lecoffre, 1856.

Bazin, Réné. *La terre qui meurt*. Paris: Librairie Calmann-Lévy, 1899.

Beausapin [Auguste Deslinières]. *Dépopulation!!! La France en péril! Exhortation véhémente aux dames! Cri d'alarme patriotique poussé par Beausapin*. Paris: Imprimérie Dubuisson et Cie, 1890.

Bederman, Gail. *Manliness and Civilization: A Cultural History of Gender and Race in the United States, 1880–1917*. Chicago: University of Chicago Press, 1995.

Béhagle, Ferdinand de. *Des moyens de combattre la dépopulation en Afrique*. Paris: Librairie Africaine et Coloniale, 1895.

Bell, David S., Douglas Johnson, and Peter Morris, eds. *Bibliographical Dictionary of French Political Leaders since 1870*. New York: Simon and Schuster, 1990.

Benoist, Charles. *La crise de l'état moderne de l'organisation du suffrage universel*. Paris: Maison Didot, 1899.

Benoit-Lévy, Georges. *La maison heureuse*. Paris: Éditions des Cités-Jardins de France, 1922.

Béquet, Léon. *Dépopulation de la France: Allocution prononcée par Mme Léon Béquet, née de Vienne, fondatrice de la société de l'allaitement maternel et du refuge-ouvroir pour les femmes enceintes*. Paris: P. Dupont, 1892.

Berenson, Edward. *Heroes of Empire: Five Charismatic Men and the Conquest of Africa*. Berkeley: University of California Press, 2011.

Bernard, Augustin. *L'Algérie*. Paris: Larousse, 1931.

———. "Le recensement de 1921 dans l'Afrique du Nord." *Annales de géographie*, January 15, 1922, 52–58.

Bert, Paul. *Lettres de Kabylie: La politique algérienne*. Paris: Alphonse Lemerre, 1885.

Bertillon, Jacques. *De la dépopulation de la France et des remèdes à y apporter*. Nancy: Berger-Levrault et Cie, 1896.

———. "Démographie." In *L'encyclopédie d'hygiène et de médecine publique*, ed. Dr. Jules Rochard, 119–304. Paris: Lecrosnier et Babe, 1890.

———. *La dépopulation de la France: Ses conséquences*. Paris: Félix Alcan, 1911.

———. "Les Français en Algérie." *La réforme économique*, March 1, 1876, 453–60.

———. *La natalité en France*. Paris: Au Siège de la Société d'anthropologie, 1891.

———. *Le problème de la dépopulation*. Paris: Armand Colin, 1897.

———. *La statistique humaine de la France*. Paris: Germer Baillière, 1880.

Bertillon, Louis-Adolphe. "Acclimatement, acclimatation." In *Dictionnaire encyclopèdique des sciences médicales*, series 1, 1:270–323. Paris: G. Masson, 1864.

———. *Atlas de démographie figurée de la France*. Paris: G. Masson, 1874.

———. "Migration." In *Dictionnaire encyclopèdique des sciences médicales*, series 2, 7:637–63. Paris: G. Masson, 1889.

Bertrand, Louis. *Le sang des races*. Paris: Paul Ollendorff, 1899.

Betts, Raymond. *France and Decolonization, 1900–1960*. New York: St. Martin's Press, 1991.

Blaise, H. *La dépopulation de la France: Le mal, les remèdes*. Alger: S. Léon, 1900.

Blondel, Georges. *La dépopulation et la guerre: Conférence donnée le 12 décembre 1916 à la société d'études économiques du département de la Loire*. Saint Étienne: Secrétariat de l'Aide aux familles nombreuses de la Loire, 1917.

———. *L'expansion de l'Allemagne dans les pays d'outre-mer*. Paris: La Société d'Économie Sociale, 1894.

———. *Le problème de la natalité et les espérances de l'Allemagne: Conférence faite le samedi 25 septembre 1920 au théâtre des arts de Rouen à l'occasion du 2e congrès national de la natalité*. Paris: Éditions de *La Femme et l'Enfant*, 1920.

Blum, Carol. *Strength in Numbers: Population, Reproduction, and Power in Eighteenth-Century France*. Baltimore: Johns Hopkins University Press, 2002.

Bock, Gisela, and Pat Thane, eds. *Maternity and Gender Policies: Women and the Rise of the European Welfare States, 1880s–1950s*. London: Routledge, 1991.

Boisson, A. F. *La colonisation française en Tunisie dédiée aux émigrants français et aux jeunes gens*. Tunis: Imprimerie Française, 1900.

Boittin, Jennifer. *Colonial Metropolis: The Urban Grounds of Anti-Imperialism and Feminism in Interwar Paris*. Lincoln: University of Nebraska Press, 2010.

Bordeaux, Henry. *La crise de la famille française*. Paris: Flammarion, 1921.

Bouscaren, Henry. *La dépopulation de la France et ses conséquences néfastes, 1908–1936*. Saint-Etienne: Dumas, 1936.

Boverat, Fernand. *Comment nous vaincrons la dénatalité par la vérité, par le devoir, par la justice*. Paris: Éditions de l'alliance nationale contre la dépopulation, 1939.

———. *La crise des naissances: Ses conséquences tragiques et ses remèdes*. Paris: Éditions de l'alliance nationale pour l'accroissement de la population française, 1932.

———. "Le danger de la dépopulation française: Rapport présenté au 18e congrès de l'alliance d'hygiène sociale, 2–4 octobre 1931."

———. *La diminution du nombre des mariages et sa répercussion sur la natalité française*. Paris: Alliance nationale pour l'accroissement de la population française, 1922.

———. *Une doctrine de natalité*. Paris: Librairie de Médicis, 1943.

———. *Famille et natalité: Spécimen de conférence de propagande*. Lyon: Alliance nationale contre la dépopulation, 1942.

————. *Patriotisme et paternité*. Paris: Bernard Grasset, 1913.

————. *Une politique gouvernementale de natalité, étude présentée, sur sa demande, à monsieur le président du conseil des ministres par l'alliance nationale pour l'accroissement de la population française*. Paris: Éditions de l'alliance nationale, 1924.

————. *La résurrection par la natalité*. Paris: Hachette, 1943.

Brau, Paul. *Trois siècles de médecine coloniale française*. Paris: Vigot Frères, 1931.

Brenier, Henri. *Le problème de la population dans les colonies françaises: Cours professé à la semaine sociale de Marseille (session de 1930)*. Lyon: Chronique sociale de France, 1930.

Brown, Mervyn. *A History of Madagascar*. Princeton NJ: Marcus Wiener, 1995.

Brunschvicg, Cécile. *Le congrès de l'alliance internationale pour le suffrage des femmes à Genève 6–12 juin 1920*. Paris: Éditions de la revue politique et littéraire, 1921.

Bugéja, Marie. *Nos soeurs musulmanes*. Paris: La revue des Études Littéraires, 1921.

Bullard, Alice. *Exile to Paradise: Savagery and Civilization in Paris and the South Pacific, 1790–1900*. Stanford: Stanford University Press, 2000.

Bureau, Paul. *Le bon citoyen de la cité moderne: Le devoir de servir, le courage de penser, la necessité d'une doctrine de vie*. Paris: Bloud & Gay, 1926.

————. *L'indiscipline des moeurs*. Paris: Bloud & Gay, 1921.

Burke, Timothy. *Lifebuoy Men, Luxe Women: Commodification, Consumption, and Cleanliness in Modern Zimbabwe*. Durham: Duke University Press, 1996.

Burton, Antoinette. *Burdens of History: British Feminists, Indian Women, and Imperial Culture, 1865–1915*. Chapel Hill: University of North Carolina Press, 1994.

Caix de Saint-Aymour, Charles-Lavauzelle de. *Questions algériennes: Arabes et Kabyles*. Paris: Paul Ollendorff, éditeur, 1891.

Camiscioli, Elisa. "Producing Citizens, Reproducing the 'French Race': Immigration, Demography, and Pronatalism in Early Twentieth-Century France." *Gender and History* 13, no. 3 (November 2001): 593–621.

————. *Reproducing the French Race: Immigration, Intimacy, and Embodiment in the Early Twentieth Century*. Durham: Duke University Press, 2009.

Campbell, Caroline. "Women and Men in French Authoritarianism: Gender in the Croix de Feu/Parti Social Français, 1927–1947." PhD diss., University of Iowa, 2009.

Cantier, Jacques. *L'Algérie sous le régime de Vichy*. Paris: Odile Jacob, 2002.

Carol, Anne. *Histoire de l'eugénisme en France: Les médecins et la procréation, XIXe–XXe siècle*. Paris: Éditions du Seuil, 1995.

Carpentier, Louis. *L'organisation de la famille et le vote familial*. Paris: M. Giard et E. Brière, 1913.

Celarié, Henriette. *Un mois en Algérie et en Tunisie*. Paris: Hachette, 1924.

Chafer, Tony, and Amanda Sackur, eds. *Promoting the Colonial Idea: Propaganda and Visions of Empire in France*. New York: Palgrave, 2002.

Chailley-Bert, Joseph. *La colonisation française au XIXe siècle: Conférence faite aux instituteurs et institutrices de la Loire-Inférieur, de l'Hérault de la Marne et du Cher*. Paris: Au Siège de l'Union Coloniale Française, 1900.

———. *Dix années de politique coloniale*. Paris: Armand Colin, 1902.

———. *L'éducation et les colonies*. Paris: Armand Colin, 1898.

———. "La France et la plus grande France." *Revue politique et parlementaire*, August 1902, 1–35.

Challaye, Félicien. *La Chine, le Japon et les puissances*. Paris: Rieder, 1938.

Chanzy, Général Antoine-Eugène-Alfred. *Conseil supérieur de gouvernement, session de 1878: Exposé de la situation de l'Algérie*. Alger: V. Gaillaud et Cie, 1878.

Chapman, Herrick, and Laura L. Frader, eds. *Race in France: Interdisciplinary Perspectives on the Politics of Difference*. New York: Berghahn Books, 2004.

Charbit, Yves. "La population, la dépopulation et la colonisation en France." In *L'économie politique en France au XIXe siècle*, ed. Yves Breton and Michel Lutfalla, 451–84. Paris: Economica, 1991.

Chaudhuri, Nupur, and Margaret Strobel. *Western Women and Imperialism: Complicity and Resistance*. Bloomington: Indiana University Press, 1992.

Chevalier, Louis. *Classes laborieuses et classes dangereuses à Paris pendant la première moitié du XIXe siècle*. Paris: Plon, 1958.

———."L'émigration française au XIXe siècle." *Études d'histoire moderne et contemporaine* 1 (1947): 127–171.

———. *Le problème démographique nord-africain*. Paris: Presses universitaires de France, 1947.

Childers, Kristen Stromberg. *Fathers, Families, and the State in France, 1914–1945*. Ithaca: Cornell University Press, 2003.

———. "Paternity and the Politics of Citizenship in Interwar France." *Journal of Family History* 26, no. 1 (January 2001): 90–111.

Chivas-Baron, Clotilde. *La femme française aux colonies*. Paris: Éditions Larose, 1929.

Choleau, Jean. *L'expansion bretonne au XXe siècle*. Paris: Édouard Champon, 1922.

Choquette, Leslie. *Frenchmen into Peasants: Modernity and Tradition in the Peopling of French Canada*. Cambridge: Harvard University Press, 1997.

Chrastil, Rachel. *Organizing for War: France 1870–1914*. Baton Rouge: Louisiana State University Press, 2010.

Clancy-Smith, Julia. "Changing Perspectives on the Historiography of Imperialism: Women, Gender, and Empire." In *Middle East Historiographies: Narrating the Twentieth Century*, ed. Israel Gershoni, Amy Singer, and Y. Hakan Erdem, 70–100. Seattle: University of Washington Press, 2006.

———. "Islam, Gender, and Identities in the Making of French Algeria, 1830–1962." In *Domesticating the Empire: Race, Gender, and Family Life in French and Dutch Colonialism*, ed. Julia Clancy-Smith and Frances Gouda, 154–74. Charlottesville: University of Virginia Press, 1998.

———. "Women, Gender, and Migration along a Mediterranean Frontier: Pre-Colonial Tunisia, c. 1815–1870." *Gender and History* 17, no. 1 (April 2005): 62–92.

Clancy-Smith, Julia, and Frances Gouda, eds. *Domesticating the Empire: Race, Gender, and Family Life in French and Dutch Colonialism*. Charlottesville: University of Virginia Press, 1998.

Cohen, William. *The French Encounter with Africans: White Response to Blacks, 1530–1880*. Bloomington: Indiana University Press, 1980.

Cole, Jennifer. *Forget Colonialism? Sacrifice and the Art of Memory in Madagascar*. Berkeley: University of California Press, 2001.

Cole, Joshua. *The Power of Large Numbers: Population, Politics, and Gender in Nineteenth-Century France*. Ithaca: Cornell University Press, 2000.

——. "There Are Only Good Mothers: The Ideological Work of Women's Fertility in France before World War I." *French Historical Studies* 19, no. 3 (Spring 1996): 639–72.

Coleman, William. *Death Is a Social Disease: Public Health and Political Economy in Early Industrial France*. Madison: University of Wisconsin Press, 1982.

Collingham, E. M. *Imperial Bodies: The Physical Experience of the Raj, c. 1800–1947*. Cambridge: Polity Press, 2001.

Comité de Lyon. *Émigration des vaudois français en Algérie: Rapport présenté aux souscripteurs par le comité protestant de Lyon*. Lyon: H. Georg, 1883.

Commission de la dépopulation: Sous-commission de la natalité, séance du 5 février 1902 sous la présidence de M. Bernard. Melun: Impr. Administrative, 1902.

Congrès de la natalité et des familles nombreuses: La journée des mères, Paris 10–13 octobre 1918. Lyon: A. Rey, 1918.

Congrès de l'exposition universelle de 1900 sous la présidence d'honneur de M. Léon Bourgeois et sous la présidence de Mademoiselle Sarah Monod: Compte rendu des travaux par Madame Pégard, chevalier de la legion d'honneur, secrétaire générale du congrès, tome deuxième. Paris: Charles Blot, 1902.

Congrès national de la natalité et des familles nombreuses: Limoges, 30–31 octobre, 1938. Paris: Charles-Lavauzelle et Cie, 1939.

Conklin, Alice. "Faire Naître v. Faire du Noir: Race Regeneration in France and French West Africa, 1895–1940." In *Promoting the Colonial Idea: Propaganda and Visions of Empire in France*, ed. Tony Chafer and Amanda Sackur, 143–55. New York: Palgrave, 2002.

——. *A Mission to Civilize: The Republican Idea of Empire in France and West Africa, 1895–1930*. Stanford: Stanford University Press, 1997.

Conseil national des femmes françaises. *Conseil national des femmes françaises, section du suffrage: Le rôle de la femme dans la société conférence de Mlle. Thérèse Mercier, institutrice publique, Avril 1908*. Paris: Charles Buquet, 1908.

——. *Dixième congrès international des femmes: Œuvres et institutions féminines, droits des femmes*. Paris: V. Giard et E. Brière, 1914.

——. *États généraux du féminisme, Paris, 14–16 février 1929*. Paris: Conseil national des femmes françaises, 1929.

——. *États généraux du féminisme, troisième session, Paris, 30–31 Mai 1931*. Paris: Conseil national des femmes françaises, 1931.

Cooper, Nicola J. "Gendering the Colonial Enterprise: *La Mère-Patrie* and Maternalism in France and French Indochina." In *Empires and Boundaries: Rethinking Race, Class, and Gender in Colonial Settings*, ed. Harald Fischer Tiné and Susanne Gehrmann, 129–45. New York: Routledge, 2009.

Corbin, Alain. *Les filles de noce: Misère sexuelle et prostitution*. Paris: Flammarion, 1982.

Corneau, Grace. *La femme aux colonies*. Paris: Nilsson, 1900.

Corra, Émile. *Les devoirs naturels de l'homme*. Paris: Édouard Pelletan, 1905.

Covell, Maureen. *Historical Dictionary of Madagascar*. Lanham MD: Scarecrow Press, 1995.

Cros, Louis. *Algérie-Tunisie pour tous, comment aller: Que faire en Algérie ou en Tunisie; Sept cent mille Français y sont déjà*. Paris: Albin Michel, n.d.

Curtis, Sarah. *Civilizing Habits: Women Missionaries and the Revival of French Empire*. Oxford: Oxford University Press, 2012.

Darrow, Margaret H. *French Women and the First World War: War Stories of the Home Front*. Oxford: Berg, 2000.

Datta, Venita. *Heroes and Legends of Fin-de-Siècle France: Gender, Politics, and National Identity*. Cambridge: Cambridge University Press, 2011.

Daughton, J. P. *An Empire Divided: Religion, Republicanism, and the Making of French Colonialism, 1880–1914*. Oxford: Oxford University Press, 2006.

———. "When Argentina Was 'French': Rethinking Cultural Politics and European Imperialism in Belle-Époque Buenos Aires." *Journal of Modern History* 80, no.4 (December 2008): 831–64.

Davin, Anna. "Imperialism and Motherhood." *History Workshop* 5 (Spring 1978): 9–65.

Davis, Diana. *Resurrecting the Granary of Rome: Environmental History and French Colonial Expansion in North Africa*. Athens: Ohio University Press, 2007.

Debury, Roger. *Un pays de célibataires et de fils uniques*. Paris: E. Dentu, 1896.

De Grazia, Victoria. *How Fascism Ruled Women: Italy, 1922–1945*. Berkeley: University of California Press, 1993.

Deherme, Georges. *Croître ou disparaître*. Paris: Perrin et Cie, 1910.

Demontès, Victor. *L'Algérie économique*. Vol. 6, *Un siècle de colonisation: Évolution historique de la colonisation de l'Algérie*. Alger: Gouvernement Général de l'Algérie, 1930.

———. "La colonie espagnol en Algérie." *Bulletin de la société de géographie d'Alger* 2 (1899): 156–79.

———. "Les étrangers en Algérie." *Bulletin de la société de géographie d'Alger* 3 (1898): 201–25.

———. *Le peuple algérien: Essais de démographie algérienne*. Alger: Imprimérie Algérienne, 1906.

———. "Le problème étranger en Algérie et les effets des lois de naturalisation." *Bulletin de la société de géographie d'Alger et de l'Afrique du Nord* 6 (1901): 288–314.

Denais, Joseph. *Pour que la France vive!*. Paris: Éditions Spes, 1926.

Dennery, Étienne. *Foules d'Asie: Surpopulation japonaise, expansion chinoise, émigration indienne*. Paris: Armand Colin, 1930.

Depincé, Charles. *Exposition coloniale de Marseille, 1906: Compte rendu des travaux du congrès colonial de Marseille*. Vol. 1. Paris: Librairie Maritime et Coloniale, 1908.

Desan, Suzanne. *The Family on Trial in Revolutionary France*. Berkeley: University of California Press, 2004.

Desbiefs, Marcel. *Le vice en Algérie*. Paris: P. Fort, 1899.

Desclozeaux, Jules. *La dépopulation, conférence*. Paris: Joseph André et Cie, 1896.

Desternes, Suzanne. *Trente ans d'efforts au service de la cause féminine*. N.p.: Union nationale pour le vote des femmes, n.d.

Deuxième congrès international des œuvres et institutions féminines tenu au palais des congrès de l'exposition universelle de 1900 sous la présidence d'honneur de M. Léon Bourgeois et sous la présidence de Mlle Sarah Monod. Paris: Charles Blot, 1902.

D'Haussonville, Gabriel-Paul-Othenin. *Salaires et misères de femmes*. Paris: Calmann Lévy, 1900.

Dictionnaire des parlementaires français: Notices biographiques sur les ministres, députés et sénateurs français de 1889 à 1940. Paris: Presses universitaires de France, 1977.

Dine, Philip. "Shaping the Colonial Body: Sport and Society in Algeria, 1870–1962." In *Algeria and France, 1800–2000: Identity, Memory, Nostalgia*, ed. Patricia M. E. Lorcin, 33–48. Syracuse: Syracuse University Press, 2006.

Direction de l'agriculture et du commerce. *Notice sur la Tunisie*. 3rd ed. Tunis: Imprimerie Générale (J. Picard et Cie), 1899.

Discours de M. Th. Steeg, commissaire résident général au conseil du gouvernement du 24 novembre 1927. Rabat: Imprimerie Officielle, 1927.

Doléris, Jacques-Amédée, and Jean Bouscatel. *Hygiène et morale sociales: Néomalthusianisme, maternité et féminisme, éducation sexuelle*. Paris: Masson et Cie, 1918.

Donzelot, Jacques. *The Policing of Families*. New York: Pantheon Press, 1979.

Dubois, Laurent. *A Colony of Citizens: Revolution and Slave Emancipation in the French Caribbean, 1787–1804*. Chapel Hill: University of North Carolina Press, 2004.

Duchambon, Charles. *L'abaissement de la natalité en France: Causes et remèdes*. Paris: Librairie Médicale et Scientifique, 1910.

Dumont, Arsène. "Aptitude de la France à fournir des colons." *Journal de la société de statistique de Paris* 1 (January 1900): 15–26; 2 (February 1900): 61–69; 3 (March 1900): 80–86.

———. *Dépopulation et civilisation: Étude démographique*. 1890. Paris: Economica, 1990.

———. *Natalité et démocratie*. Paris: Schleicher Frères, 1898.

———. "Natalité et masculinité." *Revue scientifique* 24 (June 16, 1894): 752–56.

Dunwoodie, Peter. *Writing French Algeria*. Oxford: Clarendon Press, 1998.

Duthoit, Eugène. *Comment se pose le problème social aux colonies et à quelle lumière faut-il l'étudier?*. Lyon: Chronique Sociale de France, 1931.

Echenberg, Myron. *Colonial Conscripts: The Tirailleurs Sénégalais in French West Africa, 1857–1960*. Portsmouth NH: Heinemann, 1991.

Eichner, Carolyn J. "*La Citoyenne* in the World: Hubertine Auclert and Feminist Imperialism." *French Historical Studies* 32, no. 1 (Winter 2009): 63–84.

Ellis, Jack. *The Physician-Legislators of France: Medicine and Politics in the Early Third Republic, 1870–1914.* Cambridge: Cambridge University Press, 1990.

Enfière, André. *Le vote familial, la réforme électorale.* Paris: Marcel Giard, 1923.

En mémoire de Madame de Witt–Schlumberger. Lisieux: Impr. De E. Morière, 1924.

Ezra, Elizabeth. *The Colonial Unconscious: Race and Culture in Interwar France.* Ithaca: Cornell University Press, 2000.

Falcot, Etienne. *Le péril de la dépopulation et ses conséquences économiques: Rapport présenté au nom de la commission de législation industrielle et commerciale.* Marseille: Barllatier, 1924.

Fallot, Ernest. *Le peuplement de l'Afrique du Nord.* Paris: Bureaux des questions diplomatiques et coloniales, 1906.

Faure, Jean-Louis. *La vie aux colonies: Préparation de la femme à la vie coloniale.* Paris: Larose, 1938.

Fédération des ligues des pères et mères de familles nombreuses françaises du département de Constantine. *Compte rendu du VIIme congrès tenu à Batna le 13 Mars 1927 sous la présidence de Monsieur Lecomte, président de la Ligue de Batna, assisté de Monsieur Bénos, président de la fédération et des membres du bureau fédéral.* Constantine: Impr. de M. Attali aîné, n.d.

Félice, Raoul de. *Les naissances en France: La situation, ses conséquences, ses causes, existe-t-il des remèdes?.* Paris: Hachette, 1910.

Finch-Boyer, Héloïse. "'The Idea of the Nation Was Superior to Race': Transforming Racial Contours and Social Attitudes and Decolonizing the French Empire from La Réunion, 1946–1973." *French Historical Studies* 36, no. 1 (Winter 2013): 109–40.

Fischer, Fabienne. *Alsaciens et Lorrains en Algérie: Histoire d'une migration, 1830–1914.* Nice: Jacques Gandini, 1998.

Fishman, Sarah. "Waiting for the Captive Sons of France: Prisoner of War Wives, 1940–1945." In *Behind the Lines: Gender and the Two World Wars*, ed. Margaret Randolph Higonnet, Jane Jenson, Sonya Michel, and Margaret Collins Weitz, 182–93. New Haven: Yale University Press, 1987.

Fletcher, Yaël Simpson. "'Capital of the Colonies': Real and Imagined Boundaries between Metropole and Empire in 1920s Marseille." In *Imperial Cities: Landscape, Display and Anxiety*, ed. Felix Driver and David Gilbert, 136–54. Manchester: Manchester University Press, 1999.

———. "Unsettling Settlers: Colonial Migrants and Racialized Sexuality in Interwar Marseilles." In *Gender, Sexuality and Colonial Modernities*, ed. Antoinette Burton, 80–94. London: Routledge, 1999.

Footitt, Hilary. "The First Women Députés 'les 33 Glorieuses'?," In *The Liberation of France*, ed. H. R. Kedward and Nancy Wood, 129–41. Oxford: Berg, 1995.

Ford, Caroline, "Reforestation, Landscape Conservation, and the Anxieties of Empire in French Colonial Algeria." *American Historical Review* 13, no. 2 (April 2008): 341–62.

Forth, Christopher E. *The Dreyfus Affair and the Crisis of French Manhood.* Baltimore: Johns Hopkins University Press, 2004.

————. *Masculinity in the Modern West: Gender, Civilization, and the Body*. New York: Palgrave Macmillan, 2008.

Foster, Elizabeth. *Faith in Empire: Religion, Politics, and Colonial Rule in French Senegal, 1880–1940*. Stanford: Stanford University Press, 2013.

Frader, Laura Levine. *Breadwinners and Citizens: Gender in the Making of the French Social Model*. Durham: Duke University Press, 2008.

Fribourg, André. *L'Afrique latine: Maroc–Algérie–Tunisie*. Paris: Plon, 1922.

Fuchs, Rachel. *Abandoned Children: Foundlings and Child Welfare in Nineteenth-Century France*. Albany: State University of New York Press, 1984.

————. *Contested Paternity: Constructing Families in Modern France*. Baltimore: Johns Hopkins University Press, 2008.

————. *Poor and Pregnant in Paris: Strategies for Survival in the Nineteenth Century*. New Brunswick NJ: Rutgers University Press, 1992.

————. "The Right to Life: Paul Strauss and Motherhood." In *Gender and the Politics of Social Reform in France, 1870–1914*, ed. Elinor Accampo, Rachel Fuchs, and Mary Lynn Stewart, 82–105. Baltimore: Johns Hopkins University Press, 1995.

Fuster, Joseph-Jean-François. *De la dépopulation des campagnes et des progrès de l'émigration vers l'Amérique: Mémoire adressé à l'association française pour l'avancement des sciences réunie en session à Clermont-Ferrand*. Montpellier: Imprimerie Centrale du Midi, 1876.

Galéot, A.-L. *L'avenir de la race: Le problème du peuplement en France*. Paris: Nouvelle librairie nationale, 1917.

Gallieni, Joseph-Simon. *Lettres de Madagascar, 1896–1905*. Paris: Société d'éditions géographiques, maritimes et coloniales, 1928.

————. *Madagascar de 1896 à 1905: Rapport du général Gallieni, gouverneur général, au ministre des colonies, 30 avril 1905*. Tananarive: Imprimerie Officielle de Tananarive, 1905.

————. *Neuf ans à Madagascar*. Paris: Hachette, 1908.

Gallois, William. *The Administration of Sickness: Medicine and Ethics in Nineteenth Century Algeria*. Basingstroke, U.K.: Palgrave, 2009.

Garnier, Henri. "Alliance nationale pour l'accroissement de la population française." *Bulletin de la chambre de commerce de Paris*, February 18, 1933.

Gemähling, Paul. "Pourquoi et comment lutter contre la prostitution réglementée." Cahors: De Coueslant, n.d.

————. *Vers la vie: La décroissance de la natalité et l'avenir de la France*. Bordeaux: Le comité français pour le relèvement de la natalité, 1913.

Gemähling, Paul, and Henri Strohl. *Un dossier, les maisons publiques, danger public: L'exemple de Strasbourg, documents et témoignages publiés*. Strasbourg: Pro Familia, n.d.

Gershovich, Moshe. "The Ait Ya'qub Incident and the Crisis of French Military Policy in Morocco." *Journal of Military History* 62, no. 1 (January 1998): 57–73.

————. *French Military Rule in Morocco: Colonialism and its Consequences*. London and Portland: Frank Cass, 2000.

Gibier, Mgr. *Les berceaux vides: Le mal et le remède*. 2nd ed. Paris: P. Lethielleux, 1917.

Gibon, Fénelon. *La crise de la natalité et la croisade pour la repopulation: Œuvre de salut national*. Paris, n.d.

Ginio, Ruth. *French Colonialism Unmasked: The Vichy Years in French West Africa*. Lincoln: University of Nebraska Press, 2006.

Girard, Georges-Désiré. *L'Institut Pasteur de Tananarive*. Tananarive: G. Pitot & Cie, 1930.

Godart, Justin. *Union temporaire contre la prostitution réglementée et la traite des femmes: Discours prononcés le 6 février 1931 à la salle des sociétés savantes sous le présidence de M. Justin Godart*. Paris: Éditions de l'union temporaire, 1931.

Gonnard, René. *La dépopulation en France*. Lyon: A.-H. Storck, 1898.

———. *L'émigration européenne au XIXe siècle: Angleterre, Allemagne, Italie, Autriche-Hongrie, Russie*. Paris: Armand Colin, 1906.

Good, Paul. *Hygiène et morale: Étude dédiée aux jeunes gens*. 19th ed. Issy-les-Moulineaux: Imprimérie édition "Je sers," 1931.

Gosnell, Jonathan K. *The Politics of Frenchness in Colonial Algeria, 1930–1954*. Rochester: University of Rochester Press, 2002.

Goutalier, Régine, and Yvonne Knibiehler. *La femme au temps des colonies*. Paris: Stock, 1985.

Gow, Bonar A. *Madagascar and the Protestant Impact: The Work of the British Missions, 1818–95*. New York: Africana, 1979.

Grandidier, Guillaume. *Gallieni*. Paris: Plon, 1931.

Grayzel, Susan R. *Women's Identities at War: Gender, Motherhood, and Politics in Britain and France during the First World War*. Chapel Hill: University of North Carolina Press, 1999.

Green, Nancy L. "Changing Paradigms in Migration Studies: From Men to Women to Gender." *Gender and History* 24, no. 3 (November 2012): 782–98.

———. *Repenser les migrations*. Paris: Presses universitaires de France, 2002.

Gros, H., Dr. "La mortalité et la natalité des Européens dans quelques communes rurales de l'Algérie." Pts. 1 and 2. *Janus*, July 15, 1901, August 15, 1901.

Guiard, Claudine. *Des Européennes en situation coloniale: Algérie, 1830–1939*. Aix-en-Provence: Publications de l'Université de Provence, 2009.

———. "Une presse féministe dans l'Algérie des années 1930." *Genre et colonisation*, no. 1 (Spring 2013): 232–87.

Guillou, Jean. *L'émigration des campagnes vers les villes et ses conséquences économiques et sociales*. Paris: Arthur Rousseau, 1905.

Ha, Marie-Paul. "'La Femme Française aux Colonies': Promoting Colonial Female Emigration at the Turn of the Century." *French Colonial History* 6 (2005): 205–24.

Hale, Dana. *Races on Display: French Representations of Colonized Peoples, 1886–1940*. Bloomington: Indiana University Press, 2008.

Harp, Stephen L. *Marketing Michelin: Advertising and Cultural Identity in Twentieth-Century France*. Baltimore: Johns Hopkins University Press, 2001.

Harraca, Emile. *Sur le vote familial: Le suffrage du chef de famille normale.* Paris: Marcel Giard, 1930.

Harris, Ruth. "The 'Child of the Barbarian': Rape, Race, and Nationalism in France during the First World War." *Past and Present* 141 (Fall 1993): 170–206.

Harsin, Jill. *Policing Prostitution in Nineteenth-Century France.* Princeton: Princeton University Press, 1985.

Haury, Paul. *Pour que la France vive: Éléments d'un enseignement nataliste et familial.* Paris: Éditions de l'Alliance Nationale, 1927.

Haury, Paul, and René Lugand. *Enseignement démographique et familial, classe de première: Géographie, la France par régions naturelles et l'empire colonial français.* Paris: Alliance nationale contre la dépopulation, 1944.

Hecht, Jennifer Michael. *The End of the Soul: Scientific Modernity, Atheism, and Anthropology in France.* New York: Columbia University Press, 2003.

Heffernan, Michael. "French Colonial Migration." In *The Cambridge Survey of World Migration,* ed. Robin Cohen, 33–38. Cambridge: Cambridge University Press, 1995.

Hélia, Mariel. "L'émigration féminine." *Almanach féministe* 1 (1899): 236–41.

Herriot, Édouard. *Créer.* Paris: Payot et Cie, 1919.

Heywood, Colin. *Growing Up in France: From the Ancien Régime to the Third Republic.* Cambridge: Cambridge University Press, 2007.

Hilleret, Georges. *Le problème de la population en France et le vote familial.* Paris: Marcel Giard, 1928.

Hoffmann, Stanley. "Paradoxes of the French Political Community." In *In Search of France: The Economy, Society, and Political System in the Twentieth Century,* ed. Stanley Hoffman et al., 1–117. Cambridge: Harvard University Press, 1963.

Hoisington, William, Jr. *Lyautey and the French Conquest of Morocco.* New York: St. Martin's Press, 1995.

Huard, Raymond. *Le suffrage universel en France, 1848–1946.* Paris: Aubier, 1991.

Huber, Michel, Henri Bunle, and Fernand Boverat. *La population de la France: Son évolution, et ses perspectives.* Paris: Hachette, n.d.

Huc, Paul. *L'œuvre politique et économique du protectorat français en Tunisie.* Toulouse: Imprimerie régionale, 1924.

Hunt, Lynn, *The Family Romance of the French Revolution.* Berkeley: University of California Press, 1992.

Hunt, Nancy Rose. *A Colonial Lexicon of Birth Ritual, Medicalization, and Mobility in the Congo.* Durham: Duke University Press, 1999.

Isaac, Auguste. *La propagande internationale néo-malthusienne: Rapport présenté à la séance du 26 juin 1928, académie d'éducation et d'entre-aide sociales.* Paris: Éditions Spes, 1928.

———. *Réflexions sur le dernier quart d'heure et les années qui le suivront.* Lyon: A. Rey, 1918.

Les Kabyles en France: Rapport de la commission chargée d'étudier les conditions du travail des indigènes algériens dans la métropole. Beaugency: René Barrillier, 1914.

Jackson, Julian. *France: The Dark Years, 1940–1944.* Oxford: Oxford University Press, 2001.

Jacobs, Margaret D. *White Mother to a Dark Race: Settler Colonialism, Maternalism, and the Removal of Indigenous Children in the American West and Australia, 1880–1940.* Lincoln: University of Nebraska Press, 2009.

Jennings, Eric T. *Curing the Colonizers: Hydrotherapy, Climatology, and French Colonial Spas.* Durham: Duke University Press, 2006.

——. *Vichy in the Tropics: Pétain's National Revolution in Madagascar, Guadeloupe, and Indochina, 1940–1944.* Stanford: Stanford University Press, 2001.

——. "Visions of Representations of French Empire." *Journal of Modern History* 77 (September 2005): 701–21.

Kalman, Samuel. "Le Combat par Tous les Moyens: Colonial Violence and the Extreme Right in 1930s Oran." *French Historical Studies* 34, no. 1 (Winter 2011): 125–54.

——. "Fascism and Algérianité: The Croix de Feu and the Indigenous Question in 1930s Algeria." In *The French Colonial Mind: Violence, Military Encounters, and Colonialism,* ed. Martin Thomas, 2:112–39. Lincoln: University of Nebraska Press, 2011.

——. *French Colonial Fascism: The Extreme Right in Algeria, 1919–1939.* New York: Palgrave Macmillan, 2013.

Kateb, Kamal. *Européens, "indigènes" et juifs en Algérie (1830–1962): Représentations, et réalités des populations.* Paris: Éditions de l'Institut National D'Études Démographiques, 2001.

Keller, Richard C. *Colonial Madness: Psychiatry in French North Africa.* Chicago: University of Chicago Press, 2007.

Kimble, Sara L. "Emancipation through Secularization: French Feminist Views of Muslim Women's Condition in Interwar Algeria." *French Colonial History* 7 (2006): 109–28.

Koonz, Claudia. *Mothers in the Fatherland: Women, the Family, and Nazi Politics.* New York: St. Martin's Press, 1987.

Koos, Cheryl. "Engendering Reaction: The Politics of Pronatalism and the Family in France, 1919–1944." PhD diss., University of Southern California, 1996.

——. "Gender, Anti-individualism, and Nationalism: The Alliance Nationale and the Pronatalist Backlash against the Femme Moderne, 1933–40." *French Historical Studies* 19, no. 3 (Spring 1996): 639–73.

Kranidis, Rita S. *The Victorian Spinster and Colonial Emigration: Contested Subjects.* New York: St. Martin's Press, 1999.

Lagneau, Gustave. *De la durée et de la mutation des familles rurales.* Orléans: P. Girardot, 1887.

——. *De l'immigration en France.* Orléans: P. Colas, 1884.

——. *Des mesures propres à rendre moins faible l'accroissement de la population de la France.* Paris: G. Masson, 1890.

——. *Du dépeuplement, de la décroissance de population de certains départements de France.* Orléans: P. Colas, 1883.

——. *L'émigration de France.* Orléans: P. Colas, 1884.

————. *Remarques démographiques sur le célibat en France.* Orléans: P. Girardot, 1885.

Lake, Marilyn, and Henry Reynolds. *Drawing the Global Colour Line: White Men's Countries and the International Challenge of Racial Equality.* Cambridge: Cambridge University Press, 2008.

Lambert, Charles. *La France et les étrangers: Dépopulation, immigration, naturalisation.* Paris: Delagrave, 1928.

Lamy, Étienne. *La flamme qui ne doit pas s'éteindre.* Paris: Spes, 1927.

Landry, Adolphe. *La démographie française.* Paris: Presses universitaires de France, 1941.

————. *La révolution démographique: Études et essais sur les problèmes de la population.* Paris: Recueil Sirey, 1934.

Lardillier, Alain. *Le peuplement français en Algérie, de 1830 à 1900, les raisons de son échec.* Versailles: Éditions de L'Atlanthrope, 1992.

La Roche-Aymon, le comte Georges de. *Éducation de la famille.* Paris: Librairie Saint-Paul, 1918.

Lavergne, Léonce de. "De la richesse et de la population de la France au XVIII siècle." *Journal des économistes,* December 15, 1854.

Lavigerie, Charles. *À monsieur le président et à messieurs les membres de la commission du budget au Sénat.* Saint-Cloud: Vve E. Belin et fils, 1885.

————. *L'archévêque d'Alger, ancien évêque de Nancy, primat de Lorraine, aux alsaciens et aux lorrains exilés.* Mont-de-Marsan: Delaroy, 1871.

————. *Conférence donnée dans l'église de la Madeleine, Paris par S. EM. le cardinal Lavigerie, archêveque de Carthage et d'Alger sur la necessité du maintien au point de vue national d'un clergé français dans l'Afrique du Nord.* Paris: À l'Œuvre des Écoles d'Orient, 1885.

————. *Missionaires d'Afrique, choix de textes.* Ed. Marie José Dor and J. M. Vasseur. Paris: Éditions S.O.S., 1980.

Lavorel, Jean-Marie. *Pour la résurrection de la France par la multiplicité des berceaux.* Paris: Spes, 1923.

Lebovics, Herman. *True France: The Wars over Cultural Identity, 1900–45.* Ithaca: Cornell University Press, 1992.

Le Bras, Hervé. *Marianne et les lapins: L'obsession démographique.* Paris: Hachette, 1993.

Ledoux, Eugène. *Le problème de la population française.* Besançon: Dodivers, n.d.

Lehning, James R. *To Be a Citizen: The Political Culture of the Early French Third Republic.* Ithaca: Cornell University Press, 2001.

Lemire, Charles. *Les colonies et la question sociale en France.* Paris: Challamel Aîné, 1880.

————. *Le peuplement de nos colonies concessions de terres: Madagascar, Indo-Chine Française, Nouvelle-Calédonie, Congo, Tunisie, Djibouti.* 4th ed. Paris: Challamel, 1900.

Le Naour, Jean-Yves, and Catherine Valenti. *La famille doit voter: Le suffrage familial contre le vote individuel.* Paris: Hachette, 2005.

Le Play, Frédéric. *L'organisation de la famille selon le vrai modèle signalé par l'histoire de toutes les races et de tous les temps.* 5th ed. Paris: Dentu, 1907.

Lerolle, Jean. *Le vote familial: Étude présentée à la séance du 1er avril 1924.* Paris: Spes, 1924.

Leroy-Beaulieu, Paul. *De la colonisation chez les peuples modernes.* Paris: Guillaumin et Cie, 1891.

———. "De la vraie loi de population: De l'influence de la civilisation sur la nuptialité et la natalité dans les divers pays." *L'économiste français*, November 2, 1895, 579–81.

———. *La politique française en Algérie.* Paris: Chaix, 1881. Previously published in *Journal des débats* (July 5, 1881) and *L'économiste français* (July 9, 1881).

———. *La question de la population.* Paris: Félix Alcan, 1913.

Levasseur, Émile. *La France et ses colonies: Géographie et statistique.* Paris: Ch. Delagrave et Cie, 1868.

———. "Le peuple algérien: Essais de démographie algérienne." *Journal de la société de statistique de Paris* 4 (April 1907): 105–9.

———. *La population française: Histoire de la population avant 1789 et démographie de la France comparée à celle des autres nations au XIXe siècle.* 3 vols. Paris: Arthur Rousseau, 1889–92.

Levine, Philippa, ed. *Gender and Empire.* Oxford: Oxford University Press, 2004.

Leygonie, Marcel. *Le vote familial: Rapport présenté au congrès départemental des associations de F.N. de Saône-et-Loire tenu au Creusot le 26 Mai 1929.* Le Creusot: Cure-Peteuil, 1929.

Ling, Dwight L. *Tunisia: From Protectorate to Republic.* Bloomington: Indiana University Press, 1967.

Le livre d'or du centenaire de l'Algérie française: L'Algérie, son histoire, l'œuvre française d'un siècle les manifestations du centenaire. Algiers: Fontana Frères, 1931.

Lombard, Henri-Clermont. *De la dépopulation en France: Communication faite au congrès médical de Lyon (Septembre 1872).* Lyon: Aimé Vingtrinier, 1873.

Lorcin, Patricia M. E. *Historicizing Colonial Nostalgia: European Women's Narratives of Algeria and Kenya, 1900–Present.* New York: Palgrave Macmillan, 2012.

———. *Imperial Identities: Stereotyping, Prejudice and Race in Colonial Algeria.* London: I. B. Tauris, 1995.

———. "Rome and France in Africa: Recovering Colonial Algeria's Latin Past." *French Historical Studies* 25, no. 2 (Spring 2002): 295–329.

Louwyck, J. H. *La dame au Beffroi, roman d'un flamand.* Paris: Albin Michel, 1923.

Lovett, Laura. *Pronatalism, Reproduction, and the Family in the United States, 1890–1938.* Chapel Hill: University of North Carolina Press, 2007.

Lunn, Joe. *Memoirs of the Maelstrom: A Senegalese Oral History of the First World War.* Portsmouth NH: Heinemann, 1999.

Lyautey. *Choix de lettres, 1882–1919.* Paris: Armand Colin, 1947.

———. *Lettres d'aventures.* Paris: René Julliard Sequana, 1947.

———. *Lettres du sud de Madagascar, 1900–1902.* Paris: Armand Colin, 1935.

————. *Paroles d'action: Madagascar–Sud-oranais; Oran-Maroc, 1900–1926*. Paris: Armand Colin, 1927.

MacMaster, Neil. *Colonial Migrants and Racism: Algerians in France, 1900–62*. London: Macmillan, 1997.

Mandeville, G., and V. Demontès. *Les populations européennes: Leur accroissement, leur densité et leurs origines*. Paris: Aux bureaux de la "Revue des questions diplomatiques et coloniales," 1900.

Mangin, Charles. *La force noire*. Paris: Hachette, 1910.

Mansker, Andrea. *Sex, Honor, and Citizenship in Early Third Republic France*. New York: Palgrave Macmillan, 2011.

Margadant, Jo Burr. *Madame Le Professeur: Women Educators in the Third Republic*. Princeton: Princeton University Press, 1990.

Margueritte, Victor. *La garçonne*. 1922. Paris: Flammarion, 1949.

Marine et colonies. *Port de Bordeaux: Traité de gré à gré pour le transport à la Nouvelle-Calédonie de femmes et de jeunes filles sortant les unes des maisons centrales, les autres des maisons de correction*. Bordeaux: Boussin, 1874.

Mars 1896. Tournée de Mme J. Lefébure-Fortel. Conférences sur les bienfaits que peuvent apporter les femmes françaises dans nos nouvelles colonies. Rouen: La Brière, n.d.

McClintock, Anne. *Imperial Leather: Race, Gender and Sexuality in the Colonial Contest*. New York: Routledge, 1995.

McLaren, Angus. *Sexuality and Social Order: The Debate over the Fertility of Women and Workers in France*. New York: Holmes and Meier, 1983.

————. *The Trials of Masculinity: Policing Sexual Boundaries, 1870–1930*. Chicago: University of Chicago Press, 1997.

McMillan, James. *France and Women 1789–1914: Gender, Society and Politics*. London: Routledge, 2000.

Merle, Isabelle. "Drawing Settlers to New Caledonia: French Colonial Propaganda in the Late Nineteenth Century." In *Promoting the Colonial Idea: Propaganda and Visions of Empire in France*, ed. Tony Chafer and Amanda Sackur, 40–52. New York: Palgrave, 2002.

————. *Expériences coloniales: La Nouvelle-Calédonie, 1853–1920*. Paris: Belin, 1995.

Michel, Marc. *L'appel à l'Afrique: Contributions et réactions à l'effort de guerre en A.O.F 1914–1919*. Paris: Publications de la Sorbonne, 1982.

Ministère de l'instruction publique. *Hygiène des écoles primaires et des écoles maternelles: Rapport d'ensemble par M. le Dr. Javal*. Paris: G. Masson, 1884.

Ministère des affaires étrangères. *Rapport au président de la république sur la situation de la Tunisie en 1922*. Tunis: Ch. Weber, G. Combaz & Cie, 1923.

————. *Rapport au président de la république sur la situation de la Tunisie en 1923*. Tunis: Ch. Weber, G. Combaz & Cie, 1924.

————. *Rapport au président de la république sur la situation de la Tunisie en 1924*. Tunis: Ch. Weber, G. Combaz & Cie, 1925.

————. *Rapport au président de la république sur la situation de la Tunisie en 1925*. Tunis: Ch. Weber, G. Combaz & Cie, 1926.

Mitchell, Allan. *The Divided Path: The German Influence on Social Reform in France after 1870.* Chapel Hill: The University of North Carolina Press, 1991.

Moch, Leslie Page. *Paths to the City: Regional Migration in Nineteenth-Century France.* Beverly Hills: Sage, 1983.

Mosse, George. *The Image of Man: The Creation of Modern Masculinity.* Oxford: Oxford University Press, 1996.

Nadaillac, Jean-François-Albert de. *La fin de l'humanité.* Paris: De Soye et Fils, 1897.

Ngalamulume, Kalala. "Keeping the City Totally Clean: Yellow Fever and the Politics of Prevention in Colonial Saint-Louis-du-Sénégal, 1850–1914." *Journal of African History* 45, no. 2 (2004): 183–202.

Nitti, Francesco Saverio. *La population et le système social.* Paris: V. Giard et E. Brière, 1897.

Noiriel, Gérard. *Le creuset français: Histoire de l'immigration, XIXe–XXe siècles.* Paris: Seuil, 1988.

Nordman, Jacques. "La dénatalité actuelle en France et dans le monde." Medical thesis, Faculté de médecine et de pharmacie de Lyon, 1934.

Nye, Robert. *Crime, Madness, and Politics in Modern France: The Medical Concept of National Decline.* Princeton: Princeton University Press, 1985.

———. *Masculinity and Male Codes of Honor in Modern France.* Berkeley: University of California Press, 1998.

O'Donnell, Joseph Dean, Jr. *Lavigerie in Tunisia: The Interplay of Imperialist and Missionary.* Athens: University of Georgia Press, 1979.

Offen, Karen. "Depopulation, Nationalism and Feminism in Fin-de-Siècle France." *American Historical Review* 89 (1984): 648–78.

———. *European Feminisms, 1700–1950: A Political History.* Stanford: Stanford University Press, 1999.

Osborne, Michael A. *Nature, the Exotic, and the Science of French Colonialism.* Bloomington: Indiana University Press, 1994.

Passy, Frédéric. *Entre mère et fille.* Paris: Fischbacher, 1907.

———. *Pour les jeunes gens: Avertissements et conseils.* Paris: Fischbacher, 1907.

Peabody, Sue, and Tyler Stovall, eds. *The Color of Liberty: Histories of Race in France.* Durham: Duke University Press, 2003.

Pedersen, Jean Elisabeth. *Legislating the French Family: Feminism, Theater, and Republican Politics, 1870–1920.* New Brunswick: Rutgers University Press, 2003.

———. "Regulating Abortion and Birth Control: Gender, Medicine, and Republican Politics in France, 1870–1920." *French Historical Studies* 19, no. 3 (Spring 1996): 673–98.

———. "'Special Customs': Paternity Suits and Citizenship in France and the Colonies, 1870–1912." In *Domesticating the Empire: Race, Gender, and Family Life in French and Dutch Colonialism,* ed. Julia Clancy-Smith and Frances Gouda, 43–64. Charlottesville: University of Virginia Press, 1998.

Pedersen, Susan. *Family, Dependence, and the Origins of the Welfare State: Britain and France, 1914–1945.* Cambridge: Cambridge University Press, 1993.

———. "National Bodies, Unspeakable Acts: The Sexual Politics of Colonial Policy-Making." *Journal of Modern History* 63 (December 1991): 647–80.

Peer, Shanny. *France on Display: Peasants, Provincials, and Folklore in the 1937 Paris World's Fair.* Albany: State University of New York Press, 1998.

Pégard, Mme. "L'émigration des femmes aux colonies." *Revue coloniale* 1 (1901): 252–58.

Pennell, C. R. *Morocco since 1830: A History.* New York: New York University Press, 2000.

Péricard, Jacques. *J'ai huit enfants: Roman d'un papa.* Paris: Baudinière, 1926.

Perkins, Kenneth. *A History of Modern Tunisia.* Cambridge: Cambridge University Press, 2004.

Perrot, Michelle. "The New Eve and the Old Adam: French Women's Condition at the Turn of the Century." In *Behind the Lines: Gender and the Two World Wars,* ed. Margaret Randolph Higonnet, Jane Jenson, Sonya Michel, and Margaret Collins Weitz, 51–60. New Haven: Yale University Press, 1987.

Persell, Stuart. *The French Colonial Lobby, 1889–1938.* Stanford: Hoover Institution Press, 1983.

Peyerimhoff, Henri de. *Enquête sur les résultats de la colonisation officielle, de 1871–1895: Rapport à monsieur Jonnart, gouverneur général de l'Algérie.* 2 vols. Alger: Torrent, 1906.

Pick, Daniel. *Faces of Degeneration: A European Disorder, c. 1848–c. 1918.* Cambridge: Cambridge University Press, 1989.

Pickering-Iazzi, Robin. "Mass-Mediated Fantasies of Feminine Conquest, 1930–1940." In *A Place in the Sun: Africa in Italian Colonial Culture from Post-Unification to the Present,* ed. Patrizia Palumbo, 197–224. Berkeley: University of California Press, 2003.

Pinard, André. *La consommation, le bien-être et le luxe.* Paris: O. Doin et Fils, 1918.

Piolet, Jean-Baptiste. *De la colonisation à Madagascar.* Paris: Augustin Challamel, 1896.

———. *L'empire colonial de la France: Madagascar, La Réunion, Mayotte, Les Comores, Djibouti.* Paris: Firmindidot et Cie, 1900.

———. *La France hors de France: Notre émigration, sa nécessité; ses conditions.* Paris: Félix Alcan, 1900.

Piot, Edme. *La dépopulation en France: Le mal, ses causes, ses remèdes.* Paris: Société Anonyme de Publications Périodiques, 1900.

———. *La dépopulation: Enquête personnelle sur la dépopulation en France.* Paris: Société Anonyme de Publications Périodiques, P. Mouillot, 1902.

Poinsard, Léon. *Vers la coûte ruine: Les charges d'une fausse démocratie, le règne du gaspillage, ce que coute la bureaucratie française, les excès de la fiscalité.* Paris: A.-L. Charles, 1899.

Poiré, Eugène. *L'émigration française aux colonies.* Paris: Plon, 1897.

Pollard, Miranda. *Reign of Virtue: Mobilizing Gender in Vichy France.* Chicago: University of Chicago Press, 1998.

Ponsolle, Paul. *La dépopulation: Introduction à l'étude sur la recherche de la paternité.* Paris: L. Baillière et H. Messager, 1893.

Pourésy, Émile. *La gangrène pornographique, choses vues.* Saint-Blaise and Roubaix: Foyer Solidariste, 1908.

———. *La vie morale et le respect de la femme.* Saint-Antoine-de-Breuilh, 1938.

Preschez, E. "Rapport sur le congrès national des sociétés françaises de géographie: Alger, 1899." *Bulletin de la société de géographie commerciale du Havre* (1898–99): 396–418.

Le Président Millerand dans le Nord Africain, l'œuvre de la république–Maroc–Algérie–Tunisie. Paris: Hachette, 1922.

Prévost-Paradol, Lucien-Anatole. *La France nouvelle.* Paris: Resources, 1979, 1869.

Probus. *L'organisation de la démocratie.* Paris: Bossard, 1918.

Prochaska, David. *Making Algeria French: Colonialism in Bône, 1870–1920.* Cambridge: Cambridge University Press, 1990.

Questions du temps présent: L'émigration des femmes aux colonies, allocution de M. le Cte d'Haussonville et discours de M J. Chailley-Bert à la conférence donnée le 12 janvier 1897 par l'union coloniale française. Paris: Armand Colin, 1897.

Queyrat, Louis. *La démoralisation de l'idée sexuelle.* Paris: J. Rueff, 1902.

———. *La syphilis: Conférence faite aux jeunes filles et aux mères de famille, à l'hôtel des sociétés savantes, les 15 juin et 25 juillet 1922.* Paris: A. Maloine et Fils, 1923.

Quine, Maria Sophia. *Population Politics in Twentieth-Century Europe.* London: Routledge, 1996.

Quinlan, Sean. *The Great Nation in Decline: Sex, Modernity and Health Crises in Revolutionary France, c. 1750–1850.* Burlington VT: Ashgate, 2007.

Rabary. "La chique à Madagascar (sarcopsylla penetrans) (malgache: parasintsenegaly)." Medical thesis, Faculté de médecine de Montpellier, 1902.

Rabinow, Paul. *French Modern: Norms and Forms of the Social Environment.* Chicago: Chicago University Press, 1989.

Raisin, Charles. *La dépopulation de la France et le code civil ou l'influence du régime successoral sur le mouvement de la natalité française.* Bourg-en-Presse: Courrier de l'Ain, 1900.

Rakatobé, Gabriel. "La lèpre et les léproseries à Madagascar et à la Guyane (contagion, prophylaxie, traitement)." Medical thesis, Faculté de médecine de Montpellier, 1902.

Ramisiray, Gershon. "Pratiques et croyances médicales des Malgaches." Medical thesis, Faculté de médecine de Montpellier, 1901.

Ranaivo, Charles. "Pratiques et croyances des Malgaches relatives aux accouchements et à la médecine infantile." Medical thesis, Faculté de médecine de Paris, 1902.

Ravelonahina. "Des causes de dépopulation à Madagascar et des moyens d'y remédier par la puériculture, parallèle avec l'Europe." Medical thesis, Faculté de médecine de Montpellier, 1902.

Ray, Joanny. "Les Marocains en France." PhD thesis, Université de Paris, Faculté de droit, 1937.

Raynaud, Lucien, Henri Soulié, and Paul Picard. *Hygiène et pathologie nord-africaines assistance médicale.* Vol. 1. Paris: Masson et Cie, 1932.

Rectenwald, Georges. *Les assemblées élues du protectorat français en Tunisie, édition contenant les réformes de 1928*. Alger: P. & G. Soubiron, 1931.

Renan, Ernest, "What Is a Nation?" In *Becoming National: A Reader*, ed. Geoff Eley and Ronald Grigor Suny, 41–55. Oxford: Oxford University Press, 1996.

Résidence générale de France à Tunis. *Soixante-Dix ans de protectorat français en Tunisie*. Tunis: Imprimerie Officielle de la Tunisie, 1952.

Reynolds, Siân. *France between the Wars: Gender and Politics*. New York: Routledge, 1996.

Richet, Charles. *Dans cent ans*. 2nd ed. Paris: Paul Allendorff, 1892.

———. *La grande espérance*. Paris: Montaigne, 1933.

———. *La sélection humaine*. Paris: Félix Alcan, 1919.

Ricoux, René. *Contribution à l'étude de l'acclimatement des français en Algérie*. Paris: G. Masson, 1874.

———. *La démographie figurée de l'Algérie*. Paris: G. Masson, 1880.

———. *La population européenne en Algérie, 1873–1881: Étude statistique publiée avec l'approbation de M. Tirman, gouverneur général de l'Algérie*. Alger: Gojosso et Cie, 1883.

Riley, Denise. *Am I That Name? Feminism and the Category of "Women" in History*. Minneapolis: University of Minnesota Press, 1988.

Rivet, Daniel. *Le Maghreb à l'épreuve de la colonisation*. Paris: Hachette, 2002.

Roberts, Mary Louise. *Civilization without Sexes: Reconstructing Gender in Postwar France, 1917–1927*. Chicago: University of Chicago Press, 1994.

———. *Disruptive Acts: The New Woman in Fin-de-Siècle France*. Chicago: University of Chicago Press, 2002.

Robson, Katheryn, and Jennifer Yee, eds. *France and Indochina: Cultural Representations*. Lanham MD: Lexington Books, 2005.

Rogers, Rebecca. *A Frenchwoman's Imperial Story: Madame Luce in Nineteenth-Century Algeria*. Stanford: Stanford University Press, 2013.

Rome, M. l'Abbé. *Natalité ou famille? Rapport présenté le 29 septembre 1928 à la commission catholique du Xe congrès de la natalité à Reims*. Paris: Spes, 1929.

Rommel, Dr. *Au pays de la revanche*. Geneva: Stapelmohr, 1886.

Rosanvallon, Pierre. *Le sacre du citoyen: Histoire du suffrage universel en France*. Paris: Gallimard, 1992.

Rosenberg, Clifford. "Albert Sarraut and Republican Racial Thought." In *Race in France: Interdisciplinary Perspectives on the Politics of Difference*, ed. Herrick Chapman and Laura Frader, 36–53. New York: Berghahn Books, 2004.

———. *Policing Paris: The Origins of Modern Immigration Control between the Wars*. Ithaca NY: Cornell University Press, 2006.

Rossignol, Georges. *Le rôle de l'école dans l'action contre le malthusianisme et l'immoralité sexuelle: Rapport présenté au Vième congrès de la natalité: Strasbourg, 1924*. Angoulème: Coquemard, 1924.

Royer, Clemence. *Ce que doit être une église nationale dans une république*. Lausanne: J.-L. Borgeaud, 1861.

————. *Les phases sociales des nations*. Paris: Guillaumin et Cie, 1876.

Saada, Emmanuelle. *Les enfants de la colonie: Les métis de l'empire français, entre sujétion et citoyenneté*. Paris: Découverte, 2007.

Sacco, Lynn. *Unspeakable: Father-Daughter Incest in American History*. Baltimore: Johns Hopkins University Press, 2009.

Salinas, Claire. "Colonies without Colonists: Colonial Emigration, Algeria, and Liberal Politics in France, 1848–1870." PhD diss., Stanford University, 2005.

————. "Les Non-Classées: Colonial Emigration, Gender and Republican Liberalism 1897–1900." *Proceedings of the Western Society for French History* 30 (2002): 1–9.

Saurin, Jules. *L'œuvre française en Tunisie: Le peuplement français de l'Afrique du Nord est l'œuvre nationale au XXe siècle*. Tunis: Fr. Weber, 1911.

Sarraut, Albert. *La mise en valeur des colonies françaises*. Paris: Payot et Cie, 1923.

Scham, Alan. *Lyautey in Morocco: Protectorate Administration, 1912–1925*. Berkeley: University of California Press, 1970.

Schloss, Rebecca Hartkopf. *Sweet Liberty: The Final Days of Slavery in Martinique*. Philadelphia: University of Pennsylvania Press, 2009.

Schneider, William. *An Empire for the Masses: The French Popular Image of Africa, 1870–1900*. Westport CT: Greenwood Press, 1982.

————. *Quality and Quantity: The Quest for Biological Regeneration in Twentieth-Century France*. Cambridge: Cambridge University Press, 1990.

Schweber, Libby. *Disciplining Statistics: Demography and Vital Statistics in France and England, 1830–1885*. Durham and London: Duke University Press, 2006.

Scott, Joan Wallach. *Only Paradoxes to Offer: French Feminists and the Rights of Man*. Cambridge: Harvard University Press, 1996.

————. "'L'ouvrière! Mot Impie, Sordide . . .': Women Workers in the Discourse of French Political Economy, 1840–1860." In *The Historical Meanings of Work*, ed. Patrick Joyce, 119–42. Cambridge: Cambridge University Press, 1987.

Segalla, Spencer D. *The Moroccan Soul: French Education, Colonial Ethnology, and Muslim Resistance, 1912–1956*. Lincoln: University of Nebraska Press, 2009.

Sessions, Jennifer. *By Sword and Plow: France and the Conquest of Algeria*. Ithaca: Cornell University Press, 2011.

Sghair, Amira Aleya. *La droite française en Tunisie entre 1934 et 1946*. Tunis: Publications de l'Institut Supérieur de l'Histoire du Mouvement National, 2004.

————. "La fédération républicaine, radicale et radicale socialiste de Tunisie entre 1925 et 1945." *Revue d'histoire maghrébine* 21, no. 74 (1994): 99–122.

Shapiro, Ann-Louise. *Housing the Poor of Paris, 1850–1902*. Madison: University of Wisconsin Press, 1985.

Shorrock, William I. "The Tunisian Question in French Policy toward Italy, 1881–1940." *International Journal of African Historical Studies* 16, no. 4 (1983): 631–51.

Sicard de Plauzoles, Justin-Joseph-Eugène. *La maternité et la défense nationale contre la dépopulation*. Paris: V. Giard et E. Brière, 1909.

Silverstein, Paul. *Algeria in France: Transpolitics, Race, and Nation*. Bloomington: Indiana University Press, 2004.

Slavin, David Henry. *Colonial Cinema and Imperial France, 1919–1939: White Blind Spots, Male Fantasies, Settler Myths*. Baltimore: Johns Hopkins University Press, 2001.

Smith, Andrea. *Colonial Memory and Postcolonial Europe: Maltese Settlers in Algeria and France*. Bloomington: Indiana University Press, 2006.

Smith, Paul. *Feminism and the Third Republic: Women's Political and Civil Rights in France, 1918–1945*. Oxford: Clarendon Press, 1996.

Sowerwine, Charles. *France since 1870: Culture, Politics and Society*. New York: Palgrave, 2001.

Spengler, Joseph. *France Faces Depopulation: Postlude Edition, 1936–76*. Durham: Duke University Press, 1976.

Spivak, Gayatri. *The Postcolonial Critic: Interviews, Strategies, Dialogues*. London: 1990.

Steeg, Théodore. "Contre la dépopulation: L'assistance aux familles nombreuses." *L'aide sociale, prévoyance, hygiène, travail* 23–24 (December 31, 1909): 670–80.

———. *La paix française en Afrique du Nord: En Algérie, au Maroc*. Paris: Félix Alcan, 1926.

Stewart, Mary Lynn. *For Health and Beauty: Physical Culture for Frenchwomen, 1880s–1930s*. Baltimore: Johns Hopkins University Press, 2001.

Stoler, Ann Laura. *Carnal Knowledge and Imperial Power: Race and the Intimate in Colonial Rule*. Berkeley: University of California Press, 2002.

Stoler, Ann, and Frederick Cooper, eds. *Tensions of Empire: Colonial Cultures in a Bourgeois World*. Berkeley: University of California Press, 1997.

Stovall, Tyler. *Paris and the Spirit of 1919: Consumer Struggles, Transnationalism, and Revolution*. Cambridge: Cambridge University Press, 2012.

Strauss, Paul. *Dépopulation et puériculture*. Paris: Eugène Fasquelle, 1901.

Strobel, Margaret. *European Women and the Second British Empire*. Bloomington: Indiana University Press, 1991.

Surkis, Judith. *Sexing the Citizen: Morality and Masculinity in France, 1870–1920*. Ithaca: Cornell University Press, 2006.

Sussman, George D. *Selling Mothers' Milk: The Wet-Nursing Business in France, 1715–1914*. Urbana: University of Illinois Press, 1982.

Talmy, Robert. *Histoire du mouvement familial en France, 1896–1939*. Paris: UNCAF, 1962.

Taraud, Christelle. *La prostitution coloniale: Algérie, Tunisie, Maroc (1830–1962)*. Paris: Payot & Rivages, 2003.

Tarde, Alfred de. *Le Maroc: École d'énergie*. Paris: Plon, 1923.

Thébaud, Françoise. "Le mouvement nataliste dans la France de l'entre-deux-guerres: L'alliance nationale pour l'accroissement de la population française." *Revue d'histoire moderne et contemporaine* 32 (April–June 1985): 276–301.

Thomas, Lynn. *Politics of the Womb: Women, Reproduction, and the State in Kenya*. Berkeley: University of California Press, 2003.

Thomas, Martin, ed. *The French Colonial Mind*. 2 vols. Lincoln: University of Nebraska Press, 2011.

————. *The French Empire between the Wars: Imperialism, Politics and Society.* Manchester: Manchester University Press, 2005.

Thompson, Elizabeth. *Colonial Citizens: Republican Rights, Paternal Privilege, and Gender in French Syria and Lebanon.* New York: Columbia University Press, 2000.

Torina, Martin de. *Mère sans être épouse: Pour la France et pour soi-même, étude psychologique et physiologique.* 2nd ed. Paris: Chez l'Auteur, 1917.

Toth, Stephen A. *Beyond Papillon: The French Overseas Penal Colonies, 1854–1952.* Lincoln: University of Nebraska Press, 2006.

Toulemon, André. *Le suffrage familial ou suffrage universel intégral.* Paris: Receuil Sirey, 1933.

Turquan, Joseph. *Les femmes de l'émigration, 1789–1815.* Paris: Émile Paul, 1911.

Turquan, Victor. "Contribution à l'étude de la population et de la dépopulation." *Bulletin de la société d'anthropologie de Lyon* 21 (1902): 5–165.

————. *Guide pratique des jeunes gens des deux sexes dans le choix d'une carrière: Réunion de conseils, conditions et programmes pour l'admission dans chaque profession.* Paris: Félix Ciret, 1893.

Tuttle, Leslie. *Conceiving the Old Regime: Pronatalism and the Politics of Reproduction in Early Modern France.* Oxford: Oxford University Press, 2010.

Union coloniale française. *But, moyens d'actions, résultats.* Paris: Publications de l'union coloniale française, 1900.

————. *Guide de l'émigrant en Nouvelle-Calédonie, avec une carte.* Paris: Publications de l'union coloniale française, 1897.

Usquin, Émile. *La dépopulation des campagnes.* Paris: Félix Alcan, 1910.

Vaughan, Megan. *Curing Their Ills: Colonial Power and African Illness.* Cambridge: Polity Press, 1991.

Vauthier, Louis-Léger. "Note de M. L.-L. Vauthier sur le travail de M. Arsène Dumont: Aptitude de la France à fournir des colons." *Journal de la société de statistique de Paris* 7 (July 1900): 226–34.

Verjus, Anne. *Le cens de la famille: Les femmes et la vote, 1789–1848.* Paris: Belin, 2002.

Vernes, Arthur. *Un moyen simple et rapide de faire du repeuplement.* Paris: Aux Bureaux de la Revue, 1922.

Vérone, Maria. *La femme et la loi.* Paris: Larousse, 1920.

————. *Pourquoi les femmes veulent voter.* Paris: Ligue Française pour le Droit des Femmes, 1923.

Vignon, Louis. *La France dans l'Afrique du Nord: Algérie et Tunisie.* Paris: Guillaumin et Cie, 1887.

————. *Un programme de politique coloniale: Les questions indigènes.* Paris: Plon, 1919.

Vuillermet, Ferdinand-Antonin. *Le suicide d'une race.* Paris: P. Lethielleux, 1911.

Waltz, André. *Le problème de la population française: Natalité, mortalité, immigration.* Paris: Société d'études et d'informations économiques, 1924.

Weber, Eugen. *The Hollow Years: France in the 1930s.* New York: Norton, 1994.

————. *Peasants into Frenchmen: The Modernization of Rural France, 1870–1914.* Stanford: Stanford University Press, 1976.

Weinbaum, Alys Eve. *Wayward Reproductions: Genealogies of Race and Nation in Transatlantic Modern Thought.* Durham: Duke University Press, 2004.

Wesseling, H. L. *Divide and Rule: The Partition of Africa, 1880–1914.* Westport CT: Praeger, 1996.

White, Owen. *Miscegenation and Colonial Society in French West Africa, 1895–1960.* Oxford: Clarendon Press, 1999.

———. "Miscegenation and the Popular Imagination." In *Promoting the Colonial Idea: Propaganda and Visions of Empire in France,* ed. Tony Chafer and Amanda Sackur, 133–42. New York: Palgrave, 2002.

White, Owen, and J. P. Daughton. *In God's Empire: French Missionaries and the Modern World.* Oxford: Oxford University Press, 2012.

Wildenthal, Laura. *German Women for Empire, 1884–1945.* Durham: Duke University Press, 2001.

Wilder, Gary. *The French Imperial Nation-State: Negritude and Colonial Humanism between the Two World Wars.* Chicago: University of Chicago Press, 2005.

Winock, Michel. *Nationalism, Anti-Semitism, and Fascism in France.* Stanford: Stanford University Press, 1998.

Wright, Gwendolyn. *The Politics of Design in French Colonial Urbanism.* Chicago: University of Chicago Press, 1991.

You, André. *Madagascar: Histoire, organisation, colonisation.* Paris: Berger-Levrault, 1905.

Yver, Colette. *Dans le jardin du féminisme.* 3rd ed. Paris: Calmann-Lévy, 1920.

———. *Femmes d'aujourd'hui: Enquête sur les nouvelles carrières féminines.* Paris: Calmann-Lévy, 1929.

Zahra, Tara. *The Lost Children: Reconstructing Europe's Families after World War II.* Cambridge: Harvard University Press, 2011.

Zola, Émile. *Fécondité.* Paris: Charpentier, 1899.

INDEX

Corneau, Grace, 92–93
Courrier, Mme Paul-Louis, 71–72
Crémieux Decree of 1870, 204, 282n12
Croix de feu, 223
Cros (priest), 66

Dagrand, 68
Daladier, Édouard, 237, 288n1
Dardouillet, Mme, 69
Davin, Anna, 6
Davis, Diana, 258n63
Debury, Roger, 49–50, 76, 259n96
Declaration of Rights of Man and Citizen, 164–65, 212
Declaration of the Rights of the Family, 212
déclassées, 91
de Cléron, Gabriel Paul Othenin. See d'Haussonville, Comte
decolonization, 248
de Gaulle, Charles, 174, 240, 242, 259n96
degeneration, racial, 6, 10, 28–35, 75, 78, 87, 259n93
La démographie figurée de l'Algérie (Ricoux), 45–46
Demontès, Victor, 204–5, 223, 282n12, 283n13
"departments of death," 51
"departments of life," 51–52
depopulation: and familial suffrage, 160, 164–66, 192–95, 197; in France, 28–35, 110–12, 165–66, 198; Jean-Baptiste Piolet on, 84–85; Joseph Spengler on, 5–6; in Madagascar, 113–14, 123, 131, 137–50; and migration theories, 35–45; in Morocco, 206, 208; and non-classées, 90–92, 99, 109; in North Africa, 202–8, 215–16; overview, 1–24; and pronatalist-familialist alliances, 227–34; Théodore Steeg on, 191; in Tunisia, 160, 185, 197–98, 206, 208; and UCF, 61–63
La dépopulation de la France (J. Bertillon), 146
Destour, 176
de Witt–Schlumberger, Marguerite, 172–73, 195, 282n150
d'Haussonville, Comte, 90–92, 94
divorce, 34, 132, 212, 256n30
Donzelot, Jacques, 167

dowries, 84, 94–95, 102
Dumont, Arsène, 260n104
Dunwoodie, Peter, 207
Duthoit, Eugène, 212

École coloniale, 20, 60, 65, 77, 255n53
Edict of Nantes, 28
effeminacy, 75, 81
Ellis, Jack, 155
emigrant screening, 70–71
Entr'aide coloniale féminine, 103
"Étude statistique sur les nouveau-nés" (L.-B. Bertillon), 37
extra-parliamentary depopulation commission (Commission de la dépopulation), 111, 245

Famadihana (turning of the dead), 132
familialism: family benefits in North Africa, 215–22; legacy of, 237–50; North African pronatalist-familialist alliances, 227–36; North African strategies, 222–27; pronatalist-familialist alliances, 227–34; vs. pronatalism, 16–17
familialist organizations: in Algeria, 208–15; described, 17–18; in France, 161–63; in Madagascar, 208–9; metropolitan responses to, 192–96; in Morocco, 210; in North Africa, 200–202, 208–15; in Tunisia, 200, 206, 209–10, 214–15. See also specific familialist organizations
familial suffrage, 171; and Code de la famille, 237; feminist support for, 172–73, 195, 278n58; in France, 159–74, 196–97, 275n7; in Morocco, 187–92, 197–99, 218–19, 232, 246; in Morocco, French response to, 192–96; overview, 22–23, 241; replacing universal male suffrage with, 245–46; in Tunisia, 22–23, 174–87, 197–99, 218–19, 232, 246; in Tunisia, French response to, 192–96
familles nombreuses (large families), 17, 166, 185, 187, 194, 196, 199–201, 208–29, 232–33, 246
family allowances, 7, 115, 163–64, 167, 194, 213–17, 220–21, 228, 237, 242, 249
family benefits in North Africa, 215–22
family planning, 18–19, 24, 26–27, 33–35, 58–59, 98, 106, 110–12, 119, 243, 289n23

family rights, 18, 21, 23, 211–13, 222–27, 235, 241, 246
family vote. *See* familial suffrage
fatherhood, 32, 57, 77, 224
Faure, Félix, 99
Fécondité (Zola), 54, 76, 83, 106, 206
Fédération des ligues des pères et mères de familles nombreuses françaises du département de Constantine, 223–24
Fédération marocaine des familles nombreuses, 218
Feillet, Paul, 67
feminists and feminism, 15–16, 34, 73, 97, 105–6, 168–74, 181, 195–96, 225, 230, 254n45, 254n46, 256n31, 268n161, 278n58. *See also* women's suffrage
La femme algérienne, 195
La femme et l'enfant, 172, 231
femme nouvelle (new woman), 34, 73
Ferry Laws of 1880s, 82
Fête des enfants, 135–37, *137*, 146–47, 151, 158, 241
financial incentives: for breast-feeding women, 215; for families, 2, 33, 113, 115, 120, 134, 157, 212, 222, 241, 249, 289n23. *See also* birth incentives
Fontoynont, Dr., 128, 242, 265n93
forced labor, 156
La Force Noire (Mangin), 12
the *formule*, 177–78
Forth, Christopher, 73
foundation myth, 42, 258n62
Frader, Laura Levine, 165
France: birth statistics, 1–2, 11, 110, 248; depopulation and degeneration in, 1–14, 28–35; depopulation and migration theories in, 35–45; familial suffrage in, 159–74, 196–97, 257n7; infant and child welfare reform in, 115–17; and prolific settler myth origins, 45–60; public health and hygiene reform in, 113–15; rural migration in, 51–53, 260n99, 260n102, 260n104; women's work in, 118–19
La France et les étrangers (Lambert), 80, 264n70
Franco, Francisco, 10
Franco-Malagasy War, 120–21

Franco-Prussian War, 1–2, 6, 97, 143, 238–39, 243
frapper l'imagination, 125, 154
Free French movement, 240, 259n96
French education system, 77–78
French Equatorial Africa, 65, 240
French racial identity, 7–8, 27
French Revolution, 4–5, 7, 161, 164–67, 213
French West Africa, 20, 65, 121, 143, 182
Fribourg, André, 190

Gallieni, Joseph, 22, 83, 101–2, 111–13, 119–36, 138–51, 153–58, 234, 241, 245, 265n93
La garçonne (Margueritte), 163, 276n20
gender: changing roles of, 6, 18–19, 30–33, 62–63, 73, 162–64, 239; and depopulation, 22; and emigration priorities, 89–93; and employment, 93, 239, 266n109; in Madagascar, 113, 131–35, 141, 143; and prolific settler myth, 26, 53–58, 98, 244; and race, 8–9; and Société française d'émigration des femmes, 89–103; in Tunisia, 93; and UCF, 62–63, 108; and venereal diseases, 141–42. *See also* feminists and feminism; masculinity; sexuality; women
Germany, 10–11
Gibier, Mgr, 80
Glorieux, Achille, 208
Godart, Justin, 170
Gonnard, René, 53, 59
Gosnell, Jonathan, 13, 202–3, 283n29
Grand, Sarah, 34
Grand conseil (Grand Council), 177
Grandidier, Alfred, 123, 270n26
Great Britain. *See* Britain
Great War. *See* World War I
Groupe parlementaire de protection des familles nombreuses, 201, 232
Guadeloupe, 213
Guide de l'émigrant (UCF), 67, 262n23
Guide de l'immigrant (Gallieni), 156
Guillard, Achille, 36–37

Haitian Revolution, 213
Haury, Paul, 195, 282n149
Haut comité de la population, 2, 237
homme d'attaque, 69
homosexuality, 75

Hova, 120, 129, 146, 269n22. *See also* Merina
Hunt, Nancy Rose, 125
hygiene, 77, 104–6, 118–19, 124–27, 131–32, 136, 140–41, 147, 152–55, 224
hysteria, 31–32, 75, 90

illegitimate babies, 56, 116, 132, 180, 189, 260n113, 261n114
"imperial community," 5
individualism, 15, 34, 164–65, 169, 196
Indochina, 10, 41, 100, 121, 124, 135, 157, 208, 262n27, 289n21
infant and child welfare, 112–20, 130–31, 139, 167. *See also* child care
infant mortality, 16–17, 33–34, 37–38, 56–57, 115–19, 126, 139, 147, 155, 207, 260n113
inoculations. *See* vaccinations and inoculations
internal colonization, 81,
Isaac, Auguste, 77, 192, 230–31, 233
Italy, 10

Japan, 10–11
Jourdan, Dr., 129–30
June Revolution of 1848, 36

Kabyles, 43–44
Kateb, Kamal, 207, 283n27
Kermorgant, Dr., 156
Koos, Cheryl, 239
Kranidis, Rita, 102

Lacoux, Henri, 210, 215, 219–20, 222, 228
Laignelot, General, 222
Lamartine, Alphonse de, 162
Lambert, Charles, 80, 264n70
Landry, Adolphe, 106, 237
large families. See *familles nombreuses*
Lavergne, Léonce de, 30
Lavigerie, Cardinal, 203, 282n8
Legoyt, Alfred, 29–30, 255n20
Lemire, Charles, 86–87
Lemire, Jules, 170–71
Lemire electoral model, 170–71, *171*, 180
Le Naour, Jean-Yves, 161–62, 170
lepers and leprosy, 123–25, 149, 157
Leroy-Beaulieu, Paul, 47
Ligue des familles françaises du Tonkin, 289n21

Ligue des familles nombreuses de France, 148
Ligue des familles nombreuses françaises d'Algérie (LFNFA), 209, 211, 228
Ligue des familles nombreuses françaises de l'Afrique du Nord, 210, 214
Ligue des familles nombreuses françaises de Tunisie, 219–20, 228
Ligue des fonctionnaires pères de famille nombreuse, 208–9
Ligue des pères et mères de familles nombreuses de l'arrondissement de Batna, 226
Ligue française, 161
Ligue française des pères et mères de familles nombreuses (Tunisia), 210
Ligue populaire des pères et mères de familles nombreuses, 209
Ligue pour la vie, 16, 161, 209, 211, 229
Loi d'encouragement national aux familles nombreuses, 213, 215, 218
London Missionary Society, 120
Lorcin, Patricia, 13, 279n88
low-cost housing, 212
Luce, Eugénie, 103
Lyautey, Louis-Hubert, 85, 128–31, 143–44, 182, 187–89, 200, 218, 280n114

Madagascar: birthrate in, 150–52, *151*; as colony of settlement, 65; Congregationalism in, 120, 269–70n24; decolonization of, 248; ethnic groups in, 269n22; familialist organizations in, 208–9; Fête des enfants, 135–37, *137*, 146–47, 151, 158, 241; motherhood in, 22, 111–13, 117–19, 146, 157; population growth in, 83, 120–24, 150, *150*; pronatalism in, 3, 9, 21–22, 111–13, 120–43, 143–56, 234; public health systems in, 124–31, 150; sexuality and family life reforms in, 131–35; Vichy ideology in, 241. *See also* Malagasy; Merina
Maire, Simon, 209
Malagasy, 9, 111–13, 120–23, 126, 130–34, 137–43, 146, 152, 155–57, 234, 241–42, 272n80
malaria, 123, 154, 156
male hysteria, 75
male to female sex ratio, 75

Pasteur Institute, 149
paternal authority, 166–67
paternity suits, 18, 167
Pedersen, Susan, 212–13
Peer, Shanny, 81
Pégard, Mme Léon, 16, 97–103, 105, 108, 266n113, 266n119, 266n131, 267n136, 267n138
penal colonization, 67, 82
père de famille (father of the family), 32, 166, 170, 180, 199
le péril jaune (yellow peril), 10–11, *13*, 253n31, 253n35
Pernot, Georges, 173
Persell, Stuart, 64
Pétain, Philippe, 238–39, 242
Le petit journal, 67
Le peuple algérien (Demontès), 205, 283n13
Piolet, Jean-Baptiste, 53, 84–85, 87–88
Piot, Edme, 80, 144–45, 259n94
plural vote. *See* familial suffrage
La plus grande famille, 77, 161, 170, *171*, 192, 227–29
Poiré, Eugène, 50, 259n94, 266n131
Pollard, Miranda, 239
polygamy, 181, 279n85, 283n29
polygenism, 40–41
Ponsolle, Paul, 47–48
"population reservoir" theory, 12, 247, 253n37, 253n38
pouvoir testamentaire, 276n24
poverty, 29, 96, 116, 156, 191, 222, 286n96
pregnancy, 34–35, 56–57, 111, 117–20, 127, 130–34, 140–41, 157, 245, 254–55n51
prestation (compulsory labor), 134, 272n80
Prévost-Paradol, Lucien-Anatole, 30
priests, 66, 155, 203–4, 282n8
prime de naissance, 249. *See also* birth incentives
primogeniture, 165, 266n126
prolific settler myth: and Algeria, 19, 45–60, 244; and gender, 26, 53–58, 98, 244; Joseph Chailley-Bert on, 95; and masculinity, 73; Mme Pégard on, 98; origins of, 14, 24, 26–27, 45–60; outcome of, 202; and René Ricoux, 19, 26–27, 45–60, 202, 244; and UCF, 62, 66, 106

pronatalism: in Algeria, 9, 21, 226, 235; background of, 1–14; British, 6; defined, 14–15; and Jacques Bertillon, 144–47; and L. A. Bertillon, 18–19, 26, 29, 243–44; legacy of, 237–50; in Madagascar, 3, 9, 21–22, 111–13, 120–43, 143–56, 234; in Morocco, 9, 21–23; in North Africa, 200–236; overview, 14–24; pronatalist-familialist alliances, 227–34; and race, 9, 222–27, 235; and recruitment of settlers, 61–109; theories of, 30–45; in Tunisia, 9, 229–30; vs. familialism, 16–17; women's role in, 15–16, 33–34, 146, 254n45, 254n46
property rights, 115
prostitution, 15, 31, 52, 94, 96, 116, 142, 273n104
Protection des familles nombreuses (Protection of Large Families), 161, 232
public transportation discount cards, 221, 286n93
puériculture (science of child care), 119, 139, 147. *See also* child care

Quintard, Dr., 225
La quinzaine coloniale, 64–65, 67, 99, 262n27

Rabary, Dr., 138, 141
race: and acclimatization, 26–27; and birth incentives, 249–50; and birthrates in North Africa, 44, 47–48, 183–84, 190, 208, 223, 226, 234–35, 247; and degeneration of French population, 30–31; and familialism in Algeria, 222–27; and family life in Madagascar, 131–35; and French masculinity, 73–74; and gender, 8–9, 133, 143; and poverty, 222, 286n96; and pronatalism, 9, 235; and public health care in Madagascar, 127–31; and reproduction, 6–7; and settlers' image in the colonies, 69, 262n27; and venereal diseases, 141–43
race suicide, 9, 63
racial degeneration. *See* degeneration, racial
racial mixing, 87–88, 265n91
racial purity, concerns about, 7, 228, 249
Rainilaiarivony, Prime Minister, 120
Ramisiray, Gershon, 139–41

The Moroccan Soul: French Education, Colonial Ethnology, and Muslim Resistance, 1912–1956
Spencer D. Segalla

Silence Is Death: The Life and Work of Tahar Djaout
Julija Šukys

The French Colonial Mind, Volume 1: Mental Maps of Empire and Colonial Encounters
Edited and with an introduction by Martin Thomas

The French Colonial Mind, Volume 2: Violence, Military Encounters, and Colonialism
Edited and with an introduction by Martin Thomas

Beyond Papillon: The French Overseas Penal Colonies, 1854–1952
Stephen A. Toth

Madah-Sartre: The Kidnapping, Trial, and Conver(sat/s)ion of Jean-Paul Sartre and Simone de Beauvoir
Written and translated by Alek Baylee Toumi
With an introduction by James D. Le Sueur

To order or obtain more information on these or other University of Nebraska Press titles, visit nebraskapress.unl.edu.